Animating Film Theory

Karen Beckman, editor

DUKE UNIVERSITY PRESS
DURHAM AND LONDON 2014

© 2014 Duke University Press
All rights reserved
Printed in the United States of America on acid-
free paper ♾
Typeset in Chaparral Pro by Tseng Information
Systems, Inc.

Library of Congress Cataloging-in-Publication Data
Animating film theory / Karen Beckman, editor.
pages cm
Includes bibliographical references and index.
ISBN 978-0-8223-5640-0 (cloth : alk. paper)
ISBN 978-0-8223-5652-3 (pbk. : alk. paper)
1. Animated films—History and criticism.
2. Animated films—Social aspects.
3. Animation (Cinematography) I. Beckman,
Karen Redrobe
NC1765.A535 2014
791.43'34—dc23 2013026435

Animating Film Theory

In memory of Ruth Wright (1917–2012)

Contents

Acknowledgments

Over the last few years, many people have helped me to think more carefully about animation, and their ideas and suggestions have given energy and life to this book. First, I am grateful to the volume's wonderful contributors. They have all been eager and inspired participants from the very beginning, and I thank them for their intellectual vibrancy, good humor, and grace. What a pleasure it has been to work with each one. Thanks also to the volume's three readers—they gave great advice and enthusiastic support. Lacey Baradel helped me prepare the manuscript with meticulous care and incredible efficiency, and I am most grateful to her. In addition, I've had the good fortune to consider the topic of animation in a number of different venues and with a variety of interlocutors. These include Dudley Andrew, Nancy Davenport, Erna Fiorentini, Maureen Furniss, Vinzenz Hediger, Joshua Mosley, Susan Napier, Jayne Pilling, Dana Polan, Jason Potts, Bella Honess Roe, Marc Siegel and his students, Vivian Sobchack, Sheila Sofian, Dan Stout, Orkhan Telhan, Rick Warner, Paul Wells, the members of the 2012–13 Penn Humanities Forum, the participants of the Enchanted Drawing conferences (parts I and II), and the members of the "Art of Animation" seminar. Duke University Press has been enthusiastic in its support of the project since its inception, and I'm especially grateful to Ken Wissoker and Elizabeth Ault. Penn's Program in Cinema Studies and the Department of the History of Art have provided me with collegial and thought-provoking environments for almost a decade, and I appreciate all my colleagues' friendship and support. In Cinema Studies, I am especially fortunate to be able to work with Tim Corrigan, Peter Decherney, Kathy DeMarco Van Cleve, Meta Mazaj, and Nicola Gentili. Dean Rebecca Bushnell and Provost Vincent Price could not have been more supportive during my time at Penn, and I thank them for their constant encouragement. I also thank

Leo Charney and Brooke Sietinsons for their collaborative, energetic, and innovative spirits. Robert, Merrilee, Mari, Eric, Dieter, Jane, Robin, Lucy, Suzanne, Claire, Torben, Janek, Mikkel, Freya, and mum—thanks for sharing your lives with me. Michael, Siduri, Lua, and Bruno—how did I get to be so lucky to be animated each day by you?

Animating Film Theory: An Introduction

KAREN BECKMAN

Animating Film Theory begins from the premise that cinema and media studies in the early twenty-first century needs a better understanding of the relationship between two of the field's most unwieldy and unstable organizing concepts: "animation" and "film theory."[1] As the increasingly digital nature of cinema now forces animation to the forefront of our conversations, it becomes ever clearer that for film theorists, it has really never made sense to ignore animation. Tom Gunning has recently described the marginalization of animation as "one of the great scandals of film theory."[2] Marginalization, of course, is not the same as total neglect; and in order to respond productively to this apparent scandal, we need to consider both where and when this marginalization has happened in the history of film theory, and where and when it *hasn't* happened.

Flipping through the available film theory anthologies, one could easily assume that film theorists have utterly neglected the topic of animation.[3] Yet as both Suzanne Buchan and Oliver Gaycken point out in their contributions to this volume, animation has been a sustained if dispersed area of interest for a surprisingly substantial and prominent list of authors. Part of the fragmentary nature of film theorists' engagement with the term may stem from the fact that *animation* signifies in so many different ways. At different moments, it becomes synonymous with a whole range of much more specific terms and concepts, including *movement, life itself, a quality of liveliness* (that doesn't necessarily involve movement), *spirit, nonwhiteness, frame-by-frame filmmaking processes, variable frame filmmaking processes*, and *digital cinema*, as well as a range of mobilized media that appear within animated films, including sculpture, drawing, collage, painting, and puppetry. These divergent terms do not always sit easily with each other, and though the tensions among them are important and interesting, they have not been explored as fully as they might, in part because our critical paradigms may have foreclosed such lines of inquiry. Film theory and history both frequently rely on a series of binary terms, including *continuous* versus *noncontinuous*, *narrative* versus *experimental*, *indexical* versus *handmade*, and *animated* versus *live action*. Though these oppositions can be useful, they can lead to inaccurate presumptions in that they do not always accurately reflect the differences contained within any one of these terms, such as *experimental* or *narrative*. This volume aims to unearth and think through some of these inaccuracies, blind spots, and structural inhibitors to clear some space, pose some questions, and set some priorities for the future as well as the retroactive work of animating film theory.

It would be close to impossible to organize film theorists' meandering thoughts on this sprawling term into any kind of coherent category that would work as well, for example, as *realism*, *montage*, *spectatorship*, *ideology*, or *sound* seems to do on a film theory syllabus. Yet, as the examples demonstrate, by seeking out those places where film theorists have grappled with animation, we often stumble upon ideas that complicate those concepts we think we can more easily corral into the straitjacket of the textbook (this may help us to understand animation's marginalization). No doubt, it would also be difficult to extract and anthologize, for example, writing on animation from the body of work known as *classical film theory* because of the way animation seems to wind in and out of the theorization of other aspects of the experience and materiality of cinema. Animation's persistent yet elusive presence within film theory's key writings makes it both easy to overlook and essential to engage.[4] By briefly surveying some of animation's cameo appearances in the history of film theory, I hope to encourage readers to frame today's theoretical work on the digital's relation to animation (a synonymous relationship is too easily presumed) within a longer history of thinking about what cinema is and how it works. I also hope to reclaim and reanimate some of the interesting but underdeveloped questions and ideas to which earlier and overlooked musings on animation and its relation to broader categories such as "film" or "cinema" gave rise. These questions cannot be limited to the realm of animation studies as if they were irrelevant to the broader study of moving images; as Edgar Morin, one of the important bridge figures between earlier and later film theories, suggests: "It is obviously the cartoon that completes, expands, exalts the animism implied in the cinema. . . . The cartoon only exaggerates the normal phenomenon."[5]

Movement

Paul Wells suggests that abstract animated films always prioritize "abstract forms in motion," but a close look at experimental film theory complicates this claim.[6] For sure, Norman McLaren's statement that "animation is not the art of drawings-that-move, but rather the art of movements-that-are-drawn" seems to confirm that movement is always the priority of frame-by-frame processes, but even for McLaren, things are never that simple. In 1948 McLaren distinguishes between techniques that lend themselves "more readily to creating *visual change* rather than to action (side to side, and to and fro displacement of image on the screen)," leading us to wonder what the relationship between visual change and movement is.[7] I don't think that change and movement are the same thing, but the tensions contained within the term *animation* provide us with an opportunity to think about what these two concepts share and how they differ, particularly within the context of the visual image.[8] Similarly, writing about the technical process of making *Blinkety Blank* (1954), McLaren explains his need to alternate between small clusters of discontinuous frames and continuous frames that allowed for flow and motion. Here he makes clear that motion is not a given in animation, and that discontinuous and continuous, as well as single- and multiple-frame, approaches often appear within the same experimental film:

> Sometimes . . . I would engrave *two* adjacent frames, or a *frame-cluster*, (that is, a group of 3, 4 or more frames); sometimes a frame-cluster would have related and continuous image within it and would thus solidify some action and movement; at other times the frame-cluster would consist only of a swarm of disconnected, discontinuous images, calculated to build up an overall visual "impression." Here and there, to provide much needed relief from the staccato action a single-frame images and frame-clusters, I introduced longer sections of contiguous frames with a flow of motion in the traditional manner.[9]

The Frame and the Shot

Taking a more extreme position in relation to the question of movement in frame-by-frame processes, Peter Kubelka, in "The Theory of Metrical Film," asserts: "Cinema is not movement. This is the first thing. Cinema is not movement. Cinema is a projection of stills—which means images which do not move—in a very quick rhythm. And you can give the illusion of movement, of course, but this is a special case."[10] Kubelka resists the idea that cinema *has to be* equated with an illusion of movement while simultaneously rejecting the assumption that the shot is necessarily the dominant location of cinema's articulation. Thus, he invites us to think more precisely about the language we use to describe editing and rhythm, particularly in relation to the grammar of animated and experimental films. Kubelka demonstrates that it can at times be much more important to attend to the individual frame and the relationship between single frames than to the unit of the shot; yet as he shifts our attention toward one definition of *animation*—a frame-by-frame process of filmmaking—movement is never presumed as a desired outcome. The point, rather, is to revise accepted understandings of experimental film grammar, rhythm, and editing through a recasting of the frame as a primary unit of production:

> It can be a collision, or it could be a very weak succession. There are many many possibilities. It's just that [Sergei] Eisenstein wanted to have a collision—that's what he liked. But what I wanted to say is: Where is, then, the articulation of cinema? Eisenstein, for example, said it's the collision of two shots. But it's very strange that nobody ever said that *it's not between shots but between frames*.[11] It's between frames where cinema speaks. And then, when you have a roll of very weak collisions between frames—this is what I would call a shot, when one frame is very similar to the next frame, and the next frame, and the next frame, and the next frame, and the next frame—the result that you get when you have just a natural scene and you film it. . . . This would be a shot. But, in reality, you can work with every frame.[12]

Animism and Objectification

In *The Art of the Moving Picture* (1915), one of the earliest extended pieces of writing about film, Vachel Lindsay introduces an observation about film's animistic power that persists in the writings of many of his contemporaries. In chapter 11, devoted to the topic of architecture in motion, Lindsay writes: "I have said that it is a quality, not a defect, of the photoplays that while the actors tend to become types and hieroglyphics and dolls, on the other hand, dolls and hieroglyphs and mechanisms tend to become human. By an extension of this principle, nonhuman tones, textures, lines, and spaces take on a vitality almost like that of flesh and blood."[13] With impressive economy of style, these two sentences highlight cinema's capacity to anthropomorphize inanimate objects, including humanoid dolls as well as signs and machines; turn actors (presumably human) into lifeless dolls or signs; and, in what is perhaps the most conceptually challenging of these claims, imbue abstract tones, lines, and spaces with a sense of life in addition to corporeality.[14] While Lindsay does not explicitly mention the term *animation*, he identifies early in the medium's history a few preoccupations that are pertinent to this volume's interest in how the discourse of film theory has engaged animation, and how that engagement could enrich contemporary film theory. These preoccupations, which often take on a mystical dimension, repeatedly return to cinema's capacity to reframe the relationship between humans and objects; to evoke, through animation, whether of letter, object, line, or space, attachments and emotional responses to nonhuman things; to make us think carefully about what movement is and where it is located—in the object, on the screen, or in the mind-body of the spectator; and to alter our perception of time and space through framing, camera movement, and montage, all of which have the capacity to endow supposedly still objects (animation sometimes makes us question whether true stillness in the world actually exists) with a sense of liveliness and mobility, or at least *potential* mobility, even when the object in question is not being animated in the traditional sense of this term.[15]

Prefiguring André Bazin's sense of nature's on-screen agency, Jean Epstein declared in 1926 that cinema's greatest power lies precisely in this quality of "animism": "On screen, nature is never inanimate. Objects take on airs. Trees gesticulate. Mountains, just like Etna, convey meaning. Every prop becomes a character."[16] Cinema, for him, is an "animistic" language that "attributes a semblance of life to the objects it defines," and this magical, animating force, along with its impact on the conceptualization of realism, the role of the actor, and the difference between humans and objects or abstract lines and shapes on screen, are all primary preoccupations for early film theorists.[17]

The German-Hungarian theorist Béla Balázs is no exception. While Epstein emphasizes the liveliness of objects, Balázs, like Lindsay, seems at least as interested, and at times more interested, in how film turns people into objects, and in the role of the cartoon in illuminating the difference between the film image and other types of images, particularly where the image's relationship to reality is concerned.[18] Balázs's most significant discussion of animation occurs in a chapter titled "The Absolute Film" in *The Spirit of Film* (1930), where he opens numerous suggestive lines of inquiry. First, he writes of American slapstick comedy as if the bodies on screen *actually were* cartoon bodies, and he argues that slapstick discovers its tempo thanks to what Gaycken in this volume describes as time-lapse photography's decomposition of time. Balázs writes, "For it was the tempo of time-lapse that determined the tempo of the typical mad chases of the slapstick comedy. And similarly, their non-psychological, purely mechanical confusion and chaos expressed the exuberance of a technology that can do with its creatures as it likes because they possess no gravity of their own or any autonomous logic." (We might note here that for Stanley Cavell, writing in 1979, it is cartoon characters' "abrogation of gravity" that places them outside of the world of "movies.")[19] For Balázs, slapstick comedians and not cartoon characters have no gravity, and it is in the context of slapstick, not cartoons, that he discusses the absence of danger and death in cinema:

> Events in slapstick seem unthreatening because they are, after all, no more than mere images. . . . This complete absence of danger is what makes these old-style comic scenes the absolute products of the image. For every (written) fairy tale, however comic, always contains the possibility of someone losing his life or something being destroyed. But the worst that can happen to images is that they can be erased or faded out or painted over — they can never be killed off.[20]

Here again we find a direct contrast with Cavell, for whom the impossibility of death is one of the hallmarks of cartoon characters in particular: "Their bodies are indestructible, one might almost say immortal."[21] Midway through this chapter, Balázs, in order to explain the "absolute image" and the "absolute film," compares a legend about a Chinese painting to the world of cartoons created by Pat Sullivan. This extended passage provides an important precedent to the "cartoon physics" that Scott Bukatman discusses later in this volume. Balázs begins by illustrating the centrality of animation to film theory's meditations on the nature of film realism in comparison with realism in other art forms: "There is an old Chinese legend that tells of an old Chinese painter who has painted a landscape. A beautiful valley, with mountains in the distance. The old painter likes the valley so much that he walks into the painting and disappears into the mountains, never to be seen again." Balázs then proceeds to contrast the Chinese painter with Felix the Cat and Oswald the Lucky Rabbit, arguing that with them, "the matter is not so simple."[22]

[Pat Sullivan's] pictures do not create a natural reality into which the artist might enter like the old Chinese painter. This world is populated only by beings sketched with a pencil. Yet their outlines are not so much representations of the shapes of independent beings; the lines themselves are those beings' only substance. Unlike what happened to the old Chinaman, there is no transformation here of appearance into reality. . . . Art is not transformed into nature. Instead, there is absolutely no distinction between appearance and reality. . . . There are no miracles in this world. There are only lines that function in accordance with the shape they assume.[23]

The Line and the Letter

The cartoon line, as the thing itself, has for Balázs as much utopian possibility as it does in Eisenstein's more frequently cited writing on "plasmaticness," a concept taken up in this volume by Esther Leslie and Gertrud Koch in particular. Balázs suggests, "Lines are lines and where lines can be drawn, everything is possible."[24] But Balázs also cautions readers against abstract films in which these lines of possibility become nothing but "ornaments in motion" without any further purpose or meaning.[25] If film theory has paid little attention to the interest that Balázs expresses in cinema's "first innovation" of bringing "movement into drawn lines," Andrew R. Johnston explores the possibilities of that mobile line in this volume in his chapter.[26] While Balázs rejected what he considered to be the purely ornamental animations of the abstract film, there are nevertheless effects derived from the abstract film that promise to make possible "directly materialized meaning."[27] He sees this potential particularly in the realm of animated letters and intertitles, which are both explored further in this volume by Yuriko Furuhata and Tess Takahashi, as well as by Mihaela Mihailova and John MacKay, who expand the existing English-language work on Dziga Vertov's use of and writing about animation within the 1920s Soviet context.[28] Balázs thinks about animated letters' symbolic force and he compares the effect of movement and directionality with the effect of changes in volume levels in the context of sound: "Letters that hurl themselves at us, assaulting our eyes just as a scream assaults our ears?" He also explores the affective quality of moving text and variable typefaces: "Living letters are the graphic traces of an emotional movement. They are not abstract. They are the direct reflections of an inner state."[29]

Evolution and Utopia

Mihailova and MacKay argue that Aleksander Rodchenko's spinning intertitles have a revolutionary component; but this concern with transformation is not only found within the Soviet context. Indeed, for Epstein, cinema's animated force is inextricably linked to change. For him, when the moving image is animated "as much as its nature compels it to be," it shows "that everything is diversity and evolution." Evolutionary and frame-by-frame, cellular paradigms ultimately lead Epstein to the same conclusions about cinema: "Whether we think about the cinematographic space according to its discontinuity, from cell to cell, or according to its continuous evolution, the visual data—which is, here, the sole information—indicates that most forms do not remain equal to themselves, neither in their transposition from one frame of discontinuity to another, nor during their passage from one moment of continuity to another."[30]

This association of the animated image with constant evolution provides the foundation for many utopian theorizations of animation, and they are explored here in different ways by Bukatman, Koch, Esther Leslie, and Mihailova and MacKay. For sure, cinema's animistic force disrupts conventions of time and space, but as Epstein points out in a passage on variable-speed cinematography, where the scientific experiment plays a central role (as it does for several of the authors collected here, including Alexander R. Galloway, Gaycken, Gunning, and Koch), cinema's disruption of the natural is to be found in all new ways of thinking: "One may object that it is an artificial result. But is there an experiment or even an advanced observation that does not employ a device and that does not more or less disrupt natural phenomenon while at the same time communicating new appearances? And yet, we do not consider those to be false."[31]

Kinesthetic Thinking and Feeling

Germaine Dulac, in "Aesthetics, Obstacles, Integral *Cinégraphie*" (1926), offers an extended meditation on how cinema's engagement with movement changes between the 1890s and the 1920s. This essay provides rich terrain for engaging the phenomenon of movement in cinema as a physiological experience, as well as a catalyst for both analytic thought and emotion. She states that if cinema is only "an animated reflection" of "the expressive forms of literature, or of music, sculpture, painting, architecture, and the dance," then "it is not an art." Dulac distinguishes between cinema as "a mechanical invention created to capture life's true continuous movement" and as "the creator of synthetic movements." Furthermore, Dulac here maps an interesting, complex, and perhaps surprising set of affinities among different types of movement, narrative fiction, and documentary. Soon after the arrival of the Lumières' train, she suggests, "sympathetic study of mechanical movement was scorned" (it is worth noting here that it is the loss of the study, not the recording, of mechanical movement that she bemoans).[32] Dulac continues, "In the hope of attracting an audience, the spiritual movement of human feelings through the mediation of characters was added." Distancing itself from the "actual experience" of movement, cinema becomes subordinate to "bad literature," as "one set about arranging animated photographs around a performance." In the course of the essay, Dulac explores what she considers to be the proper and improper role of movement or animation by introducing several different forms of movement: the novel's movement of ideas and situation; theatrical movement that allows for the "development of moods and events"; the movement of human feelings; and the "concept of movement in its plain and mechanical visual continuity as an end in itself." She critiques the focus on characters as the "principal objects of concern when, perhaps, the evolution and transformation of a form, or of a volume, or of a line would have provided more delight. . . . The meaning of the word 'movement' was entirely lost sight of, and in the cinema it (movement) was made subservient to succinctly recounted stories whose series of images, too obviously animated, were used to illustrate the subject."[33] Dulac's observation that the "composed" films in which movement is subordinate to narrative offer none of the "psychical and visual sensation" of prenarrative cinema provides an interesting early precedent and useful starting point for contemporary theorists exploring cinema's corporeal and affective dimensions. This kind of theoretical resonance is particularly rich in Dulac's inquiry into the spectator's emotional response to nonhuman and even nonorganic moving forms, as when she wonders: "Can lines unwinding in profusion according to a rhythm dependent on a sensation or an abstract idea affect one's emotions by themselves, without sets, solely through the activity of their development?"[34]

She extends this passage in a way that opens up interesting questions about the relationship between variable-speed cinematography and cinematic "truth," and also about the relationship between motion and what she calls "a purely visual emotion":

In the film about the birth of sea urchins, a schematic form, generated by greater or lesser speeds of time-lapse cinematography, describes a graphic curve of varying degrees that elicits a feeling at odds with the thought that it illustrates. The rhythm and the magnitude of movement in the screen-space become the only affective factors. In its embryonic state, a purely visual emotion, physical and not cerebral, is the equal of the emotion stimulated by an isolated sound.[35]

Classical film theory is often distinguished from later theories concerned with questions of identity, subjectivity, affect, and ideology. But here, through a mode of cinematic movement decoupled from both the human and narrative, we find an opportunity for unexplored continuities between early and postclassical film theories and among Dulac's emotion-inducing line, Lindsay's flesh-and-blood lines and spaces, Eisenstein's plasmaticness, Walter Benjamin's theorization of play and innervation, contemporary interest in "thing theory" and object relations, and Judith Halberstam's queer celebration of Pixar films as places that enable the development of an "animated self" that disrupts the idea of "a timeless and natural humanity." These are sites for people "who believe that 'things' (toys, nonhuman animals, rocks, sponges) are as lively as humans and who can glimpse other worlds underlying and overwriting this one."[36]

Our ability to recognize these types of affinities owes much to the late Miriam Hansen, whose pioneering work, like that of Esther Leslie, has done so much to help us understand the way in which for Benjamin and Theodor W. Adorno, "Disney films became emblematic of the juncture of art, politics, and technology debated at the time."[37] These imbrications are important because they enrich the context in which we might read the chapters collected here, such as Koch's discussion of animation in relation to kinesthetic and emotional thinking, Takahashi's exploration of the intersection of video-animation techniques and identity politics in experimental documentaries of the 1980s and 1990s, and Johnston's exploration of the energy of Len Lye's "wiggling" lines. But by drawing out such continuities, these chapters also offer a counterdiscourse to the influential model for thinking about animation's relation to the world that is proposed by Cavell in his 1979 addendum to *The World Viewed*. Cavell describes a shared world that contrasts with the childish world of cartoons. The inhabitants of the former are, apparently, quite certain of "when or to what extent our laws and limits do and do not apply"; this is a real world populated by people who are universally recognized as possessing a soul and being vulnerable to death, a world in which all bodies are "fed" and not "stoked."[38] For Halberstam, certain kinds of animation, like Pixar, encourage not so much escapism from the so-called real world as critiques of the fictions of equality and permanence that undergird the unchanging reality that Cavell describes. On this question, Hansen is particularly helpful, for she highlights Mickey Mouse's affinities with a contemporary world that resists the clear division of human and non-human on which Cavell relies:

> Benjamin's Mickey Mouse points toward the general imbrication of physiological impulses with cybernetic structures that, no longer confined to the domain of cyberfiction, has become standard practice in science and medicine, architecture and design, and a host of other areas. This cyborgian quality brings Mickey Mouse into the purview of Benjamin's reflections on the body: the problematic of the psychophysiological boundaries supposed not only to contain the subject "within" but also to distinguish the human species from the rest of creation.[39]

Worlds and Spaces

In her own exploration of "Micky-Maus," Hansen sees no need either to assert a hierarchy between live action and animated cinema or to determine whether animation belongs "inside of" or "under" cinema. But many other participants in this conversation about the relationship between film theory's proper object (cinema) and its freaky cousin (animation) have often been drawn to this type of spatial mapping. These geographic narratives tend either to insist on a total separation of realms, as we see in Cavell's distinction of "worlds," or to map out areas of overlap between cinema and animation in the context of paradigms where one term is always dominant. In 2001 Lev Manovich, in *The Language of New Media*, made this oft-cited claim: "Born from animation, cinema pushed animation to its periphery, only in the end to become one particular case of animation."[40] Although Alan Cholodenko, as he points out in his contribution to this volume, made a similar claim about all cinema being a subset of animation more than a decade before Manovich, it is only within the context of the rise of digital cinema, and the intense critical focus on cinema's changing role as what Koch describes as a "membrane" that enables us to experience the world, that the radicality and inherent interest of this claim has been properly taken up. However provocative these spatial metaphors that draw on the language of geography and

Venn diagrams can be, they also run the risk of becoming defensive, of "fixing" different types of cinema, of generating and enforcing laws in order to maintain a particular idea of cinema instead of allowing the experiment of cinema's mediation of life to provoke our philosophical reflections through its evolution.

Dudley Andrew struggles valiantly to resist this temptation in his recently articulated sense of "what cinema is." Yet even as he emphasizes cinema's adaptation, he still pursues a more stable sense of cinema, one that has gathered over time, noting that "identity accumulates."[41] He positions what he calls Bazin's "aesthetic of discovery" "at the antipodes of a cinema of manipulation, including most animation and pure digital creation," and later celebrates Jia Zhangke for his ability to "deploy animation, but always in the service of cinema, not trying to exceed it."[42] At odds with the general spirit of his own book, Andrew's mapping and ranking end up linking "discovery" to a rather narrow sense of cinema, and this volume pushes back against that narrowing, primarily because it occludes important sites of discovery that help us better understand our own moment.

We find another potent form of mapping in David Bordwell and Kristin Thompson's *Film Art: An Introduction*, which in many cinema and media studies programs provides students with their foundational paradigms and terminology for further study. The authors locate documentary, experimental, and animated films in a shared space that functions as an alternative to the fictional, apparently mainstream, and live-action fare that constitutes the primary focus of the book's other chapters.[43] There are multiple problems with this approach. First, it leaves unquestioned and unhistoricized certain assumptions, such as the one that *cinema* usually refers to "live-action film" unless otherwise specified, an assumption that also undergirds large sections of Manovich's argument about the disappearance and return of "manual construction" over the course of twentieth-century film history.[44] For as Hervé Joubert-Laurencin (a scholar who has elsewhere underscored the importance of animation for Bazin) demonstrates in his chapter on André Martin, the division of cinema into live action and animation, and the assumption that *cinema* means all films *except* animation films, occurs at a very particular moment, one almost coincident with the fall, and not the rise, of the Hollywood studio system. Joubert-Laurencin explores the consequences of this in the pages ahead.[45] Writing in France in the mid-1950s, Martin asked of those cinephiles who were resistant to animation a question that should be reiterated for today's cinephiles (who are often nostalgic for Martin's era): "How can one love the Cinema so much, to what end can it serve to see ALL films, if one is incapable of seeing and following ALL Cinemas?"[46]

Like Joubert-Laurencin, Mihailova and MacKay illuminate a further terminological conundrum that threatens to trouble the boundary between live-action and animation film by focusing our attention on the writing of another important film theorist who has been ignored or underrecognized within the English-language context, Aleksandr Bushkin.[47] Bushkin, they point out,

> in particular, took issue with the odd application of the term *multiplication* to animated film (still today normally called *mul'tiplikatsiia* in Russian), noting that it was *live-action* film that involved the shooting of "multiple" frames with each turn of the camera's handle, in contrast to the frame-by-frame fixing of every constituent part of a movement typical of animation. In that sense, Bushkin argues, animation would more precisely be termed "frame shooting" (*kadro-s'ëmka*), where the basic units of the film are taken to be frame-sized modules, rather than shots of unpredictable duration.

As we ponder the mathematics of specific animation practices, like the variable-frame, live-action process of Norman McLaren in *Neighbours* (1952), it becomes clear that, at least from a mathematical point of view, cinema has always been a bit more similar to an algebraic expression with changing values than a knowable formula. This is why, when it comes to thinking about film, we will never be posttheory. Film theorization involves testing out those shifting values at the borders of a cinema that evolves across time and space, and as this volume demonstrates, animation, like theory, seems to provide a way of grappling with these changes before they are properly understood.

A second problem with Bordwell and Thompson's system of categorization is that it constructs an intellectual paradigm in which students and teachers are encouraged to ignore the differences and interactions among experimental, documentary, and animated films, to think of them only, or at least primarily, in comparison with the live-action fiction film. The organizational structure discourages readers from considering the experimental documentary, animated documentary, or animated experiments, and one of the goals of this volume is to invite more attention to these overlooked or marginalized spaces.[48] Thomas LaMarre's chapter, for example, shines a spotlight on an important film theorist, Imamura Taihei, who may not be well known to English-language readers. In doing so LaMarre foregrounds how, via the concept of "the apparatus," Imamura simultaneously thought about animation *and* documentary, always emphasizing the (often overlooked) photographic dimension of cartoons.

Koch explores how animation, like the experiment and like theory itself, becomes a way to think at the limit of understanding in an attempt to get past that limit, a useful corrective to the notion that contemporary film theorists should stop trafficking in spaces of confusion.[49] Drawing on the examples of Eisenstein's writing on plasmaticness as well as Siegfried Kracauer's reflections on movement as "the alpha and omega of the medium," Koch explores the role of "motor-sensory knowledge" and "moods" as filters by which we understand the world and develop a sense of both life and being alive. Yet even as she explores what we can know of life and liveness through "the experiment of film," Koch distinguishes this from scientific experiments, with their demand for "identical reproducibility," by noting that the aesthetic experiment is temporally open and interminable.

While Koch distinguishes the scientific from the aesthetic experiment in a manner that is analogous to Bukatman's distinction between "cartoon physics" and the "physics of the real world," other contributions make clear just how important a role animation has played in scientific experimentation and visualization, and they explore where modeling fits in relation to film theory's discussions of time and space, revelation and creation. Drawing primarily on the writing of Epstein, Gaycken examines what scientific uses of cinema have in common with "the traditional understanding of what constitutes animation." "Here," he continues, "the scientist uses cinema in a process that is explicitly opposed to recording or reproducing an already evident phenomenon. These creations are acts of creation, thaumaturgic." While Gaycken illuminates the overlooked ways in which three-dimensional modeling has a long history within the cinematic context, Galloway's contribution generates some productive tension within the volume by placing the three-dimensional model outside of, or even against, a cinematic narrative. He states provocatively: "The goal then, to give away the ending before barely having gotten under way, will be to reconstruct a genealogy not for the moving image but for the information model, not for serial animation but for parallel animation, not for the linear but for the multiplexed; in short, not for the cinema but for the computer." Galloway's counternarrative focuses on François Willème's experiments with twenty-four cameras mounted in a rotunda, with shutters opened simultaneously with the ultimate goal of producing an object that Willème, in 1860, would patent as *photosculpture*, an object relying on "discrete photographic impressions" that are "segmented" *not* across time, as in the chronophotographic processes that have received quite substantial attention (particularly in the context of animation's relation to the comic strip and serial photography) but rather "in a spindle of space." This, Galloway argues, posits an "alternative history of photography in which point of view has no meaning." We are dealing here not with camera movement or the illusory re-creation of it in animated films, but rather with the construction of a virtual point of view that, at least for Galloway, constitutes "an *anticinematic* way of seeing," a mapping of space that preempts computer modeling and sidesteps cinema. Without doubt, this is a contentious claim, but it is one that draws our attention to the question of whether film theory's language for describing camera movement, editing, and cinematic space and time is adequate for the task of describing recent image-making practices that often (and perhaps unhelpfully) come under the spacious umbrella of "animation." Furthermore, Galloway asks us to consider what other media histories, in addition to film history, need to be included, or excluded, when animation is the object to be theorized.

Furuhata, Gunning, and Marc Steinberg all raise this same question about how animation needs to be thought in relation to media beyond film, even though these authors approach the question in quite distinct ways. Furuhata explores how for experimental Japanese xerox artists in the 1960s, graphic design's material ephemerality was at once countered by animation through the process of rephotography, a form of archiving, and translated into a temporal format—the image became newly ephemeral, not because it was in danger of crumbling or fading away, but because it was set into motion. Steinberg, drawing on the writing of two of Japan's main animation critics, Ōtsuka Eiji and Azuma Hiroki, suggests that in order for film theorists to understand how realism functions in anime, it has to be placed within a broader "media ecology" that includes both manga and the culture of *otaku* (hard-core fans) of the intertwined media landscape that includes "books, comics, magazines, and animation programs." Steinberg pushes film theorists to expand "the canons of film and animation theory to include writers from as yet underexplored critical milieus" because "it is in these milieus that we may find the potential to overturn some of the most naturalized assumptions in the canons of film and animation theory—such as the continued presumption that realism has to relate to the unmediated 'real.'"

Ducks: Theory, Politics, History

By separating our thinking about animation from our thinking about other crucial terms like *realism*, and also *genre, framing, point of view, editing, rhythm, continuity*, and the *photographic image*, we lose the possibility of thinking about these perhaps overly familiar terms in a new light. While Bordwell and Thompson discuss at length Chuck M. Jones's 1953 masterpiece, *Duck Amuck*, within the context of their chapter on documentary, experimental, and animated films, the analysis they offer persistently delimits the film's inventiveness to the realm of animation. Remarking on the film's reflexivity, they state: "It gradually becomes apparent to us that the film is exploring various conventions and techniques of animation."[50] By contrast, Richard Thompson's superlative 1975 essay on *Duck Amuck* recognizes the extent to which the cartoon is simultaneously "extremely conscious of itself" as "an *act of cinema*," an introductory film studies textbook (but more fun), and a theoretical reflection on what film is and how it works.[51] He writes, "It is at once a laff riot and an essay by demonstration on the nature and conditions of the animated film and the mechanics of film in general. (Even a quick check of film grammar is tossed in, via the 'Gimme a closeup' gag.)"[52] Resisting the urge to defend the borders between animated and live-action film, allowing them to be considered alongside each other while still marking the differences, Thompson notes a whole variety of features — about camera movement, revelation, the frame line, off-screen space, space and time, intertextual reference, genre, and the relationship between film actor and character — that make this essay an unusually rich starting point for thinking about animation within, and as, film theory. Indeed Thompson's work becomes the foundation on which Dana B. Polan builds another exemplary film theory essay that engages animation in a discussion whose pertinence extends far beyond the realm of cartoons. In "Brecht and the Politics of Self-Reflexive Cinema" (1974), Polan's analysis of *Duck Amuck* plays a central role in his exploration of the distinction between political and purely formal uses of self-reflexivity. Crucially, Polan judges *Duck Amuck* to be an example of "nonpolitical art" *not* because it is an animated film but rather because it remains within the realm of fictive characters: "If DUCK AMUCK is a metaphor for the confusions of life (as Thompson suggests), it is a disengaged metaphor at best, for it fails to examine confusion through a politicized perspective. Indeed, the source of Daffy Duck's *angst* reveals itself to be none of the agents of social domination in the real world, but merely Bugs Bunny—another fictive character, whose power is tautological in origin. The film opens up a formal space and not a political one in viewer consciousness."[53]

Vachel Lindsay, writing of ducks on screen, associated the film version of this particular animal with "the finality of Arcadian peace" and insisted that "nothing very terrible can happen with a duck in the foreground."[54] He obviously hadn't met Donald. For Adorno and Max Horkheimer, this duck actively participated in the violent oppression of the proletariat by the forces of capitalism: "Donald Duck in the cartoons and the unfortunate victim in real life receive their beatings so that the spectators can accustom themselves to theirs."[55] Ariel Dorfman and Armand Mattelart agree, as they make clear in their Marxist publication *Para leer al Pato Donald* (1971), which was translated into English and republished as *How to Read Donald Duck: Imperialist Ideology in the Disney Comic* in 1975 after it had been banned and burned in the wake of the Chilean coup d'état of 1973. The book's potent critique of the use of cartoon characters for the purpose of colonization—a blurb from John Berger on the cover describes the work as a "handbook of decolonization" and compares it to the writings of Franz Fanon—highlights the importance of expanding the purview of Third Cinema and ideological film theory's concerns to the realm of animation.[56] A number of scholars have already done important work on how animation has been used for propaganda purposes, usually within a frame where the emphasis is more historical than theoretical. Eric Smoodin's *Animating Culture: Hollywood Cartoons from the Sound Era* (1993) offers an exemplary model of this type of work, and several chapters in this volume—particularly those of Christopher P. Lehman and Bishnupriya Ghosh—continue to explore the ideological operations of animation within a historical framework. These two chapters also intersect with and are enlivened by more general theoretical speculation about animation and film. Ghosh, for example, builds on the pioneering work on scientific animation and microcinematography by people such as Scott Curtis, Christopher Kelty, Hannah Landecker, and Kirsten Ostherr by putting these scholars of the scientific image in conversation with theorists of global capital as she explores the interaction between the individual unit of the cell and the extracellular environment in her close analysis of the U.S. military's "malaria films" from 1942 to 1945. Like Ghosh, Lehman finds those moments when live action and drawn animation combine on screen to be rich sites of ideological work.

He demonstrates the unusual frequency with which African Americans appear on screen through this type of combination. His analysis of this phenomenon expands in significant ways the existing work of Rey Chow and Sianne Ngai on how the animated body gets subjected to power and manipulated by external forces precisely because of the quality of plasmaticness that Eisenstein, Benjamin, and others frame as a source of utopian possibility. As Ngai states, "Although in the last instance Chow's pessimistic reading of the animated-technologized body as a Taylorized body seems more persuasive than Eisenstein's optimistic one, the two perspectives point to a crucial ambivalence embedded in the concept of animation—ambivalence that takes on special weight in the case of racialized subjects, for whom objectification, exaggerated corporeality or physical pliancy, and the body-made-spectacle remain doubly freighted issues."[57] Ghosh and Lehman both illustrate the importance of film history and theory as inseparably intertwined enterprises; but their chapters can also be read as two possible responses to Leslie's questions about whether animation has a history and how it registers the time of its making.

Cinema without Photography?

Leslie's question is in part motivated by a recognition of the way live-action film "reflects its age into itself" through the photographic capturing of "every detail, the fashions, the hairstyles, the makeup (even if the film purports to be a historical one), the attitudes," and so on. Animation reflects its age differently, although as Lehman's discussions of the use of rotoscoping make clear, not always that differently. Furthermore, as Gunning points out, there is a "secret symmetry" between animation and photography that we need to recuperate in order better to understand how animation works. Although he recognizes that "valorizing animation as the 'anti-index' played an essential role in shifting theoretical focus from a narrow obsession with photography," he goes on to ask, "does opposing animation to photography really provide our best understanding of its nature?" Gunning makes the crucial point that "most film animation depends on photography"—and this includes cameraless animation, which relies on photographic processes in order to be transferred to the filmstrip. The fate of some of Harry Smith's unphotographed material makes clear what happens when this stage of animation is bypassed. In 1965 Smith says of the film that Jonas Mekas called *The Magic Feature (#12)*:

There was also an enormous amount of material made for that picture. None of the really good material that was constructed for that film was ever photographed. . . . On that Oz film, that expensive one, of course, I had quite a few people working; so that all kinds of special cut-outs were made that were never photographed. I mean really wonderful ones were made! One cut-out might take someone two months to make. They were very elaborate stencils and so forth. All of my later films were never quite complete. Most of the material was never shot, because the film dragged on too long.[58]

No wonder, then, that Smith would ultimately decide: "I don't think I'll make any more animated films. They're too laborious and bad for the health."[59]

Although the photographic process is essential for the very survival of certain kinds of ephemeral visual material, as both Smith and Furuhata make clear, Gunning explains that animation's symmetrical relationship with photography goes beyond the recording function. Whether or not the filmmaker pays attention to the limits of the frame on the strip when producing the images, these images are, Gunning points out, inevitably "translated into the discontinuous rhythm of the machine" in the moment of projection. Developing two distinct but complementary definitions of animation, Gunning uses the difference between these meanings to explore the shared terrain of animation and still photography, which for him lies in their mutual fascination with the instant. In a key sentence, he explains: "Animation reveals the dynamic nature of the instant through motion, while photography reveals its potential through stillness—but considered together these technological processes also reveal that stillness and movement depend on and transform into each other in the production of the instant."

This volume's call for the animation of film theory is not a question of special pleading on behalf of marginalized practices or special-interest groups, although much writing on animation has this activist dimension to it (and understandably so). Rather, in this volume, the primary goal is to explore the kinds of theoretical questions that have remained underexplored because we have allowed ourselves to be constrained by too narrow a sense of what cinema is. By not exploring our critical terms within the richest possible context, our analytic language has become impoverished and stuck. The consequences of this narrowing have become increasingly visible within discussions of the digital turn, and this is the fertile terrain out of which these chapters spring to life.

Notes

1. Suzanne Buchan points out in the opening to *Animated "Worlds"* that *animation is a term* whose precise meaning often eludes us, possibly referring to a style, a technique, a technology, or a way of experiencing the world (vii).
2. Gunning, "Moving Away from the Index," 38.
3. I am obviously excluding anthologies that are dedicated to theorizing animation, such as Alan Cholodenko's *The Illusion of Life* and *The Illusion of Life 2*.
4. Here I will not focus on the volumes dedicated exclusively to the topic of animation, many of which have emerged out of the context of animation studies, and which tend to adopt an approach that is more oriented toward history and practice than theory. There are now, however, a growing number of authors whose work crosses over between the worlds of cinema studies and animation studies. Several of them, including the contributors to this volume, as well as Maureen Furniss, Chris Gehman, Judith Halberstam, Peter Hames, the late Miriam Hansen, Norman M. Klein, Laura U. Marks, Gerald and Danny Peary, Steve Reinke, Bella Honess Roe, Robert Russett, Eric Smoodin, Vivian Sobchack, Cecile Starr, Paul Ward, and Paul Wells, very actively engage the intersection of film theory and animation theory, practice, and history, and this volume builds on their pioneering work.
5. Morin, *The Cinema, or The Imaginary Man*, 68. Karl Schoonover offers a useful summary of Morin's place in the landscape of film theory in Schoonover, "*The Cinema, or The Imaginary Man* and *The Stars* by Edgar Morin."
6. Wells, *Understanding Animation*, 44.
7. Russett and Starr, *Experimental Animation*, 123; emphasis added.
8. Colin Williamson's dissertation, "Watching Closely with Turn-of-the-Century Eyes," engages this difference in an interesting way by thinking about animation and trickery in the histories of time lapse, the substitution splice, and CGI.
9. Russett and Starr, *Experimental Animation*, 127.
10. Kubelka, "The Theory of Metrical Film," 140. Kubelka's contribution to P. Adams Sitney's *The Avant-Garde Film* is not a single essay but a compilation extracted from recorded and transcribed lectures given at New York University in 1974–75, combined with statements he made in preparation for a 1966 interview with Jonas Mekas. The passages cited here are both taken from the 1966 statements.
11. Several years earlier, at the 1961 Vancouver Film Festival, Norman McLaren uttered what is probably the most frequently cited statements about animation, which Kubelka both forgets and, through echoing, recalls: "What is the essence of animation? It is what happens *between each frame of film*—this is what is all-important." Quoted in "The Craft of Norman McLaren: Notes on a Lecture Given at the 1961 Vancouver Film Festival," *Film Quarterly* 16, no. 2 (Winter 1962–63): 17.
12. Kubelka, "The Theory of Metrical Film," 141.
13. Lindsay, *The Art of the Moving Picture*, 133.
14. Linsday's statement resonates in interesting ways with McLaren's later experi-

ments with pixilation, which Maureen Furniss defines as "animation that is created by moving a live human or animal figure incrementally." Furniss, *The Animation Bible*, 265. When shooting *Neighbours*, McLaren explains that he had to use animators as the actors because "they knew exactly how to move themselves, for instead of making a series of drawings they made a series of postures." Quoted in Furniss, *The Animation Bible*, 270.

15. Furniss writes the following about "stillness" in relation to realism within the context of animation: "In real life, living beings are never completely still because bodily functions such as breathing and heartbeats cause at least minute amounts of movement at all times. Seeing an animated figure that is completely still—that is, to see a single image that is photographed for more than, say, half a second—might strike the viewer as being unrealistic. Most animation contains constant motion, even if only at the level of blinking eyes and moving lips, or a camera movement across a still background.... Absolute stillness can work against one of the central attractions of animation, the illusion that inanimate objects have been 'endowed with life'; it could be said that, when an image within an animated production becomes still, its lifelessness is readily apparent." Furniss, *Art in Motion* (2007), 79.

And Paul Wells, for example, opens his useful book *Understanding Animation* with the following working definition of *animation in practice*, even as he is aware of the definition's insufficiencies: "A film made by hand, frame-by-frame, providing an illusion of movement which has not been directly recorded in the photographic sense." Wells, *Understanding Animation*, 10.

16. Epstein, "The Cinema Seen from Etna," 289.

17. Epstein, "The Cinema Seen from Etna," 295.

18. Alan Cholodenko's work here and elsewhere explores the dialectical tension between film's uncanny capacity to turn both the object and the live being into "the living dead." See, for example, Cholondenko, "The Crypt, the Haunted House, of Cinema." Will Schmenner's dissertation in progress (University of Pennsylvania) also addresses this issue in interesting ways, and I am grateful to him for being a wonderful interlocutor.

19. Balázs, *The Spirit of Film*, 172; and Cavell, *The World Viewed*, 170.

20. Balázs, *The Spirit of Film*, 172.

21. Cavell, *The World Viewed*, 170.

22. Balázs, *The Spirit of Film*, 173.

23. Balázs, *The Spirit of Film*, 173–74.

24. Balázs, *The Spirit of Film*, 174.

25. Balázs, *The Spirit of Film*, 175.

26. Balázs, *The Spirit of Film*, 174.

27. Balázs, *The Spirit of Film*, 175.

28. "Drawings in motion. Blueprints in motion. Plans for the future. The theory of relativity on the screen. WE greet the ordered fantasy of movement," Dziga Vertov declares in his 1922 text, "WE: Variant of a Manifesto." Vertov, *Kino-Eye*, 9. For earlier discussions of Soviet animation in English, see, for example:

Leslie, *Hollywood Flatlands*, esp. "Eisenstein Shakes Mickey's Hand in Hollywood," 219–50; Mjolsness, "Dziga Vertov's *Soviet Toys*"; and Tsivian, "Turning Objects, Toppled Pictures."

29. Balázs, *The Spirit of Film*, 175.
30. Epstein, "The Cinema Seen from Etna," 397, 398.
31. Epstein, "The Cinema Seen from Etna," 401.
32. Dulac, "Aesthetics, Obstacles, Integral *Cinégraphie*," 389–90. In 1928 Dulac reinforces the importance of the study of movement over the illusion of movement when she writes of cinema's "decomposition" of movement, which allows for analytic vision. See Dulac, "From 'Visual and Anti-visual Films,'" 32.
33. Dulac, "Aesthetics, Obstacles, Integral *Cinégraphie*," 390–91.
34. Dulac, "Aesthetics, Obstacles, Integral *Cinégraphie*," 396.
35. Dulac, "Aesthetics, Obstacles, Integral *Cinégraphie*," 396.
36. Halberstam, *The Queer Art of Failure*, 46, 27–28.
37. Hansen, *Cinema and Experience*, 163.
38. Cavell, *The World Viewed*, 170, 172.
39. Hansen, *Cinema and Experience*, 176.
40. Manovich, *The Language of New Media*, 302.
41. Andrew, *What Cinema Is!*, 140.
42. Andrew, *What Cinema Is!*, 42, 59.
43. Bordwell and Thompson, *Film Art*, 110.
44. Manovich, *The Language of New Media*, 307–8.
45. See Joubert-Laurencin, *La lettre volante*.
46. Martin, "Films d'animation au festival de Cannes," 39.
47. Bushkin was responsible for the production design of Vertov's animated short stories that appeared under the title *Humoresques* (1924). See Tsivian, "Vertov's Silent Films," 407.
48. Bordwell and Thompson do dedicate one subsection of chapter 5 in *Film Art* to "An Example of Experimental Animation: *Fuji*," but my argument here is that the overall organization of the book actively discourages thinking about these three categories—experimental, animation, and documentary—as anything other than various alternatives to the mainstream. Bordwell and Thompson, *Film Art*, 149–51.
49. See Turvey, "Theory, Philosophy, and Film Studies," esp. 119.
50. Bordwell and Thompson, *Film Art*, 148.
51. Thompson, "Duck Amuck," 41; my emphasis.
52. Thompson, "Duck Amuck," 41.
53. Polan, "Brecht and the Politics of Self-Reflexive Cinema."
54. Lindsay, *The Art of the Moving Picture*, 174.
55. Adorno and Horkheimer, "The Culture Industry," 1023.
56. Dorfman and Mattelart, *How to Read Donald Duck*.
57. Ngai, *Ugly Feelings*, 101.
58. Sitney, "Harry Smith Interview," 94–95.
59. Sitney, "Harry Smith Interview," 102.

I :: Time and Space

1 : : **Animation and History**

ESTHER LESLIE

Animation's Ahistory

Does animation have a history? Does it evolve as would any other
medium that is born and grows up, all the while refining and developing
its techniques? This appears to be how film developed. Film moved from
the front-on static-camera view to the dollying and swooping camera
eye; from black-and-white, through hand tinting, to color; from silent
to noisy; and from 2-D to 3-D, while developing editing techniques and
honing its acting styles. Then came the day, quite recently, when film
merged, through CGI, with animation. This thing that was called film,
and still is, evolves from simplicity to complexity, blaring out a narrative of progress, at least in the commercial realm. Each new film is to be
bigger, better, more immersive, more expensive, more profitable, and
more "life-like" (if not more realistic) than the last. The latest gambits
are 3-D and HD, though they are also part of the increasing entwine-
ment of film and animation via the digital. In its quest to be ever more
real, film mobilizes the irreal arts of animation. Does animation proceed
through time and technique in the same progressive way, rarely looking back? Can one tell for sure when any one animation was made? Can
one date a single animation by its technique, its ideas, its structure, the
quality of its coloration or film stock? Of course, it is possible to perceive
celluloid's deterioration and posit oldness. Of course, the coloration or
absence of color may give a clue. The technical properties of the strip
along with the music and the ideas may well indicate the date when it
was made. But animation is not as clear-cut as film, because in film the
passing fads of a world out there impress themselves upon the medium
more definitely through a technical and a social reaction. Every detail,
the fashions, the hairstyles, the makeup (even if the film purports to
be a historical one), the attitudes, the quality of color, the pace of the
editing, the rhythms of the soundtrack, the clarity of the image, the

shape of the bodily gestures, all this bears a date stamp. Film, in general, bears a rigidly progressive relationship toward both social and technical developments (though now part of that technical development has absorbed into itself the technical capacities of computer-generated animation). Film reflects its age into itself. But animation does not, or not quite so straightforwardly. It would be barely possible to place in any chronological order, in some line of responsible historical development, the myriad flimsy fragments that make up animation's legacy, for these fragments, by their very (different) nature, are so detached, reattached, and misattached from and to the world outside of them that they pose only questions, riddles, essays. Animation makes many starts. It makes many false starts. Animation starts and stops, by nature. It combines and cuts and undercuts, and reconstructs and constructs, tricks and reveals the trick and perhaps all at once. Film may do this too, but it tends to obscure the traces of the work upon it. In the mid-1930s Walter Benjamin described the output: "The equipment-free aspect of reality here has become the height of artifice."[1]

Animation is too obviously manifold to set out upon a single line of development. It begins with shadow play or with thumb cinemas, with zoetropes or magic lanterns, with lightning sketches or cel animation, with hidden wheels and pulleys or with stop-motion photography. It starts and stops in many places. It is at one and the same time a beginning and a culmination. To accept a thought such as this could explain the never-flagging bounciness of Walter Ruttmann's cavorting shapes of the early 1920s. Or it could allow an understanding of why Disney's feature cartoons are reissued periodically, not as historical items but as entities to occupy the present, even if nowadays morphed into 3-D. The banal way to put this is stated by Alan Bergman, the president of the Walt Disney Studios, in a press release: "Great stories and great characters are timeless, and at Disney we're fortunate to have a treasure trove of both."[2] In wayward terms, the sentiment taps into something of the otherworldly character of animation, which makes it truly ahistorical in relation to our world.

But this is not to say that animation always exchanges its relation to its moment for an arrival in ours. Its moment of making marks itself on the animation too, but perhaps more covertly than film's historical moment does. What does Ruttmann's outburst against Lotte Reiniger and her silhouette animation suggest about animation's particular hold on its moment of making? Reiniger animated cutouts, black delicacies set in flat fairy-tale worlds of filigreed detail. Ruttmann was a collabora-

tor on what is now labeled the oldest surviving feature-length animation. Reiniger's fairy tale, *The Adventures of Prince Achmed*, was released
in 1926. Ruttmann sat assembled with the other animators for the first
time to watch the marked copy and is reported to have exclaimed, "What
has this to do with 1923?"[3] What did the dancing shadows, trapped in
a flat world of genies and demons, caught only with sidelong glances,
have to do with the spectacular collapse of the German economy in the
epoch of hyperinflation? This was a time when, as Benjamin notes, "for
this nation [Germany], a period of just seven years separates the introduction of the calculation with half-pfennigs (by the postal authorities
in 1916) from the validity of the ten thousand mark note as the smallest
currency unit in use (1923)."[4] But Ruttmann was wrong to think that the
fairy-tale film was simply at variance to the economic devastations of
the epoch and only a frivolous play of paper and light. In any case, paper
in those charged years of billion-mark banknotes and financial ruin was
far from a frivolous topic. Perhaps indeed this animation had *everything*
to do with the crisis years, re-presenting, in graphic form, a fading out
of all life's color, a distancing from the graspable three-dimensionality
of reality, the world or life as bare, a shadow of its former self.[5] Perhaps Reiniger's animation steps toward satisfying the needs of a new
audience—composed of those who Georg Simmel had earlier termed
the "blasé" type of industrialized modernity, for whom overstimulation
promotes a withdrawal from the distinctions between things—in order
to favor that which is homogenous.[6] Perhaps this withdrawal anticipates
what Herbert Marcuse would later call the "One Dimensional Man."[7]
Arguably, Reiniger's animation dramatizes a local, historical alienation
of life through mobilization of its shadow forms by unseen hands and
unseen technologies. Except, sometimes, the scissors make their appearance—and they reveal the whole confection to be a dance of light
and paper and agile hands. Snip snip: the film is made of cuts. The film
presents, through another nature, a sidelong reflection on ours.

Perhaps it is also true that the animation had nothing specifically to
do with 1923. Animation, the one by Reiniger, just like countless others,
always asks the viewer to take a leap out of now, out of physics, out
of time, out of this world, in short, a leap of faith, to don the seven-
league boots of folklore and replace the substance with the silhouette,
the shadow. Animation is not a depiction of a recognizable world. The
mission of animation is often to tarry with the shadow side, the "night
side of nature," that obscured realm in which all unexplained and magical, illogical events occur.[8] Animation goes, in all its superficiality, deeply

into the substance of being, the hidden realms, the crevices beneath usual exposure, the constructions and reconstructions. Animation as the visualization of the shadow side is also an allegory of filmic actuality, albeit a truth that film most usually works to obscure. For film, the secret must be maintained: film asks viewers to believe in those shadows cavorting in two dimensions on the flat screen in the "kingdom of shadows," who all too often seem to live for us.[9] Film is the unknowing suspension of disbelief in stand-ins, doppelgangers, avatars, things that only pretend to be real, full-blooded, breathing, but are in fact chemical confections, celluloid compositions. Which is also to say, film is and has always been just a subset of animation—in contrast to how critics presented the relation—if animation is understood to be the inputting of life, or the inputting of the illusion of life, into that which is flat or inert or a model or an image. Reiniger, intentionally or not, made an emblem of this spectacularity, in a cine-world that was also incidentally—with the victories of the culture industry—flattening out into platitudes, façades, surfaces, and flimsiness. In giving the shadows delicate life, she made a virtue of film's flimsy flattening, decried its dull mimetics, and opened it, through animation, onto fantastic speculation and the possibility of revelation.

Telling Fairy Tales

In "Better Castles in the Sky," an essay from 1959 in *The Utopian Function of Art and Literature*, Ernst Bloch wrote of how clouds are a "fairy tale qualit[y] of nature."[10] They are, so think children, "distant mountains," entities in "a towering and wonderful foreign land above our heads," a Switzerland in the sky. The cloud is not only a "castle or ice-mountain to the fairy tale gaze." It is also an "island in the sea of heaven or a ship, and the blue skies on which it sails resemble the ocean." In the child's mind, the fluffy clouds turn into solid mountains. The airy blue sky is imagination's watery sea. The heavens are like a mirror, reflecting the Earth's inversion. All this transformation is a fundamentally animational principle. And so, if down below on earth is the world of body and action, then up there above is the world of mind, thought, imagination, and other histories, including better ones. Clouds are the fuzzy matter of utopian speculation for Bloch. They are moving screens onto which can be projected a revolutionary "not yet," the contents of an unbounded "anticipatory consciousness." This anticipatory consciousness as cloud is the antithesis of the clouds that Leni Riefenstahl allows to frame Hitler in *Triumph of the Will* (1935). These filmic clouds are the backdrop for one who is to be seen as a new god come down to earth from his airplane. The nebulous clouds of blue-sky thinking are also unlike the swastika-shaped clouds of Nutzi Land, projected by Disney in *Der Fuehrer's Face* (1942). But these Nutzi clouds, in their twisting of nature into political form, do illustrate an astute recognition that even, or especially, nature is not immune from the fascist colonizing impulse. The cloud-scape, castles and mountains in the sky, the crystals of ice that make up those clouds—these are the indistinct, magical, fuzzy places of waiting and longing. For Bloch, the vague awareness of a liberated life that blurrily takes shape in our daydreams is a stimulus for the real-world political action that seeks to fix the wishes. In his revolutionary eschatology, the clouds themselves are to be brought back down to earth. Our new, improved selves, lives, and political arrangements will roll in from the clouds and lodge on our ground—and not as Hitler's airplane does, as spectacle. Animation is the medium that allows for a dramatization of a skirmish with nature. This skirmish is not the fascistic one of subjugation. It is rather a wrestling with what is natural about nature, and what is historical, which is to say, changeable, about it. In the cartoon world, people, buildings, cars, and other inanimate objects swell suddenly, or run away, talk and leap, fly and fall without pain. Cartoons and trick films produced to entertain the city hoards were experimental and crazy from the start, using cinematic tricks and visual gags that defied logic. It was all these aspects of transformation, transmutation, alogicality, antiphysics, and nonrealism that appealed to the many intellectuals and artists—Dadaists and revolutionaries in Europe foremost among them—who fell in love with cartoon product and the outputs of American popular modernity in the first half of the twentieth century. Early comic strips and young animation processes broke open the self-understanding of the image, fracturing it into absurdism. In the cartoon world, all the laws of physics are defied or mocked. Even physics—the science of physical experience in the world—is made provisional. In animated nature, technology and magic are one.

The animated world is one in which nature is remolded, made different. Cartoons, modernized versions of folk and fairy tales, mobilize this nature in their presentation of overlively objects, or cows that turn into musical boxes, skirts that become parachutes when needed, or church steeples that crunch themselves up so that the crazy plane can avoid crashing into it with Mickey and Minnie Mouse on board. Animation reminds us of the life in other things that is like and unlike the life in us. Taken as a document of utopian thinking, animation shows a nature that is reformulated according to imagination and social prompts from a world that could one day and in some form become ours. This animated nature may assume any form and usually does in its presentation of hybrids of human and animal, coagulations of machineries and bodies, scenarios in which natural law is overturned or maliciously asserted. As the expressionist director Paul Wegener put it in 1916 in a lecture attended by Reiniger, the aim for "absolute cinema," an exploratory cinema beyond the subtheatrical version that threatened to dominate, was "a kind of cinema which would use nothing but moving surfaces, against which there would impinge events that would still participate in the natural world but transcend the lines and volumes of the natural."[11] Animation appeared to fulfill this cultured wish.

Animation depicts a nature that is hybridized: speaking animals, flowers that blush, fruits that ripen in the blink of an eye, people who shrink and twist and deform and swell. Animation's nature does not obey the laws of physics. Rain may fall upward. The sun may smile. But sometimes it *is* also just nature—redrawn and conceptualized, but mediated, with just a heightened element of drama, a potential that borders on the animistic. A shorthand version of such a definition of animation claims that animation is, in the phrases coined by Benjamin to describe the reproduced and constructed worlds of photography and film, "eine andere Natur" (different nature), an other nature.[12] Animation is "different nature" because its nature is of a different kind to the one we inhabit, and yet it is not distinct from it. Animation presents a parallel world. It presents a nature recognizable to us processed through concept, imagination, and technology. It is our nature returned back to us through mediations. Animated nature's otherness is, by and large, not one of absolute difference. Instead it is an alternativity. Animation's objects and images, drawn or modeled, are motile, flexible, open to possibility, and able to extend in any direction and undertake any action or none. Animation does not depict antinature, but "other nature," which might indeed be the noninstrumentalized nature that we would commune with, were we not so far along the route to ecological disaster. Animation's animistic approach to its objects awakens life and voice in stilled and silenced objects. It reinvents not only nature but our relationship with nature. It is therapeutic and utterly necessary. In "Experience and Poverty," from 1933, Benjamin indicates Mickey Mouse's ability to embody utopian aspiration for a technology-ravaged, yet technology-dependent, populace.[13] The existence of Mickey Mouse is labeled by

Benjamin a dream for today's people. Mickey Mouse's existence is full of miracles, and these miracles outdo technical wonders, and satirize them too. In Benjamin's view, Mickey Mouse enacts the wish for a harmonious reconciliation of technology and nature. The wish is born of an age in which technological change threatens to destabilize the existence of nature, including humans, and destroy all in spectacular acts of annihilation. But the compassionate union of technology and nature must be banished to the dreamtime world of comics and cinema, where machinery entertains and consoles humans, just as it dissects and recomposes images of humans, and the rest of the object and natural world. In the noncinematic world of industrial capitalism, technology and nature (in other words, machinery and humans) pursue different ends, are vectors of abuse and exploitation.

Sergei Eisenstein devised a category of "plasmaticness" that he evoked in order to stress the originary shape-shifting potential of the animated, the way in which an object or image, drawn or modeled, strains beyond itself, and can potentially adopt any form, thereby proposing an expansion beyond current constraints.[14] Where Benjamin observed the antiphysical, antinaturalist aspects of animation, Eisenstein focused on its renditions of the physical world. For Eisenstein, it was animated fire, which, he observes, "is capable of most fully conveying the dream of a flowing diversity of forms."[15] For Eisenstein, fire is formless. Fire is pure transformation. Fire is restless. It was the fire behind the mirror's mask in Disney's *Snow White and the Seven Dwarfs* (1937) that evoked these thoughts. Eisenstein's name for this mutability, echoing but altering Walter Benjamin's, is "non-indifferent nature."[16] Animation is for Eisenstein an ecstatic form. Its objects are ecstatic (which is to say, displaced or unstable), and it induces ecstasy in its viewers. It makes the viewers be besides themselves. Animation forces transition, a difference in quality. As Eisenstein puts it in *Non-indifferent Nature: Film and the Structure of Things* (1945): "To be beside oneself is unavoidably also a transition to something else, to something different in quality[,] . . . to be out of the usual balance and state, to move to a new state."[17] Such movement to a new state is made analogous to a physical process. If fire is a transformation, formless form, so too is water. Water may be steam, ice, liquid, and water is always passing between any of these states, when subjected to processes of heating, cooling, agitation, pressure, and so on. In *Non-indifferent Nature* Eisenstein states that "if water, steam, ice, and steel could psychologically register their own feelings at these critical *moments* — moments of achieving the leap, they would say they are speaking with *pathos*, that they are in ecstasy."[18] Animation is compelling because it is the "if" of water, steam, ice, and steel registering their own feelings at critical moments. The artist, at the same time, notes Eisenstein, creates "the necessary conditions"—specifically the construction of pathos—for the transformation of the spectator into an ecstatic state. It makes the viewer restless. This thought came from a man who had proposed "Kino-Fist," an assault on the viewer, as the appropriate mode of a new political cinema.

Animated nature appeals to us pathetically, by inviting us into its particular world. Animated nature's appeal is mediated via technology and is a shuttle between the image world of a new or second nature and us, who may be addressed as nature or as nature's other. We are invited in for the duration of the show and the rattled and super-lively objects are to make us rattled and super-lively in turn. Animation's small worlds propose certain stances on the part of viewers, encouraging them to be at least minimally alert to the ways of the image world unrolling before them, especially as it compares to the world in which they sit. They are aware too, on some, if only subliminal, level, of the differences within the image world, that is to say, the gaps between the cels or poses. These gaps, key to animation's structure, enable the excessive or implausible movements that characterize animation and mark it as seemingly unlimited and full of infinite potential. The animated form presents a dynamic image world in which, in much the same way as Eisenstein describes the dialectical cinema that he hoped to develop as his contribution to postrevolutionary culture, there is manifested a condensation of tensions that appeals, or may appeal, in a particular and cognitive way to its viewers. This is because, in propelling the viewer from image to thought, from percept to concept, the animated form models the motion of thinking itself—such that viewers are invited to complete the film through an act of appropriation of its new, and subverted, nature.

Animation and Capital

But it is not all mountains, clouds, flickering fires, and fairy tales. Animation—as Reiniger's work intimated with its flat, dark figures—has its negative face. In fact, this account would all be fairy tale were there not something else that animation as form could absorb. Animation may not readily expose its links in a progressive history of unfolding forms, but it can absorb and retransmit the motive energies of its moment. Indeed, along with the trick in film, or special effects (e.g., montage, superimposition, and negative printing), which is always in some way or another an introduction of animating principle into film, animation was the realm in which all sorts of experimenting artists found that they could develop a film language that communicated with and took hold of modernity. Through photographic media's barrage of special effects, Reiniger and Ruttmann alike developed an animated language that spoke to modernity, to its objectifications, its abstractions, and its flattening out of everything to fit into the industrial template. In this they mapped out the parameters of a system that was experienced as abstract and rationalized. They also made the system dance and overturn itself. They stretched out its time and probed its space and logic. But this work was not limited to the art experimenters—and this is another appeal of the animated. Value is less of a paranoid concern for it. It is *animation*. Or it is *cartoon*. Or it is eye music, "living pictures," "kinetische Lyrik," "optical poetry," or cinematic lyricism. At a premiere of Oskar Fischinger's *Study No. 12* in Berlin, the critic Bernhard Diebold gave a speech titled "The Future of Mickey Mouse." If cinema was to be an art form, he argued, it needed animation, because that made possible a cinema that had broken free of a naturalistic template and conventional storylines. Animated film defied the inherited artistic genres. Animation was proposed as the medium to translate into movement Wassily Kandinsky's restful points and dynamic lines in tension. Animation is—or was—always outside the frame of bourgeoisified art, though oftentimes special pleading is made for it to be let in. And yet early critics and makers certainly sensed that more united than divided were the popular works of Disney or Max Fleischer and the absolute films, or artworks, of Hans Richter or Lotte Reiniger or Walter Ruttman or Oskar Fischinger, or indeed the many advertisements they all made.

Winsor McCay, from 1911 onward, tried his hand at animation. His comic strip *Little Nemo: Adventures in Slumberland* had thematically set the city in motion. His first animation transferred Little Nemo to the screen, tentatively. First we see live action, and we see the animators and the backers of the industry in its moment of formation inside the new structures of the supercity. Inside the boxes of offices in New York, men conspire to give flat shapes life and color. There is little narrative in this animation, which consists of an unmotivated, illogical squashing and stretching, enacting the very principle of cartooning. This animation could be described as an example of the optical illusion of movement, though it is honest about its source and does not seek to deceive. It might better be described as a rumination on the passage between living and drawing, between lifelessness and life, identity and nonidentity. This animation is an image of the origin of animation itself. It is not the illusion of movement but, rather, presents movement itself, as a feat, rushing through the projector, the result here, as the film makes clear, of thousands of drawings and gallons of ink.

The motion generated in these first studio offices of mass cultural production could also be seen as a modeling of the dynamic, ever-changing forms of modernity, translated here into as lithe and as wild a form as the innovations of the prized treasures of high modernism. More specifically, the motion is a modeling of modern capital's motive force, the commodity economy, whose endless replications and innovations and commodity fetishism are analogously evident in the animated objects' push beyond their own static objectivity. Every week a new comic strip. Every month a new cartoon. The capitalist machine needs its supplies.

Animation's animatedness can be seen as a rendition of the apparent liveliness of commodity-fetishized objects. This is why advertisers loved cartoons from the start—that illusory hyperliveliness of objects, a topsy-turvy negation of the value that stems from labor. What is animation but objects coming seemingly to life, without human intervention, so it appears (but only appears—just as in commodity fetishism, the real source of value is obscured from usual view and knowledge). In the same way that commodities are correlated to exchange values, so too are those who make the commodities. Their energy, all that makes them alive, is directed toward making useful things, but it is also calibrated as abstract labor, as quantities of labor—x amount of labor hours at y amount of cost carried out by z. Indeed it is significant that, stuck on his lonely desert island, Robinson Crusoe is much concerned with saving a ledger, a pen and ink, and a watch. To be the perfect capitalist he must keep a stock book of items, a record of their mode of manufacture, and, crucially, a note of "the labour-time that definite quantities of those objects have, on an average, cost him."[19] But think what an animator does with the same equipment. Animation can be the realm in which such graphic rendition might make social forms available to knowledge, by redrawing or reshaping the rules, erasing the lines, twitching that which has become static, reconstructing or just constructing the movement, as a conscious afterimage of what we do and what the world does and what nature does daily and forever. Animation absorbs, digests, and reconfigures something of its moment of making.

Cartoon Manifesto

Animation is subversive of nature, which has so often been mobilized as ideology. Animation is subversive of order, of logic, of stasis, of every-thing that would insist that things are so and must be so—the reaction-ary mode that has more latterly been labeled by politicians as *neorealism* and is partnered with neoliberalism. Animation is an art of metamor-phosis, of transformation, and it is as if the ways in which the animated form shifts from one state to another proffers an inkling of a transfor-mation that could be undergone by all—politically, socially. Therein lies the utopian axis of animation—motility and mobility is its propulsive force, its opening onto an infinite, antigravitational other-space. Ani-mation is subversive of progress as understood in its ahuman, limited sense—as in the idea of endless perfectability in techniques and tech-nologies. Animation does not necessarily eschew the low-tech. Anima-tion is subversive of tastefulness—though it must be said that it has truly wormed its way into art galleries these days. Animation is subver-sive of itself—ever changing, ever shifting. Animation is subversive of separation. It is made and seen collectively. It unites the artisanal, the artistic, and the mechanical.

Animation has a history, naturally. Everything has a history, but, un-like film, animation, with its multiple forms (stop frame, puppet, drawn, CGI), with its low-tech and commercial practices, and with its multiple origins in zoetropes, zoopraxiscopes, shadow theater, flip-books, and the like, evokes a history that is as crowded and indistinct as a phantas-magoria. Animation does to history what it does to nature. Animation evokes history, plays with it, undermines it, subverts it, but it does not have it, just as it does not have nature. It has second nature. Or different nature. It has different history. It models the possibility of possibility.

Notes

1. Benjamin, *The Work of Art in the Age of Its Technological Reproducibility, and Other Writings on Media*, 35.
2. "Disney Re-releasing Films in 3D: 'Beauty & The Beast,' 'The Little Mermaid,' Others Coming Back," *Huffington Post*, October 4, 2011, accessed July 1, 2013, www.huffingtonpost.com/2011/10/04/disney-re-releasing-films-3d_n _994701.html.
3. Ruttmann quoted by Reiniger in Bendazzi, *Cartoons*, 33.
4. Benjamin, from a draft of "Imperial Panorama," in *Gesammelte Schriften*, vol. IV.2, 934.

5. Simmel, "The Metropolis and Mental Life," 14.
6. Simmel, "The Metropolis and Mental Life," 14.
7. Marcuse, *One-Dimensional Man* (1964).
8. For example, see the nineteenth-century Romantic scientist Gotthilf Heinrich von Schubert's *Ansichten von der Nachtseite der Naturwissenschaft* (Views on the Night-Side of Natural Science) (Dresden: Arnold, 1808).
9. This is Maxim Gorky's description upon experiencing the Lumière Cinematographe in July 1896. Richard Taylor and Ian Christie, eds., *The Film Factory: Russian and Soviet Cinema in Documents, 1896–1939* (London: Routledge, 1994), 25–26.
10. Bloch, *The Utopian Function of Art and Literature*, 175.
11. Paul Wegener, from a lecture given on April 24, 1916, at an Easter Monday conference, and printed in Kai Möller, *Paul Wegener* (Hamburg: Rowohlt Verlag, 1954). Quoted in Eisner, *The Haunted Screen*, 33.
12. Benjamin, "Little History of Photography," in *Selected Writings, Volume 2*, 510, 512.
13. Benjamin, "Experience and Poverty," in *Selected Writings, Volume 2*, 734–35.
14. Eisenstein, *Eisenstein on Disney* (1988), 11.
15. Eisenstein, *Eisenstein on Disney* (1988), 24.
16. The phrase *non-indifferent nature* is to be found where Eisenstein found it: in Hegel, in his discussion of chemism in the *Science of Logic*, where it is crucial to a discussion of motion, transformation, and affinity in natural processes. G. W. F. Hegel, *Science of Logic* (Blackmask Online, 2001), 120–24.
17. Eisenstein, *Non-indifferent Nature*, 27.
18. Eisenstein, *Non-indifferent Nature*, 35–36.
19. See Marx, "The Fetishism of Commodities and the Secret Thereof," in *Capital* (Harmondsworth, UK: Penguin and New Left Review, 1976), 164–65.

2 : : Animating the Instant: The Secret Symmetry between Animation and Photography

TOM GUNNING

The Discontinuous Photography of Continuous Animation

After being marginalized—or outright ignored—animation moved to the center of a new theorization of the moving image brought on by the rise of new media. Pioneers of new media theory such as Lev Manovich promoted animation in opposition to the focus on cinema's links to photography, which was so central to the great film theorists' work that emerged after the silent era: André Bazin, Siegfried Kracauer, Stanley Cavell, and even, in a sense, Walter Benjamin. For Manovich, digital media, with its control over pixels, reveals cinema "as a subgenre of painting," exhibiting a freedom of image creation rather than the supposed indexical enthrallment to reality that photography entails.[1] Valorizing animation as the anti-index played an essential role in shifting theoretical focus from a narrow obsession with photography and opened a new exploration of animation as a form, but does placing animation in opposition to photography really provide our best understanding of its nature?

Most film animation actually depends on photography, at least technically, even when photography does not supply animation's imagery. Keeping animation and photography separate seems nearly impossible. The animation theorist Alan Cholodenko claims that "every encounter with film is an encounter with animation—cinema, that is, live action film, included."[2] This is first of all a technical fact. As David Rodowick has stressed (or any technical description of cinematic animation points out), animating drawings in classical animation involves photographing them onto a filmstrip: "We are mistaken if we use the concept of animation to refer to the hand drawing of sequential images; it refers, rather, to photographing such images frame by frame and producing the illusion of motion by projecting them at a constant rate of movement."[3] Rodowick may slightly overstate the case if we consider such devices as flip-books or zoetropes, but cinematic animation always involves at least a projector and usually a camera. Even animation that employs drawing and painting directly on the filmstrip, often called *cameraless animation* (which has yielded so many extraordinary works by Len Lye, Norman McLaren, Stan Brakhage, Harry Smith, and recently Jodie Mack), commonly involves the making of a projection print through photographic processes. Thus, at the minimum, most animation requires photography as a means of mechanical reproduction. Therefore, animation's relation to the manual (and auratic) aspects of painting (valorized by Manovich) becomes technically mediated. While seemingly only a technical process, this transformation from manual drawing to mechanically produced filmstrip represents a fundamental transformation. By photographing onto the filmstrip, the continuous gestures of the hand employed in drawing or other manual processes are translated into the discontinuous rhythm of the machine.

The technical nature of cinema—producing continuous motion from discontinuous instants (frames)—reveals the common grounding of photography and animation in their control of time, which is what I will call the *manufacture of the instant*. Rather than maintaining the difference between animation and so-called live-action cinema, based in the manual or photographic origins of their images and consequent relation to the indexical, I want to point out not only their common quality as moving images but also their common transformation of time: their creation of the pulse of an instant through the discontinuity of the machine.

Cameraless animation highlights this dialectic relation of the continuous synthesis of movement and the discontinuous parsing of time at the heart of cinematic animation, even in its most "direct" form. In the 1920s the constructivist artist Hans Richter learned that his abstract scroll paintings (which were inspired by the temporal unrolling of the filmstrip—as well as Chinese scroll paintings and musical scores) could not be simply transferred to a filmstrip but had to be subjected to frame-by-frame photography in order to become a projectable film. Filmmakers may ignore or pay close attention to the way the apparatus (at the minimum the filmstrip and the projector, even if a camera is not used in making a print) will process their drawings, paintings, scratchings, or other markings on the actual surface of filmstrips into individual pulses, but they cannot avoid it. The animator Jodie Mack wrote me in response to my question to her about this:

Cameraless animation, free from the constraints of the camera's shutter, can either ignore or embrace the frame-by-frame divisions of the film-strip imposed by the sprockets. In frame-less animation legato-drawn gestures, sections of pattern, or blades of grass can cover long sections of film producing animation, perhaps unexpectedly, when projected.

Frame-by-frame (staccato?), cameraless animations borrow from the mechanics of cinema to achieve motion through purposeful sequencing of multiple images. A filmmaker could treat one foot of 16mm film as one long canvas or forty tiny individual canvases.[4]

Mack sets up the issue beautifully: the filmstrip viewed as succession of frames yields a staccato rhythm of passing individual instants, which the direct animators can either ignore in their processes, *or* use to structure their markings on the film. In either case, however, the process of projection (the intermittent frame-by-frame movement and projection through a shutter that are essential to all cinema) will endow the images with a continuity of movement borne of the discontinuity of individual frames (or, at the minimum, the rhythm of the projector shutter). This dialectic of continuous perceptual synthesis of what are technically discontinuous individual frames describes the process of motion in all cinema. Animation arguably makes this *production* of motion more evident.

Animation[1] and Animation[2]:
Cinematic Motion at Work and Play

This fusion of discontinuous instants, which defines film movement technically, plays a backstage role in our reception of cinema, whose dominant phenomenological effect is the perception of the flow of motion. The perceptual conditions of cinema rest on the fact that we do not, in standard projection, perceive the individual frames. The frame rate of the cinema surpasses a threshold of human perception in order to produce motion and efface our awareness of individual frames. (Some theorists call this the illusion of motion, but I feel that this begs a question. We are not tricked into seeing motion; we perceive it through an encounter between a specially designed machine and the processes of human vision.) But if the still frames become invisible, animated films, from cartoons to experimental work, constantly visualize and act out the process of producing motion. Cartoons from animators like Emil Cohl to Hayao Miyazaki show objects coming to life.[5] Indeed, the art historian Erwin Panofsky saw this as cartoons' essence: "The very virtue of the animated cartoon is to animate, that is to say, endow lifeless things with life or living things with a different kind of life. It effects a meta-morphosis."[6] Further, animated films frequently display their own pro-cesses by the baring of their devices. From Cohl to Winsor McCay to the Fleischer brothers, animators frequently portray on screen their creation of images and motion, which is a gesture that the historian of animation Don Crafton calls "self-figuration" and claims as emblem-atic of the animated film (e.g., *Fantasmagorie* [1908], *Little Nemo* [1911], and *Out of the Inkwell* [1918–29]).[7] In these caprices, animation displays cinema's otherwise invisible discontinuous frames.

It might be useful to bisect our term *animation* into two related but separable meanings. The first I call animation[1]; it refers to the techni-cal production of motion from the rapid succession of discontinuous frames, shared by all cinematic moving images. I define animation[2] more narrowly, referring to the genre of animation as commonly under-stood: moving images that have been artificially made to move, rather than movement automatically captured through continuous-motion picture photography. Nonphotographic images are most common in animation[2], but still photographs can also be animated, as in Norman McLaren's *Neighbours* (1952) or the collage films of Stan Vanderbeek in the 1950s and 1960s. I would describe animation[2] as not only displaying but also *playing* with the production of motion of animation[1]. I mean by this to invoke the ludic attitude that animation nearly always embraces. But I also reference the more technical meaning of *play* often applied to the muscles of the body or the parts of a machine or device, given in the *Oxford English Dictionary* as "freedom or room for movement; the space in or through which a thing can or does move."[8] One could state tautologically that all moving images *move*, but that animation[2] also *plays* with movement; it directs our attention to the effect of movement and explores its limits, its "room for play," the freedom of its move-ment.[9] Animation[2] plays with movement with an affect of wonder and draws attention to its own process. Animation[2] arouses some curiosity about how it is done, though this does not require a thorough technical understanding. Animation[2] restores to the moving image the sense of wonder at movement that the first projections of moving images occa-sioned.[10]

By foregrounding the process of producing motion, animation[2] bares the device of the motion-picture camera and projector and returns the vanished discontinuous frames to consciousness. This might be dis-puted, since our experience of animation[2] most often sweeps us up in a world of movement, rather than making us speculate on its technology. I argue that the wonder triggered by animation[2] comes from its pivot from stillness to motion, not simply conceived of as a technical process but experienced as a fundamental manipulation of time, which I call the *production of the instant*. Animation reveals the single frame, the brief incremental of time, through the *possibility* of motion, animation's ability to transform from static image to moving moment, from inanimate picture to animated image. Our core experience of animation[2] corresponds to the old fantasy of drawings brought to life. We wonder at the motion more than we posit the animation stand, camera, or filmstrip. However, erasing the camera from our understanding of the process not only distorts our technical understanding but also eclipses a full exploration of the wonder we experience at this genesis of motion. Probing animation in relation to the processes of photography actually allows us to more fully grasp the adventure in time and movement that all cinema invites us, as viewers, to join: the technological manipulation of time through the discovery of the instant as the seed of motion.

How does animation[2] delight us and draw our curiosity to the processes of animation[1], which underlies all cinematic moving images? As Panofsky claimed, wonder at the effect of animation increases with the animation of something otherwise perceived as inanimate (drawings, painting, geometrical figures, objects, puppets). The process of animation[1] carries an implicit fascination, an element of wonder, which animation[2] unfolds before us. Therefore, the very playfulness of animation[2] propels a theoretical project, following both Plato's and Aristotle's observations that all theory (*theoria*) begins in *thauma*, the Greek term for "wonder."[11] If theory begins as an affect of astonishment, it develops through curiosity, and the wonder triggered by animation[2] leads us to consider the nature of time in cinema through the technological production of the instant, the minimal increment of temporality.[12]

I want to use animation[2]'s devices of defamiliarization to rediscover the processes of cinema, not as a primitive stage of technical development now surpassed in the digital age but as an essential move in the modern technological transformation of time. In this context, rather than opposed to each other, animation and photography both create a novel image and experience of time and movement through technology. Both discover a way to experience the most elusive of the concepts associated with time: the instant. Animation reveals the dynamic nature of the instant through motion, while photography reveals its potential through stillness—but considered together these technological processes also reveal that stillness and movement depend on and transform into each other in the production of the instant.

Photography and the Production of the Instant

We experience animation[1] as a visible quality of movement given to images by cinematic devices. This chapter seeks to probe the technical processes that makes this production of movement possible: the succession of individual frames and the parsing of time into instants, frame-by-frame animation, and the creation of an apparatus that presents these manipulations to human vision. Although the experience of movement as the goal of animation[1] can never be forgotten, I want to probe as well its relation to immobility—not, as is often done, to expose animation and cinematic movement as an illusion based in our fallible sense of vision (the old myth of the persistence of vision), but rather to remind us of the wonder of the *transformation* that underlies animation: the production of motion through the instant, the metamorphosis of continuity from discontinuous frames.[13] While the rapid movement of discrete frames through an animation device achieves apparent motion, instantaneous still photography reveals how the seed of motion can be contained in an apparently static instant.

Photography has a long history and cannot be reduced to the recording of an image through optical and chemical means. Photography extends the process of making an image into a representation of time. I will offer a brief sketch of photography's complex and evolving engagement with time, especially the length and control of exposure time and its relation to the instant of movement. An oscillation between stillness and movement (the discovery of one in the heart of the other) shapes this story. As the historian of photography Joel Snyder has observed, rather than producing an image of the world, photographers initially tackled a more technical task, embedded in previous technology: preserving the image produced by a camera obscura.[14] This first era of fixing an image precedes the later period, the production of the instant. The still cameras of Nicéphore Niépce, Henry Fox Talbot, and Louis-Jacques-Mandé Daguerre derived from and fundamentally transformed the camera obscura. The ability of a small aperture to project a real image into a dark container (camera obscura) had been observed since antiquity, when it was used primarily for astronomical observations, and perfected since the Renaissance as a way to generate a highly detailed image. But as is too often forgotten, the camera obscura projected a *moving* image, conveying all the complexity of motion, from staged pantomimes to leaves moving in the breeze.

Talbot, the British inventor of modern photography, after trying to use a camera obscura as an aid to sketching landscapes lamented: "How charming it would be if it were possible to cause these natural images to imprint themselves durably, and remain fixed upon the paper!"[15] The first era of photography sought to fix this image, exploiting the tendency of certain chemicals to darken on exposure to light and then taking on the even more difficult task of arresting this process before the image produced was swallowed in total obscurity. Photography intended to capture these fairy pictures and transform them into material, graspable objects imprinted with still images separable from their apparatuses. The dancing image of the camera obscura had to learn to pose, and time had to learn to stand still. The photographic camera and its product rendered the camera obscura's moving image a static one. The photographic image was fixed in two senses: a frozen image was obtained from the inherent mutability of the camera obscura; and this image in turn was delivered from a progressive darkening, arresting the very chemical process on which photography was founded. These victories over time depended on embalming the moment, eliminating all movement and change. The historian of photography Michel Frizot has even declared that "the whole history of the medium could be described as a race against time."[16]

But after this initial victory of fixing the image, another battle with time loomed: reducing the actual period of exposure during which the photochemically sensitive surface within the camera had to be exposed to light in order to form an image. Rather than the monumental immobility and drama of preservation staged in early photographs, this next temporal threshold introduced the discovery of the instant. The early photographic exposures by Niépce in the 1820s took hours to imprint themselves on his chemically treated surfaces. Even as the exposure time was gradually reduced to minutes, photographers still had to limit their subjects to static objects and architecture. The emblematic image of this slow process of photographic exposure is the famous photograph of the Boulevard du Temple that Daguerre took in 1838, in which the normally busy street filled with pedestrians and carriages appears deserted. None of the moving figures that actually thronged this street could leave an impression on the photographic plate, due to the ten minutes of exposure time needed to make the image. The exception is the lone figure of a man standing still and having his boots blacked (and possibly the blurred figure of the bootblack as he performs this task) whose relative immobility allowed him to imprint himself.[17]

Overcoming this opposition between photography and a mobile world motivated photographic innovation in the nineteenth century. It also opened a new realm of time to human culture. The threshold for the photographing of motion (i.e., for shooting a moving scene without blurring) was set at one-tenth of a second (an instant of time that would take on mythic status in the nineteenth and the early twentieth centuries as the marker of the technical and scientific measurement of time, as Jimena Canales's recent book has described beautifully).[18] As photographers cleared this threshold in the late 1870s, the nature of photography transformed radically, perhaps even fundamentally. Frizot refers to the years from 1880 to 1910 as "the era of instantaneity."[19] Reducing exposure time so that human expression appeared more spontaneous, moving vehicles no longer produced an unsightly blur, and processes of nature, such as a waterfall or ocean waves, could be represented constituted goals that photography inherited from aesthetic ideals of realism (i.e., similarity to human perception) and compositional harmony. But if achieving a reassuring resemblance to normal perception constituted one of the goals of nineteenth-century photography, it also had an unstable relation to technical progress. A combination of factors soon allowed photographers to further reduce speed of exposure to one-hundredth and even one-thousandth of a second, domains of temporality only a machine could measure, beyond (or beneath) human experience. A new realm of time, the temporality of the instant, was opened by such mechanical precision and brevity. Photography made this temporality available to the human experience. The mechanical shutter, surpassing both manual coordination and visual perception, provided, as Frizot puts it, the master key to this new photographic process of brief exposures.[20]

The rapidly closing shutter literally produces the instant, slicing into the continual flow of time like a guillotine, and both instantaneous photography and early animation devices employ it, in somewhat different manners (arguably the shutter appears in animation devices, such as the phenakistoscope and zoetrope, before it appears in the camera). Due to the relatively insensitive photographic chemicals used before the 1870s, the human gesture of removing and replacing the lens cap had sufficed to determine exposure time. The new emulsion speeds of the era of instantaneity demanded the mechanization and precision, as well as brevity, of a mechanical shutter.[21]

The shutter opens on an era of technological precision, rather than simple human vision, as human perception becomes redefined through its encounter with technology. As any visual representation would, a photograph can invoke and engage visual perception, but photography can never be simply identified with the act of human perception. Shorter exposure times may eliminate certain technical artifacts that contradict our image of human visual perception (such as blurred outlines or transparent objects), but other startling deviations from human perception appeared in the new instantaneous photographs—bodies floating above the ground, liquids taking on solid forms. Instead of recalling our normal vision, this instantaneous image exceeds it. It is human vision *plus*, an alien vision in which time is stopped or reduced into an uninhabitable brevity in which the flow of motion in its physical familiarity is replaced by static poses of an ungainly sort. As Snyder, speaking of Étienne-Jules Marey's chronophotography, said: "Chronophotographs then, can bring us into a domain we cannot see; yet at the same time, they can also show us what we do see, though we cannot warrant having seen apart from the pictorial evidence produced by precision instruments."[22] Instantaneous photography revealed a world no human had ever seen. An experience of time beyond the limits of human perception is broached by an optical apparatus.

Rather than simply embalming time, fixing it through a chemically stable image, the new instantaneous photography processed time mechanically—sliced and diced it, if you will. Instantaneous photography developed alongside new modes of temporal measurement in the sciences, where, as Canales demonstrates, the tenth of a second came to mark the limits of the "human factor" (the individual variability in response time) in scientific observation—a factor that only mechanical operations could remove.[23] A new domain of time, the time of the machine, seemed to open by the end of the nineteenth century. To dip beneath the tenth of the second, therefore, overcame the human, all-too-human, aspect of time and inaugurated the regime of mechanical precision. Such an unfamiliar experience of instantaneity belonged as well to new forces of energy, such as electricity, which seemed to surge across space as if it did not exist. Indeed, Eadweard Muybridge announced his instantaneous images in 1877 as "automatic electric photographs," referring to the electrical triggering of the camera shutters.[24] This new temporality was systematic, measured and produced by precision machinery, and could only be expressed by abstract mathematic measurements (what person could discern the difference between one-hundredth of a second and one-thousandth?).

The Instant: Denial of Motion or Its Origin?

Here we encounter an apparent paradox about photography's mastery of motion and a new phase in the oscillation between stillness and movement within the medium. Motion mastered is, at least in a phenomenological sense, motion destroyed. Frizot even speaks of time being murdered by instantaneous photography.[25] Apparently bereft of our traditional sense of time and movement, the photograph no longer represented a familiar world. But is this new world truly motionless and timeless, or does it reveal new dimensions of time and new ways to conceive of motion?

Let me trace this new phase in the oscillation of stillness and motion by focusing on one of the earliest and most famous of these unfamiliar images (in addition to being inscribed in film history, since the 1970s it has nearly been an emblem for animation): Muybridge's photograph of a horse in full gallop. This photograph not only revealed all four of a horse's hooves suspended above the ground at the same instant (a fact already established scientifically by Marey's graphic method) but also portrayed the position of those legs in a totally unfamiliar and previously unseen configuration. As is well known, this photograph was initially received with skepticism, if not outright rejection, especially by those whose observation of horses had been most intense: equestrian painters. The positions of the horses' legs in Muybridge's images were considered absurd, ungainly, and impossible. Indeed, Muybridge employed his device, the zoopraxiscope (a retooling of a projecting phenakistoscope), to animate his photographs of animal locomotion, in order to prove that these odd positions could be synthesized into a continuous visible movement. At this moment painting and photography dramatically confronted each other with radically different conceptions of the image of movement. One could claim that modern animation emerged from this conflict. Here the limitations of Manovich's alignment of animation with painting as opposed to photography come sharply into focus. Rather than following the alleged freedom of traditional painters, animation drew its inspiration—and its technical process—from the *photographic* visualization of the instant. Animation[2], however fanciful, roots itself in analytical instants especially as defined by instantaneous photography.

Even before submitting itself to the lesson of the instant as taught by photography, animation had pursued the parsing of time into brief increments though submitting human vision to the effect of a rapid shutter. In the 1830s scientists such as Michael Faraday and Peter Roget had systematically investigated the temporality of human visual perception using revolving shutter-like devices. In Roget's case these studies directly led to the first device of animation, the phenakistoscope, which used a revolving-shutter effect combined with a series of drawn images that portrayed stages of motion to create a moving image. As Manovich points out, the first devices of image animation predated photography. Although early animation devices are practically simultaneous with the early experiments in photography, the achieving of the instant in photography occurred some decades later. But my story here is not about claiming the precedence of one medium over the other; instead, I stress that both participate in and explore an era of instantaneity.

It may seem perverse to refer to these devices, designed to produce a moving image, as relating to the instant, since my discussion of instantaneous photography has emphasized suspending or freezing motion. Early animation devices such as the phenakistoscope and the zoetrope used the shutter to punctuate the circular succession of images that revolved within their devices, allowing the human eye to seize them as separate images and thus synthesize them into a flow of motion. Certainly the effects of the instantaneous photograph and the early animation devices are different, even opposed. The camera uses the shutter to freeze the motion of the world in order to fix the image of an instant; animation devices, in contrast, spin still images into a continuous flow as the shutter transforms this continuity into a discontinuous presentation of images to the eye, in order to create a single evolving motion rather than a blur. But both processes use their devices to manipulate the temporal aspect of vision and create new temporal regimes of imagery through the manufacture of the instant.

The instant so brief that motion is stilled had been imagined since antiquity, as the speculations of Parmenides and Zeno testify; mathematics and Zeno's concept of the infinite division of time supplied a way to conceive of this paradoxical unit. But the instantaneous photograph and the phenakistoscope are not concepts; as devices they do things, and they do them in relation to human perception. Logic opposes concepts, whereas perception transforms one into the other. Instantaneous photography supplied an image of a time beyond ordinary human reach, now captured through technology. The instantaneous photograph opened the way to experiencing the realm of the tenth of the second, the new microtemporality in which modern technology operates at an ever-accelerating pace beyond immediate human experience, yet arguably made visible to us through new media (through, as Snyder put it, "pictorial evidence produced by precision instruments") even as it reshapes human life and culture.

The modern instant as visualized in both photography and animation devices differs from the concept found in ancient philosophy. While the conceptual instant of antiquity in the Parmenidean tradition might have excluded motion, the instant of instantaneous photography does so only in a most literal fashion. The instantaneous photograph is an image, not an abstraction, and its relation to motion depends on its imagery. It is as revolutionary in its relation to imagery as it is to time. The traditional static image of painting since the Renaissance strove after a self-contained autonomy, an aesthetic coherence, while the frozen image of instantaneous photography struck observers as ugly, unaesthetic, and uncanny due to its incomplete and restless nature (a claim often made at the time about impressionist painting as well). Although still and frozen, these photographs invoke motion as much as they deny it. Their visualizing of an apparent defiance of gravity, the strain of outstretched limbs and the suspended trajectory of drops of water or tossed balls, displays movement in a more radical manner than had baroque or impressionist painting. These images hardly portray a Parmenidean eternity of total oneness. Rather, they present an often unbearably incomplete moment, filled with potential movement, an instant torn from an unseen (but imagined) continuity whose contours they evoke almost painfully. The neuroscientist Thierry Pozzo, writing on the effect of Marey's images, evokes Theodor Lipps's concept of empathy, in which the viewer seems to experience the physical sensation that he or she witnesses in a performer or image.[26] This empathetic sense of kinesthesia renders the frozen positions of the instantaneous image as more of a cramp begging to be relieved than a timeless moment. I believe it is nearly impossible to see an instantaneous photograph of motion without continuing the frozen motion in our imagination. These instant images practically demand animation[1].

Historically speaking, instantaneous photography's impulse toward motion becomes most visible in chronophotography.[27] It is not simply the positions of Muybridge's and Marey's mobile subjects that summon up motion; their placement within a continuous series of images do so as well. Images in series demonstrate the profound relation between practices of instantaneous photography and early animation devices. Phenakistoscope disks or the strips drawn for zoetropes and praxinoscopes also presented a series of still images in stages of motion. Still images serving as sections of motion are designed for these animation devices (which first emerged in the 1830s, an era when photographic exposure remained far from brief). However, these drawn representations of stages of motion remained necessarily speculative reconstructions and record no actual temporal relations. Their primary purpose was not the analysis of motion but the mechanical production of a moving image. The individually drawn image had little significance outside of its role in the mobile device.

Instantaneous photography and chronophotography do not imagine speculative segments but actually record an instant (or a series of instants), rendered visible by abstraction from the flux of time. We see in these images not a conception of the stages of motion but rather an image of the material form that bodies take in a specific instant of time. The chronophotography of the late nineteenth century invokes and invites animation[1] not only because the arrangement of images within a series clearly portrays the trajectory of movement but also because the series both follows and breaks down an action in strict temporal order. While animation[2] certainly aims at the reconstitution of movement, it fascinates us because we seem to see movement take place before our eyes. Animation[2] reproduces motion and also displays its origin, its birth, so to speak, the emergence of motion out of stillness, of continuity out of discontinuity.

Philosophical Dilemma, Visual Resolution

I will resist wandering too far into the philosophy of time and try to remain focused on the technical production of a temporal image rather than speculating on the nature of time itself, with its notorious aporia. (As Augustine beautifully put it in *Confessions*: "What then is time? I know what it is if no one asks me what it is; but if I want to explain it to someone who has asked me, I find that I do not know.")[28] The ambiguous term I have used throughout this chapter, *the instant*, remains crucial to both philosophical debates and the new image of time that instantaneous photography and animation offer. But I differentiate between these meanings. Within philosophy, the instant has primarily been conceived of as a unit of time, expressing a view of time as discontinuous and successive.[29] For Parmenides and his student Zeno, time is indivisible, and consequently change and motion are impossible, philosophically speaking. Plato posited a distinction between a transcendent timeless realm and a mutable world as a means of overcoming the immobility of Parmenides's system. Robin Durie asserts that the instant arises in Plato's system as a means of explaining change and the passing of time.[30] In his dialogue *Parmenides*, Plato writes: "There is no change from rest while resting, nor from motion while moving; but this instant, a strange nature, is something inserted between motion and rest and it is no time at all; but into it and from it what is moved changes to being at rest, and what is at rest to being moved."[31] Aristotle, in contrast, sees time as fundamentally continuous and claims that conceiving of time as an accumulation of discrete instants is incoherent. In place of instants, Aristotle finds the essence of time in the "now," which expresses the inherent continuity of time in the process of change and movement.[32] Time is not inherently made of discrete instants; instead, its continuity is potentially divisible. The concept of *potentiality* determines for Aristotle both the continuous nature of time and allows its passing. Rather than a discrete unit, the now functions both to divide and connect time, like a point in a line. Time is related to motion, stretching into the future, which defines its potentiality.

The philosophy of time recurrently encounters this dilemma. How can we imagine the dividing of time in such a way that its continuity and passing are not denied or rendered impossible? Does dividing up time stop it in its tracks? Inversely, does seeing time as simply continuous betray our sense that time changes radically, that it produces novelty, not just an endless succession of the same? This dilemma seems to recur in the modern era, whether as Henri Bergson's championing of duration versus Gaston Bachelard's valorization of the instant, or Alain Badiou's promotion of the event over Gilles Deleuze's defense of Bergson's duration.[33] I am interested in the issues that these controversies articulate more than adjudicating the contest (which I could never do).

The alternative models of time as a succession of discrete instants or as a pure continuity may seem to parallel the opposition between the frozen image produced by instantaneous photography (or its succession in the chronophotographic series) and the continuously moving image produced by animation devices, including the cinema. But this comparison seems to me to dissolve the opposition between models of time rather than heighten it. The instantaneous photograph may seem to embody the instant as a discrete unit of time and action, while the moving image expresses the continuity of duration. But a close examination of the technology of these images reveals that each seems to derive its effect from the other. Within its stillness the images of instantaneous photography strain toward the portrayal of motion. On the other hand, animation devices all employ still images that, when the device is operated, yield a perception of movement. In Aristotelian fashion, animation[1] demonstrates the potential of motion in stillness (and vice versa). In Plato's view, the instantaneous photograph possesses a "strange nature" in which "what is moved changes to being at rest, and what is at rest to being moved." Animation (both definitions) does not exist simply in the appearance of motion; animation is in the transformation of stillness into motion. It is this potential that one senses within the tense stasis of the instantaneous image; it is this transformation that produces the wonder of animated movement, Panofsky's metamorphosis.

Thus, the understanding of the instant that I propose here does not resemble a discrete unit of time, which somehow paradoxically adds up to motion and the flow of time. The instant embodies the potential to move between the regimes of stillness and motion. I am not sure that this statement is philosophically coherent, yet it describes our experience of both the instantaneous photograph, which may murder time but cannot deny it, and the perceptual experience of animation that resurrects time from its grave of immobility. I do not argue that these images reveal to us the true nature of time, but I would maintain that they produce experiences of the instant that avoid viewing time as inertly static. These images visualize the instant's inherence in motion and time, either by artificially abstracting it from that flow or by mechanically producing that flow. The suspended gestures and actions of the instantaneous photograph complement the moment when the static images passing through an animation device become a moving image. Each process engages with our experience of time and motion in a defamiliarizing manner. Rather than simply conceived of as reproductions of motion, both instantaneous still photography and motion picture cinematography play with our perception of motion in order to produce the instant as a wonder.

Notes

For Jodie Mack, sprite of motion.

1. Manovich, *The Language of New Media*, 295.
2. Cholodenko, "The Animation of Cinema," 1. Likewise, Giannalberto Bendazzi, in the standard reference source on animation, states: "A precise separation between animation and other media is not easily identifiable." Bendazzi, *Cartoons*, xvi.
3. Rodowick, *The Virtual Life of Film*, 121. See also the definition of *animated cartoon* from *The American Heritage Dictionary of the English Language* (fourth edition): "A motion picture or television film consisting of a photographed series of drawings, objects, or computer graphics that simulates motion by recording very slight, continuous changes in the images, frame by frame."
4. E-mail from Jodie Mack to Tom Gunning, June 8, 2012.
5. Lynda Nead has brilliantly explored this theme, especially in relation to drawing and painting coming to life in early trick films, in her book *The Haunted Gallery*.
6. Panofsky, "Style and Medium in Motion Pictures," 160.
7. Crafton, *Before Mickey* (1982), 11, 347.
8. *Oxford English Dictionary*, s.v. "play," accessed June 22, 2012, http://www.oed.com/.
9. I am referencing here the late Miriam Hansen's brilliant explication in her book *Cinema and Experience* of the German term *Spielraum*, as used by Walter Benjamin (see esp. 192–94).
10. See the description of first projections of Lumière films by O. Winter (reprinted in Harding and Popple, *In the Kingdom of Shadows*, 13) and Maxim Gorky (reprinted in Leyda, *Kino*, 407–8).
11. In *Theaetetes* Plato argues that wonder is the beginning of philosophy (155d), while in the *Metaphysics*, Aristotle says that wonder is the source of theory (982b12–13). My understanding of thauma is indebted to the brilliant discussion by Richard Neer in his work *The Emergence of the Classical Style in Greek Sculpture*, 57–68.
12. Colin Williamson, in his excellent dissertation, "Watching Closely with Turn-of-the-Century Eyes" (2013), in the Department of Cinema and Media Studies at the University of Chicago, discusses the close relation of animation with magic and wonder and also the role that wonder plays in provoking curiosity in Enlightenment projects of education, especially René Descartes's account of wonder in *The Passions of the Soul* (1649).
13. For the best concise account of this theory, see Anderson and Anderson, "The Myth of Persistence of Vision Revisited." For my critique of this theory's application to animation devices, see Gunning, "The Play between Still and Moving Images."
14. Snyder, "Visualization and Visibility," 392.
15. Coe, *The Birth of Photography*, 22.

16. Frizot, *Le temps d'un mouvement*, 7.
17. See Snyder, "Visualization and Visibility," 392, as well as the fascinating blog entry on this photograph by Nicholas Jenkins of Stanford University, "Traces," *Day by Day: A Blog*, August 22, 2007, accessed June 22, 2012, http://www.stanford .edu/~njenkins/archives/2007/08/traces.html.
18. Canales, *A Tenth of a Second*.
19. Frizot, *Le temps d'un mouvement*, 9.
20. Frizot, *Etienne-Jules Marey chronophotographe*, 70.
21. See accounts of instantaneous photography in M. Braun, *Picturing Time*; Frizot, *Le temps d'un mouvement*; Prodger, *Time Stands Still*; and Snyder, "Visualization and Visibility," as well as the recent book by Josh Ellenbogen, *Reasoned and Unreasoned Images*. I have also treated these issues before; see Gunning "Never Seen This Picture Before: Muybridge in Multiplicity"; and Gunning, "New Thresholds of Vision."
22. Snyder, "Visualization and Visibility," 394.
23. Canales, *A Tenth of a Second*, 21–58.
24. Frizot, *Etienne-Jules Marey chronophotographe*, 237.
25. Frizot, *Le temps d'un mouvement*, 13.
26. Pozzo, "La chronophotographie scientifique," 18, 20.
27. Chronophotography produces instantaneous photographs in a temporally regular succession in order to chart a motion through a series of images. Thus, Frizot quotes the official definition of chronophotography from the 1889 International Photographic Congress: "Production of successive photographic images taken at precisely measured intervals of time." *Etienne-Jules Marey chronophotographe*, 233.
28. Augustine, *Confessions*, book 11, chapter 14, 267.
29. See the excellent anthology of essays collected in Durie, *Time and the Instant*.
30. Durie, "The Strange Nature of the Instant," in *Time and the Instant*, 9–11.
31. Plato, *Parmenides*, 156d–e; quoted in Durie, "The Strange Nature of the Instant," in *Time and the Instant*, 11.
32. Aristotle, *Physics*, especially chapter IV, 217–20 (*The Basic Works of Aristotle*, 288–94).
33. See especially these essays in Durie, *Time and the Instant*: Gaston Bachelard, "The Instant," 64–95; Durie, "The Strange Nature of the Instant," 9–11; Keith Ansell Pearson, "Duration and Evolution: Bergson contra Dennett and Bachelard," 144–76; and David Webb, "*The Complexity of the Instant*: Bachelard, Levinas, Lucetius," 190–216.

3 :: Polygraphic Photography and the Origins of 3-D Animation

ALEXANDER R. GALLOWAY

The Parallel Image

It is now something of a cliché: in order to speak about the images of the present one feels obligated to come to terms with the nineteenth century, weighing in on the old arguments about cinema's origins; raising a glass to those brave souls anxious about the growing technological alienation within art, to Baudelaire or Benjamin or Heidegger or Adorno according to taste; and pointing out how this or that historical detail was overlooked in the grand developmental evolution of the image from mind and memory to the plastic and visual arts, to the automatic camera, to the moving image, and ending up with the digital. Nowadays even the responses to such pat histories are themselves well rehearsed. To speak of nineteenth-century optical toys as "precinematic" offends on many levels, for not only does this reduce the specificity of real history to a mere instrumental prehistory within a process that can and must unfold in one particular way—Hollywood as destiny—it also smacks of a certain presentism within which the past is cast to play the various theatrical roles required to narrate *our* special story. So Eadweard Muybridge and Étienne-Jules Marey play their respective parts because they mean something to us today, no matter that chronophotography was only one chapter in Marey's life's work, no matter that Marey wanted first and foremost to decompose movement, not sew it back together again, no matter that neither of the two men can claim to have invented the technique outright, no matter that the most interesting chronophotographer was most certainly Albert Londe.

Was this not the problem that structuralism was supposed to solve? Recall Michel Foucault's famous concept of the historical a priori:

> An *a priori* not of truths that might never be said, or really given to experience; but the *a priori* of a history that is given, since it is that of

things actually said. The reason for using this rather barbarous term is that this *a priori* must take account of statements in their dispersion, in all the flaws opened up by their non-coherence, in their overlapping and mutual replacement, in their simultaneity, which is not unifiable, and in their succession, which is not deductible; in short, it has to take account of the fact that discourse has not only a meaning or a truth, but a history, and a specific history that does not refer it back to the laws of an alien development.[1]

How un-Foucauldian this historical a priori. The scandal is not so much that discourses have histories, a notion that the discipline of history is still warming up to, but that Foucault is so willing to give priority to the prior, what others call, using equally barbarous terms, the *real* or the *factual*. The great Foucauldian compromise, then, is between the anti-anthropocentricity of worldly data données, which is a benefit of structuralism's scientific method, and the fact that all these data are really part of a contingent, historical (read quasi-anthropocentric) discourse subject to its own laws and systems of management. The trick is that Foucault's a priori is not exactly a Kantian one; in Kant the a priori is a question of running prior to experience, yet in Foucault it is a question of running prior to knowledge. One puts the stress on the subject, the other on discourse. And while the Kantian framework dominated for two centuries at least, we have most certainly been living within a Foucauldian framework for some time now, a fact that shows no indication of changing any time soon.

So journey back again into Foucault's historical a priori, back again to the nineteenth century, only this time in search of a different kind of knowledge, what Foucault might have called a subjugated knowledge. Not political subjugation of course, but a knowledge from an occluded past, a discourse overlooked and downplayed, tidbits of evidence left behind as unimportant, or hitherto unresolved. Ever since the noble contributions of authors such as Friedrich Kittler, media theory has been shackled to an ignoble narrative of the modern media: the year 1900 marks the age of seriality; the anxiety of the nineteenth century is the anxiety of reproduction; noise and nonsense are not just threats to meaning, they are its very substrate; the image is fundamentally a mechanized image that fires forward in a line, like the rat-a-tat-tat of a machine gun.

This story of things need not be contested outright. In many ways Kittler is correct about the media of 1900. Nevertheless, I wish to tell an alternate story, parallel to the first, a story that must remain apart from the Kittlerian corpus because it has a different origin and a different end. The goal then, to give away the ending before barely having gotten under way, will be to reconstruct a genealogy not for the moving image but for the information model, not for serial animation but for parallel animation, not for the linear but for the multiplexed—in short, not for the cinema but for the computer.

Petrified Photography

The history of chronophotography is reasonably well documented. But even as photography experimented with time and movement in the late nineteenth century, the photographic apparatus also migrated in another direction seldom discussed. Not just a migration into the moving image but a migration toward the plastic arts. Not just toward the protocinematic optical toys but toward that oldest of art forms, sculpture. In fact, photography's migration into sculpture predates chronophotography by several years.

In the early 1860s, a sign with large lettering appeared on the façade of a modern four-story building in Paris. The building was newly constructed in iron and glass on what was then called the Boulevard de l'Etoile, stemming northward away from the Arc de Triomphe. The sign touted "Portraits—from mechanical sculpture: Busts, medallions, statues." According to the art historian Robert Sobieszek, "when a large circular cupola was first erected at 42, Blvd. de l'Etoile, constructed of metal mullions with blue and white panes of glass, it was thought to be a conservatory, a zoo for small animals in the English style, an aquarium and, only finally, a photographic studio."[2] When the poet Théophile Gautier visited the building and its central dome in 1863, a large chamber forty feet wide and thirty feet high (see figure 3.1), he likened it to "an Oriental copula, a weightless dome of white and blue glass."[3]

The author Paul de Saint-Victor, who also surveyed the premises, was impressed by the hollowness of the domed photographic studio: "Imagine a vast glass rotunda containing no instruments of any kind, no apparatus visible to the naked eye, nothing to offer any indication of the wonderful operation about to transpire."[4] Gautier advanced to the middle of the rotunda, up two steps onto a pedestal, and positioned his head under a silver pendant hanging to mark the exact middle of the dome: "Leaving his hat on the coatrack, he tucked his hand into the lapel of his large jacket and gazed off into the distance."[5] An operator blew a

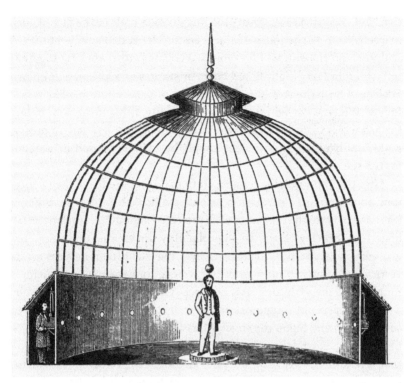

FIGURE 3.1 François Willème's glass dome, housing a perimeter ring of cameras directed inward at a central subject. Source: Théophile Gautier, *Photosculpture* (Paris: Paul Dupont, 1864), 5.

whistle and twenty-four cameras opened at once. The twenty-four apparatuses were safely hidden behind false walls occupying the perimeter of the chamber: "Each camera had a primitive shutter arrangement in front of the lens; these shutters, in turn, were all interconnected, so that a single cord could be pulled to obtain two dozen simultaneous exposures."[6] A second whistle sounded, and the exposure was complete. The entire procedure lasted less than ten seconds.

The strange new building on the Boulevard de l'Etoile was in fact not a zoo for small animals but a studio combining the arts of photography and sculpture. Bearing the name Photosculpture de France, the studio was a new commercial endeavor initiated by the artist François Willème. Willème filed a French patent on August 14, 1860, titled "Photosculpture Process," which described a technique for producing portrait sculptures relatively quickly and cheaply.[7]

It was wonderful to think of the sun as a photographer, believed Gautier, "but the sun as a sculptor! The imagination reels in the face of such marvels."[8] Or as the journalist and editor Henri de Parville put it: "A sculptor and the sun will become two collaborators working together to fashion in forty-eight hours busts or statues of a hitherto unknown fidelity, of such great boldness in outline, of such admirable likeness."[9] Indeed Willème played up the magical quality of his invention, hiding the apparatus from the sitter, who likely had no idea how such a precise sculptural likeness could appear simply by bathing oneself in sunlight for ten seconds.

After the photographic session, crafters projected each of the twenty-four photographs in succession using a magic lantern.[10] A pantograph was used to trace the outline of each projected silhouette, cutting the silhouette into a clay blank: "In all probability the manual input required was very substantial."[11] Artisans turned the clay fifteen degrees on its vertical axis for each number of the twenty-four tracings, producing a rough cut of the sculpture: "It is now necessary to smooth by hand, or by a tool, all the slight roughness produced by the various cuttings, and to soften down and blend the small intervals between the outlines or profiles. This is a most delicate part of the process; for it must be understood that it requires an artist of taste and judgment to perform it satisfactorily, and to impart to the work all the finish possible."[12] The technique was pure magic to Gautier: "Each number carries its own essential line, its own characteristic detail. The mass of clay is scooped out, thinned down, and given shape. The traits of the face appear, the folds of the clothing are drawn out: reflection transformed into form."[13] The hand of the sculptor had been replaced by a mechanized technique, aided by the intermediary of photography, and ultimately by the light of the sun. *Solem quis dicere falsum audeat?*

Before working in clay, Willème began his research with a prototype of a woman's head fashioned from thin slats of wood (see figure 3.2):

> This wooden head was probably shown to the Société Française de Photographie by Willème in May 1861, during the session at which he explained his new photographic process. However, the head was produced using a different technique from the one he subsequently developed and marketed. According to Willème, after taking fifty different angle shots of a statue, one hundred strips of wood were assembled two by two so that they could be cut out according to the profiles of the photographs.[14]

As in the science of psychophysics and its concept of a "just noticeable difference" in the human sensorium, Willème experimented with the

FIGURE 3.2 François Willème, *Portrait of a Woman* (ca. 1860). Demonstration specimen used by François Willème in a presentation of the photosculpture technique on May 17, 1861. Courtesy of George Eastman House, International Museum of Photography and Film.

width of the digital segmentation in order to achieve an optimal size. His wooden head of 1861 had a "resolution" of 3.6 degrees around the vertical axis. Later, once the technique was established using twenty-four cameras, the resolution had been degraded by a factor of four to fifteen degrees.

With Willème's *sculpture instantanée* (instant sculpture) in mind, we are now in a position to compare and contrast photosculpture and chronophotography. Both techniques are digital techniques; that much is clear. The difference lies in their divergent employments of the digital. In the case of chronophotography, digitality appears as a result of discrete photographic impressions segmented across time. For photosculpture, however, digitality appears as a result of discrete photographic impressions segmented in a spindle of space. Instead of a sum of pictures, there is a sum of profiles.

Willème's technique reveals something profound. It reveals that there is an alternate history of photography in which point of view has no meaning. The point of view, whether single or multiple, as in the case of montage, has so dominated how one thinks of photography, cinema, and visual culture in general that it is initially quite difficult to understand the ramifications of Willème's technique. There are two key aspects that must be underscored. First, one must proliferate the number of points of view dispersed within a space — proliferated not simply to two or four but to a mathematically significant number like twenty, or a hundred, or a thousand. Second, one must conceive of the multiple points of view as temporally synchronous; in other words, one must reject the basic premise of chronophotographic animation (and later cinematic animation), which multiplexes the image through time. In multiplying the number of views, one is proliferating them along a set of spatial coordinates, not along the axis of time. Willème opening and closing all the camera apertures at the same moment is crucial. The point of view does not move, as in the cinema. Instead, the view is metastable, spanning all twenty-four cameras at once. Willème's mode of vision exists as the cumulative summation of twenty-four points of view fixed at the same instant in time. But twenty-four is no special number: once the shackles of monocular or even binocular vision have been removed, in other words, the shackles of the one or the two, it is trivial for twenty-four to become a hundred, a thousand, or indeed a virtual totality of "all-vision," like the Panoptes monster in Greek myth.

It is not difficult to see how this mode of vision did not contribute much to what would become cinematic animation. In fact, one might go so far as to label this an *anticinematic* way of seeing. In the cinema the multiplication of views leads to choice or synthesis. It leads, in other words, to montage or collage: one either montages a scene together by choosing which view to sequence at which time, or one composites two or more image layers together to synthesize a new image. It leads, thus, to the serial image or the recursive image. By contrast, Willème's mode of vision is neither choice bound nor synthetic. It is metastable. Willème multiplies the view into a virtual view, a virtual camera existing synchronically across twenty-four discrete apparatuses. Willème did not choose or sequence these twenty-four streams; he did not composite them backward into a single image. He maintains the metastable view as such, maintaining the view as manipulable model.

For Paul de Saint-Victor such metastases of the photographic view led not to an immaterial, omnipresent gaze but to a pure materiality, an immanent image — but a dead one too: "The true mission of this useful and humble art form will be to bring sculpture into private life and to perpetuate the photographic image — by petrifying it."[15] To petrify photography means to transform it from a visual art to a plastic art. In other words, Willème's petrified photography is a kind of photography that has finally escaped the long shadow of the camera obscura. And in escaping the limitations of the camera obscura's single aperture, photography smears itself across a limitless grid of points, neutering the axis of time while emboldening the axes of space.

Photographic Modeling

If Londe did not aim to model the world with his multilens devices from 1883 and 1891 (only photograph it), a slightly different technique, owing perhaps more to Muybridge and Willème than to Londe, was revealed in the early 1890s in Germany. Christian Wilhelm Braune and a student thirty years his junior, Otto Fischer, developed a technique for capturing the motion of a body and modeling it in three dimensions. Today it would be called a motion-capture animation device. Where photographers such as Londe, André-Adolphe-Eugène Disdéri, and Augustin Le Prince unknowingly took small steps in this direction, Braune and Fischer took a giant leap into the realm of parallel optical dimensionality, continuing the evolution begun by Willème. I leave it to Siegfried Zielinski to describe the details:

> The male test person wears a tight-fitting, black-knit suit and, for safety reasons, thick leather shoes. His entire body appears to be wired, including his head. The electric supply is connected to the wires at his head, which enables the test person to move relatively freely. Technically, the thin white lines running down the sides of the body, called Geissler tubes, are the decisive feature of the suit. . . . Braune and Fischer's experimental design sought to solve a problem associated with Marey's method. The test persons in Marey's experiments had white or shiny metal strips attached to their limbs when he photographed them in motion, but these strips left light trails in the photographs and tended to blur the images. Exact registration and reconstruction of movements was not possible. The Geissler tubes in Braune and Fischer's experiment ran parallel to the rigid parts of the limbs and were held in place by leather straps. In all, there were eleven tubes. The advantage of this experimental design was that, since the Geissler tubes used induction current, they could produce short flashes of light in quick succession. Further, when the thin tubes filled with nitrogen flashed, they emitted much photochemically active light and, in a darkened room, it was possible to take photographs in which the individual limbs appeared as

separate lines. This equipment also enabled precise recording of how the movements of arm and leg related to each other or how the head related to the feet.[16]

What begins as chronophotography ends as dimensional modeling. Similar to the way in which stereometric cameras were used in photogrammetry, Braune and Fischer deployed a multilens technique consisting of four different cameras located in a geometrical arrangement around the subject, in the front, at the side, and so on. All cameras fired together, and measurements from the resulting photographs were correlated. In fact, Braune and Fischer's goal was *not* simply to produce a photographic image, chronographic or otherwise. Their goal was to record precise mathematical coordinates in x, y, and z dimensional space for the shoulders, knees, and other parts of the body in motion. So in this sense, Braune and Fischer are miles away from Marey or Muybridge (even though most history books would group them all together under the heading of chronophotography). To achieve the desired level of precision, Braune and Fischer would inspect the resulting chronophotographs under a microscope, measuring the precise positions of the test subject to several decimal points of accuracy. Using the registration marks that appear in each image and by correlating each measurement across all four cameras, extremely precise spatial coordinates could be recorded along three-dimensional x, y, and z axes. In fact, the long tables of vertex coordinates recorded by Braune and Fischer in their 1895 publication are surprisingly similar to today's 3-D animation formats. Braune and Fischer were more data hounds than photographers.

What was innovative, however, was the use that Braune and Fischer made of their heaps of data. Marey's bird in flight had been made into a three-dimensional geometric model, it is true, but at the end of the day Marey was no plastic artist. Braune and Fischer instead restaged their scores of vertex coordinates into actual three-dimensional models of human locomotion (see figure 3.3). If Marey's ultimate métier was geometric chronophotography, Braune and Fischer added dimensionality to the mix and produced something quite different, geometric *chronomodels*. The goal here is object modeling, not world simulation. The goal is a diffuse omniscient gaze engulfing a precisely modeled object world, not simply multiple points of view through time (cinema). Cinematic animation is never spatially synchronous within a single frame; its achievement is diachrony. Any sense of spatiality achieved by the cinema is an epiphenomenon. Braune and Fischer on the other

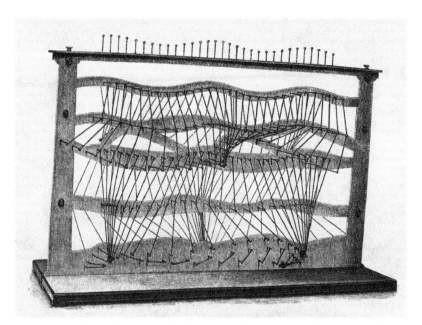

FIGURE 3.3 Three-dimensional chronomodel of human locomotion. Source: Wilhelm Braune and Otto Fischer, "Der Gang des Menschen, 1 Tiel, Versuche am un-belasteten und belasteten Menschen," *Abhandlungen der Mathematisch-Physischen Classe der Königlich Sächsischen Gesellschaft der Wissenschaften 21* (Leipzig: Hirzel, 1895): 153–322, 270–71.

hand achieved both spatial synchrony and diachrony. The object can be spun around, manipulated at will. This is a fundamentally anticinematic mode of mediation; likewise it is antiphenomenological, since complete spatial synchrony is prohibited within the cinematic and phenomeno-logical systems, themselves forever beholden to the singular experi-ences of a central gazing subject (or lens eye), however much it may be complicated by montage or the use of two or three concurrent cameras. The Braune and Fischer model presents a diffuse totality of the object. And in this sense, it is aggressively antiphenomenological and aggres-sively anticinematic. So just as Marey's geometric work pointed away from the cinema (even if his moving-plate work pointed toward the cinema), Braune and Fischer's dimensional models push elsewhere too. They point to a very different mode of mediation, and a very different kind of device. They point to 3-D animation. They point to the computer.

FIGURE 3.4 Graffiti Research Lab, "How to Enter the Ghetto Matrix (DIY Bullet Time)" (2008). Courtesy of Graffiti Research Lab and Dan Melamid. Photographic animation of the producer and rapper Large Professor, featuring the light graffiti of 2ESAE (a.k.a. Mike Baca).

The Multiplexed Camera

In order to understand the repercussions of this argument, it will be necessary to take the provocation quite literally: Braune and Fischer were doing three-dimensional "computer animation" in the 1890s. Consider the celebrated "bullet time" sequences from *The Matrix*, or the interesting reuse of the effect by the Graffiti Research Lab (see figure 3.4). A certain high-tech mythology has grown up around this technique, yet in actuality there is nothing particularly high-tech about it. The ability to freeze and rotate a scene within the stream of time is easy to perform with normal cameras. No computer is necessary. One simply needs to arrange a battery of cameras along the rotation arc and have the technical wherewithal to trigger them at exactly the same instant (which Willème accomplished one hundred and forty years earlier). Slice the individual frames together into a movie strip to achieve the effect. Thus, there is nothing lacking *technologically* that would have prevented bullet time from appearing a hundred years before the Wachowski brothers.[17] Braune and Fischer didn't use twenty-four cameras, and their resulting models were plastic not photographic, but it requires no great mental leap to see how they too were effectively staging the same bullet-time effect.

So the determinist argument—"it wasn't technologically possible to do three-dimensional animation in the 1890s"—doesn't hold water. It was possible; it was done. And it certainly wasn't a question of the human sensorium: the stereoscope had already primed large swaths of the viewing public for the marvels of dimensional media. The interesting pursuit therefore is not so much the chase after the technological roots of this or that device, but the inquiry into the conditions of possibility for a given mode of mediation, and to try to make some sense as to why one thing happened instead of another, when the *technical* conditions were ripe and ready for each. In the case of Marey's famous photographic gun of 1882, the sequence of bullet chambers was remediated as individual photographs, creating the modern convention of a photographic filmstrip.[18] The device creates multiple images of the same scene from the same point of view, but divided into separate photographs and extended through time. It took one hundred years for Marey's time bullets to be transformed into the bullet time of computer animation.[19] If the cinema became dominant in the early part of the twentieth century, while three-dimensional computer modeling did not until the late twentieth century, we must find the answer beyond the standard volumes of industrial and technical history.

The photographic gun is on the side of cinema; bullet time is on the side of modeling. So it would not be out of place to pose the question in reverse: why did *cinema* get invented around the turn of the twentieth century and not modeling? Why does cinema precede 3-D modeling when there does not appear to be any obligatory reason why it should? Perhaps the phenomenological framework determined the technical one, green-lighting the cinematic modality of the photographic gun and sidelining the informatic modality of the photographic array. If that be the case, then bullet time is the road not taken of late nineteenth-century Euro-American media, sidelined by a stronger phenomenological paradigm that pegged visuality to the standard of one viewer, standing in one place (or moving chronologically through multiple places via the rational sequences of montage), oriented with its own special perspective on its own special world.

By 1900, Kittler's symbolic year, bullet time goes into hibernation, and time bullets take center stage. Marey's time bullets settle time, regularize it into fixed frequency. By 1900 time becomes the natural infrastructure of cinematic animation, while spatial representation and visual expression become variables. But in the case of bullet time (whether in the 1890s or the 1990s), time is the variable, and space is withheld in synchrony. Mine is thus a story of selection and suppression: the cinema automates time, making it irrelevant (and thereby elevating the value of worlds); the computer automates space, again making it irrelevant (thereby elevating something else again, action perhaps). Volumetric representation becomes the so-called natural infrastructure of computer animation; whereas in painting or photography space is expressive, never infrastructural. By contrast, discrete temporality becomes the natural infrastructure of the cinematic image.[20]

This is why Willème's photosculpture or Braune and Fischer's chronophotography can be considered protocomputational. The classical chronophotography techniques of Marey or Muybridge do not have much to contribute to the prehistory of computer animation. Only through the multiplexing of vision, in Muybridge's multiple synchronic images or in Londe's grid cameras, do we see a new pathway emerging. The earlier systems deployed multiple lenses in order to move the test subject. Willème and Braune and Fischer deployed multiple lenses in order to animate the *camera* (by making it metastable and virtual). By modeling the spatial coordinates of the test subject, it became possible to translate the movement (of the camera) into spatial dimensionality, and in doing so, translate photography into sculpture.

Only polygraphic photography can explain the origins of computer modeling, and by extension computer animation, because this photography introduces a way of seeing completely foreign to the cinematic legacy: the virtualization of the eye into a metastatic virtual camera able to view an object from any point of view whatsoever.

Notes

A number of people have given me valuable feedback on portions of this chapter, including Finn Brunton, Jeff Guess, Tom Gunning, Miriam Hansen, James Hodge, Ben Kafka, and Kirsten Thompson. Nevertheless, the claims (and shortcomings) of the present argument are my own responsibility. All unattributed translations from the French are mine.

1. Foucault, *The Archaeology of Knowledge*, 127.
2. Sobieszek, "Sculpture as the Sum of Its Profiles," 621.
3. Gautier, *Photosculpture*, 5. This short booklet was excerpted from *Le Moniteur Universel* (January 4, 1864).
4. Paul de Saint-Victor, "Photosculpture," *La Presse*, January 15, 1866, quoted in Gall, "Photo / Sculpture," 65.

5. Drost, "La photosculpture entre art industriel et artisanat," 113.
6. Sobieszek, "Sculpture as the Sum of Its Profiles," 621.
7. François Willème, "Photosculpture Process," French patent number 46,358, August 14, 1860. See also additions filed April 6, 1861; September 9, 1863; and June 14, 1864.
8. Gautier, *Photosculpture*, 4.
9. Henri de Parville quoted in Sobieszek, "Sculpture as the Sum of Its Profiles," 622.
10. "Willème almost always used a quarter-plate camera which accommodated a negative slightly less than ten and one-half centimeters high." Sobieszek, "Sculpture as the Sum of Its Profiles," 619.
11. Sorel, "Photosculpture," 82.
12. "Photo-Sculpture," *The Art-Journal* 3 (May 1864): 141.
13. Gautier, *Photosculpture*, 8.
14. Sorel, "Photosculpture," 81.
15. Quoted in Gall, "Photo / Sculpture," 76. The phrase *petrified photography* is Gall's.
16. Zielinski, *Deep Time of the Media*, 245, 248.
17. As James Hodge has pointed out to me, others had been experimenting with this mode of vision well before it ended up in Hollywood. In the early 1980s, Tim Macmillan developed what he calls a "time-slice" camera, which he would eventually use in a video projection titled *Dead Horse*, which exhibited at the London Electronic Arts Gallery in 1998.
18. Marey was not the first to marry camera and gun. See Eder, *Die photographische Camera und die Momentapparate*, for any number of exotic devices, such as Dr. Fol's photographic gun (p. 587) and E. von Gothard's photographic gun (p. 589).
19. A number of articles narrate the mid-twentieth-century passage from a traditional photographic image rooted in perspectival, Renaissance techniques to a computer-enhanced photographic image oriented around the techniques of volumetric capture, multiple points of view, and world simulation. See in particular Cartwright and Goldfarb, "Radiography, Cinematography and the Decline of the Lens."
20. This is the only reason why someone such as Gilles Deleuze can speak of the "time cinema" as a kind of art cinema. See in particular *Cinema 2* and the end of *Cinema 1*. Deleuze's book on Francis Bacon is also interesting here, since, as is well documented, Bacon was cognizant of Muybridge and even incorporated the chronophotographic aesthetic into his paintings, including the nondiegetic registration marks and the rounded ring as a kind of photographic stage. See Deleuze, *Frances Bacon*.

4 :: "A Living, Developing Egg Is Present before You": Animation, Scientific Visualization, Modeling

OLIVER GAYCKEN

Cinema historians have indicated how a wide variety of contexts are part of the "wonderfully variegated area" of early animation, ranging from cartoons and caricature to vaudeville and theater.[1] Scientific visualization has figured only rarely in histories of animation, however, and the devices that are usually mentioned—optical toys (thaumatrope, zoetrope, phenakistascope) and chronophotography—are characterized as precursors. The relationship between scientific visualization practices and animation is more complicated and sustained, however. Late nineteenth- and early twentieth-century scientists used serial images in myriad ways, and a consideration of the links between scientific visualization practices and the history of animation can expand the terrain of animation studies.

Common to these disparate uses of serial images is a relationship to the practice of modeling, which provides a rich vein of overlap between scientific visualization and animation techniques. In the examples under discussion here, the serial image primarily functions to re-create or replicate volumetric space. This tendency allows for a modification of a widely held contention regarding the early scientific moving image, namely, its "penchant for flatness," which is linked to an argument about "a disciplinary scientific visual apparatus" that obscures the links between early scientific uses of cinema and animation.[2] As Soraya de Chaderavian and Nick Hopwood have pointed out, the turn to "visual languages" and "working objects" in the history of science also has emphasized flat objects.[3] Their interest in three-dimensional models is relevant for an understanding of the use of 3-D models in "pedagogy or popularization," which also has implications for the "mainstream of the history of science." Chaderavian and Hopwood write, "Not only was teaching the centrally important means of ratifying and conveying knowledge, and addressing wider audiences crucial to establishing scientific authority, the movements of models also exemplify the impossibility of separating these activities from research." Models, a form of "rational recreation," "were a key medium of traffic between the sciences and the wider culture."[4]

The mobility of models indicates their participation in a boundary layer between professional and nonprofessional scientific audiences. Another ramification of the traffic in models is the recognition of a dense relationship between two- and three-dimensional representations. Models served as the sources for textbook pictures, for instance. And models could in turn be made up of pictures, consisting of individual images that constituted a larger structure, as in embryology, electron-density maps, or archaeology. These instances of animation, which are not representational in the sense of attempting to provide a fully mimetic experience, nor inventive in the tradition of animation's tendency to create fantastic and metamorphic worlds, schematize movement and objects, creating a selective reduction of visual information that leads to a clearer understanding of the phenomenon under investigation.

Considering the importance of three-dimensional models in the sciences opens up a pathway in film history that has rarely been explored, namely animation's use as an educational medium. E. G. Lutz's *Animated Cartoons* (1926) primarily served as a how-to guide for people interested in entering the nascent industry; the book provided a source of information and inspiration to Walt Disney and the Fleischer brothers.[5] What typically goes unnoticed about this book is how it frames its detailed discussion of how to make comic cartoons with thoughts about animation's destiny as an educational medium. Lutz begins the book by employing the rhetoric of "visual instruction," and his final chapter is titled "Animated Educational Films and the Future." He underscores both the importance and relative neglect of this issue when he writes: "On the making of animated screen drawings for scientific and educational themes little has been said. This is not to be taken as a measure of their importance."[6] Further stations along this path would include the development of this mode of animation, which is largely part of popular-science filmmaking and incorporates the disciplines of medical illustration and technical drawing; some notable examples from the silent era include Percy Smith's animated war maps, the instructional films from Bray Studios, and the use of animated sequences in Soviet cinema, such as Vsevolod Pudovkin's *Mechanics of the Brain* (1926).[7]

Wingbeats, Heartbeats, and "A Living, Developing Egg"

In addition to the aforementioned assumption of a "penchant for flatness," another familiar, and related, component of the reception of early scientific cinema is the supposition that the synthesis of movement was of no interest from a scientific point of view. So, for instance, Lisa Cartwright writes of "[Étienne-Jules] Marey's mistrust of cinematography as a physiological technique," asserting, "the moving image was of little use to [Marey's] project precisely because it did not facilitate the analytical and disciplinary task undertaken in chronophotography."[8] The moving image did play a role in Marey's research, however, and an appreciation of the uses to which Marey put the moving image allows the constellation of scientific visualization, modeling, and animation to emerge more clearly.

Chronophotography and graphic abstraction played a multivalent role in Marey's work. On the one hand, the reduction of phenomena to graphic traces did relate to and allow for the stilling and disciplining of movement, as is perhaps best represented by the image that has become an icon of Marey's method, the *homme squelette* (skeleton man). The graphic registration of movement also was related to the re-creation of movement in Marey's work, however. Marey had a variety of interests in the synthesis of movement that ranged from being able to show movement to an audience to making movement portable and reproducible.[9]

Conjoined to the graphic rendering of movement was Marey's interest in re-creating objects volumetrically. In the final chapter of *Le mouvement* (1894), which is dedicated to a discussion of the value of synthetic movement, Marey discussed his stereoscopic zoetrope. This device was created to counteract the drawback introduced by previous zoetropic methods whose flattening of the phenomenon into images introduced distortions. The *zootrope à figures en relief* (zoetrope with figures in relief) overcame these distortions by using three-dimensional figures instead of flat images. Using chronophotographic images as a guide, Marey had ten small wax sculptures of a gull in the successive postures of a single wingbeat placed inside a zoetrope (see figure 4.1). Marey describes the result in the following terms: "The illusion is thus complete and one can see turning in the apparatus birds that fly in a circle and that first seem to move away from, then pass before, and return to the observer."[10] The stereoscopic zoetrope combined an illusion of movement with the reduction of that movement to a single wingbeat cycle. Marey, in other words, created a generalized movement as opposed to a specific move-

FIGURE 4.1 Stereoscopic zoetrope depicting a gull's wingbeat cycle. Source: E.-J. Marey, *Movement* (1894; New York: Arno Press, 1972).

ment. Or, rather, he extracted a generalized model of gull-wing movement from a series of specific chronophotographic observations.

Ludwig Braun's work on the dynamics of the heart provides another example of the importance of animated movement in the framework of a scientific project that is quite similar to Marey's. According to Cartwright, Braun also used cinema primarily as a method of graphic inscription: "The use to which Braun put his images suggests that he, like [John] Macintyre, regarded his film as something akin to a kymographic trace, a graphic register of change over time. . . . Braun's film is a precise, incremental index of life and death—a register that is, in very important ways, a graphic trace and not a moving picture."[11] But here too the graphic trace contains an important relationship to volume; the two-dimensional image lies in intimate contact with the three-dimensional image.

Braun, like Marey, was interested in creating a model of the ideal/normal heartbeat. The cinematic image was a method that allowed him to measure and thereby establish the volumetric parameters of "a single cardiac cycle."[12] Braun saw in the chronophotographic series the ability to establish not only and not even primarily the temporal rhythm of the heartbeat but rather its spatial displacements. He provided a brief history of chronophotography, explaining that Eadweard Muybridge's chronophotographic images were insufficient because they were only silhouettes that did not allow for the apprehension of their "plastic modeling."[13] Braun claimed, however, that his camera's optics allowed for "exact, quasi-three-dimensional reproductions [reliefartige Wiedergaben] of the beating heart."[14] And he used these sequences in order to extract volumetric data from the flat images. By laying successive cinematographic images on top of each other, he measured the displacement of the moving parts of the heart: "Thus one can *recognize the spatial displacements, judge them better than before*, and to a certain degree also measure and calculate them."[15]

Braun and Marey thus used serial images to create models of limited temporality, idealized movement cycles.[16] These cycles were as much about re-creating objects in volumetric space as they were about creating a temporal sequence. The graphic register of these images is not primarily a matter of stilling and disciplining but rather a re-creation, or animation, of a virtual object that can be measured and understood both temporally and spatially.[17]

The use of serial images to re-create volumetric depth was not always coupled with the synthesis of movement, however; serial imaging also could re-create atemporal objects. Ludwig Münch provides an instance of this kind of animation. Münch created more than twenty-five films on mathematical subjects that ranged from a graphical demonstration of the Pythagorean theorem to an animation of Copernican astronomical movements (see figures 4.2–4.5).[18] These films appeared in 1912, but a review mentioned that they were the result of "four laborious years," which means Münch began work on them in 1908, contemporaneous with the appearance of Emile Cohl's earliest animated films.[19] Indeed, Münch's method of hand drawing large images on paper and directly photographing them is similar to Cohl's method. Furthermore, Münch's use of clear, simple line drawings makes his films' fluid transformations resemble Cohl's metamorphic aesthetic.[20]

These coincidences should not be taken as indicating an argument about influence; rather, they mark the presence of an alternate animation practice running alongside other, more familiar traditions.[21] For as much as Münch's films may resemble Cohl's, their significant differences are worth underscoring. Whereas Cohl's films demonstrate a series of changes motivated by an oneiric logic, Münch's geometrical demonstrations are essentially depictions of atemporal, ideal objects. Münch's

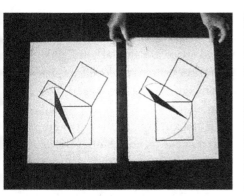

FIGURE 4.2 Original drawings used for Ludwig Münch's animated geometry films. Source: Virgilio Tosi, *Cinema before Cinema*.

FIGURE 4.3 Video still of animated geometry film, Ludwig Münch, ca. 1912. Source: Virgilio Tosi, *Cinema before Cinema*.

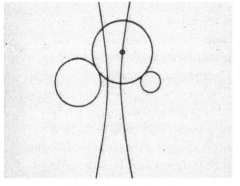

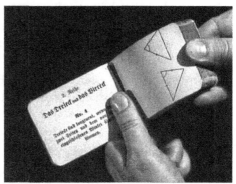

FIGURE 4.4 Video still of animated geometry film, Ludwig Münch, ca. 1912. Source: Virgilio Tosi, *Cinema before Cinema*.

FIGURE 4.5 Münch's geometry animations published as a flip-book. Source: Virgilio Tosi, *Cinema before Cinema*.

films animate geometrical concepts that exist out of time, a point underscored by the fact that three-dimensional objects were also used to illustrate and teach these same geometrical concepts.[22]

Embryologists prominently employed serial imaging to generate atemporal forms as well, and embryological models exhibit points of contact with later animation practices. Nick Hopwood has written extensively about the history of embryology's use of models and has noted that the microtome was a key instrument because of its ability to create identical slices of samples. Chronophotography and cinematography provided a similar kind of benefit, allowing for the creation of precisely separated photographic images. The space between the images on the perforated film stock is similar to the thickness of the individual embryological slices cut by the microtome; the difference is that the interstices between images on a filmstrip are temporal while the thickness of microtome slices are spatial. Time and space are similarly fungible with these methods, however. The registration system employed in Gustav Born's method of model construction consisted of notches on one edge of the plate that kept the plates in alignment, which functioned similarly to both the perforations in film stock as well as the perf-and-peg system that was such a significant part of the technical innovations leading to classical cel animation (see figures 4.6–4.9).

Other scientists used cinema in the service of modeling as well. In 1907 Karl Reicher, a neurologist at the Charité Hospital in Berlin, wrote about wanting to extend the benefits of photography's "technical achievements" to medical science. Reicher was particularly interested in the ability to demonstrate neuroanatomy in a new way, and he used cinematography to create an animated record of a portion of an adult human brain stem (from around the decussation of pyramids at the beginning of the medula oblongata to the middle of the pons) by photographing a series of slides. Reicher was most interested in how this method of visualization might allow for new insights, although he was hesitant to predict what such insights might be (one suggestion was that slowly following individual nerve groups could contribute to the understanding of nerve pathways).

His article spends a fair amount of time describing the painstaking process of centering the slides, and he apologizes for the jitter [Zittern] that the first series displayed, which consisted of 1,060 images.[23] Even though he uses a significant part of the article to enumerate the difficulties encountered and promise impending improvements in image quality, he does express confidence in one aspect of the endeavor: "One thing seems certain even today, the didactic usage of such cinematograms [Kinematogramme]." His reasons for this confidence were linked to the perceptual qualities of the animation. He declares that "one has the impression of active processes" and that "it is precisely its activeness [of the moving image] that impresses itself better on the learner and also provides better spatial representations of paths and centers than the viewing of even an expanded series of cross sections."[24] This assertion of the moving image's power resonates with Hopwood's description of the effects of embryological models when he writes about their "vividness and tangibility that no flat picture could match," and it resonates more generally with the discourse of visual education and its endorsement of the pedagogical superiority of the visual.[25]

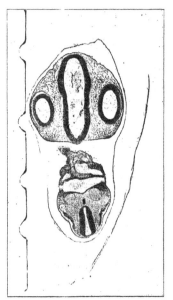

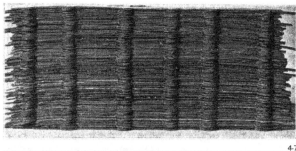
4.7

4.6
4.8

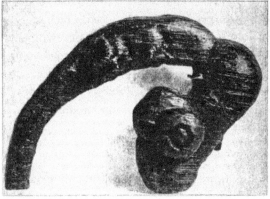
4.9

FIGURE 4.6 Gustav Born's wax-plate method of "plastic reconstruction." This is an individual section whose image will be transferred to a wax plate. Note the registration line on the left of the image. Figure 12 in Karl Peter, *Die Methoden der Rekonstruktion* (Jena, Germany: Fischer, 1906).

FIGURE 4.7 A stack of the wax plates from the side of the registration line. Figure 34 in Karl Peter, *Die Methoden der Rekonstruktion* (Jena, Germany: Fischer, 1906).

FIGURE 4.8 The same stack as in figure 4.7 from the opposite side, where the model, in this case of a lizard embryo brain, is visible. Figure 35 in Karl Peter, *Die Methoden der Rekonstruktion* (Jena, Germany: Fischer, 1906).

FIGURE 4.9 The nearly final product, after extraneous material has been cut away from the model, which was then smoothed and painted. Figure 36 in Karl Peter, *Die Methoden der Rekonstruktion* (Jena, Germany: Fischer, 1906).

Hopwood also notes that models came to be seen as "too static" for the next generation of embryologists, whose interests lay in experimentation.[26] This observation accords with Christopher Kelty's and Hannah Landecker's observations about how static and animated views of the cell have alternated in prominence over the course of the twentieth century in the cultures of microscopic imaging.[27] Their discussion of Julius Ries's use of cinema to create a record of the development of the sea-urchin egg demonstrates the importation of embryological modeling into the domain of the cinematic image. Ries's comment, "You actually believe a living, developing egg is present before you," testifies to the cinematic image's ability to create a living presence, which involves a tangibility indebted to both temporal and spatial qualities.[28]

Ries's film does not capture new knowledge; the sea-urchin egg was a model organism, in large part because its developmental stages were comparatively clear and easily visible. Kelty and Landecker note about Ries's film: "Theory animates observation. . . . A machine is built to animate observation's codification, and the resulting moving image is perceived as an animation of theory."[29] Like Marey's and Braun's employment of serial images, these images had to be projected, which is to say animated, for them to be useful. And even though the developmental process was well known from countless observations, the projection led to new insights: "The return to the perception of movement is not a circle right back to the starting point but is itself a new cycle of observation, revealing previously 'unperceived details' of movement."[30]

"Relief in Time"

The revelation of new details in Ries's film was partly due to its temporal selectivity, which is to say that certain periods of the developmental process were compressed through time-lapse photography. Marey and Braun also used this feature particular to temporal modeling, namely the ability to vary the time scale. Immediately after Marey's discussion of the zoetrope's ability to slow down the time of observation, he mentions the possibility of moving time into the realm of movements too slow to be observed by human perception. In other words, if one ramification of the cinema's ability to model movements was to slow them down, another option was to accelerate movements too slow for human perception to register.

In one of the first reflections on this possibility for scientific photography, Ernst Mach introduces the concept of time lapse in a series of analogies. A notebook entry strings together a number of concepts and serves as an outline for an essay that he would publish in 1888:

Photography
Stereoscopy. Transparency.
Expansion of the senses.
Magnification
Diminution
Temporal diminution
Temporal magnification
Expansion of the sensory field.
Kepler's laws.
Plant growth. Embryo. Mvt.
[Instantaneous photography]
who knows how much would reveal itself to us
Flying
Marey[31]

This series indicates that the moving image for Mach is one of a number of technical devices to produce knowledge—intellectual prostheses that help to generate what he calls mental strength. Above all, he addresses sensual perception; he says that recording a number of observations that come from sensual perception provides knowledge that remains wedded to the singular. The intellectual insights that interested Mach in time-lapse imaging are similar to what he had been working on in various ways earlier—his conception of stereoscopy as providing an enhanced view of a thing, a "seeing-at-once" view (seeing more than one side of an object). It is a matter of using technology to show things that have never been seen before or to show known things in a manner that is strikingly new.[32] And, indeed, Mach analogized the process of time lapse with other processes in a way that made clear that he saw no fundamental difference between the manipulation of time or space. This point is further underscored by the fact that he uses two different neologisms for time lapse—*Zeitverkürzung* and *Zeitverkleinerung*—both of which apply to time as well as space. The animation that time lapse provides thus emerges as a form of modeling, a process that reveals an object, a phenomenon, or a process in relief. Time lapse shows things that are usually perceived as motionless moving, and by extension, it allows for a phenomenal understanding of how the seeming fixity of space is undone by the flux of time.

Classical film theory contains occasional considerations of these issues. One of the more remarkable passages takes place in Jean Epstein's "On Certain Characteristics of *Photogénie*," where he writes: "To the elements of perspective employed in drawing, the cinema adds a new perspective in time. In addition to relief in space, the cinema offers relief in time. Astonishing abridgments in this temporal perspective are permitted by the cinema—notably in those amazing glimpses into the life of plants and crystals—but these have never yet been used to dramatic purpose."[33] These uses of cinema as a scientific tool have much in common with the traditional understanding of what constitutes animation; here the scientist uses cinema in a process that is explicitly opposed to recording or reproducing an already evident phenomenon. These creations are thaumaturgic. As much as animation has been associated with an anthropomorphic tendency, here the opposite tendency appears. As with Marey's use of the zoetrope, it is not simply a choice between showing what the eye already sees versus something the eye cannot grasp without the new technology; instead, the technological enhancement to vision becomes tied to conceptual growth—Mach wrote about this type of technically aided vision as "invigorated."[34] Time lapse reveals the flux of life in new places, leading to a novel form of perception that participates in what Katrin Solhdju terms "a strategy of concrete pluralization of experience and therefore of reality."[35] When Mach invokes an "ethical" dimension of time-lapse imaging, he gestures toward the opening it provides for access to a new domain of alterity.

Immediately after invoking time lapse, Epstein describes the cinema as "animistic; it attributes, in other words, a semblance of life to the objects it defines." He continues:

> It is hardly surprising that it should endow the objects it is called upon to depict with such intense life. . . . I would even go so far as to say that the cinema is polytheistic and theogonic. Those lives it creates, by summoning objects out of the shadows of indifference into the light of dramatic concern, have little in common with human life. . . . If we wish to understand how an animal, a plant, or a stone can inspire respect, fear, or horror, those three most sacred sentiments, I think we must watch them on the screen, living their mysterious, silent lives, alien to the human sensibility.[36]

This passage indicates a way of thinking of cinema as animation that is related to its use as a mode of scientific visualization. To animate in this sense means something other than to reproduce or to caricature; the practices of scientific visualization foreground the cinema's ability to create a view of something—a process, an object—previously invisible.

Notes

I would like to thank Karen Beckman for her patient editorial guidance. I also would like to thank Hannah Landecker and Scott Curtis for their helpful responses to a draft of this chapter. Unless otherwise noted, all translations are my own.

1. Crafton, *Before Mickey* (1993), 5.
2. Cartwright, *Screening the Body*, 33, 29. Cartwright does take care to qualify this judgment: "I may be overstating my case here by considering only the tendency toward the flat and the digital in Marey's work. One could certainly point to counterexamples—for example, his sculptural models of birds in flight. However, even these dimensional objects were perceptually contained and flattened" (37). As the last sentence makes clear, however, this qualification is raised only to be dismissed.
3. The authors cite Bruno Latour's memorable sentence: "There is nothing you can dominate as easily as a flat surface." Latour, "Drawing Things Together," 45. See also Latour's concept of the "immutable mobile," a graphical representation that reduces the complexity of a phenomenon and allows it to circulate more easily, in *Science in Action*.
4. Chadarevian and Hopwood, "Dimensions of Modelling," in Chadarevian and Hopwood, *Models*, 3, 6.
5. See Barrier, *Hollywood Cartoons*; and Crafton, *Before Mickey* (1993).
6. Lutz, *Animated Cartoons*, viii. He also writes, "Photography and the rendering of sounds by the phonograph have both been adopted for instruction and amusement. The motion-picture also is used for these purposes, but in the main the art has been associated with our leisure hours as a means of diversion or entertainment. During the period of its growth, however, its adaptability to education has never been lost sight of. It is simply that development along this line has not been as seriously considered as it should be" (vii).
7. Further along this path lie photographic processes that are not usually seen as part of cinema history, such as the Lumière brothers' process of *photo-stéréosynthèse*, the tomographic photography of Dr. Eugene Doyen, and X-ray tomography. For more on the intersections between cinema and tomography, see Cartwright and Goldfarb, "Radiography, Cinematography and the Decline of the Lens." An obvious continuation of the practices of modeling in embryology that has received considerable attention from media scholars is the Visible Human Project. See also Alexander Galloway's chapter in this volume for a consideration of how nineteenth-century imaging techniques may be thought about in relation to contemporary computer animation.
8. Cartwright, *Screening the Body*, 22, 38.
9. For counterpoints to the supposition that Marey had no use for the synthesis

of motion, see Gaycken, "'The Swarming of Life'"; and Tortajada, "The 'Cine-matographic Snapshot.'"

10. Marey, *Le mouvement*, 304.
11. Cartwright, *Screening the Body*, 22–23.
12. Braun, *Über Herzbewegung und Herzstoss*, 13. Braun picked the dog because it was sufficiently close to the human heart to allow for extrapolation; his pri-mary interest was to help clinicians understand the heart in order to aid in the diagnosis of abnormalities.
13. Braun, *Über Herzbewegung und Herzstoss*, 15. Later Braun uses a very similar phrase to denote the kind of image that is useful to the physiologist, "plastically modeled bodies [*plastisch modellierte Körper*]" (15).
14. Braun, *Über Herzbewegung und Herzstoss*, 25. Braun used a Viennese copy of the Lumière cinematograph equipped with Zeiss lenses.
15. Braun, *Über Herzbewegung und Herzstoss*, 29. This procedure of superimposing successive images is similar to the working method of traditional cel animators.
16. This dynamic is similar to traditional animation's attention to walk cycles; see Lutz, *Animated Cartoons*, 40, 132–33. Lutz advises animators to study chrono-photographic series in order to better understand movement.
17. For an analysis of the scientific film that foregrounds the still/moving dialectic, see Curtis, "Still / Moving."
18. See Tosi, *Cinema before Cinema*; see also Nicolet, *Intuition mathematique et des-sins animés*.
19. "Lebende Mathematik," *Die Lichtbild-Bühne*, no. 15 (April 13, 1912): 28; cited in "1912: Mathematische Trickfilme," entry on the website of the Deutsches Institut für Animationsfilm; http://diaf.tyclipso.de/de/home/rubriken/Blog_Detailseite.html?b=289; accessed June 28, 2013.
20. In an early response to Emile Cohl's films, a reviewer for the *Motion Picture World* mentions that *Love Affair in Toyland* (*Un Drame chez les fantoches*) (1908) "recalled the 'geometry at play' games from a few years prior." *Moving Picture World* 3, no. 25 (December 19, 1908): 500; cited in Crafton, *Before Mickey* (1993), 85. What exactly "geometry at play" refers to is not clear; it may refer to flip-books that animated drawings of geometrical proofs (Münch's drawings were also published as flip-books), or it may refer to another type of rational amuse-ment, probably visually similar enough to forge the associative link in the re-viewer's mind. Noteworthy in any case is that a film routinely cited as one of the first animated films was understood in terms of a popular-scientific prede-cessor. See Crafton, *Emile Cohl, Caricature, and Film*, for the contextualization of Cohl's films within traditions that range from comic strips to theater to cari-cature to the popular press.
21. As Crafton notes, "There are many other animation histories, though, besides the cultural series encompassed by the classical cinema. Examples include the abstract and avant-garde works of the 1920s, independent animation through-out the century and 'orphan' animation from industrial and sponsored films." Crafton, "The Veiled Genealogies of Animation and Cinema," 105.
22. See Mehrtens, "Mathematical Models."

23. This number of frames would result in a duration of one minute and six seconds at a projection speed of sixteen frames per second.

24. Reicher, "Kinematographie in der Neurologie," 235.

25. Hopwood, "'Giving Body' to Embryos," 463. For an account of the rhetoric of vividness used in relation to early education cinema, see Gaycken, "The Cinema of the Future." Inspired by Reicher's presentation of his films in Dresden in 1907, V. Widakowich announced his own experimentation with the cinematographic process, in which he directly applied slices of a preserved rat embryo onto clear 35mm film stock. Widakowich, "Über kinematographische Vorfürung von Serienschnitten durch Embryonen." This procedure calls to mind certain avant-garde cinema practices, particularly *Mothlight* (Stan Brakhage, 1963). My thanks to Hannah Landecker for sharing the citations to Reicher's and Widakowich's work.

26. Hopwood, "'Giving Body' to Embryos," 495.

27. Kelty and Landecker, "A Theory of Animation."

28. Ries, "Kinematographie der Befruchtung und Zellteilung," 6.

29. Kelty and Landecker, "A Theory of Animation," 38.

30. Kelty and Landecker, "A Theory of Animation," 38. Soon after Ries's work, three-dimensionality became an explicit feature of time-lapse embryological films. See Gräper, "Die Methodik der Stereokinematographischen Untersuchung des lebenden vitalgefärbten Hühnerembryos," which contains a bibliography with further citations to his work with stereoscopic imaging. My thanks to Christian Riess for alerting me to Gräper and sharing the citations with me.

31. Ernst Mach, Notizbuch B22 (August 19, 1884), Ernst-Mach-Institut, Freiburg im Breisgau; quoted in Stiegler, "Ernst Machs 'Philosophie des Impressionismus' und die Momentphotographie," 268.

32. For other accounts of uses of photography that further illuminate this position, see Cartwright and Goldfarb, "Radiography, Cinematography and the Decline of the Lens"; Ellenbogen, "Educated Eyes and Impressed Images"; and Frizot, "Le temps de l'espace." Finally, the use of cinema in time-lapse applications is similar to the use of the series in medical thought; see Curtis, *The Shape of Spectatorship*.

33. Epstein, "On Certain Characteristics of *Photogénie*," 316.

34. Mach, "Bemerkungen über wissenschaftliche Anwendungen der Photographie," 285.

35. Solhdju, "L'expérience 'pure' et l'âme des plantes," 93.

36. Epstein, "On Certain Characteristics of *Photogénie*," 316, 317.

II : : **Cinema and Animation**

5 :: André Martin, Inventor of Animation Cinema: Prolegomena for a History of Terms

HERVÉ JOUBERT-LAURENCIN

TRANSLATED BY LUCY SWANSON

In 2000, Bernard Clarens published the only work to date that collects even a small portion of André Martin's (1925–94) fundamental body of critical work. A third of the book (more than ninety pages) is dedicated to Norman McLaren and constitutes a veritable forgotten monograph. The entirety of the anthology, titled *Pour lire entre les images* (Reading between the images), such as it was conceived, also situates the intriguing and important place of animation cinema as an experience and an *idea* in the history of the twentieth century.[1]

Before his death in 2006, Clarens entrusted me with the articles and documents that he had systematically collected in hopes of publishing other volumes. I have therefore recently come to possess an archive solely devoted to André Martin, which I have named the Fonds Bernard Clarens (Bernard Clarens Collection) and presented publicly at a conference in January 2011 at the University of Picardie. I supplemented the archive with my own collection, which I began prior to 1990 in support of my doctoral thesis offering a preliminary reading of Martin's comprehensive discursive production. And my collection was immediately enhanced, notably by the contribution of Pierre Hébert, an animator from Quebec as well as a true researcher in this case, who discovered important traces of the Canadian period of the French critic and researcher.[2]

The place of Norman McLaren throughout Martin's writing can thus be grasped in its entirety. The Bernard Clarens Collection also brings to light another important director worthy of examination—not a distant contemporary like McLaren (temporally close, but spatially far from Martin) but a pioneer and fellow Frenchman: Emile Cohl (culturally similar, but temporally distant from the critic), who is better known by cinema historians today than he was during Martin's time.[3]

It is possible, thanks to two sets of Martin's writing—twenty-four notations on the creator of *Fantasmagorie* (1908) and thirty-four studies and notations on that of *Blinkity Blank* (1955)—to write a page in cinematic history otherwise little examined by historians: the invention of animation cinema. This history is little known because of its peculiar resistance to the chronological imperative, and thus its failure to present (either in order or according to common logic) two chapters typically found in histories of animation cinema: those dedicated to so-called precursors, inventors, and pioneers, which never fail to leave a place for Cohl, and those dedicated to McLaren. I offer an overview of another history, that of the expression *animation cinema*, that is to say, an act of naming, a *formative* statement, to borrow a term recently introduced by a historian in another field.[4] This linguistic act and its implementation in reality is based on the events of the 1950s—McLaren's glory years, a fact that certainly had something to do with the possibility of such an invention—and yet it is simultaneously retrospective, oriented toward the rediscovery of pioneers. Within the system created by Martin, Cohl operates from a distance as an archaic model of singular invention, toward which McLaren's modernity will return. In sum, what is at stake here is the affirmation that the birth of animation cinema should not be situated in the 1870s, 1890s, or 1910s but rather around 1955.

The Invention of Animation Cinema

The expression *animation cinema* appeared for the first time, at least in Martin's writing (although I have yet to find any examples prior to his use of the term), in the body of a *Cahiers du Cinéma* article from July 1953: "Films d'animation au festival de Cannes" (Animation films at the Cannes festival). It is a report on the first specialized international meeting, organized by the Association française pour la diffusion du cinéma (French association for the promotion of cinema), which organized the "Journées du cinéma" (Days of cinema).[5] The article is an explicit attempt to impose "this adventurous *animation cinema* which insists that a film . . . cannot be anything other than a work felt and arranged frame by frame."[6] In reading the article, it becomes clear that that in the time and place in question, the use of the expression was not self-evident and represented a verbal problem that could not be resolved, even among cinema specialists: "At the international meeting of Cannes [in 1953], animation films, as always, disconcerted enthusiasts and made specialists misspeak. Once again, advertisements, press releases, technical specification sheets, blithely mixed everything together, confusing marionettes and animated cartoons. As soon as animation film was being discussed, whether they were English or Japanese, translators no longer knew their language and gave in to the same incompetent Esperanto." Here Martin addresses the cinephile community and clearly underlines the distinction between cinema and films, which thus reveals itself to be one of the historical markers of the invention: "Nevertheless, how can one love the Cinema so much, to what end can it serve to see ALL films, if one is incapable of seeing and following ALL Cinemas."[7]

Martin took up the expression again with more success the following year and subsequently in all his writings in the 1950s, until the name took hold in common speech, although with some difficulty, since it appeared pleonastic and complicated to commentators. With the third "Journées internationales du cinema d'animation" or "JICA" (International days of animation cinema) in 1960, the phrase became the official, institutionalized name of a grouping that had never been conceived of as such, because the films categorized under this rubric had previously been designated by a variety of expressions: *animated cartoons, children's films, trick films, puppet films, Chinese shadows* (for silhouette films), and a few other variations.

Without having undertaken systematic international research—a task that would be impossible for me to do alone—I believe it is possible to locate this terminological dispersal on either side of a worldwide caesura that took place around the year 1955. It is not only a question of word-for-word translation. Even if there is little doubt that the French word *animation* has been exported directly to other languages, this fact is no more decisive than finding a "first occurrence" of the term. It is, rather, a question of knowing whether there was a spread, during the 1950s (or later) of three characteristics: (1) the use of a noun (*animation* in French and *animation* in English) in place of an adjective (*animé* in French, found in *dessin animé*, and *animated* in English, present in *animated cartoon*); (2) the association of *animation* with *cinéma* rather than with *films* (*animation cinema* in English); (3) the beginning of a rivalry between the new term and *dessin animé* (*animated cartoon* in English), when it is a question of defining a group of films broader than the genre of the animated cartoon, including nongraphic films that were regarded as more or less composited or manipulated and in this way opposed to the typical recording style perceived as the norm; and (3b) the appearance of a new term, *prise de vue directe* in French, *live action* in English, to designate not *all cinema* but all *cinema* except for *animation cinema*.

The association implied by the term *animation cinema* was new because it suggested, beyond the technical correlation between the films, a grouping that might allow for organized screenings and the existence of a community of interest, of spectators (in 1960 the "JICA" were held in Annecy by the militant cinephiles of the largest film club in France) or of artists (the Association internationale du film d'animation [International Association of Animation Film] was created there the same year). To my knowledge, the oldest work that uses the term in its title is Italian, and it ends with a chapter on McLaren and an acknowledgment of the "Journées du cinéma": *Il cinema di animazione, 1832–1956* by Walter Alberti.[8] The progressive birth of innumerable specialized festivals in the world, and the country-by-country development of the Association internationale du film d'animation, rendered the progressive dissemination of the new expression possible.[9]

McLaren's Invention

From the first specialized public display of *animation cinema* in 1953, which took place then in the form of a thematic projection in a room of the Cannes festival, until the institutionalization of an autonomous festival in the city of Annecy in 1960, Martin himself composed the press releases, programs, and major reports in the French press. He was judge and jury, organizer and critic, almost a lobbyist for animation cinema.

In 1960 the name *animation cinema*, taken up repeatedly from that point on, still had not become established, nor had it entered into common usage: "Thus"—writes Martin again—"a new Festival has just appeared dedicated to animation cinema. This expression might upset the purists who feel it is an annoying pleonasm. Is cinema not inevitably the art of movement, of animation par excellence? Why organize another festival devoted, as it would appear to cinema-cinema or to animation-animation?"[10]

Several historical facts pertaining to McLaren's career played an undeniable role in the invention. The official position that he was offered by John Grierson in Canada (the creation of an "animation service" in 1942–43, soon after his arrival in 1941, when he was only a simple, unknown experimental filmmaker emigrating in the midst of a war) and what resulted from it in the following decade laid the groundwork for his career.[11] It truly began to take off in the period from 1952 to 1958, which saw the successive release of *Neighbours, Two Bagatelles, Blinkity*

Blank, *Rythmetic*, *A Chairy Tale*, and *Le Merle*. It was the golden age of his filmography. In 1954 his film *Two Bagatelles* was screened at Cannes, and in 1955 a foundational moment occurred: *Blinkity Blank* was awarded the Palme d'Or for best short film. Finally, by entrusting, or abandoning, to Martin a few famous lines drafted on "invisible interstices" and "drawn movements"—lines that long served as a flag for the small world of animation—McLaren assured their global transmission in a few short years. Among other places, Martin had them reproduced in their calligraphic form (equal to an illustrated or filmed work) in the special edition of the journal of the French federation of cinema clubs, *Cinéma 57*, which was created exclusively in order to launch the new form of cinema as defined by the first JICA.[12]

One likely hypothesis is the historical influence of the film *Neighbours* on Martin (the film was released in 1952, the year he began writing about cinema). The use of pixilation following more classical techniques was also an invention and a rediscovery of practices used in the early days of cinema. Like animation cinema, pixilation (stop-motion animation of human beings) had always been there but had also been forgotten: it had no name.

Neighbours restored photographic recordings of human bodies to animation; that is to say, at least nominally, it reinserted live-action cinematography into the fabricated, artificial space of stop-motion animation. Pixilation historically brings our understanding of *recorded cinema* back to our understanding of *drawn cinema*.

Martin alone was in a position to take full stock of the paradoxes at play—and to allow himself to be submerged by them.[13] *Neighbours* is not merely an example—it is not even paradigmatic of stop-motion animation cinema. It is the blind spot, the impossible space, or rather the utopian nonspace of the term *animation cinema* championed by Martin. The neighbors in this film, based entirely on doubling and reversal, are revenants because they bring about the return of animated photography (*revenant* is the first name in French for "cinema"), but also because animation cinema appears as a return of the first days. Cohl used pixilation at least in *Le mobilier fidèle* (His faithful furniture) (1910) and in *Jobard ne ve pas voir les femmes travailler* (Jobard doesn't want to see women working) (1911).

What, precisely, did Cohl represent, in the age of McLaren, in the discourse of Martin?

Emile Cohl's Invention

Fantasmagorie (1908)

The historian Christophe Gauthier has demonstrated that in France the early 1930s saw the discursive "invention" of precursors, in this way authorizing a rereading of cinema history that reverses the aesthetic genealogy accepted up to that point.[14] French ancestors (primarily Georges Méliès, but also Max Linder) were found for the American directors Cecil B. DeMille and D. W. Griffith, in order to posit them as founders of world cinema as a language. Méliès was not only redeemed but became a founding father of cinema.

The history of animated cartoons that emerged throughout the 1930s, in particular through the dispute over attributing its invention to Cohl, was based on the same premises, adds Gauthier.[15] The new decade began with an article rehabilitating Cohl, exactly contemporaneous to the Méliès Gala on December 16, 1929, and written by a co-organizer of the event, Jean-George Aurio.[16] The conditions for the birth of *Fantasmagorie* in 1908 and Cohl's beginnings at the Gaumont film company were discussed, notably in a series of articles in *Comoedia* in early 1936. And the year 1938 opened with the deaths of Cohl and Méliès, a few hours and a few kilometers apart, after difficult, almost miserable ends, which attest to a truly communal destiny. The idea of a possible commemoration of the anniversary of the "first animated cartoon" arose in part from this double coincidence: the concurrent death in 1938 (January 20 and 21) of two patriarchs with the same pointed white beard, and the affirmation of the 1908 birth of the new cinematic genre of the animated cartoon with *Fantasmagorie.*[17]

The commemoration fell flat. A monument to Cohl and Méliès was conceived of and financed before the wars, following their simultaneous deaths, but it was never built. Twenty years later, after another world war and another postwar period, the year 1958 marked the fiftieth anniversary of Cohl's alleged invention, although this memory was not yet truly visible outside of specialist circles. However, the difference twenty years after 1938 was that these specialists existed and the term *animation cinema* had been introduced. For these reasons, Martin attempted a media operation in the summer of 1958, more or less on his own, likely thanks to the space freed up in the journals during the season.

The Fiftieth Anniversary (1958)

Martin lead a campaign for the commemoration of August 17, 1908, the exact date of the first screening of *Fantasmagorie* in Paris, in three rather significant journals—*Arts, Radio-Cinéma-Télévision,* and *Cahiers du Cinema.* His procedure can be summed up in three coherently articulated points: (1) the French would have fatally forgotten to commemorate in a dignified manner the anniversary of the worldwide birth, in their country, of the animated cartoon;[18] (2) all the signs of the decline of the classic American animated cartoon, which had until then dominated world production, were in 1958 clearly perceptible and definitive;[19] and (3) a renewal was already visible but, with a few exceptions, it was under way outside both France and the United States (see all the conclusions to the articles of the second stage). This transnational modernity, constituted by "young Czech, Canadian, Polish, Hindu or Yugoslavian productions" (the last words in the September 7 article in *Radio-Cinéma-Télévision*), or "happy Russian surprises" (the last heading in the May 18 issue of *Arts*), crossed borders, notably including the iron curtain of the cold war.[20]

Finally, the legend to an illustration concisely sums up Martin's three-part logic in which a central place is occupied by the reactivation of the national myth of a certain Cohl, worthy of international merit but forgotten by the state: "No celebration or homage for the Fiftieth Anniversary of the French Animated Cartoon. No more animated cartoon in the Americas. Yet frame-by-frame Cinema continues."[21]

April 1953

A few years earlier, Martin's first text published in *Cahiers du Cinéma* appeared, the manifesto for the "Journées du cinéma" (the principle behind these "days of cinema" was to wholly dedicate a provincial city to cinema for an intensive week), cosigned by Pierre Barbin and Michel Boschet. Although the text did not yet constitute a defense of animation, it already proposed screenings devoted to Cohl and Méliès, identifying them together by the same vivid term: "Makeshift screens, set up on street corners, offer impromptu showings of rapid and energetic films: phantasmagoria by Cohl or Méliès, illustrated poems by Paul Grimault."[22] But *phantasmagoria* is neither capitalized nor italicized in the original edition.[23] It is certainly a question of a reappropriation of Cohl's title to make a lexical equivalent of *trick films.*

The Hundred-Year Anniversary (1977)

In 1977, that is to say twenty years after this period of invention, Martin wrote a small book at the behest of Raymond Maillet, an independent archival historian and the first Cohl specialist who was at the time director of the eleventh JICA in Annecy. Martin expresses in the book, retrospectively, and with more clarity, the place that his historical system accorded to Cohl. In the form of a fictive daily newspaper, the short work titled *Image par image* (Frame by frame) was placed under the following auspices: "Fondateur: Emile Reynaud. 100e année. Directeur : Emile Cohl" (Founder: Emile Reynaud. 100th year. Director: Emile Cohl).[24] The coupling of Reynaud and Cohl is classic in the histories and accounts of animation enthusiasts. It creates a cinematic counterhistory through the use of wordplay, since it makes it possible to avoid placing any definitive birth of the animated cartoon or of the animation film in 1895: the first Emile preceded this threshold by fifteen years, a fact that the second was unaware of when his invention followed it by more than twelve years. In this historical panorama of French animation cinema, Martin left the task of writing the report on Cohl to the specialist Maillet, but he evoked elsewhere the filmmaker's "seriousness" in his "responsibility to new combinations," making the rather striking comparison between Cohl's puppets and schemata taken from the notebooks of a contemporary, Ludwig Wittgenstein.

Anachronisms

Martin views Cohl as a pioneer. In this case, a solitary worker who values the everyday invention of new, expeditious techniques commensurate with one man, a singular island in an economy that could not assimilate him nor make him fit into its framework.

But a pioneer or, according to Martin, a "primitive," is not the protagonist of a nationalist discourse on the past. Cohl was not, in himself, a patrimonial resource to be profited from, a treasure of French history or a genius who gave everything to the Americans. On the contrary, he was a present energy, a nonchronological event that returned in the current McLarenian moment of international creation, more precisely in its most advanced stage, which was geared toward the future of the art of animation, an art that invents new techniques consistent with a poetics and a concrete, expressive necessity. Regarding McLaren, Martin asserts in an article titled "N'oublions pas le mode d'emploi" (Let's not forget the owner's manual): "In the same way, browsing through the reel of unreleased negatives of that other pioneer, Emile Cohl, I was not surprised to discover (notably in *Le peintre néo-impressionniste* [The neo-impressionist painter]) an example of that discontinuous animation which, forty-five years later, would impassion Norman McLaren when he had pushed his attempts at drawn-on-film animation to the limit with *Blinkity Blank.*"[25]

The movement of an anachronistic history continued with a word from McLaren reported and commented on by Martin in January 1958: "When he saw himself ranked among the pantheon of avant-garde creators, Norman McLaren, more aware of origins, protested: 'Put me, rather, with the rear-guard, after Cohl, Fischinger and Len Lye.' In fact it was Emile Cohl who, long ago, first gave the example of solitary animation, of schematic drawing, and of analogical freedom in the development."[26]

In a more theoretical passage on McLaren, Martin evokes Stéphane Mallarmé and Paul Valéry to situate the "problem of the subject" specific to animation, the precise location where it moves away from the rest of cinema, all the while digging deeper into the central question (the philosophical basis of Martin's contribution was to invent, for cinema, such an "outside thought"). Against "dramatic, oratory or comedic" contemporary cinema, McLaren sustains interest with purely abstract material "because movement is enough to make him happy." And Martin adds: "Emile Cohl, possessed by the *demon of analogy*, also directed films of pure, perpetual movement *that had no beginning and no end.*"[27] For our part, we could name this magnificent intuition that Cohl's work offers to Martin "the demonic analogy." Because, in effect, the realist strength of the movement of objects and bodies in animation constitutes an analogical force no less important than that of photomechanical reproduction (if animated images resemble each other to the point of passing from one to another imperceptibly, then they can just as well transform, in the spectator's experience, into real bodies and objects). Paradoxically, this idea opposes the autonomy of an animation cut off from cinema; on the contrary, it comes full circle to locate a troubling effect at the edge of cinematographic realism.

Moreover, the fact that Cohl's films have "no beginning and no end" recalls a more general question brought to light by Martin, one pertaining to community and cinematography: animation cinema's capacity for national and chronological unmooring. One could say, effectively, that Martin's specific ideological contribution can be located in the affirmation of the art of animation's fundamental *absence of chronological inevitability*, and in the instinctive negation of the traditional history that went hand in hand, in his writing, with a refusal of geopolitics and established national borders. This study of his discourse reveals a temporality less subject to chronology, in order to return to Martin's instinctive practice of a history that goes against the grain.

Notes

1. Clarens, *André Martin*. It is a remarkable critical anthology, accompanied by contextualization that gives several precise and original historical points regarding the history of French cinema culture. It brings together critical articles spanning, without exception, 1952 to 1965. Nevertheless, the collection represents less than a third of Martin's complete works.

2. Martin published his first article in 1952 in *L'Âge du Cinema*, and his last written publication known to date is an encyclopedia entry published in 1987 in *L'encyclopaedia universalis*. After this date, a debilitating illness prevented him from working. In France, beyond his activity in film criticism in the 1950s (forty-nine articles in *Cahiers du Cinéma* between 1953 and 1960), and more occasionally in *Radio Cinéma Télévision, France Observateur, Le Cinéma Chez Soi, Le Cinéma Pratique, Artsept, Cinéma Quebec, Images et Son, Banc-titre*, and a few other locations, he was a general delegate of an association for the promotion of cinema subsidized by the state (the Association française de diffusion du cinéma), in which the current festival in Annecy has its origins. He was also present at the creation of the Groupe de recherche image (Image Research Group) in 1961 at the Office de radiodiffusion-télévision française (French Office of Radio-Television); was producer and director of animation films in association with Michel Boschet (with the company Les films Martin-Boschet); and then, in 1970–80, upon his return from a visit to Canada, was a research engineer at the Institut national de l'audiovisuel (National Audiovisual Institute), charged with reflecting on the future of images and in particular CGI. To this end, he contributed to the founding of Imagina in Monte Carlo in 1981. In Canada, after a first trip at the invitation of the festival in Montreal in 1961, Martin was brought on by Pierre Juneau in 1965 as the director of research services at the Canadian Radio-television and Telecommunications Commission, and he lived in Montreal from 1966 to 1974 with his family. He directed films there and prepared the International Retrospective of the Cinema of Animation that the Cinémathèque canadienne (future Cinémathèque québécoise) offered on the occasion of the 1967 International and Universal Exposition in Montreal; his fabulous giant synoptic chart "Origin and Golden Age of the American Cartoon from 1906 to 1941" was exhibited at this occasion. He conversed with Marshall McLuhan, whom Martin helped to introduce in France in a long article documented in *Image et Son* in 1965, and he made an unpublished series of recorded and transcribed interviews with Northrop Frye in 1968–69.

3. On Cohl, see Crafton, *Emile Cohl, Caricature, and Film*; and for recent French works, see Courtet-Cohl and Génin, *Émile Cohl*; Vignaux and Courtet-Cohl, *Emile Cohl*; and Vimenet, *Emile Cohl*.

4. See Dufoix, *La dispersion*, 14–28. These pages in particular offer a useful panorama of the diverse schools of thought—historical, philosophical, and philological—that have worked on a historical semantics that has proposed histories of the word. See also, in the artistic sphere, Roque, *Qu'est-ce que l'art abstrait?* Neither of these two studies ever anticipates a predefined object that would exist before its naming and the use that its interpreters would make of it. The first part of the work that came out of my doctoral thesis followed the same approach, interrogating the term *animation cinema*. See Joubert-Laurencin, *La lettre volante*, 35–68. In critiquing the reprisal of the Austinian notion of "performativity" by the French sociologist Pierre Bourdieu, which he judges erroneous, Stéphane Dufoix proposes the idea of the "formativity" of words to designate, in their progressive polysemic dispersal, their influence on reality when they are successful and widely revived in different places and times.

5. See Clarens, *André Martin*, 25.

6. Martin, "Films d'animation au festival de Cannes," 39; emphasis added.

7. Martin, "Films d'animation au festival de Cannes," 39.

8. Alberti, *Il cinema di animazione, 1832–1956*.

9. What followed this history is not the subject of this chapter, but it is notable that the definition and the delimitation of *animation* was followed by violent modifications: the end of the institutional restriction to frame-by-frame animation in 1980 by the Association internationale du film d'animation during the Zagreb festival (see Joubert-Laurencin, *La lettre volante*, 41–42), and the end of the trenchant break between animation cinema and live-action cinema as a result of the advent of the digital age (see Joubert-Laurencin, "Le cinéma d'animation n'existe plus").

10. Clarens, *André Martin*, 133.

11. Before 1953 *animation* and *animated film* existed in specialized vocabulary. It is possible to follow the slow modification of the vocabulary in the revisions to the small volume *Technique du cinéma* in the scholarly paperback series of the Presses Universitaires de France, titled "Que sais-je?" written by Joseph-Marie Lo Duca, also the writer of the trailblazing book *Le dessin animé*. In the first edition (1943), the chapter "Technique du dessin animé" ("Animated Cartoon Technique") aims to be prophetic ("Animated cartoons tend to evolve. The 'one turn, one picture' technique has just begun") and proposes an initial rough classification of stop-motion films, described as a "branch of cinematography." Lo Duca, *Technique du cinéma* (1943), 115. The return of the same classificatory table in Lo Duca's specialized 1948 work is unchanged, as is the 1956 edition, but the 1971 edition adds a name to this "branch," which is still not "animation cinema," but "animation films" (113).

12. Norman McLaren, *Cinéma 57*, no. 14 (January 1957): 12. Martin's published reproduction of McLaren's calligraphy can be found, followed by a commentary, in Joubert-Laurencin, *La lettre volante*, 52, among other places. The text, as

presented by Martin, is the following with underlining and the lapsus of the crossed out *that*: "Animation is not the art of DRAWINGS-that-move but the art of MOVEMENTS-that-are drawn. What happens between each frame is much more important than what exists on each frame. Animation is therefore the art of manipulating the invisible ~~that~~ interstices that lie between frames. Norman McLaren."

13. In fact, Martin must have had a belated awareness, or perhaps was never able to see *On the Farm* (directed by McLaren in 1951), in which the word *pixilation* appeared for the first time in the closing credits, based on *pixie* or *pixilated*, a word found in a philological discussion in *Mr. Deeds Goes to Town* (directed by Frank Capra in 1936; the word appears ninety-four and ninety-five minutes in). Martin uses circumlocutions rather than *la pixillation* in 1953, and again in 1958. See Martin, "Films d'animation au festival de Cannes," 39. And, exceptionally, one of his final encyclopedia entries in Passek, *Dictionnaire du cinéma*, "Animation (techniques de l')" (22–25), which is dedicated to the subject, manages neither to spell (he only puts a single *l*) nor to define the technique (he cites two animations of objects in two of Cohl's films, whereas pixilation is defined, precisely, in opposition to the animation of objects, by the presence of human bodies in the field of vision).

14. Gauthier, "L'invention des 'primitifs' à l'orée du parlant," 164. This is the first publication of the results of his doctoral thesis, "Une composition française."

15. Gauthier, "L'invention des 'primitifs' à l'orée du parlant," 172 n. 52.

16. Auriol, "Les premiers dessins animés cinématographiés."

17. On December 21, 1937, a few weeks before the death of the two French pioneers, the animated cartoon saw renewed interest worldwide with the American release of Disney's *Snow White and the Seven Dwarfs* at Carthay Circle Theatre in Hollywood. On the film's reception in France, see the indispensable, encyclopedic dissertation of Sébastien Roffat, "L'émergence d'une école française de dessin animé sous l'Occupation (1940–1944)," 116–28 and appendixes 7, 11, 12, and 15.

18. For Martin, "Cinquante ans après, le dessin animé revient à ses origines," *Arts*, no. 684 (August 20, 1958), see Clarens, *André Martin*, 127–31; for Martin, "Le 17 Août 1908," *Radio-Cinéma-Télévision* no. 448 (August 17, 1958), see Clarens, *André Martin*, 177–78; and for Martin, "Un cinquantenaire par comme les autres," *Cahiers du Cinéma*, no. 86 (August 1958): 42, see Clarens, *André Martin*, 55–56.

19. For Martin, "L'Amérique a perdu le monopole du dessin animé," *Arts*, no. 672 (May 28, 1958), see Clarens, *André Martin*, 125–27; for Martin, "Le dessin animé américain est-il mort?," *Radio-Cinéma-Télévision* no. 451 (September 7, 1958), see Clarens, *André Martin*, 179–80; and for Martin, "Feu l'animated cartoon," *Cahiers du Cinéma*, no. 86 (August 1958): 43–44, see Clarens, *André Martin*, 54–55.

20. Martin, something of a legal activist, certainly thinks of animation and its festivals (the triangle Annecy-Zagreb-Ottawa of the 1960 to 1980s) as a means of saving the artists from the countries under the yoke of communism.

21. André Martin, "Pour faire partager son indignation et remuer les foules ciné-philes," *Cahiers du Cinéma*, no. 86 (August 1958): 43; cited in Clarens, *André Martin*, 52 (there is an identification error added by the publisher Dreamland).

22. Clarens, *André Martin*, 38.

23. The original edition is *Cahiers du Cinéma*, no. 22 (April 1953).

24. The twenty-four-page pamphlet published on the occasion of the eleventh annual "Journées Internationales du Cinéma d'Animation: 14–18 juin 1977," alongside the exhibition *Cent ans de dessins animés 1877–1977*, which was held at the Musée-Château d'Annecy, summer 77, Bernard Clarens Collection; it is not reproduced in Clarens, *André Martin*. The year 1877 represents when Emile Reynaud received the patent for the praxinoscope, which marks, according to Martin, who justifies this date on the first page, "not only the beginning of the idea of animated cinema but also the beginning of this very particular form of cinema in France."

25. André Martin, "N'oublions pas le mode d'emploi," *Cinéma 57*, no. 14 (January 1957): 36; cited in Clarens, *André Martin*, 254.

26. Quoted in Clarens, *André Martin*, 191.

27. André Martin, "III. On a touché au cinema," *Cahiers du Cinéma* no. 82 (April 1958); cited in Clarens, *André Martin*, 240; emphasis added.

6 :: "First Principles" of Animation

ALAN CHOLODENKO

All my publications on animation of the last twenty-three years are dedicated to *animating film theory*—not only addressing what animation adds to the theorizing of film but doing that adding, while trying to redress the marginalization of animation by film studies, film history, and film theory. For animation has been their blind spot. My animating (of) film theory as *film animation theory* applies especially to the theorization of live action film through animation and responds to late 1960s French Marxist film theory and the Anglo-American film theory derived from it.[1] Given that there is no way I can offer here a comprehensive rehearsal of my interventions over those twenty-three years, I ask the reader to consult my publications, especially my introductions to the anthologies I edited—*The Illusion of Life: Essays on Animation* (1991), the world's first book of scholarly essays theorizing animation, and *The Illusion of Life 2: More Essays on Animation* (2007)—which directly address film studies and film theory, as well as animation studies and animation theory.[2] In this chapter I offer my key results to date, my "first principles" of animation.

To ask the question, "By not writing about animated films, have theorists simply been prioritizing the live action film while still producing theory that is applicable to animation?," misses the key first point of my 1991 introduction in *The Illusion of Life*, which I reiterated in my essay in that anthology.[3] It is a claim I still find to be radical, and it was made ten years before Lev Manovich's similar assertion.[4] Let us call it our first "first principle" of animation: not only is animation a form of film but all film, film "as such," is a form of animation.

Given *all film* by definition includes live action, live action is a form of animation. Consequently, film theorists have never not been writing about animated films and film (as) animation, knowingly or unknowingly. I say *animated films* to designate that genre or mode of films traditionally defined as "animation" and treated as the least significant form of film or even not a form of film at all, rather a form of graphic art, by film studies, film history, and film theory.[5]

It is not only recently, with the advent of digital film, that animation has become the paradigm for all forms of cinema, and its study consequently become the study of cinema's basic ontology overall. For me — our second principle — this has never not been the case (with the caveat, as I shall explain, that I do not subscribe to a simple ontology of cinema, much less of animation). And that primacy includes necessitating the *reversal* of the historical and theoretical prioritization, by those speaking for film, of film over animation. Such a reversal results in the privileging of the heretofore degraded animated film for film animation, for all film, for film "as such," for which, as a result, *the animated film becomes the paradigm.*

Put simply, historically as well as theoretically, film is the "stepchild" of animation, not the other way around. This is a second radical claim that I posed in *The Illusion of Life*, in terms that included the film animator Emile Reynaud, creator of the praxinoscope and, most crucially here, the Théâtre Optique of 1892–1900. Reynaud is the most singular figure in film forgotten by both film studies and animation studies — and whose name, work, and achievements I sought to resurrect, *reanimate*.[6] Indeed, Reynaud's key term, *animated*, used in all his publicity, passed on to the term *animated photographs*, a term by which cinema was in its earliest years known, at least in France, England, and England's colonies.

These two principles have a radical consequence. First: to theorize film without theorizing animation is to not theorize film. And a second, even more radical, one: to theorize film, including live action, without theorizing it through animation is to not theorize film. That theorizing *of* and *through* animation has been my project of the last twenty-three years.[7] At the same time, insofar as live action is the special case, the conditional, reduced form of animation, what has been written about live action is by definition applicable to animation, in obviously a conditional, reduced way. By definition what has been written about animation is applicable to live action, since animation subsumes live action, is the unconditional, unreduced form of live action. Therefore, animation theory is by definition theory of live action, of what live action has come to denominate: cinema and film. And animation theory, like the film it animates, is more. For animation film and film animation operate within, at, and beyond the limits of live action. Not only is animation never not operating within live action, the expanded field of live action is animation.

Here it is imperative to note the decades-long existence of scholars, scholarship, and publications in animation history and theory, including the ongoing, increasingly burgeoning, and increasingly animated existence of the Society for Animation Studies, founded in 1987. That scholarship in animation must be acknowledged by film historians and theorists, for it is crucial to understand that we are not at a zero-degree state in animation scholarship. Far from it.[8] Nor are we at a zero-degree state in terms of film theorists theorizing animation. Here I reference not only my work but that of fourteen other authors in my two anthologies who have come out of film studies and film theory, accounting for twenty of the twenty-seven essays in the two volumes.[9]

In sum, film studies needs to engage with animation studies, as animation studies needs to engage with film studies.[10] Animation scholars have much to learn from film studies scholars, especially from the theorizing of film and from the history of that theorizing. Put simply, for me film studies is by definition the conditional, reduced form of animation studies, and animation studies the unconditional, unreduced form of film studies. These constituencies are commingled, inextricably so, despite the lack of general acknowledgment of that on the part of either. So, yes, theorists prioritizing the live action film are still producing theory that is applicable to animation; but the specifics need to be teased out, examined, and assessed.

The questions are: first, how has animation been marked and inscribed in live action theory? And second, is this marking and inscription adequate to animation? For me, live-action theory must by definition be so marked, including with terms derived from and associated with animation, not just with the lexical forms of *animate* itself but with cognate terms such as *authoring* and *engendering*, and cognate expressions too, such as something has *a life of its own*, is *coming to life*, *brought to life*. Such terms appear often in discussions of film but are used without any awareness of, much less inquiry into, what they point to and open up as something substantive in its own right: animation. So, in response to the question, "Exactly where is film theory lacking in its consideration of animation?," I would say: in the general absence in that theory of a direct address of animation! Theorization of live action qua live action can only get one so far in terms of theorizing animation, not just in the theory's consideration of live action but in the operations within that theory of animation.

For what is the point of a fixed, static—inanimate—theory of animation? Or at best a conditionally, reductively animated theory of it? What is called for is a theorization of live action, and of theories past and present of live action, *through animation*, even as animation calls for an animated and animating theory of itself, an animating / reanimating film animation theory, as it were, indeed an animatic theory of it, whose purport I shall elucidate.

To answer these questions, we must posit what animation is, including offering its two major definitions: the endowing with life and the endowing with motion.[11] Any theorizing of animation cannot limit itself to that endowing with life and motion but must consider the full cycles of each, that is to say, their metamorphoses, their diminutions, and their terminations—death and nonmotion—as well as their inextricable commingling throughout their cycles.[12]

Of course, *animation* immediately imbricates Latin *anima* (air, breath, soul, spirit, mind), Latin *animus* (mind, soul), and animism, even as animism is never not inextricably commingled with its opposite, mechanism.[13] The inextricable, deconstructive commingling of animism and mechanism (and therefore of the institutions and discourses each privileges and is privileged by—the arts and humanities and the sciences and technology, respectively) in film animation makes the cinematographic apparatus the *animatographic apparatus*, indeed the *animatic apparatus*, what I dubbed *animatic automaton*, "ur," "defining" technology of animation for me.

Animating not only the illusion of life but the life of (that) illusion, the vital machine that is the animatic automaton has as consequence: any theorizing of film animation only in terms of motion (and mechanism) while excluding life (and animism) is reductive, doing an injustice to animation, as is any theorizing that theorizes film animation only in terms of life (and animism) while excluding motion (and mechanism), as is any theorizing that theorizes the cinematographic apparatus without theorizing the animatographic apparatus, as is any theorizing that theorizes the animatographic apparatus without theorizing the animatic apparatus, the animatic automaton.

Given that Latin *anima* is a translation of Greek *psyche*, it crucially opens up the relation of Plato's *psyche* (air, breath, soul, spirit, mind) *and* its ontological and ontotheological inheritance both by Western metaphysics and Christianity—and, crucially, *by ontological and onto-*

theological film theory, most notably André Bazin's—to Homer's *psuché*, his simulacral spectre wandering as a flitting shade in Hades.[14] I shall return to this.

Insofar as animation privileges the primitive, the savage, the primal, the nutty, the loony, the child, the nonhuman (including all other organic forms, as well as the inorganic), and the object *over* what for us cinema has privileged—the civilized, the sane, the adult, the human, and the subject[15]—the cartoon is the privileged example of what operates within animated film. The cartoon is therefore the privileged example of animated film, and the privileged example of film animation and of what operates therein—the animatic. While late 1960s French film theory (including as taken up in Anglo-American film theory, itself strongly influenced by and influencing cultural studies) privileged the subject, production, and identity, including self-identity, it neglected what is superior to them, superior to the subject and its desires: the object and its games, the world and its play.[16] Which is to say *all* the things that animation for us privileges. Their vital, unmasterable life of illusion is privileged for us by animation, animation as the animatic, a life never not operating within live action and its zone of reality. Consequently, one must theorize not only the illusion of life but also the life of that illusion (*illusion* is from the Latin *ludere*, meaning "ludic" and "play"). For animation is not delimited to film.[17] It is idea, concept, process, performance, medium, and milieu. As I wrote in 1991:

> To seek to account for animation film, the theorist would be compelled to approach the idea of animation precisely as not delimited to and by the animation film (and conventional ideas of it) but as a notion whose purchase would be transdisciplinary, transinstitutional, implicating the most profound, complex and challenging questions of our culture, questions in the areas of being and becoming, time, space, motion, change— indeed, life itself.[18]

There is a privileged relation between film animation and philosophy, a privilege I have posited as the second key neglect of film studies, and as the key neglect of animation studies too, a neglect that a number of us have been working to remedy. Which is to say that we are not at a zero-degree state in theorizing film animation in terms of "philosophy," in treating film animation as a mode of "philosophizing," and, let me add, "philosophizing" as a form of animation. But with this caveat: our embrace of "poststructuralist" and "postmodernist" approaches means not simply an espousal of the ontological, of Western philosophy as a metaphysics of presence, of fullness of living being, but rather a challenge to them, especially for me from the perspective of Jacques Derrida and Jean Baudrillard. Of course, for Derrida, deconstruction is not philosophy; it is aphilosophy, on both sides of the horizon of philosophy at the same time, at once the philosophy of nonphilosophy and nonphilosophy of philosophy. In other words, deconstruction is an in-betweener—privileged in and for the theorizing of film as form of animation, of the animatic. This makes deconstruction isomorphic with animation, and with my aphilosophy of animation.[19]

For animation—animation as the animatic—is an in-betweener, coming between any and every thing, including all oppositions, confounding all either / or-isms, as well as operating within any and every thing, as well as forming the milieu, the medium, for any and every thing, *thing* including *one*.[20] But here I need to explain the animatic, as there is more to animation than animation! For the past twenty-three years, I have been working between and across film studies, film history, and film theory *and* animation studies, animation history, and animation theory, *reanimating* them, even the very idea of film, *through the animatic*. And this means working to turn animation theory and film theory into film animation theory, to turn animation studies and film studies into film animation studies, to turn animation and film into film animation, and thereby to turn the cinematographic apparatus into the animatographic apparatus, even the animatic apparatus. And this includes working to mark their never not being so reanimated, as well as to mark the blind spot of the animatic as never not operative therein.

I theorize the animatic as the very singularity of animation, anterior and superior to animation, not only the very logics, processes, performance, and performativity of animation but the very "essence" of animation—the animation and animating of animation. The animatic subsumes animation, is its very condition of possibility and at the same time impossibility—at once the inanimation never not in and of animation and the animation never not in and of inanimation. Making animation never totally animate and inanimation never totally inanimate, the animatic is that nonessence that at once enables and disenables animation as essence—including Sergei Eisenstein's *plasmaticness*, his animistic essence of film (as) animation[21]—as it does all essentialist theories of film and / as animation. This is why I put the word *essence* in quotation marks, under erasure. Put simply, the animatic indetermines and suspends all things, including animation. Including "itself."

The animatic is to animation what *psuché* is to *psyche/anima* (and to all derived from *psyche / anima*), what specter is to soul, what for Derrida *différance* is to presence, what dissemination is to essence, what the hauntological is to the ontological. Not simply different but radically, irreducibly Other—the animatic is "ur" *in-betweener* (with "ur," henceforth marking nonessence)—animation itself gifting us this term *in-betweener*! So while Norman McLaren declared that "*difference* . . . is the . . . soul of animation," for me, Derridean *différance* is the specter of animation, is animation as the animatic.[22]

Insofar as there is no essence to the animatic, animation is not intrinsically anything. Meaning there is no essence to film animation, including cinema. Insofar as there is no proper, propriety nor property to it, animation is always already, never not, expropriated, as is any fixed, final definition of it. As expropriated, animation cannot be appropriated by or to anything.

The animatic: what conjures animation (cinema, live action, included) and what animation seeks to conjure away but cannot, what uncannily haunts animation as its ghost, its specter, its death, cryptically incorporating, deconstructing, disseminating, and seducing it. Put simply, what is at stake in animation, including film animation, is life and death, as well as their inextricable commingling. And animation's own life and death.

As I have written: "Animation—the simultaneous bringing of death to life and life to death—not only a mode of film (and film a mode of it) but the very medium within which all, including film, 'comes to be.' The animatic apparatus—apparatus which suspends distinctive oppositions, including that of the animate versus the inanimate—apparatus of the 'uncanny.'"[23] This uncanny simultaneous bringing of death and the dead to life and life and the living to death is what, after Derrida, I call *lifedeath*, at once the life of death and the death of life—both alive and dead, neither alive nor dead, at the same time. In consequence, one can never know life or death, motion or nonmotion, as such.

Lifedeath, cryptically incorporated in and deconstructing the life and death of film animation, necessarily implicates the spectator (including author, reader, analyst, and theorist)—drawing the spectator, returning it, toward death even as it draws forth, returns, toward life those dead imaged in the film. In other words, film animation, as animatic in-betweener, occupies that in-between space, that "meeting ground"— that haunted house, that crypt[24]—between life and death, between motion and nonmotion.

Insofar as film animation puts life and death at stake, films and film genres that explicitly stage and perform that stake are privileged for and as animation. This privileges the horror genre, with its family of specters of the living dead (the vampire, the zombie, the mummy, and so on), and science fiction too (with its automata, robots, and cyborgs, and aliens)—and their remakings, their metamorphosings, of the human and the nonhuman.[25]

But that putting of life and death at stake is already there in Maxim Gorky's paradigmatic (for Tom Gunning and me) July 4, 1896, review of the Lumière brothers' program at the Nizhny Novgorod fair. Gorky's is a traumatic experience and review that places cinema, film animation, in what he calls the "Kingdom of Shadows." For me, this is the kingdom of specters, of *psuché*, of lifedeath, and the animatic. Through reference to this canonical review, I have repeatedly posited a privileged relation between animation and its apparatus and Freud's uncanny (in both its psychological and anthropological modes) for the theorizing of film animation. Along with Gunning's "An Aesthetic of Astonishment: Early Film and the (In)credulous Spectator" (1989), this review enabled me to posit as first, last, and enduring attraction, even primal, "ur" attraction, of cinema, of film animation . . . animation itself! The astoundingly attracting and attractingly astounding endowing with animation by means of a mechanical apparatus, marked by Gorky's famous Frankensteinian words: "Suddenly a strange flicker passes through the screen and the picture stirs to life."[26] Not just motion but life!

And these two texts enabled me to characterize as "first, last and enduring attraction of animation," including film animation . . . the animatic "itself"! And to posit the specter as "ur" figure of film animation as the animatic. And to posit as "ur" experience of film animation "the Cryptic Complex," "ur" complex, composed, after Derrida, of the uncanny, the return of death as specter, endless mourning and melancholia and cryptic incorporation.[27] It is a complex of the shocking return of the dead as specters and of their attraction[28] to and *for* the spectators, and of the aftershocks felt by the spectators. Put simply, the "ur" experience, "ur" attraction, of cinema is that of animation as the animatic, as the Cryptic Complex, as the shocking, traumatic, uncanny reanimation of the dead as living dead. And at the same time, the shocking, traumatic, uncanny reanimation of the living, including the spectator, as living dead, turning spectatorship (including analysis and theorizing) into *spectership*, into haunting and being haunted, encrypting and being encrypted—the cryptic incorporation of the living dead specters in the spectator, and vice versa—accompanied by mourning and melancholia in perpetuity, *no matter what other affects might be generated to cover them over.* The animatic lifedeath of the Cryptic Complex is for me the "foundation," the foundation without foundation, of cinema and movies—of film animation. As the animatic is of all animation, its singular attraction, the "life" of its illusion.

The Cryptic Complex of animation as the animatic enabled me to recast Gunning and André Gaudreault's "cinema of attractions" as "animation of attractions," Gunning's "cinema of narrative integration" as "animation of narrative 'integration,'" and Gunning's return of the cinema of attractions in the "Spielberg-Lucas-Coppola cinema of effects" in the 1970s and 1980s as the reanimation of the animation of attractions, as the hyperanimation of hyperattractions.[29] Marking the increasingly pervasive impact of digital film animation as well as anime,[30] such hyperanimation is of the order not of the hauntological nor of the ontological but of what I call the *oncological.*

Insofar as animation is never not informing film in all its registers, animation recasts not just the classic realist text but also the cinematic text "as such" as what I call *the animated text,* indeed *the animatic text,* text animated by the Cryptic Complex, by lifedeath. Thus, it becomes necessary to conceive of cinema, of film, as *spectrography* (the writing of the specter—ghost writing), as *cryptography* (the writing of the crypt), as *thanatography* (the writing of death).

But crucially, after Baudrillard, the return of death and the dead, and as specters, means yet more, for it is the return of the "ur" radical, irreconcilable, irreducible, excluded Other—the model of all radical, excluded Others. While animation privileges the simple other of what live action privileges, the animatic privileges the Other, the radical Other, the Other irreducible to simple other, simple other to the same, of both animation and film. This is the animatic—radical Other of animation, animation *as* radical Other—as what I call "death the animator."

But as many of my articles after Baudrillard propose, it is not enough to theorize animation and the animatic. One must also, where applicable, theorize *hyperanimation*—the pure and empty form of animation, where the animate becomes more and less inanimate than inanimate and at the same time the inanimate becomes more and less animate than animate—and the *hyperanimatic*—the pure and empty form of the animatic.[31] Hyperanimation and the hyperanimatic are for me of the order of the oncological, of Baudrillard's disillusioned, disenchanted, hyperreal third and fourth orders, orders of virtual, viral, metastatic, pure and empty forms. One must theorize hyperanimation and the hyperanimatic most especially in terms of post–Second World War film and of course computer animated film, including live action, where film becomes hyperfilm, live action becomes hyperlive hyperaction, or, better, hyperlivedead hyperaction nonaction — the pure and empty forms of film, life, the living, death, the dead, lifedeath, the living dead, action, and nonaction.

Arguably, since the Second World War, we live increasingly in the era of the hyper, of hyperreality, where hypertelia rules. Here all things push and are pushed to their limits, where they at once fulfill and annihilate themselves, including all the components of the Cryptic Complex, therefore the Complex too, which morphs into the hyperCryptic hyperComplex. It is no longer the era of lifedeath but of hyperlifedeath, and hypermotion, of hypermotion nonmotion, where the human passes into the posthuman, the hyperhuman, figured for Baudrillard by the clone, the clone figured by me as the zombie,[32] the cyborg, and the replicant in *Blade Runner*.[33] Here death takes on the form of hyperdeath, the absence of death, absence of the radical Other, and therefore of all others. Here hyperlifedeath reigns, where life and the living are more dead than dead, and death and the dead are more alive than alive. In other words, not only life but death has died, each replaced by cold, clonal hyperimmortality, fulfilling the human's wish for escape from death — escape from the uncanny valley, valley for me of the shadow of death — the death of death, by definition, an escape from the human itself.

Hyperanimation and the hyperanimatic increasingly present themselves as the most compelling and singular processes of not only contemporary "film" but the contemporary "world" and "subject." The implication is clear: we need animation film theory, film animation theory, animation theory "as such," and especially hyperanimation hyperfilm theory and hyperfilm hyperanimation theory, to attempt to understand film, the world and the subject, especially in their hyperforms. And we need television, video, and especially computer animation theory, because these media, these technologies — like film, by definition animators / reanimators, including of the world and the subject — increasingly pervade and reanimate the mediascape, or rather immediascape, of the world and the subject, an immediascape, world, and subject that are increasingly hyperanimated, hyperanimatic. For today not only do we swim in a sea of hyperanimated hypermedia, hypertechnologies, but that sea swims inside hyperanimated, immediated, hypermediated, hypertechnologized, hyperremediated, hyperirradiated us.

To conclude, but alas with a few caveats: whether Baudrillard's first order of the Radical Illusion of Seduction (for me, the animatic) has been annihilated in the passage into the Perfect Crime of Virtuality of his third/fourth orders of hyperreality, virtual reality (for me, the hyperanimatic), or the hyperanimatic is but *the avatar* of the animatic is for me, as it was for him, undecidable, irresolvable.[34]

This is a reminder of the hypothetical nature of the "principles" I have proposed—speculations, indeed specters, spectering, cryptically incorporating, *this* specter-speculator-spectator-analyst-theorist, and I they. Specters never laid to rest, never resolved, never reconciled. In fact, a specter, an evil demon, after Baudrillard, keeps pressing me to propose: thanks to the animatic, the only first principle of animation is *there is no first principle of animation.*

And there are never not more specters, crypts, analyses to come.

Notes

A nod of acknowledgment to John Grierson's famous "First Principles of Documentary." But unlike the essentialist Grierson, I put First Principles *in quotation marks to show their deconstructive nature, undoing themselves in their very inscribing.*

1. My animating (of) film theory also, in my own small way, responds to cognitive film theory. See Cholodenko, "Animation (Theory) as the Poematic: A Reply to the Cognitivists."

2. In addition to the introductions to my two animation anthologies, see the following for my discussion of film studies and film theory, as well as animation studies and animation theory: "Animation (Theory) as the Poematic"; "Animation—Film and Media Studies' 'Blind Spot'"; "The Animation of Cinema"; "*Who Framed Roger Rabbit*, or the Framing of Animation"; and "Why Animation, Alan?"

3. See Cholodenko, "*Who Framed Roger Rabbit*, or the Framing of Animation."

4. See Cholodenko, "Introduction," *The Illusion of Life 2*; and Cholodenko, "The Animation of Cinema." In both texts I acknowledge those who I discovered have theorized film as a form of animation *before* both Manovich and I did: Alexandre Alexeieff, Ralph Stephenson, Taihei Imamura, and Sergei Eisenstein.

5. I abandon here what I have done in a number of publications over the years, that is, to capitalize film studies to mark it, unlike animation studies, as an established discipline, only then to deconstruct film studies consistent with my claim that all film is a form of animation. Put simply, film studies must be obedient to (the very "principle" of) animation itself, never fixed, static, immobile, such as a capital letter might be thought to denote.

6. See Cholodenko, "The Animation of Cinema."

7. That theorizing includes the necessary (re)theorizing *through animation* of all modes, forms, registers, and aspects of film and its apparatus. As examples of my retheorizing of authorship, auteur theory, and genre theory, see "Intro-

duction," *The Illusion of Life*; "(The) Death (of) the Animator, or: The Felicity of Felix," part II; and "The 'ABCs' of B."

8. See Cholodenko, "Introduction," *The Illusion of Life 2*; and Cholodenko, "Animation—Film and Media Studies' 'Blind Spot,'" 16.

9. I also reference the work of Vivian Sobchack and that of authors in this volume. Many more are to come, led there by digital film animation.

10. See Cholodenko, "Introduction," *The Illusion of Life 2*; and Cholodenko, "Animation—Film and Media Studies' 'Blind Spot.'" For my critique of the animation studies we encountered in 1991, see Cholodenko, "Introduction," *The Illusion of Life*, 14.

11. See Cholodenko, "Introduction," *The Illusion of Life*, 15. A student, Dominic Williams, once nicely noted for me that the term *live action* contains both pertinences of animation—life and motion.

12. See Cholodenko, "Introduction," *The Illusion of Life 2*; and "Speculations on the Animatic Automaton." Metamorphosis is a privileged figure in and for animation.

13. See Cholodenko, "Speculations on the Animatic Automaton."

14. See Cholodenko, "(The) Death (of) the Animator, or: The Felicity of Felix," part II.

15. See especially Cholodenko, "The Nutty Universe of Animation, the 'Discipline' of All 'Disciplines,' and That's Not All, Folks!" Animation as the animatic privileges the "life" of inorganic objects.

16. See Cholodenko, "Introduction," *The Illusion of Life 2*. On the enchanting, magical, seductive life of objects, see Cholodenko, "Introduction," *The Illusion of Life*, 32–33 n. 23.

17. For my "principles" drawing the longest reach possible for animation, see Cholodenko, "Introduction," *The Illusion of Life 2*, 67–68. See also "The Nutty Universe of Animation, the 'Discipline' of All 'Disciplines,' and That's Not All, Folks!," where I posit a privileged relation between animation as the animatic and quantum physics and quantum cosmology; and "(The) Death (of) the Animator, or: The Felicity of Felix," part III, where I relate animation to biogenetics.

18. Cholodenko, "Introduction," *The Illusion of Life*, 15.

19. For me, the work of Derrida offers the richest ways to theorize film animation, offering not only a theory of film animation as the animatic but an animated, indeed animatic, theory of it. See below.

20. Norman McLaren apprehended the key nature of the in-between for animation when he made the foundation of animation the "invisible interstice" that lies between frames. Cited in Sifianos, "The Definition of Animation," 62.

21. Eisenstein, *Eisenstein on Disney*, 21.

22. Sifianos, "The Definition of Animation," 66. Also quoted in Annemarie Jonson, "Porky's Stutter: The Vocal Trope and Lifedeath in Animation," in *The Illusion of Life 2*, edited by Cholodenko, 445.

23. Cholodenko, "Introduction," *The Illusion of Life*, 29.

24. See Cholodenko, "The Crypt, the Haunted House, of Cinema"; and "(The) Death (of) the Animator, or: The Felicity of Felix," part III.

25. See Hutchings, "The Work-Shop of Filthy Animation"; and Trahair, "For the Noise of a Fly."

26. Quoted in Gunning, "An Aesthetic of Astonishment," 34.

27. On cryptic incorporation, see Cholodenko, "The Crypt, the Haunted House, of Cinema." Cryptic incorporation (i.e., incomplete, failed mourning) makes the self forever for Derrida a "lodging, the haunt of a host of ghosts," as is for me the movie theater. Derrida, "Fors," xxiii.

28. Here I must highlight *attraction* as a term of drawing, from the Latin *trahere*. But the attraction of the animation of attractions is animatic, at once attraction and repulsion / retraction. This is to mark, too, the privileged relation between the graph (from Greek *graphein*, meaning *both* writing and drawing) and animation, of what I call the *graphematic* (the inextricable coimplication of writing and drawing) and the animatic. The graphematic and the animatic are themselves inextricably coimplicated, making writing / drawing a form of animation and animation a form of writing / drawing. In "The Animation of Cinema," "The Illusion of the Beginning," "Still Photography?," and "*Who Framed Roger Rabbit*, or the Framing of Animation," I demonstrate why drawing and animation have priority over live action, over cinema, as *photo-graphed* film, making live action cinema ironically a form of the graphic too! In response to film theorists who posit photography as the foundation of cinema, including Siegfried Kracauer and Bazin, there are two key "foundations" *before* photography, including and subsuming it: graphics and animation, thereby deconstructing and seducing photographic "indexicality."

29. Gunning, "The Cinema of Attraction," 70.

30. On anime, see Cholodenko, "Apocalyptic Animation"; and Cholodenko, "Introduction," *The Illusion of Life 2*.

31. See Cholodenko, "The 'ABCs' of B"; Cholodenko, "Apocalyptic Animation"; Cholodenko, "(The) Death (of) the Animator, or: The Felicity of Felix," part III; Cholodenko, "The Nutty Universe of Animation"; Cholodenko, "'OBJECTS IN MIRROR ARE CLOSER THAN THEY APPEAR'"; and Cholodenko, "Speculation on the Animatic Automaton." See also Cholodenko, "'The Borders of Our Lives'"; and Cholodenko, "Jean Rouch's *Les maîtres fous*."

32. Or rather, as the hyperzombie, George A. Romero's zombie, to be distinguished from the classic voodoo zombie. On the hyperzombie, see Cholodenko, "The 'ABCs' of B"; and "(The) Death (of) the Animator, or: The Felicity of Felix," part III. On the cyborg and replicant, see Cholodenko, "Speculations on the Animatic Automaton."

33. In terms of animism and mechanism, film animation has passed from Baudrillardian first order seductive, enchanting animatic automaton and second order productive, animated, automatic robot to third and fourth order hypersimulacral, disenchanting, hyperanimated, hyperautomated cyborg, hyperzombie, and replicant. See Cholodenko, "Speculations on the Animatic Automaton."

34. See Baudrillard, *The Perfect Crime*, 5, 74; and Baudrillard, *The Vital Illusion*, 53, 55.

7 :: Animation, in Theory

SUZANNE BUCHAN

Most of us today are aware of the many ways that animation has in-
filtrated our visual culture. For scholars and the public, exposure and
access to commercial and especially independent animation film —
through broadcast television, online archives, artist and studio websites,
and new media platforms — have dramatically increased. While animation studies has been active for more than fifty years, film studies is
only beginning to deeply engage with a cinematic form that has more to
do with sculpture, algorithms, or painting than with the genres of narrative cinema. As a film studies scholar who specializes in animation
and experimental film and digital media, I have examined film theory
texts over the years for gaps and queries that seemed to address animation — or not. These trawled fragments formed the origins of *animation:
an interdisciplinary journal*, published since 2006. This chapter traces the
intellectual genesis of the journal, locating it in a historical and theoretical framework that, with some exceptions, spans the 1970s to the mid-
2000s. In doing so, I take the long view — without Plato there would be
no Gilles Deleuze, without Émile Cohl no *Wall-E*, and, in my view, without Jean Mitry, Heinrich von Kleist, Noël Carroll, and Stanley Cavell
no animation theory. I reflect on past achievements but also write to
appeal to future researchers and makers of animation to be sensitive to
the historical continuum of authorship and creating in the (mainly digital) striving ahead. I will not address writing about commercial canons
or digital animation (Disney, Aardman, Pixar, and others) and will focus
on some theoretical writings. This doesn't mean that others are less important; the selection is based on queries and positions that are relevant
to my premise of "animation, in theory" that entails a skeptical but pro-
active attitude to theorizing animation.

Animation Studies: The Long View

My discussion here of some past developments in animation studies does not suggest this is the only way to survey this legacy.[1] Early writing on animation was composed of a dispersed and international authorship from various disciplines, professions, and national or cultural contexts, published in festival catalogues and specialist screening supplements, with little or no reference to film theory. Some of these writings set the tone and direction for later research, forming an eclectic primary-knowledge base. Scholars working on animation often did so as a tangent to their disciplines, more often than not cultural studies, languages and literature, or art history, frequently providing historical and contextual information; but there were few research-specific or theoretical book-length publications on animation. The 1990s was a period of expansion of animation practice programs at universities and art schools, accompanied by a rash of animation publications: historical, national, and stylistic surveys; general introductions, and overviews of production systems, specific eras and studios, and individual filmmakers. Animation film also enjoyed critical attention in experimental film theory. Some scholars explored aesthetic implications of techniques other than planar (painted and drawn) animation, intersections with the avant-garde, and experimentation in animation by fine-art practitioners. The industrious scholar will also find a range of articles relating to animation film in the FIAF *Index to Film Periodicals*, and will also look for keywords in the indexes of nonfilm publications.

Authors increasingly explored the vast richness of animation film using frameworks of critical theory, semiotics, postcolonialism, and gender studies. These were and are frequently published as chapters in thematic or theoretical anthologies in film, media, and cultural studies, often as the "animation" chapter, and often working with established (and tired) canons. Sometimes it is the case that, in admirably trying to do too much, authors achieve the opposite effect. Gone awry, it can result in writings that skim colonialism, queer theory, feminism, cognitive theory, and spectatorship within a single chapter or article, and without much evidence of these being applied to animated film.

Others engaged more specifically with structuralism, realism, semiotics, psychoanalysis, national cinemas, and with postmodernism, not least because of the potential in animation for parody and merging high and low art. In the last decade, book-length publications and collections with film's theoretical subareas such as formalism, critical theory, apparatus, and spectatorship are on the increase, and an observable phenomenon is a strengthened interdisciplinarity in these writings. This could be expanded: there are dozens of theoretical book-length publications on animation in French, German, Japanese, Korean, Chinese, and Russian. When texts by Christian Metz, the Cahiers group, Mitry, and Deleuze were made available in the academic lingua franca, their impact on developments in cinema theory were significant. Similarly, English translations of writings outside the Anglo and Euro intellectual landscape (of publishing) that introduce new approaches to animation would provide a new impetus and enrich academic communities with works that communicate through other cultural lenses and intellectual traditions.

The "Problem" of Animation

Much like the term *experimental film, animation* is an imprecise, fuzzy catchall that heaps an enormous and historically far-reaching, artistically diverse body of work into one pot. In 1997 Philip Denslow made a point that is still valid: that a single definition is incomplete and "that no matter what definition you choose, it faces challenges from new developments in the technology used to produce and distribute animation."[2] He goes on to explain how studio ideology, production hierarchy, union contracts, special effects hybridization, and independent film affect the definition of animation. Denslow's discussion leads to a topic that Christian Metz also mentions in this context: "The rubric of special effects will obviously form, for the semiologist, a heteroclitical group. Jean-Louis Comolli is quite right in remarking that the notions of technicians—who sometimes have a *professional*, and therefore corporate, personality—cannot automatically be considered as theoretical concepts. Each case must be examined separately."[3] One method to describe what animation *is* within the diversity of cinema is to treat animation as a heteroclitical group of films (ultimately, an animation filmmaker working alone is a technician in complete control of the image), and to examine each film as an individual case.

In a search for a unifying definition, Maureen Furniss reviews a number of proposals made by filmmakers and theorists, and she concludes that a "lot of energy was spent to reach this point, but little has been achieved."[4] Furniss then proposes a continuum between mimesis and abstraction: "A continuum works with similarities to position items in relation to one another, while a definition seeks difference, to separate items in some way. Using a continuum, one can discuss a broad range of materials without qualifying the extent to which each example belongs to a precisely defined category called 'animation.'"[5] Furniss widens the scope of animation to include the diverse overlaps between animation and live action, but in my view her definition remains too broad and without a differentiation between items. Noël Carroll comments on criticism are helpful here: he regards central activities of criticizing artworks to be "description, classification, contextualization, elucidation, interpretation, and analysis,"[6] and he emphasizes artistic evaluation as the *primus inter pares* central to the critic's role.[7] To undertake this kind of critical work, each technique requires its own unique description, classification, and a set of suitable and applicable formal parameters that would allow analysis based on distinctive aesthetic qualities and technical properties of artistic media. For example, a material taxonomy (oil painting, collage, sculpture, watercolor, etchings, drawing, etc.) differentiates the technical definitions of planar animation, clay animation, painting on glass, object animation, and so forth. These qualities not only affect production; they also have profound ramifications for the critic's (and viewer's) experience and interpretation of the work.

In the introduction to *The Illusion of Life* (1991), Alan Cholodenko addresses animation as an object of theoretical inquiry: "In terms of scholarship, animation is the least theorized area of film. In neglecting animation, film theorists—when they have thought about it at all— have regarded animation as either the 'step-child' of cinema or as not belonging to the cinema at all, belonging rather to the graphic arts."[8] At the time of publication, few readers would have paused at this statement—the anthology was, after all, a major contribution to animation studies at the time. Yet Cholodenko's concern that animation not be regarded as part of cinema ends with a revealing assumption that when we talk about animation, we usually mean graphic animation (planar 2D drawn, cel, or digital). The published collection and other lectures listed in the book's overview of "The Illusion of Life" conference[9] focused almost exclusively on planar and computer animation. This reveals how graphic animation did and still does dominate the understanding of what animation is. Writing on cinema made before 1906, Tom Gunning observes: "The history of early cinema, like the history of the cinema generally, has been written and theorized under the hegemony of narrative films."[10] Similarly, the hegemony in theorizing animation primarily through graphic and cel techniques determines canons and influences topics in the quickening of animation theories.

In the two decades since Cholodenko's publication, much has changed to improve the low profile of animation in cinema theory, but at a price for predigital and nongraphic animation. In 2001 Lev Manovich made a now well-known polemical assertion for cinema as a particular case of animation, provocatively proposing that we need to reverse the traditional hierarchy and position digital animation as the general, higher-order category for the cinema.[11] The notion of animation as the paradigm for all cinematic production, and for the study of its ontology overall, is an assertion that film studies has begun to seriously challenge or support. But again, we must pause. Manovich's argument is based on the premise of cinema as digital, and on graphic cinema, and he doesn't account for animation that uses manifold other techniques like object or puppet animation. Alla Gadassik argues, "[Manovich] admires animation's hand-crafted tradition, and yet his vision of digital cinema does not foreground the constructed character of the early animated image. . . . In this network of digital technologies, the hand of the animator is seen as an antiquated curiosity, which has been rendered obsolete by faster, more powerful machines."[12] What is largely missing in this debate is an approach to animation films that elaborates on the solid work that has been achieved regarding history, techniques, and aesthetics. Animation is, after all, a cinematic form that can be analyzed through almost all formal and stylistic cinematic parameters and theorized using many film studies approaches. In a critical discussion of what he calls the two constructions of British and American cultural studies, Stuart Hall remarks: "In Britain, we are always aware of institutionalization as a moment of profound danger."[13] The "danger" of institutionalizing animation "theory" in a hegemony of graphic animation, digital or otherwise, within film theory is the risk of neglecting other techniques and their analyses when developing specific questions pertinent to individual films. This omission could also thwart opportunities to discover new and innovative ways of theorizing animation that don't nominally fit in the formal, stylistic, and theoretical frameworks of film studies.

Microanalysis and Methods

In film studies, animation was a tangential object for research and teaching for many years, but this is changing. As universities become mass-educating "multiversities," they are forced to respond to market demand, and the number of animation programs is rising, as animation is now pervasive on other platforms than cinema screens, for example in apps, games, the web, and advertising. While much of film theory could be instrumentalized for theorizing animation to enhance curricula — cognitivist, queer, formalist, reception, sociocultural, feminist, semiological, immersion, narrative — many chapters and articles on animation film lack specificity, and they tend to use idiosyncratic or tired, self-perpetuating canons to prove or disprove an element of cinema theory. David Bordwell has suggested, as Alissa Quart points out, that "the true business of film scholars is to account for craft of filmmaking and the experience of film viewing — and not to cull examples from the movies in order to illustrate sweeping theories of the human psyche or society."[14] This is as true for animation as it is for film studies. I have found *microanalysis* (a term used in the sciences for analysis of minute quantities of materials) to be a useful bottom-up method to initially unpack the craft and construction of an animation film in a way that elegantly fits with film studies methods. By describing formal cinematic parameters in detail (shot length, image composition, lighting, camera movement, point of view and angle, lenses, music, sound, transitions), it is then possible to work with this stylistic information and use film theory to develop sustained discussions about the experiential complexity of a single animated film, sequence, or scene.[15] In planar animation, visual parameters are rendered through artistic techniques, exceptions being perspective created using multiplane setups and transitions, and puppet and object animation that is shot in miniature stage sets, which in most cases uses the same equipment and principles as live-action filmmaking.[16] Such microanalyses can serve as methodological models for theorizing about other animation films and augmenting animated film criticism and theory, mitigating what Paul Coates describes as the isolating effect of writing without comparison.[17] A method I have found especially useful in tandem with microanalysis is the philosophical and practical method that Carroll calls "piecemeal theorizing," a process of "breaking down some of the presiding questions of the Theory into more manageable questions, for example, about the comprehension of point-of-view editing, instead of global questions about something vaguely called suture. As compelling answers are developed to small-scale, delimited questions, we may be in a position to think about whether these answers can be unified in a more comprehensive theoretical framework."[18] Because animation as yet has no comprehensive theory equivalent to what Bordwell ironically calls "SLAB Theory" (Saussure, Lacan, Althusser, Barthes), new theory will not have to defend or discern itself from dominant film theory.[19] On the other hand, animation theory must also develop its own contexts while seeking embedment within film theory and try to avoid the heterogeneity of piecemeal theory that could mean that no unified theoretical base is formed at all.

Fragments: Useful Film Theory

The introduction of digital technologies was also a developing force in animation production, but film scholars left its precursor—predigital animation—by the wayside, and to articulate an ontology of animation—digital or otherwise—means revisiting these (celluloid) casualties. There are many film theorists who are useful for developing animation theory (Rudolf Arnheim, Béla Balázs, André Bazin, Walter Benjamin, Donald Crafton, Deleuze, Mary Ann Doane, Sergei Eisenstein, Gunning, Siegfried Kracauer, Mitry, Hugo Münsterberg, Laura Mulvey, and others), and some appear regularly in writings on animation. During studies at the University of Zurich, I began the detective work that I continue to do of scanning indexes and tables of contents of thousands of books and journals on film theory for animation-related themes, key words, filmmakers, and film titles. More often than not, what I found expressed a puzzling attitude toward animation as a cinematic form. I sensed that animation's marginalization in academia did not take into account animation's influence in private and public domains, and I began thinking about animation's aesthetic, perceptual, and ideological values, meanings and impacts. Sometimes I found a sentence, a paragraph, and rarely more, but these brief mentions of animation—or no mention at all—offer fecund territories as springboards for theorizing animation. I have used the exemplars of Cavell, Alexander Sesonske, Dudley Andrew, Mitry, Carroll, Deleuze, and Sobchack in my own writing (other scholars will have their own lists of names), and in the following (for reasons of space) I concentrate on concepts around figures and worlds.

In the final section of Cavell's *The World Viewed: Reflections on the Ontology of Film* (1979), there are more than thirty mentions of cartoons. In a debate with Sesonske, Cavell describes cartoons: "[They are] a region of film which seems to satisfy my concerns with understanding the special powers of film but which explicitly has nothing to do with projections of the real world—the region of animated cartoons. If this region of film counters my insistence upon the projection of reality as essential to the medium of movies, then it counters it completely."[20] While Sesonske raises a number of ontological ideas about cartoons, he addresses a key concept of worlds: "There is *a* world we experience here, but not *the* world—a world I know and see but to which I am nevertheless not present, yet not a world past. . . . It exists only now, when I see it; yet I cannot go to where its creatures are, for there is no access to its space from ours except through vision."[21] Cavell describes Sesonske's "rebuttal" as "[a] negation or parody of something I claim for the experience of movies." One of many epistemologically tantalizing remarks that Cavell makes is this: "But on my assumption (which I should no doubt have made explicit) that cartoons are not movies, these remarks about their conditions of existence constitute some explanation about *why* they are not."[22] Though he makes some concessions, for Cavell cartoons completely counter his insistence on the projection of reality as essential to the medium of movies. In other words, Cavell seems to consider cartoons (again, a symptomatic omission of other animation techniques) as not belonging to the domain of his conception of cinema, and he puts forth that maybe we can't consider them as films at all.[23] Sesonske's hypotheses on how animation differs from reality are especially interesting: he points out that Cavell omits that projection enables the illusion of movement and the experience of these drawings as a "reality" particular to the "region" of animation. We need to develop a more precise definition, an ontology, of what Sesonske means by "*a* world."

This led me to Andrew's phenomenological questioning in 1978 of the concept of cinematic worlds: "What exists beyond the [film] text and what kind of description can be adequate to it? Here we encounter the exciting and dangerous term 'world.' A film elaborates a world which it is the critic's job to flesh out or respond to. But what is this cinematic world?"[24] Animation can visually represent endless possible worlds, each of them often unique and often with little or no relation to the phenomenal world that surrounds us. I found a way to understand these worlds, and a method to describe them, through Deleuze: "A work of art always entails the creation of new spaces and times (it's not a question of recounting a story in a well-determined space and time; rather, it is the rhythms, the lighting, and the space-times themselves that must become the true characters). . . . A work of art is a new syntax, one that is much more important than vocabulary and that excavates a foreign language in language."[25] Many animation films create visual equivalents to neologisms in the particular animated space-times—the worlds—that are the true characters of the films, and theorists need to develop a new syntax in the stylistic and critical language used to describe these works.

Animation evokes many diverse phenomena in its reception that have little to do with our experience "in the world." Andrew's formulations on the usefulness of experiential, phenomenological approaches to cinema and "the constitution of a cinematic world" can help to develop a framework that takes into account the spectator's lived experience of animated films, of animated worlds that might not exist in the natural world, but that have a very real existence in projection for the viewer.[26] Sobchack sees the appeal of phenomenology in "its potential for opening up and destabilizing language in the very process of its description of the phenomena of experience."[27] Opening up and destabilizing may also lead us toward a new theoretical syntax, but this must be done via a "well-made language." More than sixty years ago, Étienne Souriau wrote of the challenges facing the French filmology movement that, according to David Rodowick, "approached the cinema from the outside, carrying out research on cinematographic facts through the domains of psychology, psychiatry, aesthetics, sociology, and biology."[28] Souriau writes: "Since filmology is a science, it must be and must want to be one. And if a science is not, in the famous words of [Étienne Bonnot de] Condillac, simply a 'well-made language,' then it clearly requires one as its precondition."[29] One of the so-called problems that the theorizing of animation needs to resolve is the definition of a well-made language — comparative and interdisciplinary criticism is implicit in this.

These animated worlds are populated by animated figures that also pose ontological puzzles; writing within film studies on animation often discusses animated figures with the same terms and descriptors as for human actors. Although Mitry refers minimally to animation films in his profound aesthetic and psychological analysis of cinema — it may be for him that the animated image is, simply, a cinematic image — here I will use his writing on figures as an example for how concepts in film theory not specific to animation can be used to theorize about animation. Mitry discusses relationships between the literary author's personality that "is always evident in his characters" and the cinema, which "presents only actions. Though the characters are the creation of the filmmaker, at least they are there, present and active, 'in the flesh.' Dissociated from creative imagination, they seem to have an independent, exclusive existence which is objective and no longer merely conceptual."[30] The animated figure is not "dissociated from creative imagination"; it embodies just this, in that the figure's existence and character are defined entirely by the conceptual, stylistic, and technical processes of its design, construction, and animation.

Mitry makes an observation about actors that is thought-provoking for animated figures. "However basic [the actor's] psychology, it is always 'located.' The characters are drawn according to circumstance and their development always depends on an effectively 'experienced' reality. They are human beings 'in the world'; they act and are acted upon." The scare quotes Mitry uses throughout these passages are meant to incite curiosity: if Mitry means that the character's psychology is located in the living actor, then the psychology of an animated figure is located in the filmmaker whose personality and psychology are transmuted into the character, "ascribing to it [the filmmaker's] thoughts and emotions."[31] The character's psychology is read by the audience using codes of behavior and gesture. Another concept from Mitry that is promising for animation that uses abstract, nonanthropomorphized figures is his proposal that "one might say that *any object presented in moving images gains a meaning* (a collection of significations) *it does not have 'in reality,' that is, as a real presence.*"[32] A related insight into the viewer's engagement is Christine N. Brinckmann's exploration of empathy in abstract forms in the Absolute films of Walter Ruttmann and Viking Eggeling. Brinckmann describes how movement creates alliances and choreographies between the figures, and she then queries the audience's engagement: "In light of such cinematic processes the temptation is there, both to identify the moving forms and to animate them with characteristics and intentions."[33]

A defining feature of many animation films is that figures are often composed of a combination of physically incompatible elements, and in projection they and the spaces they are in can visually defy physical, optical, and natural laws of gravity, electromagnetism, perspective, and entropy (an obvious example is Chuck Jones's 1953 *Duck Amuck*). While we can say the same for live-action films that employ profilmic special effects (I am not considering digital or in-camera effects) to create impossible figures, worlds, and events, these retain an indexicality that represents the physical world and the materials that the effects are created in and of. Carroll's "A Note on Film Metaphor" elegantly and effectively takes on this conundrum. Referring to a range of examples, from Fritz Lang's *Metropolis* (1927) to Popeye cartoons, Carroll introduces two terms with great potential for describing animated figures and worlds, and the remainder of his text elaborates on conditions that explain how and why we engage with what we see on screen.[34] The first term is *physical noncompossibility*: "It is not physically compossible with the universe as we know it that muscles be anvils, that people be cassette recorders or that spies be foxes."[35] Carroll discusses drawn animation, but his concepts also work for a range of techniques that animate objects and matter from the phenomenal, physical world—disparate elements that can be fused together in composite figures. He then explains why we understand this noncompossibility by introducing another incisive term, *homospatiality* (elements copresent in the same figure). Homospatiality is a prerequisite for what he describes as visual metaphors, as it "provides the means to link disparate categories in visual metaphors in ways that are functionally equivalent to the ways that disparate categories are linked grammatically in verbal metaphors."[36] Carroll suggests that "metaphors interanimate the relations between classes or categories."[37] As one of many possible categories of a taxonomy and ontology of animated figures, noncompossibility interanimates between disciplines and categories of fine arts and commodity culture and disciplines of film theory, philosophy of perception, and literary theory.

Animation, in Theory

Perhaps it is time to ask some questions. The first is: what is the problem of animation that it requires a theory? I see a partial answer in Deleuze's remarks that "the encounter between two disciplines doesn't take place when one begins to reflect on the other, but when one discipline realizes that it has to resolve, for itself and by its own means, a problem similar to one confronted by the other."[38] The discipline of animation studies is riddled with what amounts to an avoidance of resolving the problem of animation within the larger scope of film studies. It has been informed in part by discourses that weakly lean on cinema theory and are driven by the legacy of an innate difference between live action and animation film that animation studies has tried to solve. Deleuze goes on to suggest that "the same tremors occur on totally different terrains. The only true criticism is comparative (and bad film criticism closes in on the cinema like its own ghetto) because any work in a field is itself imbricated within other fields."[39] The marginalization of animation studies is often referred to by its own authors as a "ghetto"—and it is pertinent to consider Deleuze's idea that the ghetto of bad criticism is due to it not being comparative. Historically, many animation studies texts do not use the critical, comparative approaches that Deleuze suggests are necessary to solve the problem, just as film studies often does not take key queries about properties of animation into account. This may help us to understand animation scholarship's slow integration into film studies.

A second question is: why the recent interest in animation "theory"?

Hall suggests that "movements provoke theoretical moments. And historical conjunctures insist on theories: they are real moments in the evolution of theory."[40] The Chinese term for crisis (*weiji*) is formed of two characters that mean crisis and crucial point:[41] the crucial point for animation was the digital shift, a commercially motivated historical conjuncture, and this rupture caused a crisis in film studies—the loss of its material object, celluloid, and of photoindexicality—through cinematic production's increasing reliance on digital animation techniques. Already in 1998 Thomas Elsaesser suggested that "any technology that materially affects [the status of indexicality] . . . and digitisation would seem to be such a technology, thus puts in crisis deeply-held beliefs about representation and visualization, and many of the discourses— critical, scientific or aesthetic—based on, or formulated in the name of the indexical in our culture, need to be re-examined."[42] While many authors initially engaged primarily with technological marvels and popular feature-length film, responses to this so-called crisis are manifold (the second Chinese character for the term crisis understood here in the more common [mis]perception as opportunity), provoking valuable debates to move on from Manovich's polemic. There are other themes in this crisis of film studies that have the potential to embed animation in rigorous and well-developed critical disciplines. I see the digital's complex ethical relationship to realism and its aesthetic, political, and technological impacts on the moving image in a continuum with Andrew's "exciting and dangerous term 'world.'" The aesthetic representation of worlds is thematized in philosophical, cognitive, and psychoanalytic discourses with impacts on almost all areas of the humanities, and animated worlds can visualize worlds in ways that photoindexical cinema cannot.

So, in theory, what could a theory of animation look like? This is an impossible question, and I'd like to work with what Hall describes as a tension that arises for theory and culture. In this context I'm thinking about theory and the visual culture of animation—about the impossibility of getting "anything like an adequate theoretical account of culture's relations and its effects."[43] The cultural impact of animation is impossible to funnel into *a* theory of animation for a number of reasons. It is not a single profession or discipline, and academic understanding and inquiries both originate from and extend into other disciplines. We must ensure that we can extend acquired knowledge to develop "theory" without losing the dispersed wealth of existing scholarship. In my view, we need to

- consider fine-art practice in conjunction with cinematic representation using parametric description and microanalysis;
- work with paradigmatic films to develop central queries based on film theory;
- draw on interdisciplinary methodologies to contextualize the making of animation films in related practice areas;
- understand how nonhuman figures and animated worlds affect a different spectatorial experience in terms of perceptive modalities; and
- approach high-flowing generalities by a roundabout (piecemeal) route and work across multiple fronts and disciplines in dialogical exchange.

animation: an interdisciplinary journal

Peer-review journals incite, foster, and disseminate critical reflection on diversity in practice; challenge or expand existing canons; and provide a platform for exploratory hypotheses and developing theories that have not yet found their ways into themed anthologies or monographs. These journals also provide opportunities for the growing number of international PhD students to publish their innovations and contributions to new knowledge. Concepts and ideas from the film studies theorists I mentioned earlier, and from others, were fertile ground for the intellectual genesis of *animation: an interdisciplinary journal*. Its core editorial aims are closely linked with my own research into animation's relationship to moving-image practice and the epistemological question of how animation helps us know the world. Because intellectual endeavors thrive best in a constituency, this research is collaborative in nature, and is informed in part by the journal's editorial team and board. The journal aims to reveal animation's pervasive impact on other forms of time-based media expression—past, present, and future—and illuminate how these affect our lives. It also, crucially, regularly publishes writings from artists, to ensure a dialogue between practice and theory. Many of the articles originate in informal discussions with film studies scholars and other academics about how they could shift their focus askew and apply their expertise, specialisms, and research interests to explore animation, analogous to how scholars of art history, philosophy, and literature in the 1950s and 1960s explored cinema to develop film studies as a respected academic discipline. Perhaps animation studies, like film studies, will eventually have a variety of journals on diverse subgenres for developing readerships, and we need to anticipate their needs. This would help open up the field and encourage specific research in inter-related yet unique creative areas.

Journal authors have contributed a variety of articles and themes that question and grow the field of animation theory. For instance, some authors are engaged in debates around loosening assumptions of anima-tion's medium specificity and purist essentialism, as Andrew Darley con-vincingly argues in his polemic "Bones of Contention." His main topics are "inflated claims of medium superiority; essentialist and reduction-ist definitions of the form; exaggerated claims that animation is inher-ently, somehow, a more expressive or imaginative visual medium than others."[44] Darley makes some interesting correctives to this by point-ing out similarities and differences and freedoms and constraints that animation shares with a diversity of media; he also effectively critiques the detrimental effect of usurping animation in the name of "Theory." Many of the journal's authors work with film theory and are develop-ing the "well-made language" crucial to formulating queries and ap-proaches to an intentionally wide concept of animation across platforms and media.[45] Some of these questions are direct responses to writing that doesn't overtly theorize animation much at all. Sean Cubitt's re-view of the anthology *The Cinema of Attractions Reloaded* (2006), which celebrates Tom Gunning's writing, engages with Gunning's seminal concepts and asks the question: "For readers of *animation: an interdisci-plinary journal*, the key issue must be: what relevance do these concerns have for our field of enquiry?"[46] Over the course of his article, Cubitt answers this himself, finding relevance in animation works from early cinema to postmillennial architecture installation and generously pro-viding topics for further research.

Other contributions expand existing notions of animation in terms of culture, technology, ideology, and aesthetics, some from film studies and some from animation studies or other disciplines. Pan-Asian au-thors introduce cultural and philosophical perspectives to theorize about animation made within these cultures and for their indige-nous populations. Others discover relations between animation, early cinema, and consumer culture in international contexts (a special issue was on animation, precinema, and early cinema). Artists theorize their own work (Gregory Barsamian on sculpture and perception, Dennis Dollens on biomimetic architecture, Thorsten Fleisch on chemistry and physics): such multidisciplinary animation artworks that lie outside the traditional canons of animation studies are key to encouraging dis-courses that center on, for instance, animation used in so-called high-art practice, in architecture, or in the sciences. The journal also revisits and recontextualizes artists who have slipped off the radar: a special issue from July 2010, guest edited by Mark Bartlett, on Stan Vanderbeek demonstrates intersections with early computer and communication technologies and artist-thinkers. It situates his politically and poetically informed and technologically enabled texts—moving images, artworks, writings—both within and distinct from the received histories of animation from which he is often elided. One area that is recently taking on substantial theoretical form is documentary animation. In a 2011 special issue, *Making it (Un)real: Contemporary Theories and Practices in Documentary Animation* (guest edited by the filmmaker and theorist Jeffrey Skoller), authors not nominally associated with animation studies engage almost exclusively with single films or works by a single filmmaker.

Conclusion

As animation increasingly defines our visual moving image culture, the number of researchers and students of animation studies, and animation theory, is growing, and the boundaries between film theory and animation theory are diminishing. Although rarely invoked in animation studies, the notion of blending media is implicit in animation filmmaking because it has always been a collaborative part of the interdisciplinary contagion and hybridity that define so much of our visual culture, and animation is also used in many creative and scientific disciplines. From performance (Windsor McCay's "interactive" stage performances with an on-screen animated figure in *Gertie the Dinosaur* (1914) and Miwa Matreyek's *Dream of Lucid Living*) and painting (Oskar Fischinger's 1947 *Motion Painting No. 1* and Jeremy Blake's digital time-based painting) to architecture (1990s computer-aided design walk-throughs and Kas Oosterhuis's 2002 proposal for Ground Zero in New York) and electronic engineering (animated MRI images and the design and simulation of micro and nano systems), animation has always blended media. This is because while animation's predigital forms share film's photochemical base and projection processes, with few exceptions, animation is visually and materially constituted by other artistic media, including photography, theater, painting, sculpture, fine arts, graphics, and text. As practice differentiates and technologies and production methods develop, some animation is also breaking through low-art barriers to achieve high-art status and becoming an artistic partner in manufacturing and sciences. Animation's critical companion, theoretical conceptualization, will also develop and differentiate, perhaps one day forming something close to an interdisciplinary theory of animation.

Notes

1. For reasons of space I will not include titles; there are many animation bibliographies available online and in print.
2. Denslow, "What Is Animation and Who Needs to Know?," 1.
3. Metz, "*Trucage* and the Film," 153. Metz cites Comolli, "Technique et idéologie (3)," 47.
4. Furniss, *Art in Motion* (1998), 5.
5. Furniss, *Art in Motion* (1998), 7.
6. Carroll, *On Criticism*, 13.
7. Carroll, *On Criticism*, 9.
8. Cholodenko, "Introduction," *The Illusion of Life*, 9.
9. In a note at the end of his Introduction to *The Illusion of Life*, Cholodenko writes almost all essays in the collection were presented at the Illusion of Life conference held July 14–17, 1988 (29).
10. Gunning, "The Cinema of Attraction," 64.
11. Manovich, *The Language of New Media*.
12. Gadassik, "Ghosts in the Machine," 229.
13. Hall, "Cultural Studies and Its Theoretical Legacies," 273. Hall's incisive and critical evaluation of the gestation of cultural studies from multiple disciplines and their conflicts offers some interesting correlations with the interdisciplinarity of animation studies.
14. Quart, "The Insider," 36.
15. I am indebted to Christine Noll Brinckmann for introducing me to parametric film analysis in her undergraduate "Introduction to Film Analysis" classes at the Seminar for Film Studies, University of Zurich.
16. For an analysis of this in the Quay Brothers' films, see chapters 3, 4, and 5 in Buchan, *The Quay Brothers*.
17. Coates, *The Story of the Lost Reflection*, 1.
18. Carroll, "Prospects for Film Theory," 58.
19. "What we call Theory is an abstract body of thought which came into prominence in Anglo-American film studies during the 1970s. The most famous avatar of Theory was that aggregate of doctrines derived from Lacanian psychoanalysis, Structuralist semiotics, Post-Structuralist literary theory, and variants of Althusserian Marxism." Bordwell and Carroll, *Post-theory*, xiii.
20. Cavell, *The World Viewed*, 167.
21. Cavell, *The World Viewed*, 167–68.
22. Cavell, *The World Viewed*, 168.
23. For an extended discussion of Cavell's concept of cartoons and the realism of puppet animation's use of real-world objects, see Buchan, "The Animated Spectator: Watching the Quay Brothers' 'Worlds,'" in Buchan, *Animated "Worlds,"* 17.

24. Andrew, "The Neglected Tradition of Phenomenology in Film Theory," 47.
25. Deleuze, "The Brain Is the Screen," 370.
26. Andrew, "The Neglected Tradition of Phenomenology in Film Theory," 49.
27. Sobchack, *The Address of the Eye*, xviii.
28. Rodowick, "A Care for the Claims of Theory," 31–32.
29. Souriau, "Die Struktur des filmischen Universums und das Vokabular der Filmologie," 141; my translation.
30. Mitry, *The Aesthetics and Psychology of the Cinema*, 50.
31. Mitry, *The Aesthetics and Psychology of the Cinema*, 50.
32. Mitry, *The Aesthetics and Psychology of the Cinema*, 45.
33. Brinckmann, *Die anthropomorphe Kamera und andere Schriften zur filmischen Narration*, 265; my translation.
34. As just one example for how a few theoretical sentences or concepts provide fruitful terrain for generating interdisciplinary approaches, to explain viewer comprehension and cocreative engagement with the Quay Brothers' films, I expanded on Carroll's concepts using writings from Trevor Whittock (*Metaphor and Film* [Cambridge: University of Cambridge Press, 1990]), Deleuze (*The Logic of Sense* [Logique du sens, 1969], trans. Mark Lester [London: Athlone Press, 1990]), Deleuze with Félix Guattari (*Anti-Oedipus: Capitalism and Schizophrenia*, trans. Robert Hurley, Mark Seem, and Helen R. Lane [London and New York: Continuum, 2004]), Fritz Senn (*Joyce's Dislocations: Essays on Reading as Translation*, ed. Jean Paul Riquelme [Baltimore: Johns Hopkins University Press, 1984]), and Benjamin (his poetic concept of "detritus" in "Old Forgotten Children's Books" [a translation of "Alte vergessene Kinderbucher" (1924)], *Walter Benjamin: Selected Writings*, trans. Rodney Livingstone, vol. 1 [Cambridge: Harvard University Press, 1996], 406–13). See chapter 2, "Palimpsest, Fragments, Vitalist Affinities," and chapter 4, "Metaphysical Machines," in Buchan, *The Quay Brothers*.
35. Carroll, *Theorizing the Moving Image*, 213.
36. Carroll, *Theorizing the Moving Image*, 214.
37. Carroll, *Theorizing the Moving Image*, 219.
38. Deleuze, "The Brain Is the Screen," 367.
39. Deleuze, "The Brain Is the Screen," 367.
40. Hall, "Cultural Studies and Its Theoretical Legacies," 270.
41. Victor H. Mair, "Danger + Opportunity ≠ Crisis: How a Misunderstanding about Chinese Characters Has Led Many Astray," http://www.pinyin.info/chinese/crisis.html (access date June 26, 2013).
42. Elsaesser, "Digital Cinema," 201–22.
43. Hall, "Cultural Studies and Its Theoretical Legacies," 271.
44. Darley, "Bones of Contention," 72.
45. Journal contributors and editorial board members include a number of authors from this collection (Karen Beckman, Scott Bukatman, Alan Cholodenko, Yuriko Furuhata, Thomas LaMarre, Esther Leslie, Marc Steinberg, and Tess Takahashi).
46. Cubitt, "The Cinema of Attractions," 276.

III : : The Experiment

The property

8 :: Film as Experiment in Animation: Are Films Experiments on Human Beings?

GERTRUD KOCH

TRANSLATED BY DANIEL HENDRICKSON

The goal of experiments, according to the optimistic, empirical definition, is to reveal rules, if not also laws. In the way that experiments are
arranged, they define x conditions, under which y occurs. If y occurs, it
is inferred that in the arrangement x there are generally applicable conditions for the appearance of y. The general applicability is temporally
defined through repetition. Whenever x, then y. According to skeptics,
however, since conditions are *defined* by the arrangements in the experiment, the experiment turns into experimentation, that is, it is itself already a hypothetical action that interferes in the field that it is meant
to research by induction. Gaston Bachelard summarizes this in a bon
mot: "Un fait est un fait" (a fact is a fact). And Hans-Jörg Rheinberger
proposed the nifty German translation that draws attention to the relation between the being-done of the fact and the action, the doing: "Eine
Tat*sache* ist eine Tat*sache*."[1] The experiment thus once again comes out
of the fantasmatic realm of pure empiricism and into the contaminated
zone where human beings and nature overlap. The experiment, the empiricism of which is itself made relative in the experiment's quality as
artifact and as something done, becomes a paradox. This originates in
the experiment's two interwoven natures, the physical one crisscrosses
the human one. The anthropological explanation of the human being as
a natural being, eccentrically situated in relation to its own physicality,
as Helmut Plessner has put it, allows us to draw further conclusions that
call into question whether hypotheses, condemned by experimental philosophy as a humanoid relapse of empiricism into metaphysics, can be
abolished, or whether it is better to take on the fact that the human is a
being that creates hypotheses.[2]

A popular television comedian from Cologne, Willy Millowitsch, puts
it succinctly: "What you yourself don't know, you have to explain to

yourself." Since we are constantly running up against the limits of our tacit knowledge (Michael Polanyi), which constantly shifts the horizon of our previous understanding (Hans-Georg Gadamer), we are also constantly forced to shift the horizon of our nonknowledge further, to form new hypotheses, while those that hold up in the current situation are expanded into a theory.[3] The beginning of expanding such theories, and this includes routine theories, scientific theories, absurd theories, and any others as well, is thus marked by an experience of lack, of a need, a need for explanation. To form a theory is to react to the experience of reaching a limit of understanding and wanting to get beyond it. Presumably, we construct theories where our curiosity runs up against something that escapes the empirical descriptive capabilities of our ordinary consciousness. This is why theories are at their cores nonempirical and speculative, even if theories refer to concrete empirical objects and incidents. At the same time, however, theories are driven by a longing for the real. It is not by chance that this brief polemic against theory originates from Ludwig Wittgenstein, who succinctly states: "Philosophy must not interfere in any way with the actual use of language."[4] And, he says, "we may not advance any kind of theory. There must not be anything hypothetical in our considerations. All *explanation* must disappear, and description alone must take its place."[5] These descriptions, however, "must not interfere in any way with the actual use of language."[6] In a critique of this apodictic thesis, which it is only almost correct to dismiss, Herbert Marcuse raises the thought-provoking objection that thinking here is "pressed into the straitjacket of common usage," and it is assumed that common-language use is always already all right—that is, in a certain sense it lies outside the experimental. "What," asks Marcuse, "remains of philosophy? What remains of thinking, intelligence, without anything hypothetical, without any explanation?"[7]

The motif of forming theories, which is a precursor to any experiment, is similar to that of forming fictions in another area, namely aesthetics. Not only can we aesthetically relate to theories, as we can to any other objects, phenomena, and ideas, but I would go so far as to say that there is an isomorphism in the affective priming of both variations to confront the impenetrability of the physical world and the contingency of the social world. When a circumstance can no longer be ascertained in the usual way and can be integrated into the operative consciousness of a possible space of action, the spheres of fantasy, imagination, and fiction begin. At this point, a need emerges to convert the imaginary, which envelops the real, into a form that we, following Wolfgang Iser, could call *fiction*.[8] Even if Iser explicitly seeks to delimit his model of the acts of fictionalizing from theories of theoretical fiction, his argument is nonetheless grounded on the affective basis of the behavior of the physical body, which makes it of vital interest to see one's own corporal frontality, and in which we go into the world, as a process of continually unlocking and opening new horizons. This is a process that does not remain bound by the limits of the physically visible but is directed at relationality: in space by assumptions about what lies far away, close by, and off to the side, and in time by the constant links between modes of time made by memory and recognition, as needing to be recognized, forgotten, and so on, in the future. The stream of consciousness permanently interweaves experiences, perceptual impressions by the senses, with linguistic and visual ideas that constitute an imaginary that pushes us onward to performative formation. Theories, hypotheses, images, and experiments in thought have a common reservoir in the real, which has to be materialized and substantiated as fact in the very act of fictionalizing.

From this store of imaginary ideas, both linguistic and visual, we form the theoretical network with which we attempt to capture the real as a kind of grid by which we perceive and orient our actions. For this reason, theories are not possible outside of visual and affective ideas and circumstances. Martin Saar, in his reconstruction of the Nietzschean model of genealogy, raises exactly this point to emphasize that theories emerge in a crisis as a critique of existing models of explanation and interpretation.[9] The fact that these theories have any bite as criticism at all is due to their temporal arrangement—that is, that they always emerge when something new turns up that we need to know more about. The mistrust of theory is much larger than that of dogmas, which have already established themselves as incontrovertible and can gather believers around them who no longer need to be convinced. Theories, on the other hand, are trophies that have to be passed on, since the horizons of our world can have no fixed limits.

The skeptical demand to mitigate the question of why (the explanation) with that of how (the description) is countered, however, by the fact that our *need* for explanation has an affective basis, which cannot be fobbed off onto any call for empirical modesty. When Sigmund Freud presents a biologically based affect theory of knowledge by assuming a "drive to knowledge," this brings a new angle to the question of how the biological materialization of thinking is connected to human corporality.[10]

I take the experiment to be a kind of *dispositif*, in which the relation between physical nature and physical bodies must always be defined and redefined in reference to the human body and its physical and mental capacities. In this context, the experiment is also always an experiment on human beings as much as it is an experiment *by* human beings. The anthropocentric dimension of the experiment, as an artificial, humanly conceived trap, in which nature is meant to show itself to us and speak to us, turns into the experimental investigation of the boundaries of the human itself. In the experiment, if an untouched nature is supposed to be animated into one that speaks to us, the human being itself soon becomes positioned in the experiment as a mystery.[11] At the beginning of the experiment is the question of the nature of nature, and at the end the question of the nature of the human being within the experiment. The fascination that the experiment has held as a technologically grounded cultural technique of desiring desire against any and all skepticism is above all emphasized where the experimental arrangement directly targets human perception, that is, the *impact* of an experiment, which is supposed to be new and take place in the interplay between the reception of the senses and the reception of affect. If the boundaries between the disciplines become fluid there, this should come as no surprise. Philosophy becomes psychology, psychology becomes aesthetics, and experimental aesthetics sets out once again to revise experimental philosophy.

In a review of Kurthian music psychology, Theodor W. Adorno points to comparable developments in music theory in the transition from the nineteenth to the twentieth century. He refers to the subjectifying power of music, which works directly against the experimental-exact models of examination:

> It is much more characteristic of [Hugo]Riemann's teachings than of the most effective of recent work that they believe they can banish the element of subjective tension in a static-objective, mathematizing schema, which was incompatible with the dynamic of the phenomena and which collapsed in the end. — Static, systematic, but always essentially didactic "music theory" figured as a supplement to a "psychology of sound," which hoped to overcome the subjective side of musical phenomena in the psychological experiment by using the measuring methods of psychophysics. It saw its central problem as the relation between basic appeal and the strength of sensation, also already essentially getting beyond the mere analysis of elements in Carl Stumpf's examinations, which were extensive and oriented to material, but still remaining for-

eign to spontaneous subjectivity, even in its themes, in the forms of musical cohesion as such.[12]

I am not so much interested in historically reconstructing the shift between philosophy, psychology, and aesthetics as I am in attempting to break down the inherent model of animation for the production of communicative expressivity as an aesthetics proper to the experiment in film. I take *animation* in film to be a process of bringing to life in a double sense: (1) through the technological setting-into-motion of individual pictures, the film itself is animated in a general sense, which exceeds the strict definition of the genre "animation film" and constitutes animation as a moving image that suggests the quality of vitality, and (2) the spectator is animated by the animation and displaced in a specific way into the state of vitality.

Materialist theories of film, which originate in the materializing film effects in the perceptual events of the recipient, tend to draw on the transformed vocabulary of experimental philosophy. This begins with the work of Gustav Theodor Fechner, whose psychophysics was strongly critiqued and rejected as a one-sided relation of causality, but whose terminology has meandered through the disciplines and the centuries ever since in a wide variety of ways. Both Freud and Friedrich Nietzsche, in the ideas they formulated, showed themselves to be open to a direct connection between the physiological and the psychological—and in individual cases it is not at all easy to detect where the terms came from in these authors. Max Weber, in his study "Zur Psychophysik der industriellen Arbeit" (On the psychophysics of industrial work), was extensively concerned with the works of labor psychology, which he sought to link to sociology's new questions and methods. Here he already cites studies on typewriter writing that resemble Siegfried Kracauer's descriptions of disciplining employees with metronomes that set the pace. Weber's study cited concerns about the so-called loss of practice, which occurs when an established routine is interrupted by a break and has to be practiced anew:

An (American) test in typewriting showed, for instance, that the level of proficiency attained after 50 days when first learning to type was later achieved, after a break of more than two years during which the test subject had completely broken off any contact to typing, after only 13 days. In this shortening of the necessary practice time to around a fourth, we can see the "practice balance." On the other hand, it seems to be demonstrable, in experimental review of familiar everyday experiences, that no level of proficiency, no matter how high, provides an immunity to "loss of practice," but that every interruption, even of the most proficient worker (typesetter, bookkeeper, piano virtuoso) makes its presence known *at once* in the continuing practice—which is of practically considerable significance for the question of diversifying work.[13]

Weber remains notably skeptical of psychophysics in connection with Fechner, Wilhelm Wundt, and Emil Kraepelin, emphasizing the discrepancy that exists between the simple assumption that it is physical appeal that triggers a parallel emotion, and the complex construction of emotions in social structures of activity, which themselves can become further triggers. Kracauer speaks of "psychophysical correspondences," which securely found their way into his *Theory of Film*, by referring back not to Fechner but to Freud and to the French psychologist Henri Wallon, who was one of the founding figures of French *filmologie* and who had been examining film from a psychological perspective since the forties. Kracauer cites Wallon in the spectator chapter, including his essay "De quelques problèmes psycho-physiologiques que pose le cinéma" (On some psycho-physiological problems posed by cinema).[14] This critique of positivism and its opposition of man and nature is taken from Wallon:

> Between it [the object] and the observer, there is no impenetrable interval as is postulated by positivism, nor all the old doctrines that go along with it, for which the universe and humanity come to be juxtaposed like two more or less distinct entities. Pushed to a sufficient degree of minutia, the measure of physics shows that observation modifies the fact observed, since there is no such thing as observation disembodied from all physical action, nor is there intelligence without an organ nor a man without a body.[15]

Kracauer refers to Wallon's film studies in order to document his own theory of cinema, which affects the spectator "with skin and hair." The center of these reflections is occupied by movement itself: "Movement is the alpha and omega of the medium. Now the sight of it seems to have a 'resonance effect,' provoking in the spectator such kinesthetic responses as muscular reflexes, motor impulses, or the like. In any case, objective movement acts as a psychological stimulus. . . . The effect itself appears to be well-established: representations of movement do cause a stir in deep bodily layers. It is our sense organs which are called into play."[16] The spectator involuntarily adapts to rhythms and movements well before any meanings arise between the shots in the montage or narrative dramaturgies—and herein lies the analogy to music that Kracauer underscores: "Aside from its meaning in each case, music has a direct effect on the senses; its rhythms directly stimulate the senses. The material phenomena represented in film and their movements fundamentally produce the same effect—indeed, film images are thus doubly allotted to this effect because without it they sink back lifelessly into the surface."[17] To sink back, "lifelessly into the surface," would spell the aesthetic end of film—it would have lost its power to bring to life. The fact that this bringing to life becomes the telos of film aesthetics in Kracauer is omnipresent in the spectator chapter.

"Life" is nature animated, and film is the experiment that exposes this. "Whitehead for one," writes Kracauer, "was deeply aware that scientific knowledge is much less inclusive than aesthetic insight, and that the world we master technologically is only part of the reality accessible to the senses." He continues, "The concept of life may also designate this reality which transcends the anemic space-time world of science."[18] The reality that Kracauer finds rescued in film aesthetics is exactly this nature, experimentally produced, brought to life, animated in our gaze. The experiment of film, however, also differs from scientific experiments in another respect. While the scientific experiment is aimed at identical reproducibility, which is basic to its claim to legitimacy, the aesthetic experiment lives from the fact that it is temporally open and its repeated reception is precisely not aimed at identical reproduction but at the interminability of a process, a process in which signs are found in relation to one another in a movement that is not fixed by any identity of meaning. Adorno shifts the focus to the open temporal horizon of the aesthetic experiment when he describes its dialectic as targeted at "realizing the demand that is recognized without forgetting the nature that conditions the demand. For neither of them ever come into accord within the existing, but merely in what is to come: dialectically. Experiments are the genuinely dialectical moments in the life of the artwork."[19]

The nature that speaks to the camera is different from the nature of the squeaking laboratory rat; what the scalpel (Benjamin's camera) cuts free are points of view and not facts. These points of view are the result of alternating standpoints, which—and this is the insight of Nietzsche's perspectivism—do not only stand open to principal alterability and ecstatic cross fading but can also be anticipated. As such, the film experiment goes after the subjectivity of reception without fixing it into a subject-object schema. In the experiment of film, therefore, it is not only the identity of the object that comes into question but also the identity of the subject. In the open temporal horizon of *what will be*, subjectivity and objectivity are experimentally interwoven with each other. The life of the artworks and the life of their recipients are ecstatically intertwined in the moment of bringing to life, which occurs in separate temporal windows. This is the criterion for the success of the aesthetic experiment, the twisting of the externality of the test arrangement with the interiority of the sensations of the senses.

Sergei Eisenstein also sees this duality as dialectically dynamic:

> The dialectic of a work of art is constructed upon a most interesting "dyad." The effect of a work of art is built upon the fact that two processes are taking place within it simultaneously. There is a determined progressive ascent towards ideas at the highest peaks of consciousness and at the same time there is a dual process: an impetuous progressive rise along the lines of the highest conceptual steps of consciousness and at the same time there is a penetration through the structure of the form into the deepest layers of emotional thinking. The polarity between these two creates the remarkable tension of the unity of form and content that distinguishes genuine works. All genuine works possess it.[20]

Eisenstein, who was fascinated by psychological experiments, never forgot that the form does not only penetrate the inner storyline of the film; the form also penetrates the spectator. "Emotional thinking" is connected to the ecstatic states of the spectators, which it exemplifies with recourse to the concept of life. And it does so in film objects, which still undermine the materialistic concept of the nature of our physical surroundings—this seems to be fundamental for Benjamin and Kracauer.

In his euphoric commentary on Walt Disney's early animated films, Eisenstein developed a poetics of film and life with the goal of connecting the permanent re-forming of the drawn line into new forms with a motif of plasmaticness. Animated films are, as he writes, "mocking at their own form."[21] The infinite life of the endlessly metamorphizing characters becomes an ecstatic celebration of a life that is continually created anew, free of the production of meaning and responsibility: "Disney is simply 'beyond good and evil.' Like the sun, like trees, like birds, like the ducks and mice, deer and pigeons that run across his screen. . . . Disney's films, while not exposing sunspots, themselves act like reflections of sunrays and spots across the screen of the earth. They flash by, burn briefly and are gone."[22] The Nietzschean citation, set in single quotes, is not the only allusion to the Dionysian celebration of merging with drives, with nature, or with whatever else will be called on as a generic primeval ground to picnic with plasma. The Apollonian trump card, which refers to the Dionysian ecstasy of borders, is nothing more than time itself:

> And if most of them did not flash by us so quickly . . . we could be made angry by the moral uselessness of their existence on the screen.
> But because of the fleeting ephemerality of their existence, you cannot reproach them for their mindlessness.
> Even the string of a bow cannot be strained forever.
> The same for the nerves.
> And instants of this "releasing" . . . are just as prophylactically necessary as the daily dose of carefree laughter in the well-known American saying: "A laugh a day keeps the doctor away."[23]

The energetic model of tension and release used here by Eisenstein is that of nerve stimulation; at a different point he relates it to another element that has an effect on the nerves by means of light and warmth, that of fire. The love of fire, and here he is following a study of pyromania by the psychiatrist Paul Näcke, is based on the following reasons: "Foremost phototropism, characteristic of all living matter—that is, the attracting power of bright light, the sun, or fire . . . thermotropism—that is, the magnetic power of warmth on the cells of an organism." Eisenstein emphasizes "the magnetic power of . . . *movement*."[24] The synaesthetic model of a connection between visual, haptic, and tactile qualities in perception is a model for film perception: it gets on our nerves. Film is an experience that we sense synaesthetically, which is subcutaneously brought into a rhythmic shaping of time through light and movement. This is the poetic plasmaticness that the material of film presents and that protects us from "ossification." There is "a rejection" at work, "of once-and-forever allotted form, freedom from ossification, the ability to assume dynamically any form. An ability that I would call 'plasmaticness.'"[25]

Eisenstein finds these poetics in Japanese woodcut prints; in Maxim Gorky's description of fire in alternating images of animals, whose forms assume the shape of flames; in the snake people who share a world with Lewis Carroll's Alice, who can become quite small and quite large in Wonderland; and more. Movement becomes a media-anthropological *tertium comparationis*, and it is movement that has an effect as the animation of drawing. The pneuma of the film, we might add, lies in the rhythm of the montage's cuts, the temporality of the twenty-four frames per second, the vibration of the flicker that is obstructed as inner agitation in the very film being screened. The film is thus similar to the attractiveness of fire, which—and here Eisenstein cites Hegel's *Lectures on the History of Philosophy*—"is physical time, absolute unrest, absolute disintegration of existence, the passing away of the 'other,' but also of itself."[26] Film goes by in physical time, but over and over again it takes on form; it burns up and is animated once again in the apparatus.[27]

If Eisenstein had simply remained with the celebration of biological life, we would probably attribute to him today a life-sciences paradigm that had quite abandoned the obstinacy of an aesthetic concept of form, jumping back once again into psychophysics. This is an option that Eisenstein rejected *expressis verbis*. Eisenstein has bigger plans for Disney. The comedic quality of the film cannot simply be explained through biological regression to plasmatic merging. The matter that becomes the material of the film cannot be plasma.

> In terms of their material, Disney's pictures are pure ecstasy—all the traits of ecstasy (the immersion of *self* in nature and animals etc.)
>
> Their comicality lies in the fact that the *process* of ecstasy is represented as an *object*: literalised, formalised.
>
> That is, Disney is an example (within the general formula of the comical) of a case of *formal ecstasy*!!! (Great!) (Producing an effect of *the same* degree of intensity as ecstasy!).[28]

The comedic as a form is based on a shift of the metaphor of metonymy, a procedure that Eisenstein also sees in effect without the shift to the comedic in the following line that he cites in German from Friedrich Hölderlin's *Der Wanderer* (The wanderer, 1797):

> Fernhin *schlich das hagere Gebirge*, wie ein wandelnd Geripper,
> *Streckt* das Dörflein *vergnügt* über die Wiesen sich aus.
>
> [Far away *crept the haggard mountains*, like a mutating carcass,
> The village *merrily stretches* out past the meadow.][29]

The fact that it is the village itself that "stretches" fascinates Eisenstein: "This kind of motor metaphor . . . is the very earliest, most ancient type of metaphor—*directly* motory. . . . Not objectively *visible*, even less 'a comparison of something with something' . . . but rather a motori-subjectively *sensed* metaphor, *par excellence*."[30] This is what fascinates him so much in the elongated necks of the Disney bestiary, in the legs that get longer as they run, for example: that the contours become independent and form themselves into a second object, which exists alongside the first and which does not simply metaphorically replace it. "And only after the contour of the neck elongates beyond the possible limits of the neck—does it become a comical embodiment of that which occurs as a sensuous process in the cited metaphors."[31] Referring to Walt Disney's *The Karnival Kid* (1929), Eisenstein at one point notes—without mentioning the title of the film—that "there are the hotdogs whose skins are pulled down and are spanked."[32] The anarchistic shifts of metaphors into metonymies are clearly shown in the film. Mickey plays a hot-dog seller, running his mobile business out of a small wagon at a fair. This is one of the first sound films in which Mickey speaks, and he intones a staccato "hooot dogggs, hooot dogggs," each time sticking a fork into one of the sausages, which then responds with a bark. As the film goes on, the hot dogs undergo different kinds of transformations, for example, from sausage to a dog that bites, to a boy that gets his behind paddled. The hot dogs that bark are not metaphors for dogs. Rather, their proper name is used metonymically: the hot dogs become dogs, the bites become biters, the sausage casing becomes a textile covering, and so on. The comedic arises at the level of a motory-sensual knowledge about how it feels to be in motion, and of the object-like representation of its intention, such as getting away quickly, or its mood, such as feeling agitated.

Eisenstein is fascinated by Émile Zola's formula: "*Une réalité vu à travers un tempérament*" (a reality seen through a temperament).[33] The world is seen through a temperament, or, one could add, following Heidegger, through a mood. Moods are ways of perceiving the world. They are not simply bad filters or distorting mirrors; they are our own membranes, which connect us to the world as we perceive it. Films, and particularly those of Disney, create this membrane, which is required for us to experience the world as one in which will and representation can appear side by side. And precisely because of this these films allow the will and the wish to come forth to color our representation of the world and provide it with its plasticity by distributing light and shadow.

The poetics of film that Eisenstein develops with Disney's animated films is thus based on a threefold conception of life:

1. Biological life as matter or plasma, which precedes any implementation of individual life as substance.
2. The artwork as an experiment of animation, which grants itself a life.

3. The artwork as an experiment of animation, which arouses the spectator to life and allows the spectator to experience himself or herself as living.

By mediating the three layers, film becomes an aesthetic experiment in which, as I proposed in the definition of the experiment, something is to be given voice in its nature. In his astute study *Ästhetik der Lebendigkeit: Kants dritte Kritik* (Aesthetics of vitality: Kant's third critique), Jan Völker has derived a principle of difference from Kant's concept of life and nature: "If we return once again to the third *Critique*, then Kant's definition of the human animal—as that animal that is an organic being and at the same time a being that can express its difference in nature—can be read differently. The specificity of the human being lies in its nonnatural life."[34] The experiment of animated film gives voice to exactly this aspect. The "ecstasy of form" is not the dull celebration of the organic around the plasmatic melting pot; it is the enhanced experience of an animated nature, a fictitious nature, which is the effect of a human act, an action that it has manufactured: "This is Kant's solution to the question of spirit. The spirit is the human faculty of negating the order of nature, and therein lies the paradoxical nature of the human being. It is its nature to negate nature."[35]

Whether it be barking sausages, talking mice, or czars drawn out in their shadows, in the film experiment of animation, the open quality of natural definition can be experienced as a permanent metonymic shift. If we define the experiment as a dispositif, it can be deployed, as Eisenstein has shown, as a basic building block of cinema aesthetics.

Notes

All translations are my own unless otherwise noted.

1. The standard German translation for "fact" is *Tatsache*, which is made up of the parts *Tat* (act, action) and *Sache* (thing, matter). Rheinberger, "Wissensräume und experimentelle Praxis," 368.
2. Plessner, *Conditio humana*; and Plessner, *Die Stufen des Organischen und der Mensch*.
3. Polanyi, *The Tacit Dimension*; Gadamer, *Wahrheit und Methode*.
4. Wittgenstein, *Philosophical Investigations*, section 124, 55e.
5. Wittgenstein, *Philosophical Investigations*, section 109, 52e.
6. Wittgenstein, *Philosophical Investigations*, section 124, 55e.
7. Marcuse, *One-Dimensional Man* (2002), 182–83.
8. See, for example, Iser, *The Fictive and the Imaginary*.

9. See, for example, Saar, *Genealogie als Kritik*.

10. Freud also speaks of "infantile sexual theory," the child's "instinct for knowledge," and the "instinct for discovery" of intellectuals and scholars. See Sigmund Freud, "Drei Abhandlungen zur Sexualtheorie," in *Gesammelte Werke*, Band V (Frankfurt am Main: S. Fischer, 1968).

11. See, for example, the writings of Robert Hooke, the curator in charge of experiments at the Royal Society: "Such Experiments therefore, wherein Nature is as 'twere put to Shifts and forc'd to confess, either directly or indirectly the Truth of what we inquire, are the best if they could be met with." Cited in Nelle, "Im Rausch der Dinge," 145.

12. Adorno, "Ernst Kurths 'Musikpsychologie,'" 350–51. Translation by Daniel Hendrickson.

13. Weber, "Zur Psychophysik der industriellen Arbeit," 188–89. Translation by Daniel Hendrickson.

14. Wallon, "De quelques problèmes psycho-physiologiques que pose le cinéma," 15. Translation into German is mine, into English from German by Daniel Hendrickson.

15. Wallon, "Le réel et le mental," 456. "Entre lui [l'objet] et l'observateur, il n'y a pas cet intervalle étanche que postulent le positivisme et, avec lui, toutes les vieilles doctrines pour qui l'univers et l'homme en viennent à se juxtaposer comme deux entités plus ou moins distinctes. Poussées à un degré suffisant de minutie, les mesures de la physique montrent que l'observation modifie le fait observé, car il n'y a pas d'observation désincarnée de toute action physique, pas plus qu'il n'y a d'intelligence sans organes ni d'homme sans corps." Wallon's essay is a thorough examination of the 1935 book by Lucien Lévy-Bruhl, *La mythologie primitive: Le monde mythique des Australiens et des Papous* (Paris: Alcan, 1935).

16. Kracauer, *Theory of Film*, 158.

17. Kracauer, "'Marseiller Entwurf' zu einer Theorie des Films," 579.

18. Kracauer, *Theory of Film*, 170.

19. Adorno, "Musikalische Aphorismen," 27.

20. This is from Eisenstein's speech to Soviet filmmakers on January 8, 1935; quoted in Eisenstein, *The Eisenstein Collection*, 80 (in Naum Kleiman's "Introduction" to the chapter "On Disney").

21. Eisenstein, *The Eisenstein Collection*, 88.

22. Eisenstein, *The Eisenstein Collection*, 93.

23. Eisenstein, *The Eisenstein Collection*, 92.

24. Eisenstein, *The Eisenstein Collection*, 107.

25. Eisenstein, *The Eisenstein Collection*, 101.

26. Hegel, *Lectures on the History of Philosophy*, 287.

27. See, for example, Lyotard's position on film aesthetics as explosion in *L'acinéma*. Lyotard, *L'acinéma*.

28. Eisenstein, *The Eisenstein Collection*, 126.

29. Eisenstein, *The Eisenstein Collection*, 141.

30. Eisenstein, *The Eisenstein Collection*, 141.

31. Eisenstein, *The Eisenstein Collection*, 142.

32. Eisenstein, *The Eisenstein Collection*, 94.
33. Eisenstein, *The Eisenstein Collection*, 158. Zola, however, does not speak of "reality" but of "a corner of creation": "J'exprimerai toute ma pensée en disant qu'une oeuvre d'art est un coin de la création vu à travers un tempérament" (I will express the entirety of my thought in saying that a work of art is a corner of creation seen through a temperament). Zola, *Mes haines*, 234.
34. Völker, *Ästhetik der Lebendigkeit*, 263. Translation is mine.
35. Völker, *Ästhetik der Lebendigkeit*, 262.

9 : : Frame Shot: Vertov's Ideologies of Animation

MIHAELA MIHAILOVA AND JOHN MACKAY

We could begin by postulating that only the technological-economic limitations plaguing Soviet art workers in the early 1920s—absence of equipment, most pertinently, along with shortages of raw film—prevented the extravagantly gifted creators associated with Soviet constructivism from engaging with animated film as seriously and creatively as they practiced (among other things) graphic, architectural, clothing, and industrial design. Indeed, if we think of constructivist animation during the movement's glory years, little comes to mind apart from the moderately well-known mobile intertitles that Aleksandr Rodchenko created, in some cases reworking some of his own "spatial constructions," for Dziga Vertov's *Kino-Pravda* (*Film Truth*) experimental newsreel series (1922–25). Not much to go on, it would seem: still, what light might these intertitles shed on the obscure relationships between animation, constructivism, and Vertov's "kino-eye" cinema?

To be sure, some of these intertitles can be called animations only in a loose sense. Near the beginning of *Kino-Pravda*'s fourteenth issue (1922), which was dedicated to the Fourth Congress of the Communist International in Moscow (November 5 to December 5, 1922), a Rodchenko construction, identified by Yuri Tsivian as *Spatial Construction 15* (1921), is shown turning clockwise around its vertical axis and bearing the words "ON ONE" on one side and "SIDE" on the other (see figure 9.1).[1] These five seconds of rotation are wedged between a shot of a globe turning counterclockwise and evidently advancing toward the camera, and a shot of another Rodchenko construction with the letters of the word "America" distributed more or less syllabically over its rotating surfaces.

Thus, it could be said that we are looking at a moving photograph of a sculpture turned into a suspended mobile rather than animation as

FIGURE 9.1 Spinning Rodchenko title from *Kino-Pravda* 14 (Dziga Vertov, 1922). Source: Russian State Archive of Film and Photo Documents 12998.

such. But surely this is a borderline case, and we might feel justified in considering it a very simple kind of stop-action (or to use the parlance of 1920s Soviet animators, *volume* [*obyomnaia*]) animation,[2] at least in light of the intention animating Vertov's decision to make his titles move:

> Considering it established that the motion picture is but a skeleton of intertitles plus cine-illustrations,
>
> In the name of the liberation of cine-spectacle from the literary yoke I propose:
> BREAK THE BACK OF THIS SCUM![3]
> . . .
> Illuminated advertisements, a slogan written in fireworks, a slogan [on] a revolving construction, and similar mobile things [*dejstvennye veshchi*] that fulfill the task they are set, are acceptable to us.
>
> In those cases when the construction of a slogan does not satisfy us, we temporarily retain the right to construct the slogan *we* need, a slogan in movement that would provide the correct interval between the shots coming before and after.
> . . .

FIGURE 9.2 First shot of *Kino-Pravda* 14: another Rodchenko construction, turning. Source: Russian State Archive of Film and Photo Documents 12998.

The mobile intertitles of *Kino-Pravda* 14 are just a bolder step in the only correct direction: toward the complete destruction of static intertitles.[4]

True, the motives behind Vertov's decision to put his intertitles into motion are not easy to grasp or summarize — they evidently derive from both his antiliterary bias and his futurist enthusiasm for speed and mobility, among other inspirations — but in the case under discussion, it seems that the intershot intervals that he is at pains to articulate involve movement and meaning at once. *Kino-Pravda* 14's very first shot is of another Rodchenko construction, a simple turbine-like affair turning in two abrupt shifts on its horizontal axis to announce the newsreel's title ("Kino / Pravda / 14") (figure 9.2). After a credits title in constructivist lettering, the spinning motif returns, along inconsistent axes and in varied directions, with the globe and the two whirling constructions, thus providing a strong "revolving" cadence as prelude to the newsreel to come.

Turning carries semantic-associative weight as well, activated above all by the globe — shown three more times, along with images of maps of both the Western and Eastern Hemispheres—and by the internationalist occasion of the newsreel itself, the Comintern's fourth congress, here announced in what the constructivists hoped would be the Left's "new international" style: their own. The rotations may well encrypt personal references (*Vertov* derives from *vertetsia*, meaning "to turn") and a political one ("revolution"), together with the more narrowly geopolitical motif.[5]

Two other features of the intertitle, slightly less obvious than its mobility, link it to constructivist practice in a more interesting way. First, it is, as Vertov puts it, "a slogan [on] a revolving construction," or rather a fragment of such a slogan, a rhetorical device that introduces a capitalist world dominated by the United States, incorporating nations "obedient to America" (*pokornye Amerike*), such as France and Britain, and contrasted with the USSR—the "OTHER SIDE," a phrase introduced on yet another spinning Rodchenko construction—about two and a half minutes into the film. And slogan making, or more generally the practical application of constructivist design to the production of announcements, propaganda posters, and (above all) advertisements, would become one of the hallmarks of the movement (especially during the years 1922 to 1925).[6]

Second, the intertitle is a quite strictly modular construction, "knocked together out of ten identical 9-inch-long square-profile wooden bars extending in three dimensions at right or 45-degree angles to each other."[7] As the art historian Maria Gough has shown, modular principles of construction—that is, the use of uniform, standardized units, whether two- or three-dimensional, to generate "things" (*veshchi*) of unpredictable scale and formal shape—became central to constructivist theory and practice beginning around 1922, particularly in the work of Rodchenko, Karl Ioganson, and El Lissitzky.[8] Indeed, we are tempted to suggest that modularity—an unimpeachably contemporary and industrial approach to construction, as well as a strategy for reducing the role of the artist's subjectivity in the creative process—is part of what is announced by the intertitle, however briefly and cryptically: a new, constructivist practice, and perhaps a new constructivist *film* practice, will take these principles of making as its own.

The twin (and, in a certain way, related) preoccupations with advertising propaganda and modularity, emerging out of the constructivist matrix of the early 1920s, underlie Vertov's own enduring interest in and practice of animation, from the *Kino-Pravda* period onward to the stop-action animations in *Man with a Movie Camera* (1929) and animated sequences planned for major late (and unrealized) projects, such as *The Girl and the Giant* (1940).[9] As a platform for propaganda, advertisement, slogan, and announcement, animation technique had the advantage of being able to generate images at once vividly distinct — distinct, that is, from more straightforwardly photographic mimeses of the world — and immediately legible, by virtue of the way that putatively basic principles, ideas, or essences, such as "the global / international" in *Kino-Pravda* 14, could be built into their visible structure.[10] The best way to practically command those basic principles — not to know them, but to mobilize them, make them manifest — was to configure them out of still more basic, essentially neutral (modular) elements, in line with the most up-to-date industrial theory and practice. Such was the method, on this reading, of animation as such, insofar as it was a way of building up a film piece by piece, in a process of "frame shooting" (*kadro-syomka*, in the parlance of the 1920s), rather than fashioned through the larger "shot" units typical of more conventional photographic cinema. However, modular animation practice had important ideological ramifications for Vertov as well, insofar as it offered certain tropes that enabled him to link his own work in film with advanced industrial labor, and indeed with the labor of machines as such.

From Agitation to Ads

In many ways, Vertov's experiments in *Kino-Pravda* set the tone for the initial development of drawn Soviet animation, not least in *Kino-Pravda*'s application to advertising and propaganda. In his memoir, aptly entitled *Kadr za kadrom* (*Frame by frame*), Ivan Ivanov-Vano — a major member of the first contingent of Soviet animators, along with Vladimir Suteyev, Valentina and Zinaida Brumberg, and Nikolai Khodataev — writes that animators should recall Vertov with gratitude for involving a small collective of animators (most notably Aleksandr Bushkin) in the production of *Kino-Pravda*.[11] The animation scholar Sergei Asenin describes Vertov's inclusion of drawn imagery in *Kino-Pravda* as inseparably linking animation in the Soviet Union "from its first steps" with political issues, political journalism, topical subjects, satirical political posters, and newspaper caricature.[12]

Commercials composed a large proportion of all early Soviet animated film. In 1926 Mikhail Boytler claimed that film advertisements (including animated ones) were already among the more widely employed, diverse, and well-developed varieties of *reklama* (commercials

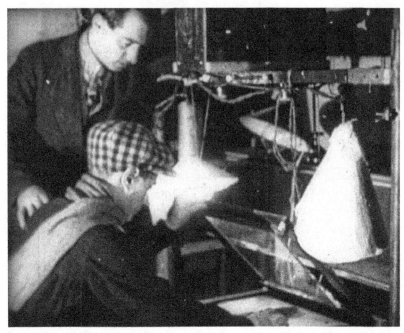

FIGURE 9.3 The cameramen Mikhail Kaufman (Vertov's brother) and Ivan Belia-kov at an animation stand. Still from *A Survey of Goskino Production in March 1924* (1924). Source: Russian State Archive of Film and Photo Documents 11622.

or ads) on view in the Soviet Union.[13] As in so many areas of early Soviet film, Vertov was one of the pioneers not only of animation and film advertising but also of their cross-fertilization. In his 1923 article "Advertising Films," for instance, he includes two examples of animated commercials, the "special-effects advertisement" (stop-action) and the "cartoon advertisement" (drawn), in his long list of extravagant and often amusing pitches (Vertov obviously had an aptitude for this sort of thing).[14] The rise of the animated ad had coincided with the great years of constructivist advertising (1923–25), with Rodchenko and the poet Vladimir Mayakovsky only the most prominent of the artists engaged in the design of posters, product labels and packaging, journal and magazine covers, logos, trademarks, and much else. This was all in an effort to at once help rebuild the shattered post–Russian Civil War economy, participate in a practical (rather than irrelevantly artistic) way in the construction of a new society, and create models for *reklama*—a representational form out of place, it would seem, in a postcapitalist country—proper to Communism.[15]

Some of the most interesting constructivist ads seem to reflexively theorize socialist advertising as such, as in the case of a remarkable 1923 mise en abyme maquette by Rodchenko and Mayakovsky for a cooking-oil ad, where the ad (in Leah Dickerman's words) "uses a smaller image of itself as the label on its central bottle of oil . . . [to conjure] a mythic socialist plenitude[,] . . . at the same time [working] to develop a coordinated system of identity between the advertising graphic and the product itself."[16] Vertov also managed to enclose his sole-surviving entirely animated film, *Soviet Toys* (1924), in a kind of self-reflexive bracket—of a type familiar from his films of the *Kino-Pravda* period, and later fundamental to the structure of *Man with a Movie Camera*—that draws attention to the power of animated advertising as such. This is perhaps not apparent on a first viewing, as the central section of *Soviet Toys* is taken up by a crude and somewhat bloodthirsty political allegory whose iconography (some drawn, some cut out) derives to a considerable extent from Russian Civil War–era models. In that main narrative, *Soviet Toys* offers a representation of the capacity of united workers, peasants, and soldiers of the Red Army to extract surplus (through taxation) from New Economic Policy–era capitalists ("Nepmen"), and eventually to remove the latter and their hangers-on (priests, prostitutes) from the historical stage entirely.[17]

What is most interesting for our purposes is the cartoon's overt if inconsistent cinematic self-reflexivity: nothing new in animation globally by 1924 (think of Dave and Max Fleischer's great "Out of the Inkwell" series of 1918–29, for example), but quite startling in the otherwise unsophisticated *Soviet Toys*. A certain self-consciousness is announced with the very first (animated) title card: two cameras, top right and bottom left, and pointed left and right, respectively, flank the names of the film and the studio ("Goskino," centered top and bottom). The names are apparently no more than logos at this point, but they preface more overt metacinematic references to come.

About eight minutes and forty seconds into the film, after the appearance of a series of ornament-like Red Army soldiers (who eventually gather into an arboreal configuration that will double as a scaffold), a strange new personage, with bulbous eyepieces and a whirling movie-camera shutter protruding from his mouth, walks on from the left. Granted one of several iris-shot close-ups included in *Soviet Toys*, this figure is identified as "GOSKINO FILM ADVERTISING" (*Kino-Reklama Goskino*), performing a cameo appearance. He then reverses direction and leaves screen left (see figure 9.4). Immediately following his departure, the bloated and much-abused Nepman also shrinks to ornament

FIGURE 9.4 "Goskino Film Advertising," from *Soviet Toys* (1924). Source: 35mm print, Yale University.

size, thus suggesting through contiguity (as Lora Wheeler Mjolsness has hinted) the power of cinema to provide different ways of imagining otherwise inert and recalcitrant realities.[18]

At the very end of the film, after the central narrative has concluded with the allegorical hanging of class enemies on the branches of the rather complicated Red Army "tree" (which converts suddenly and festively into a "Soviet Christmas tree"), a wipe reveals another (animated) scene. This scene is perspectivally relatively "realistic," showing part of the studio where the film we have just seen was presumably made and first exhibited (see figure 9.5). A man in an overcoat looking to the right watches, in seeming delight and amazement, what is apparently the conclusion of the film we have just seen (i.e., *Soviet Toys*). The goggled mascot of Goskino Film Advertising sits near him at a desk, while the man—evidently a client of Goskino Film Advertising, perhaps even a

FIGURE 9.5 Still from *Soviet Toys* (1924). Source: 35mm print, Yale University.

Nepman—comes to his senses, mugs a bit, takes a seat, and looks down at a piece of paper in his hand. That paper, the last shot reveals, is a simple flyer for "Goskino / Film Newsreel / Film Advertising / Tverskaia Street 24 / Tel. 5-70-71." Thus, *Soviet Toys* turns out to have been an animated ad for animated advertising; and the film's politically ambivalent message, on this meta level, seems to be that animated film techniques, fortified by the long agitprop experience during the Russian Civil War, might be effectively mobilized for purposes *other* than political agitation, attracting both audiences and new clients.

Units of Motion

But what can animated ads—rather expensive and labor-intensive, after all—do that other ads can't, or can't do as well? Both in Russia and abroad, and well before 1917, animated film had been identified as a valuable tool for the conveying of complex messages with clarity, force, and (sometimes) humor—sometimes in advertisements, but particularly in educational and scientific applications. (Intriguingly, some important early advertising theory identified pedagogy as one of the powers of filmed ads in general, insofar as they tended to teach audiences something about the commodities they were peddling, including details about how they were produced.)[19] When the pioneering producer Aleksandr Khanzhonkov established a scientific-educational division in his studio in 1911, he recruited Vladislav Starevich, then involved in filming insects and soon to become one of the greatest early animators, as both consultant and filmmaker. For Khanzhonkov, Starevich produced some of the first successful Russian educational animations. One of the studio's most popular productions of 1913 was *Drunkenness and Its Consequences*, starring the acting legend Ivan Mozzhukhin and incorporating a Starevich animation in which a tiny devil crawled out of a half-empty bottle of vodka — presaging a famous "trick" shot in *Man with a Movie Camera* by some fifteen years! — and then proceeded to tease and torment the drunkard (played by Mozzhukhin).[20]

By the 1920s, important Soviet writers on film, such as Lazar Sukharebsky and A. Tyagai, presented animated imagery as the most suitable means of visualizing and explaining scientific phenomena and hidden physical and chemical processes, and as a particularly powerful exploitation of that capacity to enhance "visibility" (*naglyadnost*) specific to cinema. Both authors provided examples of educational and instructional cartoons and praised their pedagogical and illustrative value. In his 1928 book *Uchebnoe kino* (*Educational cinema*), Sukharebsky discusses how animation could be used to illustrate the mechanisms of nutrient absorption in trees in such a dynamic and clear way that it would make the principle accessible and understandable to children.[21]

For his part, Tyagai mentions that animation had been used in the creation of a series of instructional films about petroleum with titles like *Drilling* and *Prospecting*.[22] He references a 1926 film titled *From Artisanal Labor to the Mechanization of the Silicate Industry*, wherein animated sequences depict the work of the most advanced glass-production machinery available in Soviet factories.[23] Tyagai extols the "practical significance" of such films and suggests that they may substitute for foreign technical literature, obviously less readily accessible due to its reliance on verbal, as opposed to visual, instruction. Animation, he stresses, allows the filmmaker to show the viewer the fundamental processes percolating beneath high-speed mechanical movement, processes virtually always hidden from the human gaze.[24]

Many of Vertov's better-known animations have clear expository motivations, such as the animated diagrams explaining radio installation in *Kino-Pravda* 23 from 1925 (a.k.a. *Radio-Pravda*), or the stop-action animations of bread in *Stride, Soviet* from 1926 (a fanciful illustration of wartime rationing and its welcome termination), or of the movie camera toward the end of *Man with the Movie Camera* from 1929 (illustrating the main parts and basic functions of the camera and tripod).[25] And his most famous animation-related statement seems to refer as much to this power of (in Donald Crafton's words) "scientifically concretizing abstract thought"[26] as to any capacity for projecting utterly novel imaginings:

> Cinema is, as well, the *art of inventing movements* of things in space in response to the demands of science; it embodies the inventor's dream — be he scholar, artist, engineer, or carpenter; it is the realization by *kino-chestvo* of that which cannot be realized in life.
> Drawings in motion. Blueprints in motion. Plans for the future. The theory of relativity on the screen.[27]

Thus, a certain rationalizing motive, grounded in the conviction that generalizable principles do subtend chaotic reality and can be legibly represented, lies behind these applications of animation.

In this light, Vertovian animation might be usefully related to its dialectically opposite number, namely the use of film by Soviet exponents of the Frederick Winslow Taylor–inspired scientific organization of labor (*nauchnaia organizatsiia truda*, often abbreviated as NOT), *not* to synthesize individual moments (or frames) into an animated illusion of movement but rather to break larger-scale movements down into what was believed to be their component parts: to do animation backward, as it were. The Taylorist method, wrote the great NOT theorist Osip Ermanskii, involved "the organization [not only] of lifeless objects, but of living humans [as well]. All movements performed by a worker . . . are broken down into elements, into single, basic partial movements [*Teilbewegungen*]." This segmentation was executed in order to measure the time and effort taken to perform each movement, with an eye to reducing them and thereby secure "some profit, some savings."[28] Film enabled both the character and the duration of movement to be analyzed: "A stopwatch is put next to a worker [who is being filmed]; the clock is filmed along with the worker. The place of the clock hand at the beginning and end of the film strip, corresponding to the beginning and end of a given partial movement, enable the determination, through subtraction, the length of time taken by this movement."[29] That is, movement is taken as ideally *modular*, as composed of basic elements that can be refined and redistributed in accord with some larger project of efficient production.[30]

We suggest, as have other scholars, that Vertov's preoccupation with the visual segmentation of work processes reflects the influence of these Taylorist practices of managerial labor analysis, an influence shared by his constructivist contemporaries (see figures 9.6 and 9.7).[31] This influence is particularly evident in the three Ukrainian features released during the period of the First Five-Year Plan: *The Eleventh Year* (1928), *Man with a Movie Camera*, and *Enthusiasm: Symphony of the Donbass* (1931). For "kino-eye" and constructivism alike, adopting the modular was one way to replace studio-based models of creative practice with those of the factory, and thus a means of undoing the distinction separating artistic from industrial kinds of production, and indeed between intellectual and manual labor.[32]

It worth noting in this connection, though perhaps unsurprising, that an important strand of Soviet animation theory of the 1920s began defining animation in effectively modular terms. Bushkin, in particular, took issue with the odd application of the term *multiplication* to animated film (still today normally called *multiplikatsiia* in Russian), noting that it was *live-action* film that involved the shooting of "multiple" frames with each turn of the camera's handle, in contrast to the frame-by-frame fixing of every constituent part of a movement typical of animation. In that sense, Bushkin argues, animation would more precisely be termed "frame shooting" (*kadro-syomka*), where the basic units of the film are taken to be frame-sized modules, rather than shots of unpredictable duration.[33]

Indeed, we wish to conclude by speculating, largely on the basis of new archival evidence, that Vertov took frame shooting—that is, a conception of filmmaking as modular—as a more general model for his mature practice (at least in the late silent period), in part because the modular was so evidently up-to-date as a method of construction, and so closely affined with industrial labor. The evidence in question is Vertov's 1929 diagram of a fragment of a montage phrase from *Man with a Movie Camera* (figure 9.8), which provides a chart or schema of a brief (thirty-one-shot) passage of extremely rapid montage from near the end of the film's fourth reel. Along the chart's vertical axis, on the left-hand side, are the main categories of represented object in the sequence: the lens of the movie camera, the man with the movie camera, "light machines," "dark machines," and so on (there are nine categories in all).

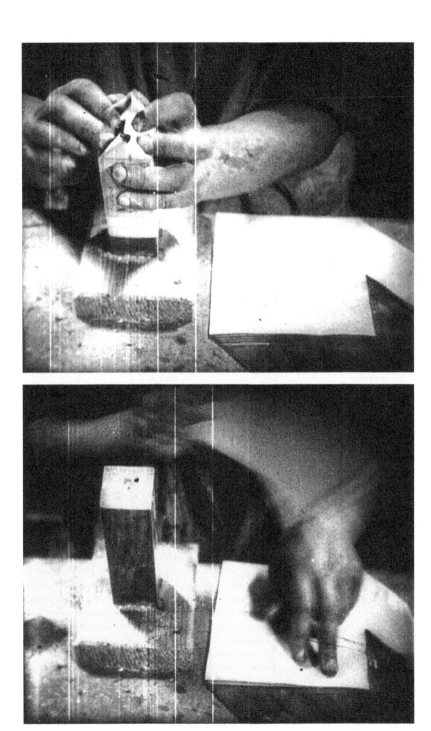

FIGURES 9.6 AND 9.7 The work of making cigarette cartons, broken into component parts, from *Man with a Movie Camera* (1929). Source: 35mm print, Yale University.

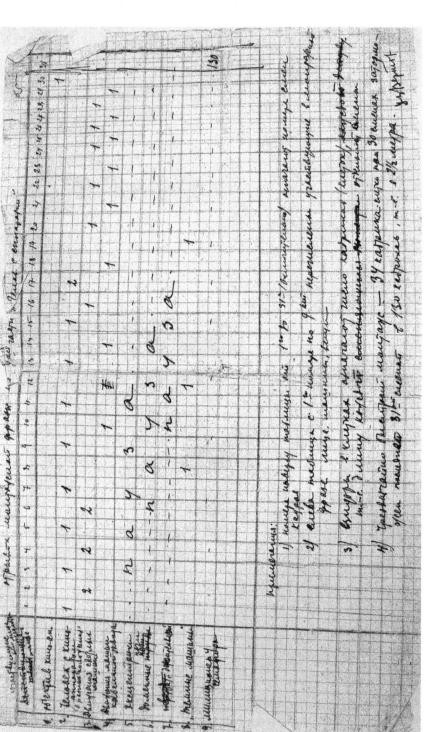

FIGURE 9.8 Vertov's handwritten "diagram of a fragment of a montage phrase from *MWMC* [*Man with a Movie Camera*]." Source: Russian State Archive of Literature and Art f. 2091, op. 2, d. 407, l. 65.

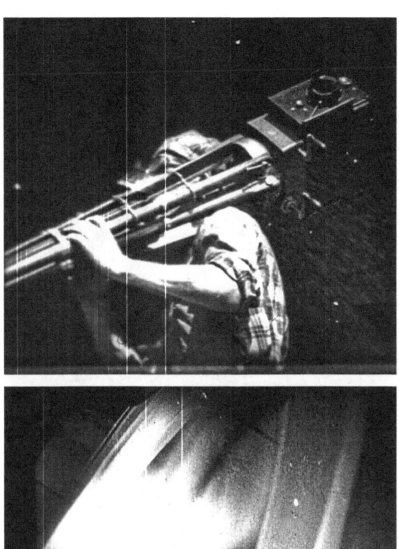

FIGURES 9.9 AND 9.10 Alternation of "man with the movie camera" with "light machines" from *Man with a Movie Camera* (1929). Source: 35mm print, Yale University.

FIGURES 9.11 AND 9.12 Alternation of "man with a movie camera" and "cable factory machines" from *Man with a Movie Camera* (1929). Source: 35mm print, Yale University.

FIGURE 9.13 Penultimate single-frame image of camera lens (filming the camera) in the "fragment of a montage phrase." *Man with a Movie Camera* (1929). Source: 35mm print, Yale University.

Along the horizontal axis at the top of the chart stretches a sequential numbering of all the shots, from one to thirty-one.

On the chart proper, Vertov has inscribed the number of frames (*not* seconds!) devoted to each shot: one frame of "the man with the movie camera" alternating with two frames of "the movement of light machines" from shots 1 to 7; a single one-frame alternation of "dark machines" and "man with a movie camera" in shots 8 and 9; one single-frame alternation of "machines in the cable factory" with "man with the movie camera" in shots 10 and 11; back to the one-frame alternations of "dark machines" and the "man" in shots 12 and 13; a complex series of one frame of the "cable factory machines" (shot 14), one frame of the "man" (15), one frame of "light machines" (16), two frames of the "man" (17), another single frame of the "cable factory machines" (18), and one frame of the "dark" machines (19); then a rapid one-frame alternation from shots 20 to 29 between "light" and "cable factory" machines, where the "man" has dropped out entirely; a single frame of the camera lens in shot 30; and, finally, 130 frames (a virtual eternity!) of a policeman directing traffic, one of the film's central motifs and self-reflexive indices.

The most remarkable parts of the schema, however, are at lines 5, 6, and 7 on the left-hand side of the graph. For the categories "cogwheels" and "blast furnaces," no indications of numbers of frames are given. Instead the simple word *pausa* (pause) is written across the page. This is peculiar at first sight, for why would an element *not* in the sequence find any place in the notation whatsoever? A moment's comparative reflection, however, makes clear the actual structural model for the notation and the sequence. That model is plainly musical, with the frames standing in for tones, and the *absence of frames* representing rests (*pausa* also means "[musical] rest" in Russian), inserted within the overall orchestration of the material. Just as a composer or arranger does not simply let the string portion of an orchestration vanish from the page when the strings are not participating in the piece, so too the elements of Vertov's visual sequence, like the blast furnace and cogwheels, inhabit the sequence even in their absence. What Vertov is trying to do here, it seems, is use existing, familiar ways of organizing artistic material heuristically, as a kind of ladder to vastly intensified powers of (in this case) visual perception. We can grasp musical (sonic) material of this density and at comparable speeds, when properly organized; why not try the same with images, even single frames?

From the perspective of ideological analysis, what is sought by this heuristic and modular technique of frame shooting (and frame editing)—where the conception of animation as radical modularity takes over ostensibly live-action cinema—is total *simultaneity*. This simultaneity is about bringing audiences up to speed, on the level of perception, with the ideal perceiver, who (actually *which*) is of course the optical machine itself, whose industrially produced units of vision are single frames. The technique involves a certain (purely ideological) reduction of the distance between intellectual (Vertovian) and manual (proletarian) labor as well, inasmuch as artistic strategy and industrial process seem to converge in the kino-eye. Is the elite filmmaker using art (music in this case) to expand and free up the perceptual capacities of the industrial proletariat, or is the film artist trying to find ways to organize materials in accord with the modularity and new, rapid rhythms of industrial production (abundantly referenced in the iconography of the sequence)? The answer, it would seem, must be both.

In tune with this musical thematic, however, we must add a final coda: a qualification, rather, that complicates or even contravenes some of what we have been saying, or at least confronts certain dissonances. Vertov's work may well be modular, and we can hardly doubt his desire to affine his practice with that of modern industry and proletarians, but surely his choices can also be read as drastically sui generis. They can be as idiosyncratic in their own way as the montage and animation experiments of the post–Second World War European and American avant-garde. And his choices can hardly be understood as the erasure through modular procedures of (to borrow the language of the constructivist ideologue Alexei Gan) "blind taste and aesthetic arbitrariness."[34] Much the same could be said of Rodchenko's revolving intertitles with which we began: garden-variety static intertitles, created with templates and much despised by Vertov, are the truly standardized form of silent movie text. Relative to these nearly invisible typographic norms, Rodchenko's constructions must be seen as highly eccentric outliers. Indeed, we could compare Vertov's frame shooting with predodecaphonic atonal composition, where the movement from each unit (note, frame) to the next is a matter of radical, moment-by-moment choice, rather than efficiently eased through adherence to paradigm or convention: artisanal (*kustarnaia*) work rather than industrial.[35] Yet Vertov's constructivist and modernizing agenda can hardly be denied. And so we can see how thinking about Vertov's work *through animation* brings to the fore the central paradox of *Man with a Movie Camera* as considered within its historical situation. In its radical and self-conscious emphasis on construction, frame by frame, it is at once a completely autonomous avant-garde work and completely participatory in the dominant production-oriented discourse of the First Five-Year Plan.

Notes

All translations are our own unless otherwise indicated.

1. Tsivian, "Turning Objects, Toppled Pictures," 102.
2. See Bushkin, *Triuki i multiplikatsiia*, 15–16. The other two types identified by Bushkin—a pioneer animator who worked with Vertov—are flat (*ploskostnaia*) or drawn and mixed (*smeshannaia*) modes incorporating live action, drawing, or stop-action.
3. Russian Civil War–era bombast, recycled for Vertov's "war" against fiction film.
4. Russian State Archive of Literature and Art (RGALI [Moscow]), f. 2091, op. 2, d. 390, ll. 7–9. "Static intertitles" here translates to *plakaty nadpisej*; the quotation is from a talk Vertov delivered in 1923.

5. The newsreel's opening section sets up a strong contrast between the U.S.-dominated capitalist West and the USSR as the seat of internationalism. For more on this issue of *Kino-Pravda* and the twin internationalisms of communism and constructivism, see MacKay, "Vertov and the Line."

6. It is worth noting that in some national varieties of Spanish (e.g., that spoken in Argentina), the Spanish word for *propaganda* is used to describe what we term *advertising*: a usage whose importation into English might well prove politically useful!

7. Tsivian, "Turning Objects, Toppled Pictures," 103. By all appearances, the intertitle introducing "the other side" is also built out of identical modular segments.

8. In her seminal *The Artist as Producer*, Gough writes of Ioganson's discovery, through the use of "the standardized modular unit," of "the possibility of potentially infinite expansion within a nonrelational progression" (86). In another essay, Gough defines "nonrelational progression" as "a structure governed by the repetition of homogeneous units rather than the compositional balancing of heterogeneous ones" ("Constructivism Disoriented," 97). See also Hubertus Gassner's description of Ioganson's structures as "made of standardized elements and homogeneous materials and rendered transformative through variable central connections or kinetic mounting" ("The Constructivists," 313).

9. For a script and storyboards of *The Girl and the Giant*—perhaps the most important of Vertov's many tragically unrealized projects—see Vertov, *Iz Naslediia*, 302–26. It seems that Vertov planned to use only stop-action animation in this film, and he was opposed by this time to the inclusion of any drawn animated sections (RGALI f. 2019, op. 2, d. 215, l. 30; RGALI f. 2019, op. 2, d. 429, l. 18).

10. Let us qualify our thesis here by acknowledging that early animation did not always strive to be distinct from photographic mimesis. Consider, for instance, Winsor McCay's *The Sinking of the Lusitania* (1918).

11. Bushkin worked with Vertov on some now-lost animations (*Humoresques*, 1924), a section of *Kino-Pravda* 23 (1925), and wrote one of the first important Russian-language books on animation (*Triuki i multiplikatsiia*). Ivanov-Vano describes Bushkin as "one of the first to sense the great potential of using animation as a means of visual agitation and cinematic propaganda." Ivanov-Vano, *Kadr za kadrom*, 22. For an overview of Vertov's work in animation, complete with filmography, see Deriabin, "Vertov i animatsiia."

12. Asenin, *Volshebniki ekrana*, 21. Good examples of animated political caricature can be found in the mid-1920s newsreel, which sometimes concluded with animated versions of Viktor Deni's satirical cartoons. See *Sovkinozhurnal*, no. 23 / 42 (1926); available at the Russian State Archive of Film and Photo Documents (RGAKFD) 816; and *Sovkinozhurnal*, no. 22 / 41 (1926) at RGAKFD 263. *Sovkinozhurnal* no. 37 / 95 (1927) ends with a folktale-like satirical animation urging peasants to open bank accounts (RGAKFD 1660).

13. Boytler, *Reklama i kino-reklama*, 3. Examples of animated advertising from 1920 to the early 1930s would include Aleksandr Ptushko's extraordinary *Sluchai na*

stadione (Incident at the stadium) from 1929 (available at RGAKFD 3924), which is actually an ad for the film *Vsesoiuznaia Spartakiada* (*All-Union Spartakiade*, 1929); and an ad for the new Palace of Arts of the USSR included in *Sovkinozhurnal* 10 / 273 (1930) (RGAKFD 2113).

14. Vertov, "Advertising Films," in *Kino-Eye*, 25.
15. See Dickerman, "The Propagandizing of Things," esp. 66–72. To be sure, the use of animation in advertising was neither a novel phenomenon nor limited to the Soviet Union. Many animators on both sides of the Atlantic began their careers by working on advertisements. While American cartoon directors often moved away from this type of production as their careers took off, their European colleagues tended to remain involved with commercial filmmaking. See Crafton, *Before Mickey* (1993), 228–30.
16. Dickerman, "The Propagandizing of Things," 71.
17. The New Economic Policy (1922–28) is a period during which limited private enterprise was encouraged for purposes of economic development. For a recent examination of this film with animation history in mind, see Mjolsness, "Dziga Vertov's *Soviet Toys*."
18. Mjolsness, "Dziga Vertov's *Soviet Toys*," 263.
19. See, for instance, Hartungen, *Psychologie der Reklame*, 195.
20. See "Spisok kinematograficheskikh kartin, kotorye dopushcheny k publichnomu demonstrirovaniiu," *Vestnik Kinematografii* 87, no. 7 (April 1, 1914): 51; and Ginzburg, *Kinematografiia Dorevoliutsionnoi Rossii*, 96; Roshal', *Nachalo Vsekh Nachal*, 58.
21. Sukharebsky, *Uchebnoe kino*, 15.
22. Tyagai, *Kino v pomoshche tekhnicheskomu podkhodu*, 16. Almost three decades later, the famous animation team Halas and Batchelor directed the animated shorts *We've Come a Long Way* (1951), which tells the history of the oil tanker and *Down a Long Way* (1954), which illustrates the functioning of an oil well.
23. Tyagai, *Kino v pomoshche tekhnicheskomu podkhodu*, 9. The Russian word for "labor" used here is *kustarnichestvo*.
24. Tyagai, *Kino v pomoshche tekhnicheskomu podkhodu*, 15. Once again, similar discussions were taking place abroad, particularly in the United States. In 1926 John A. Norling and Jacob F. Leventhal wrote that animation had "become of increasing value to every branch of industry and science." Like their Soviet contemporaries, they suggested that, in the field of education, animation is more valuable than any other mode of filmmaking, since it can show the "most intricate mechanical actions." Norling and Leventhal, "Some Developments in the Production of Animated Drawings," 60–61.
25. Vertov's animated tripod looks remarkably similar to Starevich's animated grasshopper in *The Grasshopper and the Ant* (1911), a film that Vertov exhibited many times on agit-trains in 1920.
26. Crafton, *Before Mickey* (1993), 235.
27. Vertov, "WE: Variant of a Manifesto," in *Kino-Eye*, 9; *kinochestvo* is an early term for Vertov's own "kino-eye" (*kino-oko*) nonfiction experimental practice. Esther

Leslie glosses the passage as follows: "Film must broadcast that which cannot be realized in life, and this will allow the analytical, scientific attitude, the dissection of reality. And it will allow an opening onto the future, the possibilities of the new world, on the bases of the science and technique of the present" (Leslie, *Hollywood Flatlands*, 224).

28. Ermanski, *Wissenschaftliche Betriebsorganisation und Taylor-System*, 110. This was a translation of Ermanski's highly popular *Nauchnaia organizatsiia truda i proizvodstva v sisteme Teilora*, which appeared in Moscow the same year in the first of five editions. Of course, such procedures had their roots in the classic chronophotographic experiments of Eadweard Muybridge and Étienne-Jules Marey. Marey, in particular, had been known in Russia at least since 1875, when a translation of his 1873 *Machine animale: Locomotion terrestre et aérienne* appeared as *Mekhanika Zhivotnago Organizma: Peredvizhenie po zemle i po vozdukhu* (St. Petersburg: Znanie, 1875), and he was regularly recalled in prerevolutionary film journals (e.g., "Pamiatnik frantsuzskomu uchonomu Zhiuliu Marej — pervomu izobretateliu kinematografa," *Vestnik Kinematografii* 92, no. 12 [June 21, 1914]: 13). A 1930 book on scientific uses of the movie camera, cowritten by Sukharebskii and the animator Aleksandr Ptushko, mentions Marey as the first to use the camera in physics. L. Sukharebskii and A. Ptushko, *Spetsialnye Sposoby Kinos'emki* (Moscow: Khudozhestvennaia Literatura, 1930), 3.

29. Ermanski, *Wissenschaftliche Betriebsorganisation und Taylor-System*, 155.

30. On the use of film to Taylorist ends in the United States during the same period, see Grieveson, "The Work of Film in the Age of Fordist Mechanization," esp. 30–34.

31. Among the earliest important discussions of the link between Vertov and Taylor are in Aronowitz, "Film," esp. 118–21; and Linhart, *Lénine, les paysans, Taylor*, esp. 129–33.

32. On Rodchenko's conceptualization of "construction" as the organization of modular units with a distinct utilitarian goal in mind, see Lodder, *Russian Constructivism*, 73.

33. Bushkin, *Triuki i multiplikatsiia*, 5.

34. Cited in Gough, *The Artist as Producer*, 86. For an essay that touches on some of the avant-gardists who might be considered in these terms, see Tode, "Absolute Kinetika."

35. On the problems emerging from the demands of and resistance to standardization, see Adorno, "Criteria of New Music," esp. 175–93.

10 :: **Signatures of Motion: Len Lye's Scratch Films and the Energy of the Line**

ANDREW R. JOHNSTON

Line, no matter how supple, light or uncertain, always implies a force, a direction. It is energon *work, and it displays the traces of its pulsation and self-consumption. Line is action become visible.*

ROLAND BARTHES, *"Non Multa Sed Multum"*

After a decade-long hiatus in which he mostly produced wartime documentaries and military training films, Len Lye in the 1950s once again began using the technique of direct animation that he had helped pioneer more than twenty years earlier. These previous films, such as *Colour Box* (1935), *Colour Flight* (1938), and *Swinging the Lambeth Walk* (1939), develop what Lye calls a "sensory-ballet" in which abstract forms and music are knit together with color to produce sensations of motion.[1] The point was to create a sensual experience of pleasure generated through color whose abstract and direct appeal avoided narrative forms and the kinds of associations that Lye believed plagued realistic imagery. In the early 1940s, Lye stopped producing these films, in part because of the war and an increasing scarcity of financial supporters and in part because of his growing interest in politics and a desire to counter Nazi propaganda films.[2] However, when invited to submit a film to the 1958 International Experimental Film Competition in Brussels by his friend Alberto Cavalcanti, Lye produced a direct animation but moved away from painting bold colors as he had done previously. Instead, he scratched into black 16mm film stock to produce lines, points, strokes, and zigzags that frenetically move across the screen and play not only with two-dimensional space but also with depth perspective, as some forms twist and rotate on the z-axis. The resulting film, *Free Radicals* (1958, revised 1979), is an ecstatic celebration of energy that elides any kind of figuration and instead embraces a profoundly chaotic abstraction. Producing this film was no simple task. Because of the small scale in which Lye was working, he explains in his writings that when making etchings into the filmstrip he had to keep the needle very still while affecting its direction by moving other parts of his body, so that the resulting movements of the line are registrations of his own kinesis. It is the energy and sensation associated with movement that, according to these writings, he conveys through these films, generating formally innovative works that also open spectators to a new understanding of motion and how it is sensed by the body.

Such activity is achieved through a misleading simplicity of form whose expressive power has been the subject of numerous investigations into modernist aesthetics and the power of abstraction: the line. Little criticism exists on Lye's scratch works, but what does often places them within a tradition of abstract expressionism that was popular in the artistic circles that Lye circulated through in 1950s New York. Wystan Curnow, for instance, argues that Lye's interest in atavistic thought and ideas about a possible link between the unconscious and proprioception indicates an indebtedness to the aesthetic argued over and defined by critics such as Clement Greenberg, Harold Rosenberg, and Louis Finkelstein.[3] Each of these critics, to various degrees, claim that the gestural abstractions of Jackson Pollock and others bare the afterlife of the artist's unconscious subjectivity. Associating a gestural mark or inscription with the articulation of this form of subjectivity, however, is reductive of Lye's work and, as other scholars and critics point out, the work of other artists who traditionally fall into the canon of abstract expressionism or action painting. T. J. Clark points out that though the space of Pollock's canvases reveals an autonomous, subjective realm produced outside the force of market operations, "the marks in these paintings . . . are not meant to be read as consistent trace of a making subject, but rather as a texture of interruptions, gaps, zigzags, a-rhythms and incorrectnesses: all of which signify a making, no doubt, but at the same time the absence of a singular maker—if by that we mean a central, continuous psyche persisting from start to finish."[4] If we sever the associations of Lye's gestural lines, or what he calls "figures in motion," from the divestiture of Lye's unconscious, what do we make of these raw, abstract lines that spin or wiggle frenetically across the screen? Why does Lye turn to this form of abstraction compared to his earlier direct animations? What is the relationship between animation and the dynamism or force of movement that Lye wishes to generate in viewers through these abstractions?

Furthermore, how do these abstract animations position cinema as a medium?

Lye posed these same questions to himself and was, throughout his career, very deliberate about the aesthetic, formal, and technological choices that he made in a variety of media. In his article "Why I Scratch, or How I Got to Particles" he explains that the lines in *Free Radicals*, *Particles in Space* (1960s, revised 1979), and *Tal Farlow* (1980) are meant to be formal expressions of a vitalistic energy that swirls around individuals, or "the stuff out of which we came, and of which we are." Such forces are felt by the body according to Lye and are stored in what he calls the "old brain of our primal organs," a localization of the body's capacity to sense movement that has been suppressed by human evolution, and further by contemporary culture, until, he says, movement exists as a diffused and unintelligible sensation in the body.[5] For Lye, this energy is more connected to the senses and the body than to the unconscious and repressed elements of the psyche. He explains that this energy comes from outside the body in nature, but that it is also responsible for the composition of the body. Associations or communions with this energy are what transpire unconsciously, or more exactly, outside analytic thought. This vitalistic formulation is similar in orientation to the cosmological analysis put forward by Alfred North Whitehead, especially in *Process and Reality* (1929) where he claims that all matter, both animate and inanimate, is constantly reemerging and forming, usually outside of consciousness. This process of becoming takes place through what Whitehead calls feeling, arguing that all forms of matter and life are generated out of affect and perceptual vectors, "pulses of emotion" or invisible energy that produce forms of relative unity. Objects such as rocks, people, and atomic particles affect and are affected by others and thus exist as subjects in a matrix of experience.[6]

Lye believed that certain types of abstraction tapped into a similar sensual energy that structures the inner identity of both the body and nature. Thus, the deep drumbeats on the soundtrack of *Free Radicals* represent, for Lye, an expression of energy in the same way as the mechanistic, whirling sounds produced by his metal kinetic sculptures. For this reason, he incorporated both kinds of sounds on the audio track of *Particles in Space*. The marks and lines in his scratch films visually operate in the same manner and are oriented as modulations of energy made visible through direct contact with the filmstrip. These have a deliberate force that is often structured and precise rather than generated through techniques of spontaneity that aim to perpetually hold the sense of

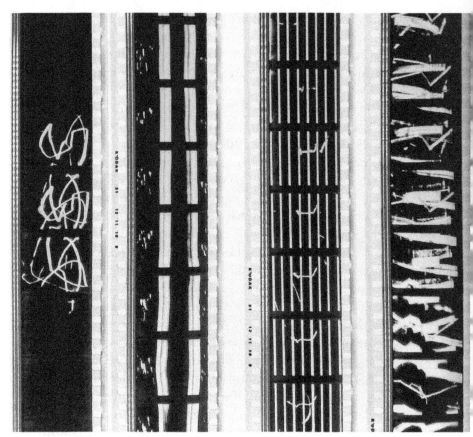

FIGURE 10.1 Filmstrip from *Free Radicals* (1958, revised 1979), 16mm. Courtesy of the Len Lye Foundation and New Zealand Film Archive.

presence and articulation of subjectivity bound up, as some argue, in Pollock's drips. For instance, in *Particles in Space*, dots congregate and sway to the sounds of one of Lye's metal kinetic sculptures, providing an animated visual projection of its oscillations. In *Free Radicals*, vertical lines many times run down the frame to create a grid that other forms oscillate within. Other marks in the film maintain a consistency of shape as they spin on the z-axis, indicating a stronger connection to Alexander Calder's mobiles than to Pollock's drip paintings (see figure 10.1).

These marks and lines reveal a play not only with dimensionality and figure-ground relations but also with the material base through which these forms are generated. Though Lye was indebted to a tradition of painterly gesture and abstraction, his primary interests were in the aesthetics of motion and cinema's privileged role as a medium in portraying motion. This emphasis on cinema as a technological and aesthetic form best suited for conveying and playing with senses of movement strays from the notion that film is defined through a photochemical material base whose indexicality aligns it with certain aesthetic modes of realism. Lye's frustration with this formulation that guided both film practice and the arguments made within what is now considered classical film theory influenced the construction of his films and theoretical writings on cinema and points to an alternative conceptualization of cinema rooted in graphic manipulations and sensations of movement. His focus on the body of the spectator in his films and writings and the empathetic relation between the senses and moving forms in cinema led him to produce increasingly extreme abstractions to both distill this connection's elements and analyze their relations. In this light, Lye's animation of graphic forms functions as a site for working through and exploring how the body sensually engages with different materials, a workshop and playground of materialist phenomenology.

Accordingly, for Lye, each type of animation contained its own specific aesthetic potentials, and scratching rather than painting lines was a key distinction between the types of direct animations he produced. The force applied to the celluloid through a technique of negation where parts of the emulsion are removed produces a work with a kinetic energy whose specificity intrigued Lye immensely. From such a seemingly anarchistic technique and reduction of form came a paradoxical explosion of vitality that Lye believed better conveyed the energy of motion relative to other abstractions. That such an exploration takes place through the abstractions and movements of the line exposes this form's own contradictory simplicity and expressiveness. And in animation these scratch lines move wildly while simultaneously isolating a sense of force in the perceptual encounter with the viewer, multiplying the kind of dynamism that Roland Barthes describes in the epigraph to this chapter. I argue that when in motion, the permutations of Lye's lines take on an animism that no longer simply bares the afterlife of his kinesis — the "action become visible" — but becomes a source of the lines' own vitality and transmission of movement in viewers. The movements of the line become, according to Lye, the line's own "life-manifestations."[7]

Lye was not alone when thinking through the qualities of different media during and after the Second World War. Questions of medium specificity and materiality were on the minds of a number of critics, especially within the arena of modern painting. Perhaps the most well-known, and belabored, formulation of medium specificity and the role of different aesthetic forms in modernity came from Greenberg, a critic who has generated both admiration and ire to the point of being so controversial that, as Caroline A. Jones explains, his name alone sparks debates and stands in for a number of ideas about aesthetics in a many times reductive fashion.[8] Without focusing here on this discourse and its polemics, Lye's abstractions and writings from this time did contain traces of these debates, though it is clear that his interest in aesthetics and abstraction lay in the perceptual address of his films and the variations in experience that different formal manipulations could produce. Similar to Rosalind Krauss's later analysis of a medium that works through this discourse, Lye viewed cinema as a form that participated in the construction of an aesthetic event, but a form that was in flux historically and open to bringing new techniques, technologies, and sensual experiences into its fold.[9] This emphasis on aesthetic effects as the final address of a medium is apparent in the opening of Lye's first published essay where he inverts the primacy given to form over movement in perception: "The result of movement is form. . . . When we look at something and see the particular shape of it we are only looking at its after-life. Its real life is the movement by which it got to be that shape. The danger of thinking of physical things in terms of form rather than of movement is that shape can easily seem more harmonious, more sympathetic with other shapes than its historical individuality justifies."[10] The consequences of such a shift result in Lye positing "movement as a medium" whose formal instantiations are more the residue of movement rather than that which conditions its possibility. In such a framework, marks in Paleolithic cave paintings speak to the contact of movement and also project in viewers a sense of motion through an intuitive force. Movement exists as vitalistic energy in this formulation and can be transferred through a "kinetic kind of osmosis" between different forms and materials, or between a body and an object, the traces of which are always visibly apparent.[11] Thus, for Lye, "to extricate movement from the static finalities or shapes which the mind imposes on living experience is to translate the memory of time back into time again — to relive experience instead of merely remembering it."[12] Shapes and forms are not static in this formulation; instead, they contain traces of action and duration constitutive of their making. The movement of the hand of the artist can become embedded within forms, and aesthetic experience is guided through a subsequent tracing of that movement, recreating the arcs, peregrinations, and pressures of the artist's hand. This aesthetic and intuitive force described by Lye operates through recognition and kinesthetic empathy along tactile and optical vectors. Just as Wilhelm Worringer explains, when a spectator traces the movement of a line in visual space, "we feel with a certain pleasant sensation how the line as it were grows out of the spontaneous play of the wrist," almost as though we had drawn the line ourselves.[13]

In this light, the scratches in *Free Radicals* exist not only as the residue or signatures of Lye's bodily motion but also as vectors along which the energy of motion exists. The title of the film came from a *New York Times* article Lye had read about the existence of highly reactive and unstable molecules called free radicals, and Lye felt that his aesthetic shared these forms' density of energy and eruptive potential.[14] He also believed that the title was appropriate given his own orientation to filmmaking and persona as an artist. Throughout Lye's career he felt a frustration with the emphasis on photographic realism in film and the continuities of space and time constructed through what he describes as "the Griffith technique." Film, like kinetic sculpture, has a privileged ability to work with the aesthetics of motion because of the way it internalizes time. But Lye found instead that film was increasingly becoming an adjunct and illustration of literature and proposed ways of "get[ting] out of the Griffith technique" in a lecture to the Film-Makers' Cinematheque.[15] One possibility he suggested was to use techniques taken from cartoon animation in live-action filmmaking, so that a hybrid aesthetic would be generated that creatively explains how movement is composed through time in cinema.

This hybridity can be seen in some of Lye's films, such as *Rainbow Dance* (1936), where colors play off one another in counterpoint as shapes and silhouettes of bodies moving about the screen dance to the musical accompaniment. His later complete abandonment of figuration was not a denial of the possibilities of this combination. Instead, this departure came about because of an increasing interest in how cinema engenders kinesthesia in viewers through the channels of empathy described above. While *Rainbow Dance* also aimed its address at sensual intensities, it did so through color patterns and an identification with the body on screen dancing and playing tennis. This produces a different aesthetic formation with its own specific "vibration-pattern," as Lye put it, which here played with the differences between static and kinetic forms and the sense of movement still attributed to a body frozen in action.[16] In contrast, the jerky, intermittently rigid, and chaotic scratches in *Free Radicals* use the gestural mark not to simply witness the body in motion but instead to feel its corporeal pressure through the lines' moving undulations.

Several writers have examined the pathways through which lines produce aesthetic effects on multiple perceptual registers simultaneously, and in animation Sergei Eisenstein's writings on Disney and the line are the most cited. For Eisenstein, animation could offer a spectacular liberation from social and physical laws by projecting a world whose fluidity of shape plays with subject and object relations as bodies, objects, and the environment constantly shift through a "plasmaticness" that destabilizes forms and mesmerizes spectators in the same manner as fire. Just as Lye argues, this nonrealistic motion can still produce physiological sensations, and Eisenstein similarly links animated action with a sensual address to the body. While the animated form of Mickey Mouse, or other figures in Disney films, continually morphs, the contour of such a transformation was always the line, which was responsible for viewers sensing that these figures were alive and for producing any kinesthetic empathy. Eisenstein explains that the movement and combination of abstract elements in animation are a manipulation of "heartless geometrizing and metaphysics [that] here give rise to a kind of antithesis, an unexpected rebirth of universal animism."[17] The source of such animism is not only the projected movement of these figures, so that one believes that "*if* it moves, *then* it's alive," but also the observer, who endows life to these forms with both the eye and the body.[18]

Traditionally, the line functions as a contour or boundary, a two-dimensional abstraction that demarcates the visible and establishes figure and ground relations in a separation that usually focuses attention on the content it delimits. That said, it hardly disappears, a point that William Hogarth makes in *The Analysis of Beauty* (1753). He explains that the line "leads the eye" around forms in a game of chase, suggesting that an imaginary ray emanating from the eye traces the contours and movements of forms, imbuing motion to the object and to the subject as well.[19] Eisenstein, possibly following Hogarth's lead, makes a similar argument about the ways that the line affects viewers sensually, but Eisenstein recognizes how perceptual activity and attention are affected by cultural and historical circumstances and how, additionally, this context can affect the development of artworks that respond to such changes. Maurice Merleau-Ponty in "Eye and Mind," a phenomenological analysis of painting and the visual arts, also tracks the historical nature of aesthetic encounters by showing how techniques and tendencies in different periods are oriented toward and affect the body in different ways, so that "every technique is a 'technique of the body.'"[20]

In the modern art of Paul Klee the line is freed from its traditional role of articulating visible forms, of being "the apparition of an entity upon a vacant background" and now functions as a modulation of a space and according structures aesthetic experience in a different way from, for instance, baroque painting. Throughout the essay Merleau-Ponty attempts to explain the power of painting and the line, arguing that they function as vehicles for the transmission of energy, or "the body's animation," between different bodies of producers and viewers. Thus, painting does not produce an imaginary field of contemplation for the mind but rather a sensual one directed toward the eye.

Variations in formal choices have important aesthetic consequences when this sensual address is foregrounded. Hogarth, for example, argues that the "serpentine line" or abstract line that does not give shape to form and does not function as a contour can produce the most aesthetic pleasure because of the way it sets the eye in motion. Similarly, Worringer argues that the Gothic line that moves in and out of figurative and abstract articulations also has a fascinating vitalistic power. In *Abstraction and Empathy* and in his following book, *Form in Gothic*, Worringer argues that two fundamental aesthetic desires drive the formation of visual art through its history: abstraction and empathy. While for Worringer empathy denotes the ways in which viewers engage with artworks where a phenomenal world is reproduced or projected in a figurative manner, abstraction pulls objects out of space and time in order to purify them from the contingencies of nature, or from what he describes as the arbitrariness, entropy, decay, and imperfections that suffuse everyday life. This is fundamentally a desire for transcendence both from the world and from the body's relation to this space. The pleasure of abstraction in this argument is generated out of witnessing a form break away from the world and become absolute in a sense, so that it is self-contained and self-perpetuating, inorganic and mechanical.[21] Gothic lines have this kind of energy. But they are not pure abstract forms in the way that Worringer sees ancient Egyptian pictographs as being a more exemplary articulation of the desire for abstraction. Instead, the Gothic line contains traces of both empathy and abstraction, so that a vitality remains within this line that is not a hard geometric figure, but one that is labyrinthine and endless, that is jagged, and that stops and starts in interruptions and pulsations that also distinguish it from a smooth, curved line found in classical Greek art. No longer bound to the urge for a figurative representation or for an absolute abstraction, the Gothic line exhibits an independent will to form with its own mechanical laws and values; it has an "expression of its own, which is stronger than our life."[22]

This story of the line's revolt and independence from figuration has been thematized by a number of filmmakers, most notably in Emile Cohl's *Fantasmagorie* (1908) and Robert Breer's *A Man and His Dog Out for Air* (1957). In these films the dialectic between figuration and abstraction through the line is literally animated and cinematically represents Klee's famous formulation of the line's own sense of deliberateness, which "the principle and active line develops freely. It goes out for a walk so to speak, aimlessly, for the sake of a walk."[23] The lines in these films never cease to oscillate, split, intersect, and take new directions, creating a geometry of peregrinations no longer solely in the service of representation. That said, their vectors still coalesce into figures whose own disintegration keeps the oscillation between abstraction and figuration moving and generates a play with expectations and form. Lye's lines in *Free Radicals*, on the other hand, are forceful graphic marks lacking any kind of figuration. These lines are insubstantial, in that they delimit nothing and serve as ends within themselves. Instead, they focus on the elements and processes through which form is generated, something that Klee's line emphasizes. In his lectures and writings, Klee explains that figuration and the projection of objects and form should not be the goal of aesthetic production. Rather, the approach to how form is constructed should be emphasized, revealing "genesis, essence, growth . . . [and] form as movement, action, active form."[24] Lye's scratch lines focus on this kind of action and take on a similarly vitalistic tenor as they dance across the dark space of the filmstrip while never operating as figurative contours. These independent abstractions instead attempt to give expression to incoherent forms of energy, reveling in a figurative void.

That these lines are constructed through Lye's bodily gestures emphasizes this point. Rather than signifying some form of unconscious subjectivity, these gestural lines articulate a play with indeterminacy and structure through the at times controlled and other times chaotic assemblage of marks. Yet the body was not the only source of energy that could generate a force upon materials. Lye locates this same power in many places throughout the natural world, describing how the abstractions seen in the cracks of rocks or in the cross sections of trees also bear witness to this force of energy in nature. His drawings and studies for his scratch animations were analyses of moving shapes affected by

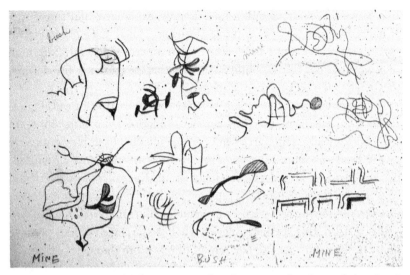

FIGURE 10.2 Len Lye's *Abstractions and Rock Paintings ('Bush-Mine')* (1933), ink on paper, 113 × 178mm. Courtesy of the Len Lye Foundation Collection, Govett-Brewster Art Gallery.

this energy manifested in the natural world, such as flames, waves, or flapping pieces of cloth. But he only worked from these transcriptions to generate ideas of how this force manifests and how motion operates, attempting to project abstractions of movement rather than the contours of specific forms in motion (see figure 10.2). As Vivian Sobchack argues, the energy of the animated line as it moves across the screen is doubled.[25] And while Sobchack's argument applies to several types of animation, this doubled expression of force is put on dramatic display in Lye's films, exponentially increasing an aesthetic pleasure of movement that once stemmed from his abstract transcriptions and now appears to be immanent to the projected lines, a spectacular autopoiesis.

That this energy can exist independently from the original source of movement, and even from the hand of the artist, is important since Lye believes that this energy can reside outside the body as a rhythm of vibration.[26] Thus, in addition to producing kinesthetic responses in spectators, *Free Radicals* and *Particles in Space* aim to render visible the sources of sensation that suffuse all matter, the literal free radicals and particles in space usually invisible to the eye. This goal became particularly important for Lye in his later work, when he was simultaneously producing his scratch films and the kinetic sculptures that he began working on in the late 1950s and into the 1960s. In his article "The Art

That Moves" he addresses this issue directly, explaining that the energy of his sculptures, such as *Rotating Harmonic* (1959) or *Fountain* (1963–76), operates and exists independently of a perceiving body.[27] Though such works house the possibility of a kinesthetic experience for viewers, they have taken on their own, independent life.

At a moment in modernism when a reexamination of ontological claims about media pressed into aesthetic practice, Lye's films that seem to technologically strip the cinema down to its most basic elements were paradoxically an attempt to open the medium up and reveal potentialities skipped over by others. Lye's focus on the force of energy that could be conveyed through film by scratching out kinetic movement in its surface was not for the sole purpose of reducing film's materiality to its zero point. Instead, this aesthetic reveals what can be done without photography in film and that the medium of film is more than a projection of moving images of the world. Though there is a play with the material of film in Lye's scratch works, he uses scratches in the black celluloid to generate senses of movement, a vitalistic activity that he argues is the medium he works in.

This is why, after many years of unsuccessfully supporting himself as a filmmaker, he turned to kinetic sculpture, since he could more easily find financial support through museums and galleries and because he believed he was performing the same kind of aesthetic operation. These works, such as *Blade* (1959), *Fountain* (1963–76), *Grass* (1965), and *Flip and Two Twisters* (1977) are composed of polished steel rods and sheets that move through concealed motors or by the force of the wind (figure 10.3). The metallic sounds produced by these sculptures are just as important as their shining visual undulations, generating an audio-visual projection of energy that articulates movement in the same way as *Free Radicals* and *Particles in Space*. *Flip and Two Twisters*, for instance, contains one loop of metal and two other straight pieces on either side of it, all suspended from the ceiling. These are twisted and attached to motors, that, when on, produce a violent thrashing and swishing to accompany the flailing metal arcs made of flexible steel. Once again, the expression of energy through the manipulation of material, by natural or mechanical forces, is the focus of Lye's aesthetic that cuts across traditional definitions of media. The articulation of force through a work becomes the focus instead. It is this state of initial impartiality, where the force behind the generation of the mark is made visible, that Lye attempts to work through in his scratches and that sets apart this aesthetic of negative force applied to black film stock from his earlier colored lines

FIGURE 10.3 Len
Lye's *Fountain III*
(1976). Courtesy of
the Govett-Brewster
Art Gallery.

painted on clear celluloid. Putting these scratches in motion through the
technology of film only increases a sense of their power, as they seem to
take on a living energy of their own, which, once imparted by the hand
of the artist, has become independent and sovereign.

Notes

1. Lye, "Experiment in Colour" (1936), in *Figures of Motion*, 48.
2. Lye was supported by John Grierson at the G P O Film Unit in the mid-1930s and
    was afterward commissioned by corporations, such as Imperial Airways, to gen-
    erate advertisements. This complicated both the production and reception of
    these films, especially since they could not be distributed in the United States
    because of restrictions on advertising films. See Horrocks, *Len Lye*, 170.
3. Curnow, "Lye and Abstract Expressionism."
4. Clark, *Farewell to an Idea*, 331–32.
5. Lye, "Why I Scratch, or How I Got to Particles" (1979), in *Figures of Motion*, 95.
    These scratch films were created and exhibited in the late 1950s and early 1960s
    by Lye, but he afterward stopped making films and dedicated all of his energy
    to kinetic sculpture, claiming that the culture of avant-garde filmmaking and

exhibition was caustic at the time. At the end of his life (he passed in 1980), he revised *Free Radicals* and *Particles in Space*, but he failed to finish the revision of *Tal Farlow*. This was completed after his death by one of his assistants, Steve Jones.

6. Whitehead, *Process and Reality*, 166.
7. Lye and Laura Riding, "Film-making" (1935), in *Figures of Motion*, 40.
8. Jones, *Eyesight Alone*, xxii.
9. Krauss, *A Voyage on the North Sea*.
10. Lye and Laura Riding, "Film-making" (1935), in *Figures of Motion*, 39.
11. Lye, "The Art That Moves" (1964), in *Figures of Motion*, 82.
12. Lye and Laura Riding, "Film-making" (1935), in *Figures of Motion*, 41.
13. Worringer, *Form in Gothic*, 42.
14. Horrocks, *Len Lye*, 266.
15. Lye, "Len Lye Speaks at the Film-Makers' Cinematheque," 50.
16. Lye and Laura Riding, "Film-making" (1935), in *Figures of Motion*, 41.
17. Eisenstein, *Eisenstein on Disney* (1988), 35.
18. Eisenstein, *Eisenstein on Disney* (1988), 54.
19. Hogarth, *The Analysis of Beauty*, 55.
20. Merleau-Ponty, "Eye and Mind," 168.
21. Worringer, *Abstraction and Empathy*.
22. Worringer, *Form in Gothic*, 41.
23. Klee, *Notebooks, Volume 1*, 105.
24. Klee, *Notebooks, Volume 2*, 43.
25. Sobchack, "The Line and the Animorph or 'Travel Is More Than Just A to B.'"
26. Lye, "The Art That Moves" (1964), in *Figures of Motion*, 85.
27. Lye, "The Art That Moves" (1964), in *Figures of Motion*, 85–87.

11 : : Animating Copies: Japanese Graphic Design, the Xerox Machine, and Walter Benjamin

YURIKO FURUHATA

When studying film theory today, one would surely encounter Walter Benjamin's essay "The Work of Art in the Age of Mechanical Reproduction" (1936) at one point or another. This seminal essay on the historical effect and the potential of technological reproduction has arguably become one of the most widely read texts in the canon of film theory, at least in Anglo-American academic circles. Benjamin's work has consistently gained attention from literary and film scholars since the English translation of *Illuminations* (1969), a collection that includes the artwork essay. Since then, this text has become a standard entry in film theory books.[1] A similar upsurge of interest in Benjamin took place in Japan during the 1960s. The artwork essay was translated into Japanese in 1965, three years prior to its English counterpart.[2] A considerable number of Benjamin's work, including fifteen volumes of the collected works, had appeared soon after. Book reviews and short articles on Benjamin appeared in Japanese newspapers as early as 1967.[3] While this situation in Japan seems to parallel that in North America, the initial reception of the artwork essay has taken a slightly different path. The essay first found its most ardent readers and critics among the ranks of graphic designers and artists, a number of whom turned to the medium of animation in the 1960s. Work needs to be done to trace the distinct path the Japanese reception of Benjamin took at its early stage. This investigation in turn offers us a unique opportunity to rethink animation's relation to film theory — in this case that of Benjamin — as well as experimental animation's relation to graphic design.

What were the discursive, aesthetic, and technological conditions that undergirded the initial reception and uptake of Benjamin's artwork essay in Japan (see figure 11.1)? One way to answer this question is to examine the writings by critics, animators, graphic designers, and pho-

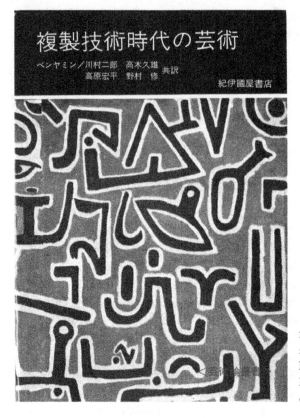

FIGURE 11.1 The 1965 Japanese translation of Walter Benjamin's artwork essay. Cover image.

tographers in the years leading up to and subsequent to the translation of this essay. More specifically, I will explore how the twin issues of reproduction (*fukusei*) and copying (*fukusha*) came to be entangled in Japanese art and media criticism during the mid-1960s and early 1970s. Crucial to note here is that the translation of Benjamin's artwork essay coincided not only with a new current of experimental animation but also with the rise of a new type of publication. In addition to art and film journals, discussions of Benjamin's artwork essay appeared in a most unlikely venue: Fuji Xerox's corporate PR magazine, *Graphication*.[4] *Graphication* offered a unique platform for art and media critics who addressed the issues of technological reproduction and duplication. I thus aim to contextualize the initial reception of Benjamin's work in relation to these various historical factors. In so doing, I tease out a productive tension between technological *play* (or playfulness) and technological *display* found in the experimental animation films of this period.

Experimental Animation

In addition to the publication of the Japanese translation of Benjamin's artwork essay, the year 1965 also saw two other notable events: the legendary *Perusona ten* (Persona Exhibition), which featured works by ten young graphic designers, and the second annual Sōgetsu Animation Festival, curated by three young animators (Kuri Yōji, Yanagihara Ryō-hei, and Manabe Hiroshi) who formed the Animation Group of Three (Animēshon sannin no kai) in 1960. I mention these two exhibitions — one for graphic design and the other for animation — since it was around this time that a new generation of now-famous graphic designers and illustrators, including Yokoo Tadanori, Uno Akira, Tanaami Keiichi, Wada Makoto, and Awazu Kiyoshi, began to push the envelope of graphic art by making forays into animation filmmaking. This crossover between animation and graphic design in the 1960s has received little attention from scholars working on the history of Japanese cinema and animation. However, this crossover reveals an intriguing aspect of this history and sheds light on the specific context within which Benjamin's artwork essay was initially discussed.

One of the key characteristics of this new generation of animators is the strong emphasis that they placed on the formal graphic features of the image, including elaborate typography. Stylized graphics take precedence over the illusion of motion, as films keep the movement within the image to a minimum. Take, for instance, Uno Akira's experimental short, *La fête blanche* (*Shiroi matsuri*) of 1964, which was screened at the first Sōgetsu Animation Festival. The film heavily relies on a series of dissolves to give the impression of movement to otherwise fairly static drawings, accompanied by a score of baroque music. Similarly, Wada Makoto's prize-winning animation, *Murder* (*Satsujin*, 1964), is a film that flaunts the style of limited animation.[5] The film toys with genre expectations associated with crime and mystery films. It repeats the exact same opening scene where a maid discovers a dead body seven times. Each iteration of the murder introduces a different detective figure and is accompanied by variations of the same jazzy tune. The film is a series of animated parodies, including a parody of *Last Year at Marienbad* (1961).[6] In spite of its extremely sparing use of motion, the film holds the attention of the spectator with its ingenious use of sound and seriality. Commenting on Wada's restraint over the expression of movement, the well-known animation critic Mori Takuya argued that *Murder* and other

FIGURE 11.2 A close-up of Yokoo's illustration. Still from Yokoo Tadanori's *Anthology No. 1* (1964).

works presented at the Sōgetsu Animation Festival are "film illustration" or "nonanimated animation."[7]

Yokoo Tadanori's *Anthology No. 1* (1964), which also screened at the first experimental animation festival, equally foregrounds the static, graphic quality of unanimated images. The film is a collage of rephotographed illustrations, most of which are publicity posters and book-cover designs he made (see figure 11.2). Rapid editing, pans, and dissolves are used to animate and give a sense of variation to still illustrations. To borrow a dictum by Marshall McLuhan, whose work was frequently cited by Japanese critics at the time, "the 'content' of any medium is always another medium."[8] Here the content of the animation is literally the print medium. In Yokoo's two other experimental animation films—*KISS, KISS, KISS* (1964) and *Kachi kachi yama meoto no sujimichi* (1965)—the graphic quality of the print medium is similarly brought to the fore. While Yokoo drew new illustrations for *KISS, KISS, KISS*, instead of simply recycling old materials, the film's overt imitation of American comics suggests its continuity with the aesthetics of remediation, which he foregrounds in his other works such as *Anthology No. 1*.[9] As Yokoo's comments on his own animation works indicate, this nesting of one medium within the other medium was intentional: "Each of these mass-produced works that appear on screen are ruins of the former works, robbed of their short life after being exhausted on the commercial front. I am playing the role of a spiritual medium who conjures their spirits from the ghostly past and confers them a new light of life."[10] Arguably, animation allows Yokoo to both preserve otherwise ephemeral works of graphic design and to breathe new life into them, all the while highlighting his investment in repetition as a central component to his artistic process. While not everyone recycled already-printed materials as Yokoo did, many of the experimental animation films presented at the Sōgetsu Animation Festival displayed a similar tendency to downplay the appeal of animated movement and to accentuate the graphic and typographic aspects of print-based illustrations.

This visible affinity between the world of graphic design and that of animation led Mori to conclude that the films screened at the festival are not really animations but "illustrations done on film."[11] Elsewhere he calls these films "graphic animation," a term he coined to describe the intermedial form of graphic design and animation.[12] Kaji Yūsuke, the advertising copywriter of the time, also took note of this new current of experimental animation filmmaking. Kaji, who worked for the leading advertising agency Nihon Design Center along with Yokoo and Uno, welcomed this tendency to blur the boundary between animation and graphic design. Unlike Mori who saw this situation as an unhappy infiltration of cinema by graphic designers, Kaji saw it as a means to transform cinema. He argued that such hybridization expands the horizon of cinema and allows it to be more competitive in light of the arrival of television.[13]

During the 1960s television did become one of the important venues for presenting experimental animation films, as exemplified by the weekly broadcasting of Kuri Yōji's animation shorts on the popular midnight television program *11PM*. While traditional venues of exhibition such as film festivals played a key role in establishing this new current of experimental animation, television also offered an effective means to disseminate it. The growing affinity between the formal qualities of graphic design and experimental animation, which Mori and Kaji acknowledge, had much to do with the proliferation of television as well. The connection between experimental animation and television was also strengthened by the fact that many of the graphic designers who participated in this new current worked within the advertisement industry. This added factor of advertising practice uniquely inflects this new current of experimental animation, which Mori calls graphic animation. Take, for instance, *Commercial War* (1971). This is one of the celebrated experimental animations made by the graphic designer and artist Tanaami. The film is a composite of print illustrations and photomontages, most of which are fragments of magazine ads. Tanaami edits these images with the audio track of Japanese television commercials. It is a work that playfully mimics the sensation of watching television advertisements. Like Wada's *Murder*, the film heavily relies on repetition, a nod to the cyclical temporality of advertisements. In a manner reminiscent of Yokoo's *Anthology No.1*, Tanaami's *Commercial War* also turns advertising ephemera into its enduring content. The fact that this short animation was commissioned by 11PM suggests a deeper connection between graphic animation and advertisement. I will come back to this issue of advertisement shortly. However, before doing so, it is worth investigating how the Japanese discourse of graphic design came to intersect that of animation.

Graphism and Technological Reproduction

How might we understand the relation between the print medium and the filmic medium? One clue is offered by the discursive currency of the term *graphic*. The notion of the graphic gained new connotations in the 1960s. Here I want to point out the novel use of the word *graphic* (or *gurafikku* in Japanese), which was used to signify not only printed illustration but also animation and cinema. The precise semantic parameter of the term *graphic* as used by artists, critics, and filmmakers during this decade is difficult to pin down. Nonetheless, since it was widely used in Japanese art and media criticism during this decade, the meaning of the term deserves scrutiny. According to the art historian Hayashi Michio, we can identify at least two axes of meaning: "One is the graphic in the sense of linear drawing, writing, or illustration (as the Greek *graphikos* and Latin *graphicus* originally implied), and the other is the graphic in its modern (post-Gutenberg) conceptual association with the technology of reproduction, as in words such as photo*graphy* and litho*graphy*."[14] The visible affinity between experimental animation and graphic design that we have observed in films by Yokoo, Uno, Wada, Kuri, and Tanaami hinges on these two axes of the term *graphic*: the manual mode of drawing or writing and the mechanical mode of drawing or writing. While the two are divided by technologies of reproduction (such as the camera), they are clearly complementary.

By calling attention to the act of tracing that binds the manual and mechanical processes of graphic production, Hayashi argues how the second process heightens the possibility of iteration implied by the notion of *trace*: "While graphic linearity provides the very basis for the act of tracing (the appearance of objects in the world or an imagined architectural plan), the act of tracing simultaneously opens up the possibility of *repetitive* tracing and its technological mediation."[15] Paradoxically, then, to trace means to follow a mark or to follow a course, as well as to leave a mark or to chart out a course. The graphic as tracing is both creative and iterative, an original act of marking and a secondary act of copying the mark.

In the essay "Thoughts on Total Design" (*Tōtaru dezain kō*, 1967), the graphic artist and filmmaker Awazu Kiyoshi articulates this duality and inverses an implied hierarchy between the manual and the mechanical. Instead of defining graphic design as an art of drawing or producing a trace, which could then be reproduced through the technical mediation of printing or photographing, Awazu inverts the logic and defines it as first and foremost as the iterative act of reproduction. Noting how the practice of graphic design must realize its promise of total visual communication, he argues that illustrators must not be limited to print and should start using the electric media of television, animation, and the neon sign, because their task as designers is to develop a means of transmitting information most suited to "the age of reproduction."[16] Awazu reiterates this view in a number of published essays, and he proposes to redefine graphic design not simply as a visual mode of communication but as a uniquely visual mode of communication that relies solely on *reproductions without originals*. "The age of technological reproduction is called graphism," writes Awazu.[17] In the essay "The Age When the Reproduction Is the Original" (*Fukusei ga honmono de aru jidai*, 1972), Awazu argues that technologically reproduced images without originals have become our environment, our second nature; the imitation has replaced the real: "In the past, a reproduction [fukusei] was an imitation, copy, or miniature model of the original, but today the reproduction is reality, that is to say, another kind of original in its own right."[18] It is precisely this inversion of the hierarchy between the original and its reproduction—to the point of the disappearance of the original as such—that Awazu describes by using neologism *graphism* (or *gurafizumu* in Japanese).

Awazu's use of the term *graphism* to describe the conditions in which reproductions or copies replace originals is partly inspired by Benjamin, whom Awazu frequently cites in his writings. But Benjamin is not the only source of inspiration. Rather, Awazu seems to have borrowed the phrase from the Japanese translation of Daniel Boorstin's influential book *The Image: Or, What Happened to the American Dream* (1962). Translated one year before Benjamin's artwork essay, Boorstin's text helped shape the Japanese discourses of cinema, animation, and graphic art. It was Boorstin's argument about the inversion of values in which copies generate a greater sense of reality than the original that gained the most popularity. This inversion of values has a precise historical origin: the modern graphic revolution. By the phrase *graphic revolution*, Boorstin means post-Gutenberg inventions of technologies of reproduction and communication, including movable-type printing presses, photography, cinema, radio, and television. Of particular interest to us is the fact that the English phrase *graphic revolution* was translated into Japanese as "revolution in reproduction technologies" (*fukusei gijutsu kakumei*).[19] This literal equation of the graphic with reproduction technologies, I think, helped Awazu to draw a metonymic association between graphic design and Benjamin's analysis of reproducible media. Other critics followed suit and used the term *graphic* to signify a surprisingly wide range of media, from print to animation. This interchangeability of the graphic and technological reproduction, prompted by the translation of Boorstin, explains why Benjamin's artwork essay attracted such attention from graphic designers who experimented with film and television.

A 1968 article published in the leading art journal, *Bijutsu Techō*, is telling in this regard. "Graphic Art in the Age of Electronics" defines graphic art simply as an "art of copy and reproduction."[20] This expanded definition of graphic art as the general art of reproduction nullifies the distinction between graphic and photographic images, and between animation and cinema, with which we are familiar.[21] Regardless of their indexical or manual processes of production, cinema and animation are both graphic in the sense that Japanese critics use the word. In this framework, the categorical distinction between the photographic image and the graphic image, which often separates live-action cinema from animation, disappears. From the perspective of the graphic (rather than the photographic), there is no ontological difference between cinema and animation. Animation is often contrasted to cinema on the basis of "manipulation" and its material process of production.[22] Similarly, the drawn is separated from the photographic. The rise of the digital is generally seen as the moment where these differences between animation and cinema, and the drawn and the photographic, break down.[23] However, the notion of graphic already breaks down the supposed ontological divisions between these practices. And it is because of the terminological slide of the graphic to encompass all arts of reproduction that Benjamin's essay becomes as productive for thinking animation in Japan as it is for thinking film.

In the context of this timely reception of Benjamin and Boorstin, it is worth noting a preceding work on technological reproduction penned by a Japanese critic. This is the literary critic Tada Michitarō's book *Fukusei geijutsuron* (On the art of technological reproduction, 1962).[24] While Tada's work may have had a lesser impact on the Japanese discourse on reproduction, it addresses one of the same issues that Benjamin's essay articulates: the impact of technological reproduction on the perception of art. Tada's title text, which was originally published in essay form in 1958, presents cinema, photography, and electronic music as "reproduction arts [*fukusei geijutsu*] without originals."[25] These modern technological media differ from older media of communication and expression (e.g., painting and theatrical performance) because of their inherent multiplicity and the absence of the original. Because of their penchant toward mass dissemination, artworks made with such technological media radically democratize art criticism, hitherto considered the exclusive domain of the select few: "The masses throughout the whole world can now have the credentials to become an art critic."[26]

Despite the remarkable similarity between his argument and the argument found in Benjamin's artwork essay, Tada was not yet familiar with Benjamin's work when he first wrote his text.[27] But when he revisited the same topic in the 1971 essay, published in the magazine *Graphication*, Benjamin not surprisingly became Tada's main interlocutor.[28] Building on Benjamin's definition of aura as the singularity of "the here and now" as well as an attribute of the sacred experienced as "the unique phenomenon of a distance, however near it may be," Tada discusses how the technological reproducibility of artwork severed its ties to religion. Tada's analysis of art unfortunately lacks the critical force of Benjamin, who warns against the process of aestheticizing politics that satisfies the masses' desire for reproduction without transforming existing class relations.[29] Instead Tada emphasizes the utopian dimension of play as the defining characteristic of art in the age of its technological reproducibility.[30] This element of play is the aesthetic telos of the secularized art. Tada's focus on play as the characteristic element of the secularized and mass-produced artwork is useful insofar as he lists Yokoo as the exemplary artist of this second phase of reproduction arts. Before investigating this question of play further, I would like to reflect on the historical

and political implications of the fact that Tada's revised essay on technological reproduction appeared in *Graphication*, Fuji Xerox's PR magazine.

The Copying Revolution

Launched in 1969, Fuji Xerox's *Graphication* was a highly successful
corporate PR magazine that presented itself as a cutting-edge publication venue for art and media criticism. The very title of the magazine
("graphic" plus "communication," defined as "methods of communicating information through the image, such as letters, signs, painting,
design, photography, comics, film, and television") conveyed its ambi-
tion.[31] This idea of graphic communication in the age of informatiza-
tion allowed Fuji Xerox to market its own product (the photocopy machine) as the latest medium of communication, and gave a new twist to
the already expanded understanding of the graphic. It was within this
historical context that Benjamin's artwork essay received notable attention from Japanese artists and critics in the late 1960s and early 1970s.
For instance, a number of essays dedicated to the issues of reproduction and aura appeared in the beginning of the 1970s. In March 1971
Graphication published a special issue dedicated to the topic of technological reproduction that included Tada's aforementioned essay.[32] Half
a year later, the art journal *Bijutsu Techō* published an issue focusing
on the exact same topic. As indicated by the essay titles, such as "After
Benjamin: Contemporary Tasks of Art and Reproduction," "Aura—The
Traumatic Experience of Art," and "From the Aura of Life: Organization
in the Age of Post-reproduction Technology," most of the essays published in this issue of *Bijutsu Techō* consciously engage with Benjamin.
Similarly, the essays published in *Graphication* make extensive references to Benjamin's artwork essay.[33]

The concurrent publications of these two journals—one from the
leading art journal and the other from the corporate PR magazine—
attest to the heightened interest in Benjamin's work. But more important, they point to the proximity between advertisement and art criticism of the time. Indeed, when *Graphication* published a follow-up issue
in 1974, a number of critics and theorists associated with *Bijutsu Techō*
contributed their articles. While it is not surprising to see Benjamin referenced in art journals, it seems odd to see his name appearing in a corporate PR magazine. One may be tempted to dismiss it as a mere historical oddity. But given Benjamin's refusal to uphold the autonomy of art
(unlike Theodor Adorno) in his artwork essay, and given that advertising

and experimental animation were already in dialogue, it would be a mistake to simply pass over this point.[34] We should take it as an opportunity to reflect on the circulation of theory itself as a mass-produced commodity, and how theory travels outside the narrow confines of academic journals. After all, it is quite suggestive that Benjamin's analysis of technological reproducibility appears in the PR magazine for Xerox, a company that sells photocopy machines. The fact that Benjamin's work was circulated through this nonacademic venue is enough to make us pause and reflect on the implication this may have on our codified assumption about film theory.

One thing to note is that the great divide between commercial and academic publications that we see in North America did not and still does not exist in Japan, where the bulk of critical theories are translated, published, and disseminated through nonacademic journals. The most telling indicator of this unique phenomenon is the introduction of semiotics and poststructuralism in the 1970s and 1980s through commercial publication venues such as the journals *Eureka* and *Gendai Shisō*. Similarly, to date it is companies such as Kashima Corporation, Dentsū, and NTT that have been major publishers of influential media and architecture journals, rather than university presses. Along with Esso's PR magazine *Energy* (which elevated the status of corporate PR magazines from publicity organs to cultural magazines), Fuji Xerox's *Graphication* was one of the earliest corporate PR magazines to publish scholarly articles on art and communication media in a style evocative of commercial journals, such as *Eureka*.[35] When we take note of the initial reception of Benjamin in Japan, this factor cannot be overlooked.

Yet if Fuji Xerox's *Graphication* succeeded in presenting itself as a cultural magazine, it is also because the novelty of the photocopying technology had already attracted the wide attention of artists and critics. Fuji Xerox's investment in art criticism and media theory, and artists' and critics' interests in the photocopying machine went hand in hand. For instance, the May 1970 issue of *Graphication* featured Xerox art pieces created by leading Japanese visual artists such as Takamatsu Jirō and Tanaka Shintarō. The artists were cordially invited to the Tokyo headquarters of Fuji Xerox to freely use its latest photocopy machines to make their artworks. The same year also saw the then-young (and now world-renowned) photographer Araki Nobuyoshi self-publish a unique photo book titled *Xeroxed Photo Albums*. To make this book, Araki used a Fuji Xerox photocopy machine at Dentsū, a major advertising agency for which he was working at the time. Similarly, the July 1972 issue of the film journal *Kikan Firumu* published a series of essays under the title "Sharing of Media and Thoughts on the Copy" (*Media no kyōyū to fukusha no shisō*), along with playful visual works all using the photocopy machine. Most of the articles published in this issue reference Benjamin.[36] This collective fascination with xerography and the persistence of Benjamin as the primary point of reference are significant for three reasons. First, Benjamin's analysis of technological reproducibility of the image was mobilized to discuss this latest medium of reproduction, the photocopy machine.[37] Second, the imbrication of art criticism and advertisement that we find in publications such as *Graphication* also extended to visual practice. Third, artists who responded to the problematic of the "copy" associated with the technology of photocopying were predominantly photographers, graphic designers, and animators.

In this regard, the avant-garde photographer Moriyama Daidō's timely contribution to the debates on technological reproduction warrants our attention. Before Araki's experiment with the Xerox photocopy machine, Moriyama had already declared that the camera was itself a mere copy machine (*fukushaki*). As exemplified by the series Accident (1968), in which Moriyama simply rephotographed then-current journalistic materials (such as press photographs of Robert Kennedy's assassination, crime prevention posters, and screen shots of television news), Moriyama's work toys with the idea of multiple copies. Photography is an art of duplication, and to photograph a photograph is to draw attention to this foundational fact. Echoing Awazu's definition of graphic design as communication based on reproductions without originals, Moriyama dispenses with the notion of the original. Instead of claiming authorship of the image, he thus signs "copy & composition by Moriyama Daidō." The word *copy* (*fukusha*) used here highlights the graphic process of remediation, of tracing a mark left by a prior moment of tracing.

Moriyama's conceptual framework for the Accident series is clearly indebted to Andy Warhol's Death and Disaster series from 1962 to 1963. For this reason, Moriyama's play with the notion of copy appears to be derivative of Warhol.[38] Moriyama's fascination with sensational subject matters, such as high-profile crimes, spectacular accidents, and celebrity gossip, would support this reading. However, if we simply write Moriyama off as a mere copy of Warhol (though this gesture of mimicry is interesting in its own right), we may miss the specific context within which he positioned his photographic work. One of the key elements of this context is Fuji Xerox's ad campaign, which helped popularize the very notion of the copy. The word *fukusha* (copy) gained currency in the media soon after Fuji Xerox launched its inaugural marketing campaign for the Xerox 914 Copier in 1962. This was the year when a joint-venture business agreement between the American company Xerox Corporation and the Japanese photography firm Fuji Film was signed. This agreement marked the beginning of Fuji Xerox. In its first marketing campaign promoting the Xerox 914 Copier, the company used the catchy slogan "The copying revolution starts today" (*Kyō kara fukusha kakumei ga hajimaru*). With this slogan the company aggressively promoted its product through an innovative leasing system wherein business and government offices would rent the machine and receive maintenance service (see figure 11.3).

Moriyama's tongue-in-cheek reference to the notion of copy, and his positioning of himself as copier or duplicator of the images, gains added significance if we consider this historical factor of the Fuji Xerox's campaign. The calculated publication of *Graphication* was part of an advertising strategy that had begun with the idea of a "copying revolution." In addition to the influence of Warhol, Moriyama's definition of the camera as a copying machine must be interpreted in relation to this specific local context. Incidentally, the influential photographer and critic Nakahira Takuma argued that Moriyama's photography intuitively responds to the decline of aura in the age of technological reproduction.[39] Published in 1968, on the cusp of what might be called the Benjamin boom, Nakahira's attempt to analyze Moriyama's work through the lens of Benjamin's artwork essay suggests how the parallel discourses on *reproduction* (within art criticism) and *copy* (within marketing) came to converge around the impact of this technology of photocopying.[40]

We thus find a surprisingly close connection between the marketing discourse and art criticism of the 1960s. This connection is historically specific, and the rise of graphic animation and the Japanese reception of Benjamin in its initial stage are deeply implicated in the connection. To wit, *Graphication* blurred the boundary between advertisement and theory, and graphic animation by designers working for the advertising industry also blurred the boundary between advertisement and art. In contrast to the highly politicized milieu of avant-garde cinema, which attracted leftist intellectuals and activists, the practice and criticism of experimental animation are more visibly and less antagonistically tied to the advertising industry.[41]

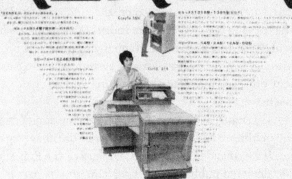

FIGURE 11.3 The first Fuji Xerox advertisement (1962) announces: "The copying revolution starts today."

Technological Play versus Technological Display

I want to push this inquiry one step further by connecting this proximity between art and advertisement to Benjamin's own reflection on two types of technologies. As Miriam Hansen and others have noted, this reference to two technologies only appears in the second version of the artwork essay, which was not translated into Japanese until the 1990s. Nonetheless, this version offers a useful framework through which to understand the centrality of play that appears in the art and advertisement discourses in 1960s Japan. This will also allow us to revisit Tada's claim that the principal characteristic of the "reproduction art" is play. In the concluding passage in the 1971 essay in *Graphication*, Tada cites Yokoo's observation about his own artwork: "At the roots [of my work] is a philosophy of mimicry, which negates the original in order to create the original."[42] This issue of mimicry is precisely what Benjamin addresses in the second version of the artwork essay.

Benjamin aligns what he calls the first technology with the ritual, magical, and auratic works that retain a beautiful semblance as well as their cult value. This first technology is linked to the singularity of the work and to the mastery of nature through the representational process of mimesis. In contrast, the second technology does not aim at mastering nature or preserving the aura. Instead, the second technology relates to the noninstrumental aspect of mimesis, which Benjamin associates with the utopian dimension of play. He writes, "What is lost in the withering of semblance and the decay of the aura in works of art is matched by a huge gain in the scope for play [*Spiel-Raum*]."[43] Works of art that are produced by technologies of reproduction place more emphasis on play than beautiful semblance. The historical transformation of art from the auratic to the reproducible is, for Benjamin, inseparable from the tension between the first and the second technologies.

But what binds the two together? According to Hansen, Benjamin's interest in the mimetic faculty connects semblance to play, and thus the first technology to the second technology.[44] Mimesis for Benjamin concerns, on the one hand, the production of semblance and thus aesthetic representations and, on the other, the repetitive structure and the creative potential of children's play acts. It is this second aspect of mimesis characterized by playful repetition that Hansen links to photography and cinema, forms of "mechanical reproduction as replication that lacks an original."[45] This idea of a replication that lacks an original is what Yokoo associates with his own art of mimicry, which Tada in turn cites as an exemplary case of playful art that basks in the glow of technological reproduction. By extrapolating from Benjamin, I would argue that Yokoo's animations heighten the playful potential of the second technology that is already at work in the medium of cinema, as they recycle original-less graphics and illustrations.

The strategy of reproduction, undertaken by Japanese graphic designers turned animators such as Yokoo reminds us of the critical potential of the second technology, though they are by no means immune to the auratic domain of semblance and the cult value aligned with the first technology. Indeed, a tension between the first and second technologies persists in their animations. This tension manifests itself in the complementary functions of display and play. For these animators' works equally rely on the first technology that generates the beautiful semblance, which Benjamin also links to the function of display and to the "phony spell of the commodity."[46] The phony spell of the commodity is an illusion of aura that lingers after the disappearance of genuine aura. This phony spell of the commodity is the phantasmagoric structure of semblance that Marx associates with commodity fetishism. For Benjamin, an exemplary instance of this return of beautiful semblance through the lure of the commodity is advertisement. In discussing the commercial use of photography for advertising purposes, Benjamin writes: "The creative in photography is its capitulation to fashion. *The world is beautiful*—that is its watchword. In it is unmasked the posture of a photography that can endow any soup can with cosmic significance but cannot grasp a single one of the human connections in which it exists."[47] The glossy veneer of advertisements that don the semblance of the beautiful appearance conceals the material conditions of production rooted in human labor. A photograph that enhances the fetishistic allure of the commodity it advertises forfeits its critical potential as the second technology and reverts back to the realm of magic. Similarly, the experimental animations by graphic designers tread the thin line between critique and publicity, as they appropriate ephemera from the world of advertising into their content. Yokoo's and Tanaami's works are exemplary in this regard. Their works are organized around the playful reproduction and citation of publicity materials, which celebrate the disappearance of the original artwork. At the same time, their works partake in the resurrection of the beautiful-semblance characteristic of advertisement.

In his 1970 essay, titled "Year Zero of Design" (*Dezain o nen*), Awazu references Benjamin's 1935 essay, "Paris, the Capital of the Nineteenth Century," suggesting that the practice of graphic design is phantasmagoric.[48] Graphic design is a practice geared toward the lure of the appearance; it is an art of *display* appropriate for advertising. The historical development of advertising is inseparable from the rise of mass media and from commodity economy.[49] The graphic animation that emerged in the 1960s shares the same phantasmagoric quality with graphic design, and oscillates between two poles of mimesis: illusory semblance (or display) and playful repetition without an original. This ambivalence on display in graphic animation symptomatically visualizes the reception of Benjamin's artwork essay in 1960s Japan. This reception also oscillated between critical engagement and fashionable consumption, as Benjamin's work reached far and wide beyond the narrow confines of academic circles. On the one hand, the artwork essay inspired critics and artists such as Awazu to theorize the relation between technological reproduction and graphic design. On the other hand, the essay also contributed to the promotion of the corporate PR magazines like *Graphication*. In this sense, this profane encounter between graphic animation and Benjamin's artwork essay should caution us against maintaining any illusions about the autonomy of theory. Indeed, as Benjamin warned us, the desire for autonomy—whether it is that of art or theory—must be both distrusted and historicized. The Japanese reception of his text may well be used to dispel and historicize our investment in the autonomy of film theory. Yet as we have seen here, the fascinating encounter between theories of reproduction and the rise of reproduction technologies such as the photocopy machine also provides an indispensable context for understanding experiments in graphic animation in 1960s Japan.

Notes

All translations are mine unless otherwise indicated.

1. Jeffrey Grossman, "The Reception of Walter Benjamin in the Anglo-American Literary Institution," *German Quarterly* 65, nos. 3/4 (Summer 1992): 417. Benjamin's essay "The Work of Art in the Age of Mechanical Reproduction" remains one of the central theoretical texts of cinema and modernity. As Gertrud Koch notes, the text also stands as an important precursor to the apparatus theory. See Koch, "Cosmos in Film." See also Mast and Cohen, *Film Theory and Criticism.*

2. The first Japanese translation of the artwork essay was included in an anthology of Benjamin's essays, which was given the title of this iconic work, *Fukusei gijutsu jidai no geijutsu*. While different versions of this essay have been variously translated into English as "The Work of Art in the Age of Mechanical Reproduction" in *Illuminations* and "The Work of Art in the Age of Its Techno-

logical Reproducibility" in *Selected Writings*, a literal translation of the Japanese title of the essay would be "Art in the Age of Reproduction Technology." See Benjamin, *Illuminations*, 217–51; Benjamin, *Selected Writings, Volume 3*, 101–38; and Benjamin, *Selected Writings, Volume 4*, 251–83. According to the translator Takahara Kōhei, the publication of *Fukusei gijutsu jidai no geijutsu* was prompted by a study group on Benjamin led by the German literary scholar Johannes Ernest Seiffert, who was teaching in Japan at the time. See Tahakara Kōhei, "Kaisetsu," in Benjamin, *Fukusei gijutsu jidai no geijutsu*, 252.

3. One of the first book reviews of Benjamin's work, referencing the German publications of *Illuminationen* (1961) and *Angelus Novus* (1966), appears in "Benyamin chosakushū," *Asahi Shinbun*, January 9, 1967, 5. The same newspaper also introduced Benjamin as one of the most influential thinkers on the current student movement in Germany under the heading "best sellers" in 1968. See "Besuto seraazu: Wakai sedai ni tsuyoi anji," *Asahi Shinbun*, June 28, 1968, 18.

4. Fuji Xerox's *Graphication* belongs to a new type of corporate PR magazine that appeared in the 1960s and that focused on cultural and artistic contents. *Graphication* published graphic works and writings by artists and critics such as Awazu Kiyoshi, Yokoo Tadanori, Kimura Tsunehisa, Nakahira Takuma, Taki Kōji, and Oshima Nagisa. Other notable PR magazines founded around this time include *Energy* by Esso and *Mugendai* by Japan IBM. For more on the history of corporate PR magazines, see Mishima, *Kōhōshi ga kataru kigyōzō*, 25–26.

5. As indicated by the music score, the sixth episode of *Murder* is also a parody of *Astro Boy* (*Tetsuwan Atomu*, 1963), the television animation series known for its use of limited animation style.

6. The seventh episode of *Murder* appears under the title "Murder for Art Theater," a tongue-in-cheek reference to the Art Theater Shinjuku Bunka, where Alain Resnais's *Last Year at Marienbad* was premiered in May 1964, two months before the Sōgetsu Animation Festival.

7. Mori, "Caatōn to gurafikku anime," in Sōgetsu Aato sentaa no kiroku kankō iinkai, ed. *Kagayake 60 nendai*, 338.

8. McLuhan, *Understanding Media*, 8. The Japanese translation of this book, *Ningen kakuchō no genri*, translated by Gotō Kazuhiko and Takagi Susumu (Tokyo: Takeuchi Shoten), appeared in 1967.

9. I wish to thank Ikegami Hiroko for bringing this fact to my attention.

10. See Yokoo, "*Anthology No. 1, KISS, KISS, KISS*," in Sōgetsu Aato sentaa no kiroku kankō iinkai, ed. *Kagayake 60 nendai*, 336.

11. Mori, "Sōgetsu anime fesutibaru o mite," 45–47.

12. Mori, *Animēshon nyūmon*, 23.

13. Kaji, "Dezainaa no eiga ni kitai suru," in Sōgetsu Aato sentaa no kiroku kankō iinkai, ed. *Kagayake 60 nendai*, 339.

14. Hayashi, "Tracing the Graphic in Postwar Japanese Art," in Chong, *Tokyo 1955–1970*, 95.

15. Hayashi, "Tracing the Graphic in Postwar Japanese Art," in Chong, *Tokyo 1955–1970*, 95.

16. Awazu, "Hōhō to hyōgen ni tsuite: Tōtaru dezain kō," 81. See also Awazu, *Dezain ni nani ga dekiruka.*

17. Awazu writes, "In the past reproduction meant an imitation, copy, or miniature model of the original, but today reproduction is the reality and has replaced the original." Awazu, "Fukusei ga honmono de aru jidai," in Awazu, *Dezain Yakō*, 124.

18. Awazu, "Fukusei ga honmono de aru jidai," in Awazu, *Dezain Yakō*, 124.

19. See Boorstin, *Gen'ei no jidai*, 96.

20. See Hinata, "Gurafikku aato," 106–7.

21. Imamura Taihei's earlier analysis of animation and documentary film relies on this distinction. See Imamura, *Manga eigaron.*

22. Andrew, *What Cinema Is!*, 42.

23. Manovich, *The Language of New Media*, 295.

24. I would like to thank Matsui Shigeru for pointing out the importance of Tada's work.

25. Tada writes, for instance: "Is there any original version of *Potemkin?* No, there is none. The film archived in Leningrad and the one imported to Japan both are equally reproductions." Tada, *Fukusei geijutsuron*, 3.

26. Tada, *Fukusei geijutsuron*, 37.

27. Tada, "Fukusei geijutsu to wa nani ka," 114. Tada also notes that the term *reproduction art* was first used by Hasegawa Nyozekan, a journalist and film critic, who wanted to differentiate the work of modern media such as radio from what he called "original art" (*genkei geijutsu*) in 1938.

28. Benjamin, "The Work of Art in the Age of Its Technological Reproducibility: Third Version," in *Selected Writings, Volume 4*, 257.

29. Benjamin, "The Work of Art in the Age of Its Technological Reproducibility: Third Version," in *Selected Writings, Volume 4*, 269.

30. Tada, "Fukusei geijutsu to wa nani ka," 139.

31. Kamiyama, "1970 nendai shotō no Nihon no zerogurafii aato," 21.

32. The essays collected in this volume approached the history of reproduction from antiquity to the present.

33. Contributors included Hariu Ichirō, Tone Yasunao, Kimura Tsunehisa, Yokoo Tadanori, Akasegawa Genpei, and Araki Nobuyoshi.

34. Adorno criticizes Benjamin for assigning "a counter-revolutionary function" to the "autonomous work of art." See Adorno and Benjamin, *The Complete Correspondence, 1928–1940*, 128.

35. Founded in 1959 by the oil company Esso, *Energy* consciously adopted a glossy cover most frequently associated with art journals. Like *Graphication*, *Energy* also published essays by leading scholars and well-known novelists such as Tada Michitarō, Umesao Tadao, and Komatsu Sakyō. See Mishima, *Kōhōshi ga kataru kigyōzō*, 92; Shiozawa, *Sengo shuppanshi: shōwa no zasshi, sakka, henshū-sha*, 104–5.

36. See *Kikan Firumu* 12 (July 1972).

37. In this regard, the Japanese translation of Hans Magnus Enzensberger's text "Constituents of a Theory of the Media" in 1971 cannot be overlooked, given

Enzensberger's extensive use of Benjamin and his discussion of the democratic and political potential of the photocopier.

38. For a comparison between Warhol and Moriyama, see Kai, "'Akushidento' no shōgeki nao," 176.

39. Nakahira and Moriyama, "Shashin to iu kotoba o nakuse," 102–7.

40. When discussing the issue of the copy and reproduction in 1960s Japan, the first and most obvious reference would be the *Model 1000-Yen Note* art project (1962) by Akasegawa Genpei, who hand-reproduced the 1,000 yen note and was charged with counterfeiting. Akasegawa's positioning of his artwork as a "model" (*mokei*), rather than reproduction or copy, adds another context to this history of reproduction art. On the work of Akasegawa, see Marotti, "Simulacra and Subversion in the Everyday"; and Tomii, "State v. (Anti-) Art."

41. Given the history of animation in Japan, however, this proximity is perhaps not surprising. As the recent studies by Thomas LaMarre and Marc Steinberg suggest, animation had historically played a key role in the development of state propaganda and the advertising industries, from animation's use in wartime to its use in postwar television commercials. The specificity of the experimental animation that flourished in the 1960s cannot be seen as a radical break from the mainstream practice of animation, but is rather its experimental counterpart. See LaMarre, "Speciesism, Part I"; and Steinberg, *Anime's Media Mix*.

42. Tada, "Fukusei geijutsu to wa nani ka," 143. My translation.

43. Benjamin, "The Work of Art in the Age of Its Technological Reproducibility," in *Selected Writings, Volume 3*, 127.

44. Hansen, *Cinema and Experience*, 184.

45. Hansen, *Cinema and Experience*, 195.

46. Benjamin, "The Work of Art in the Age of Mechanical Reproduction," in *Illuminations*, 231.

47. Benjamin, "Little History of Photography," in *Selected Writings, Volume 2*, 526.

48. Awazu, "Dezain o nen," 17. Awazu was also one of the founding members of the architectural group Metabolism as well as a principal organizer of the intermedia event "Nanika ittekure, ima sagasu: EXPOSE · 1968" and a contributor of the gigantic multiscreen projection work at Expo 70.

49. Benjamin writes: "The commodity economy reinforces the phantasmagoria of sameness, which, as an attribute of intoxication, at the same time proves a central figure of semblance." See Benjamin, "Exchange with Adorno on 'The Flaneur,'" in *Selected Writings, Volume 4*, 208.

12 : : Framing the Postmodern: The Rhetoric of Animated Form in Experimental Identity-Politics Documentary Video in the 1980s and 1990s

TESS TAKAHASHI

There are two counterintuitive aesthetic paradigms: animation and the 1980s and 1990s experimental identity-politics documentary video. By experimental identity-politics documentary, I mean the kind of work sometimes called personal documentary, domestic ethnography, or autoethnography.[1] In this work, the often-minority filmmaker's personal experience, personal memory, and personal media (in the form of family photo albums and home movies) were used to present the self in a purposefully different way. These works, frequently made on video, were self-consciously different from both mass-media representations of Otherness and from ethnographic representations, on which the works often drew and critiqued. While some of these works showcased naive voicings of identity, more often various kinds of formal fracturing complicated the autoethnographic voice, as in work by artists such as Sadie Benning, Joan Braderman, Tony Cokes, Marlon Fuentes, Mona Hatoum, Isaac Julian, Trinh T. Minh-ha, Marlon Riggs, and Rea Tajiri. Reconsideration of the experimental identity-politics video through the lens of animation offers an important counterdiscourse to standard thinking about this now sometimes-disparaged genre of film. Understanding the role of animation in this work complicates the ways in which we understand how the two dominant discourses of this decade came together in the regularly forgotten medium of video: namely, postmodern theory and identity politics.

While documentary film scholars have not talked much about animation in documentary films of the 1980s and early 1990s, many of the present anxieties about digital animation's supposed destabilization of the relationship between sign and referent in documentary are very similar to, or follow from, those anxieties raised by the proliferation of postmodern theory in the academy. At that time, theories of postmodernity were perceived as threatening established documentary guarantees by flattening not only structures of signification but also the grand narratives that held them in place. By documentary guarantee, I mean the ways in which documentaries establish their truth claims. Video technology was seen as operating hand in hand with postmodern aesthetics. Many theorists figured video technology and video aesthetics, like those of television, as slippery, malleable, flowing, and capable of flattening our sense of history.[2] Indeed, in some video work, MTV music-video aesthetics seemed to privilege a jumble of ideas via the use of found footage, animation, live action, and video keying. In the experimental identity-politics video, these forms of video special-effects animation can be seen not only as a symptom of postmodernity but as an antidote to it.

The video special effects of the 1980s and early 1990s, although not usually thought of as animation, operated rhetorically much as digital animation does today. Techniques such as video keying, the palimpsestic layering of images, the insertion or scrolling of video and computer-generated text, the use of the frame within a frame, and the manipulation of image speed through slow motion, stuttering, and looping gave documentary and experimental filmmakers alike a way of figuratively, visually, and rhetorically opening up critical space in a flattened postmodern world. These techniques of animating the image, of manipulating the image at the level of the frame, also allowed artists to open up a space of playful and transformative personal and political imagining. Animation allowed them to deessentialize notions of race, class, gender, sexuality, and nationality—and imagine other ways of being. Artists' aesthetic use of video animation tools actively theorized and historicized questions of subjectivity. In this way, artists' use of animation contributed to larger theoretical conversations on the impact of postmodern theory on subjectivity. These artists did not just represent their subjectivities but additionally enacted them through various forms of video animation. Looking at the experimental identity-politics documentary video through the lens of animation and defining forms of animation more precisely as rhetorical structures allow these practices to become visible as theoretical interventions into the critical discourse of the day. This approach encourages us to think about how aesthetics reflects and also shapes shifting epistemological discourses in the larger culture. In other words, experimental identity-politics video illuminates the way that animation both was shaped by and shapes the ways we know the world and understand ourselves.[3]

Hybrid Animation

Looking at video special effects as animation allows us to draw connections between questions about documentary in the 1980s and current concerns about animation in documentary today. With the rise of digital animation in the past decade, some documentary theorists have defined animation as a problem for documentary because documentary seems to require the indexical image to point to reality. Here I want to define animation as not limited to a problem for documentary certainty but as comprising a range of devices that work to enact specific *rhetorical* strategies within documentary. As such we can talk more specifically about particular tropes and techniques rather than talking about animation in general.

These video animation techniques function very similarly to digital animation techniques used in documentary and across moving-image culture today, where animated lines, frames, color, and moving text are embedded within live images. Lev Manovich describes these as hybrid forms of animation, forms that we have come to encounter most regularly in "commercials, music videos, motion graphics, television graphics, and other types of short non-narrative films and moving image sequences."[4] Contemporary image culture features digital composites, composed of registers of analog and digitally animated images. Hybrid images, as Manovich notes, have proliferated in the wake of cheap and accessible animation programs such as AfterEffects and Photoshop, which became widely available in the mid-1990s. Hybrid forms of the animated image, in which editing occurs *within* the image rather than *between* images, are today ubiquitous and unremarkable. We assume that most images we see are digitally animated, whether obviously so or not. Whether or not such images present themselves as seamless or foreground their hybrid status, today editing and animation within the image are taken for granted. Hybrid forms of animation challenge indexicality and also integrate different registers and forms of the image, palimpsestically layering various forms of representation, such as video, television, photographs, and 16mm and 8mm film footage.

We should remember that before AfterEffects and Photoshop, the 1980s and early 1990s witnessed an explosion of editing within the frame. As with today's digital animation, video animation was partly automatic and partly undertaken through personal manipulation of video editing tools. While clunkier than current digital editing tools, analog video editing systems allowed editors to manipulate and generate various kinds of hybrid animated images. Artists' experiments with documentary form in this period often incorporated complex integrations of images and sound. Like the image track, the soundtracks of the experimental identity-politics video documentary were often composed of multiple tracks, including found music, sound, other recordings, and voices in the forms of monologue, poetry, and interview. Rather than presenting a seamless image, these experimental identity-politics videos often seem to foreground their status as composited. At least it seems this way in hindsight compared to the relative seamlessness of current digital media.

The use of these kinds of animated special effects was not limited to experimental documentaries edited on video. In the same period, similar animated special effects were widely produced on celluloid film with optical printers. These techniques and the larger theoretical questions they addressed were not technologically determined. The optical printer, sometimes called a step printer, which invokes the step-by-step nature of the printing process, allowed filmmakers to produce complicated image effects one frame at a time on celluloid film, in a process more akin to what we think of as traditional sequentially produced animation. This can be seen in experimental work by Peggy Ahwesh, Betsy Bromberg, Bruce Elder, Nina Fonoroff, Su Friedrich, Malcolm LeGrice, David Rimmer, and Barbara Sternberg. The proliferation of experimental animation techniques across video and celluloid production in this period shows that something larger was happening throughout the culture than in just this small niche of experimental identity-politics video. It also helps to connect the aesthetics and concerns of the experimental identity-politics video to many experimental works made on film that also examined questions of personal experience and voice.

Just as hybrid digitally animated images incorporate various registers of appropriated images, the 1980s and early 1990s saw a strong turn to the incorporation of found footage from both mass media and more obscure sources. Television and video found footage were relatively easy to get and use, with improved accessibility to home-video recorders. Universities, media centers, and community groups, often organized around race, gender, or medium, provided access to cameras and editing systems. Found footage appeared in experimental and documentary work alike, whether made on film, video, photographs, or combinations thereof. Animated special effects were imbricated with artists' use of found footage. Some hybrid animated special effects in both film and video included the use of the frame within a frame (for both found footage and original footage); the manipulation of the speed of the image via slow motion, as well as the looping and stuttering of the image; and the editing, movement, and palimpsestic layering of image and text within the frame.[5] These special effects for animated video, often used in combination, gave documentary and experimental filmmakers a way of figuratively, visually, and rhetorically doing three important things: comment on postmodern flattening, open up critical space, and create spaces of playful and transformative personal and political imagining.

Documentary Theory and the Problem of Postmodern Collapse

The formal and rhetorical uses of animated special effects were significant within documentary production in the 1980s and 1990s, yet these uses were not often remarked upon by documentary theorists and critics. With the rise of postmodern theory, investment in the guarantees of observational documentary, once endorsed by direct indexical recording and the project of authoritative truth telling, met with considerable challenges. Postmodernism produced a crisis within documentary theory dominated by "discourses of sobriety" that were "devoted to certitude."[6] This crisis occurred partly in response to postmodern theory's description of a number of supposed collapses. These include the collapse of grand narratives, the collapse of history, the collapse of high and low culture, and the collapse of the avant-garde and mass cultures. Perhaps most significant for documentary were the supposed collapses between fact and fiction, between historical reality and the image, and between sign and referent. However, these convergences also generated anxiety over the possibility for generating critical art in the modernist tradition. As Fredric Jameson writes in a most influential, and anxiety-provoking, passage: "Now reference and reality disappear altogether, and even meaning—the signified—is problematized. We are left with that pure and random play of signifiers that we call postmodernism."[7]

Documentary theory showed marked anxiety about the status of documentary and its capacity for political efficacy in the context of this supposed flattening of signification and reference.[8] In particular, many documentary theorists bemoaned the limited possibilities for opening up critical space under the weight of so much historical, ideological, and semiotic flattening. The following quotations from essays written a decade apart by E. Ann Kaplan (in 1983) and Linda Williams (in 1993) demonstrate the durability of this anxiety for documentary theory. Kaplan writes, "The danger of semiology has been the sliding away from the referent that I mentioned earlier. . . . Semiologists run the danger of collapsing levels of things that need to remain distinct if we are to work effectively in the political arena to bring about change."[9] For Kaplan, the collapse of the realms of text and the material world seemed to threaten possibilities for political change. A decade later, Williams writes, "While not all theorists of postmodernity are as disturbed as Jameson by the apparent loss of the referent, . . . many theorists do share a sense that the enlightenment projects of truth and reason are definitively over. . . . We seem to be plunged into a permanent state of the self-reflexive crisis of representation. What was once a 'mirror with a memory' can now only reflect another mirror."[10] Williams describes a widespread contemporary feeling of crisis regarding the status of critical visual representation. The metaphor of reflection that had been so important to theories of critical and political modernism now signaled a collapse of space for critical reflection.

For many theorists of documentary, postmodern theory's troubling of the relationship between sign and referent threatened the status of documentary representation as a political vehicle with potentially material effects in the world. The collapses associated with postmodernity were often figured through the ways in which the increasingly dominant media of television and video presented both original and found footage. If celluloid was figured as a modernist medium with the capacity for critical juxtaposition of historically marked images, then television and video were figured as epitomizing postmodern flow and obliterating historical consciousness. Jameson notoriously describes video as the "art form . . . *par excellence*" of postmodernism and late capitalism, "ceaselessly reshuffl[ing] the fragments of preexistent texts," and collapsing the critical and political capacity associated with modernist style through a supposedly indiscriminate incorporation of found footage.[11]

However, postmodern theory was less a threat than a tool for many political artists and documentary practitioners in this period—a group whose forays into documentary tended more toward experimental explorations of political subjectivity than the tradition of modern social documentary. Theories of postmodernity became illuminating tools for groups seeking a certain slipperiness or contingency in order to change their relationships to existing power structures. Postmodern theory met identity politics in this period, in what Linda Hutcheon describes as a most productive meeting, as individuals and groups worked to deconstruct essentialist notions of racial, sexual, and gender identity. "What these various forms of identity politics shared with the postmodern,"

Hutcheon writes, "is a focus on difference and ex-centricity, an inter-est in the hybrid, the heterogeneous, and the local, and an interroga-tive and deconstructing mode of analysis."[12] Linda Nicholson and Steven Seidman also note that "it is among the American left, among neo-and-post-Marxists, feminists, queers, and Third World and postcolonial intellectuals, that postmodernism has been most enthusiastically em-braced."[13] While now sometimes disparaged as simplistic, in that histori-cal period, identity politics, feminism, and postcolonial concerns pro-duced a set of grounding political (and physically material) stakes that butted up against the seemingly relentless textual circularity of post-modern theory. This was nowhere more visible than in the experimental identity-politics documentary video, and made visible by video anima-tion techniques.

Under postmodernity, with its convergence of categories, medium specificity also became an outmoded category of analysis. Video's adapt-ability and ease of use meant that it was often figured as a nonmedium capable of blending into a larger discursive field. Even so, video still re-called Rosalind Krauss's "video narcissism" and the remnant of its early critical figuration as a mirror.[14] The nonmedium of video seemed to offer transparent access to the minority author-subject of the experimental identity-politics video. Indeed, documentary criticism has examined the experimental identity-politics video of the 1980s and early 1990s primarily in terms of authorship and identity with transparent access to even the most multiple and dispersed of subjects provided by the medium of video. In turn, many critics have tended to collapse author-ship, subjectivity, and the video into a transparently accessible autobio-graphical voice. If theories of postmodernity unsettled traditional guar-antees for documentary film theory, then via identity politics the lived experience and authentic voice of the minority subject-artist seemed to ground meaning in physical and emotional experience. In this context, for some theorists of documentary, the experimental identity-politics video appeared to offer the impression of grounded, embodied author-ship, even as these works complicated the status of that authorship and of those bodies.

Still, despite all this animation and manipulation, there remained a strong tendency to see video as a mirror of the self that reflected the author-subject rather than figuring the field of video as a complex dis-cursive space. The place of formally complex films and videos by mi-nority subjects, often taken up within the academy, was often seen as revealing a fractured psyche. Writing in 1988, Judith Williamson notes that "it is particularly striking that the black British work that's been taken up most widely in the world of theory, been most written about and also picked up at festivals, on tours, and so on, is the work that fits most obviously into that category avant-garde." And yet, as Williamson writes, and as I also note, "the formal properties of those films have somehow, in most of the critical discourse surrounding them, been subsumed into their 'blackness.'"[15] Formal inventiveness by women and blacks (not to mention black women) was seen by many critics as articulating a specifically women's—or black—aesthetics. Work by LGBT artists was likewise seen as articulating a specific point of view, where fractured aesthetics were linked to fractured identity. Further, artistic choices in experimental identity-politics work on video, far more than on film, were subsumed into categories of identity and understood as self-expression. Coco Fusco observes: "Since the early '70s, the reigning interpretation of Eurocentric film theory has led to the fetishisation of formal complexity *and* the obsessive search for visual illustrations of psychoanalytic 'truths.'"[16] In other words, academic criticism has tended to equate formal complexity with direct access to the minority subject's complex inner life and complicated subject position. In experimental identity-politics videos of the late 1980s and early 1990s, "formal complexity" and "visual illustrations of psychoanalytic 'truths'" were seen as one and the same.

Rather than simply reflecting a state of being through video, the often-minority author-subject of the experimental identity-politics video used animation to critique the notion of unified subjectivity. Special-effects animation for video was used to visually enact, rather than merely reflect, the disjunctions of that subjectivity under specifically historical conditions. In this period, these animated special-effects techniques emphasized spatial and temporal disjunction as a metaphor for disunified, fragmented subjectivity. It should be noted that the use of sound (spoken monologues, popular music, fragments of voice, sound from movies) operated in similar ways. Rather than merely reproducing the supposed collapse of history and signification under postmodern conditions, artists used video animation to pry open figurative, rhetorical, and critical space. Some of these techniques worked in Marlon Riggs's *Tongues Untied* (1989), Rea Tajiri's *History and Memory* (1991), and Tony Cokes and Donald Trammel's *Fade to Black* (1990).

Frame within a Frame

Perhaps one of the most widely used animation techniques in the 1980s and 1990s was the frame within a frame. In the present day, filled as it is with digital windows and frames, a hybrid image such as the frame within a frame so pervades our daily field of vision that it almost fails to register. Today these frames operate less as framing devices and more as portals or windows into different websites, images, photographs, texts, YouTube videos, and so on, which are layered over one another on our laptops and desktop computers.[17] In the 1980s and 1990s, the frame within a frame functioned very differently. While it sometimes served as a window to memory, it more often functioned as a critical, reflexive gesture that drew attention to the status and ideology of the media image. This media image was figured regularly through the presence of the television raster, which sometimes stood for a certain kind of ideological framing aligned with mass culture, rather than as a window through which to access images and information. The frame within a frame as a formal and rhetorical technique in experimental documentary includes more than just video and optically animated frames around found and originally shot footage and photographs. These frames also appeared as actual material television frames, picture frames, book pages, and mirrors, as can be seen in examples as diverse as the critical cable-access show *Paper Tiger TV*, Leslie Thornton's *Peggy and Fred in Hell*, Laura Mulvey and Peter Wollen's *The Riddle of the Sphinx*, and a number of pieces by Isaac Julien, including *The Passion of Remembrance*, *The Attendant*, and *Looking for Langston*.[18]

In the 1980s and early 1990s, the animated frame within a frame was a privileged formal structure that artists and documentarians widely employed in attempts to, on the one hand, figuratively pry open critical space for the analysis of images and, on the other hand, serve as portals to spaces of memory, play, and fantasy. Criticism and fantasy are of course two important functions of animation in documentary. They also help us to see the two sides of experiments with documentary in this period. The mobility of the animated image is important both in the context of postmodernist challenges to the stability of the human subject and in the possibility for playful transformation.

For example, Riggs's now-canonical *Tongues Untied* makes use of a number of animated special effects in relation to found and originally shot footage. In one instance, Riggs uses the frame within a frame as a space of fantasy to animate a high school photograph in a segment

FIGURE 12.1 Still from Marlon Riggs's *Tongues Untied* (1989). Image courtesy of Signifyin' Works.

that recalls the miracle of friendship offered by "the boy with the gray-green eyes," told in longing voice-over, against the sonorous backdrop of Roberta Flack singing *The First Time Ever I Saw Your Face*. Animated against a black field, the photograph advances, eventually filling the frame and the space of the present before receding, as Riggs narrates his story on the audio track.[19] Here the animated photograph opens not only a space of memory, fantasy, and personal history but also a space of recognition that produces a sense of wholeness for the young Riggs.

This frame-within-a-frame animation segment generates a striking rhythmic and emotional contrast with the narration of childhood experiences that precedes it. Riggs describes that childhood as spent "cornered by identities [he] never wanted to claim": "Punk—homo—faggot—freak—mother-fucking coon—niggas, go home—Uncle Tom." These stereotypical names delivered in clipped fragments come out of anonymous mouths set in partial faces, eyes cut off by the frame, flashing across the screen. These aggressive staccato audio-visual rhythms are hushed by the lush, lyrical wholeness of the song sung by Flack and the wholeness of the face of the boy with gray-green eyes, framed in a high school photo. The boy Riggs loved, who called him a friend, did not only have eyes that Riggs could disappear into. More important, they were capable of seeing him and making an alienated young black gay man feel whole. Riggs says looking into the camera: "In search of self I listened to the beat of my heart, to rhythms muffled beneath layers of delusion, pain, alienation, silence. The beat was my salvation. I let this primal pulse lead me past broken dreams, solitude, fragments of identity to a new place, a home." However, this particular use of the frame within a frame as a space of longing in *Tongues Untied* constitutes a mere moment in a complex tale of often-fractured subjective experience, articulated through a range of formal animation and editing devices. This interplay between a sense of broken, fragmented selfhood and a longed-for, if ideologically suspect, feeling of wholeness is echoed in most of the prominent experimental identity-politics videos of the day.

Slow Motion, Looping, and Stuttering

Slow motion, looping, stuttering, and repetition of both found and originally shot images also were used for multiple purposes in experimental identity-politics documentary. Sometimes slow-motion animation techniques contributed to a sense of lyrical wholeness, while at other times they constituted critical strategies that attempted to break apart the apparently obvious meaning of an image and make it signify differently. Looping and stuttering were used more often in the service of intellectual critique, but also to draw attention to feelings of displacement and alienation. Variations on these animation techniques can be seen in Trinh T. Minh-ha's *Reassemblage* (1983), Joan Braderman's *Joan Does Dynasty* (1986), Riggs's *Tongues Untied* (1989), Rea Tajiri's *History and Memory* (1991), Shashwati Talukdar's *My Life as a Poster* (1996), and many others. In part, the regular use of slow motion, looping, and stuttering of the image as critical devices helps explain why scholars of documentary were outraged during the Rodney King trial in 1992 by the defense's use of slow motion and frame-by-frame analysis to scrutinize the video footage of Los Angeles police officers beating Rodney King. The use of frame-by-frame analysis in deconstructing a grainy home video disregarded the visible evidence of a brutal beating, yes. However, even more disturbingly, the defense used a supposedly critical methodology in the service of the state.

Tajiri's exemplary *History and Memory* (1991) employs slow motion, looping, and stuttering to manipulate found footage from various sources, including army footage, government-produced documentaries, Hollywood movies, home movies, and Tajiri's own original footage, in ways that range from identificatory to poetic to critical. One segment uses the stuttered video image to point to the fragmentation of her mother's memory of past experiences in the Japanese internment camps during the Second World War. These stuttered images also gesture to Tajiri's own sense of incompleteness, "feeling a lot of pain," as she says in voice-over at one point, not knowing how the incomplete stories and fragmented images of that time fit together.

This segment begins with found footage taken from the Hollywood film *Bad Day at Black Rock*, in which the actor Spencer Tracy investigates the death of a Japanese man around the time of the internments. The animated title "wildflowers" is superimposed over a man's hands as he picks flowers. The next image features the stuttered image of Tajiri's mother laughing and leaving the frame, followed by the title "Mother's voice 1989," and scrolling white text over a black field:

She tells the story of what she does not remember
But remembers one thing:
Why she forgot to remember.

This text scrolls over audio of Tajiri's mother talking about the consequences of thinking too much about why the Japanese had been interned, as she recalls the memory of a beautiful young woman who lost her mind from the experience. As the stuttering image emphasizes its missing frames, it points to Tajiri's mother's lost memories, and the beautiful young woman's lost mind.

As the mother voice speaks on the soundtrack, two other forms of animation appear. A young boy's face in negative with an artificial bright pink glow emerges from the blackness. Over his face, the following text scrolls in glowing green letters: "Letter sent to selected members of the Japanese community post-Pearl Harbor: 'Certain Japanese persons are being considered for repatriation to Japan. You and those members of your family listed above are being so considered.'" The sequence evokes the feeling that things are not as they should have been. Black seemed white. White seemed black. The animated video's keying of an unnatural pink pervades the negative image of an innocent child who could not understand what was happening. The historical "reasons" for the Japanese interment in glowing green scroll deliberately over the image. They make no sense, but they continue their relentless animated pace.

The end of this segment returns to a clip from *Bad Day at Black Rock*. Pulling a few wildflowers out of his pocket, Tracy says: "There's something buried up there — wild flowers? That means a grave. I suppose you knew that." Following this bit of footage is a slow, stuttering image of a plant identified by the title "Wildflowers in Mother's Yard 1989," implying that something lies buried there in Tajiri's mother's memory (see figure 12.2). The stuttering image points to the lost, discontinuous spaces of not only memory but self. For Tajiri, the loss of memory implies a fragmented sense of self, one that haunts her too. Later in *History and Memory*, Tajiri says in voice-over: "I began searching because I

FIGURE 12.2 Still from Rea Tajiri's *History and Memory* (1991). Courtesy of Electronic Arts Intermix (EAI), New York.

felt lost, ungrounded, somewhat like a ghost that floats over terrain, witnessing others living their lives and yet not having one of its own." "Somehow I could identify with the search," she says, "the search for an ever-absent image and the desire to create an image where there are so few." By making a picture, she could connect to the story, Tajiri says: "I could forgive my mother her loss of memory and could make this image for her."

Editing within the Frame

Cokes and Trammel's *Fade to Black*, which appeared in the Whitney Biennial in 1992, employs a range of animated special effects in critical ways. Unlike many of the experimental identity-politics videos of its day, *Fade to Black* is more interested in exploring and evoking a fragmented sense of subjectivity than resolving it in wholeness. For this reason, I believe that *Fade to Black* has received less critical attention than it deserves.[20] *Fade to Black*'s prologue sets up its overall logic, reorganizing meaning and deconstructing subjectivity via a juxtaposition of original and appropriated sound with a sophisticated and layered image track. The image track of the prologue begins with the appropriation of the credit sequence to Alfred Hitchcock's *Vertigo*, in which a spiraling line disappears into actress Kim Novak's eye, set in a box within a larger black field. This box frames specific parts of the original credit sequence, using *Vertigo*'s animations of spirals and overlays of color to imply the themes of vertiginous experience, desire, split subjectivity, and performative identity that *Vertigo*'s narrative explores, and that likewise constitute some of the major themes explored in *Fade to Black*. Here the frame within a frame serves as a citation, zeroing in on portions of *Vertigo*'s image that Cokes and Trammel wish to isolate and emphasize. This procedure foreshadows a recurring sequence on *Fade to Black*'s image

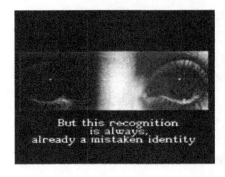

FIGURE 12.3 Still from Tony Cokes and Donald Trammel's *Fade to Black* (1990). Courtesy of Electronic Arts Intermix (EAI), New York.

track, which features a historical accounting of iconic Hollywood films, some represented through framed visual excerpts, and others represented only by text stating their titles and years of release; this offers an idiosyncratic history of race, representation, and uneasy identification across a century of image production.

Below the box that cites images from *Vertigo*, glowing animated text emerges from and fades into a black field. "In this darkened room," the text begins, "there is nothing for me to see. The plot in this darkness revolves around recognition—But this recognition is always, already a mistaken identity" (see figure 12.3). The text continues, asking questions about the writer's subjectivity and desire in relation to the film, saying: "I find my fragmented self posing questions I should have asked," for example, "what does this film have to do with me?" in this text where "no one looks like me." This animated writing seems to offer a distinct point of view, a clear voice, which the viewer might associate with *Fade to Black*'s authors. However, the work's dual authorship complicates the ascription of a clear subject position to the voice behind that text, or to any singular experience of being a black man in North America.

The sounds and voices that accompany the image track also ask questions about subjectivity, wholeness, and identification, both on the level of the human subject and on the level of the text. Like the image track, the soundtrack foregrounds the excerption and appropriation of found texts, very similar to the snippets of rap music that weave in and out. The audio track of the prologue begins with an excerpt from Public Enemy's *It Takes a Nation of Millions to Hold Us Back*, followed by an appropriated clip of a man's voice talking about the function of rap as a form. "As an art form," the voice intones, rap allows "the youth of our culture be able to pick up the bits and pieces of life as it is lived and transform mess into a message." Like its image track, *Fade to Black*'s audio track takes up bits and pieces in order to form a new whole, as rap does, even as the sampled parts remain distinct. In this sequence the sound of a tape rewinding punctuates the spoken text's ability to be excerpted. A man's voice reads from Louis Althusser's "Ideology and Ideological State Apparatuses" on the way that ideology works to transform individuals into subjects: "It transforms them all, by that very precise operation that I have called interpolation, or hailing, and which can be imagined along the lines of the most commonplace everyday police or other hailing, 'hey, you there!'" The verbal citation of Althusser on the hailing of the subject continues through *Fade to Black*'s prologue, which points to the way that differently raced subjects respond to the call. Likewise, *Fade to Black*'s use of animation continually points to the slippage between the hailing call and the subject's sense of self.

The prologue ends with the title "Fade to Black," followed by more computer-generated texts giving credits, but also citing the texts used—audio, music, voices, sounds. In this way the prologue points to the fragmented amalgamation of sources, including David Byrne and Brian Eno, Last Poets, Living Colour, Jesse Jackson, N.W.A., Pet Shop Boys, and Public Enemy, in conjunction with jokes told by the two narrators, personal stories, and quotations from people ranging from Althusser to Malcolm X. *Fade to Black* is elegantly assembled but points to the multiplicity of its sources and the difficulties of resolving them into a seamless whole.

Conclusion

By examining these animated special effects for video within the experimental identity-politics video of the 1980s and early 1990s, we are able to rethink a number of questions that were under discussion at the time. First, this examination allows us to see how the split figuration of video technology as an epistemological tool functioned. On the one hand, video was figured as a mirror, capable of rendering an accurate documentary image of its often-minority subject-author. On the other hand, video via editing and animation also was figured as the opposite of a mirror, a field of playful experimentation that could be used to render that minority subject fragmented, unstable, and critical of the notion of coherent subjectivity. Ironically, this fragmentation of self via editing and animation was often read as mirroring the subject's inner state rather than as a discursive intervention. The video representation of subjective fragmentation was seen as a most authentic mirroring. At the same time, with the category of medium specificity officially dead, the nonmedium of video blended easily into the larger discursive field.

Second, rather than seeing video special effects as a symptom of postmodern collapse, an examination of animation as a rhetorical tool within this work helps us to see artists' use of video animation as making significant theoretical interventions into contemporary discourse. As Trinh has noted, the stories and experiences of people of color tend to be relegated to the realm of the personal rather than the ideological. I suggest that in documentary theory, the experimental identity-politics video has tended to be relegated to the realm of autobiographical rather than the theoretical. Like more traditional editing, editing within the video frame by way of animation enabled artists to make a variety of rhetorical interventions. Special effects such as the frame within a frame, video keying, scrolling text, and the palimpsestic layering of images did not produce mirror reflections of fragmented subjectivity. Rather, artists and filmmakers employed special effects to negotiate the intersecting concerns of postmodern theory and identity politics. Through animation, artists enacted investigations of the personal, historical, and discursive conditions under which subjectivity was constructed.

Finally, interrogating video animation as a form of editing within the frame in experimental identity-politics video helps connect video editing practices in the 1980s and 1990s to present digital animation practices. Within the field of cinema and media studies, video and digital media were figured as similar, often appearing in the same edited collections with little distinction between them until the mid-1990s. Only toward the late 1990s, with the increased presence of the web and questions of interactivity, did documentary scholars start to distinguish video and digital media from one another. Part of what this examination of experimental video animation techniques shows is how animation has long operated as a form of editing. Such an insight asks that we reconsider the status of not only animation in this period but also editing. This insight makes us think about the shift from editing between frames to editing within the frame as a kind of critical intervention rather than simply a collapse of images upon one another. In some ways, the overwhelming nature of these visual and aural aesthetic practices was associated with the collapses of postmodernity. However, video animation in the 1980s and 1990s also points to shifting forms of critical intervention within documentary practice in a period when political modernism found itself in crisis.

Notes

1. For "domestic ethnography," see Renov, *The Subject of Documentary*, 218. For "autoethnography," see Nichols, *Blurred Boundaries*, 65.
2. For "flow," see Williams, *Television*, 78.
3. Artists and filmmakers, many of whom were familiar with theoretical discourses on postmodernity, as well as the discourse of race, gender, and sexuality that pervaded the academy, also examined the relationship between documentary guarantees and authorial subjectivity.
4. Manovich, "After Effects, or the Velvet Revolution," 7.
5. Other animated video special effects include the movement of photographs within the frame (or into and across photographs) and video keying (which inserted color and image in irregular ways into the frame).
6. Nichols, *Representing Reality*, 4; and Renov, *The Subject of Documentary*, 136.
7. Jameson, *Postmodernism*, 96.
8. In the 1980s through the 1990s, numerous theorists of documentary, including Bill Nichols, Michael Renov, Jay Ruby, Paul Arthur, Seth Feldman, Phil Rosen, Trinh T. Minh-ha, Linda Williams, Brian Winston, Katie Russell, and Laura Marks, investigated a range of challenges posed by theories of postmodernity to documentary guarantees. Among the most influential at the time were theories of documentary reflexivity, performativity, and failure as modes of producing new forms of documentary authority.
9. Kaplan, "Theories and Strategies of the Feminist Documentary," 60.
10. Williams, "Mirrors without Memories," 10.
11. Jameson, "Reading without Interpretation," 207, 223.
12. Hutcheon, "Postmodern Afterthoughts," 5.
13. Nicholson and Seidman, "Introduction," *Social Postmodernism*, 1.
14. Krauss, "Video: The Aesthetics of Narcissism."
15. Williamson, "Two Kinds of Otherness," 109, 110.
16. Fusco, "Fantasies of Oppositionality," 90; emphasis added.
17. For a broader discussion of the evolution of frames and windows in media, see Anne Friedberg's book *The Virtual Window from Alberti to Microsoft*.
18. The use of the television raster can be seen in *Paper Tiger TV*, a cable-access television show that was dedicated to the critical analysis of mass media, in particular, but not exclusively, television. Shows often took the form of academic lectures, as in "Brian Winston Reads T.V. News March 16, 1983" (1983), "Joan Does Dynasty" (1986), and "Ads, Ads, Ads! Mark Crispin Miller Journeys thru the Expanding Geography of American Advertising" (1991).
19. More colloquially known as the "Ken Burns effect," the camera's movement into the photographic image, across images, and through images is an example of mainstream usage, as in Ken Burns's miniseries *The Civil War* (1990).
20. For a very different account of *Fade to Black*, see Scott MacDonald's "Desegregating Film History."

IV :: **Animation and the World**

13 :: Cartoon Film Theory: Imamura Taihei on Animation, Documentary, and Photography

THOMAS LAMARRE

As initially developed in the 1930s, Imamura Taihei's theory of animation took American cartoons as a point of departure, especially Disney cartoons such as *Mickey Mouse* and *Silly Symphonies*, but also those of Disney's rival, Fleischer Studios, such as *Popeye the Sailor* and *Color Classics*. This is not particularly surprising: other theorists of film and mass culture such as Sergei Eisenstein, Walter Benjamin, and Theodor Adorno repeatedly turned to Disney cartoons in articulating their reflections.[1] Yet Imamura's film theory is unusual in its equal emphasis on animation and documentary. While his publications tend to treat them separately, animation and documentary were for him two faces of cinema, interrelated and inseparable. Moreover, he did not relegate animation in advance to the realm of fantasy in contrast to the reality of live-action cinema, nor conversely did he see documentary in terms of objectivity in contrast to the subjectivity of fiction. His film theory was ultimately able to work across animation and documentary because it centered on an unusual conceptualization of photography, which led to his distinctive approach to cartoons as a form of realism.

Imamura's reflections used American cartoons not only as a point of departure for theorizing the realism of animation but also as a practical model for improving the quality of Japanese cartoons. Imamura's 1938 essay, "For the Sake of Japanese Cartoon Films" ("Nihon manga eiga no tame ni"), opens with such concerns: "I recently went into a theater for short films, and there was but one cartoon. Surprisingly, it was a Japanese cartoon, *Kaeru no kenpō* [Frog swordplay]. Accustomed to seeing cartoons like *Mickey Mouse* and *Popeye the Sailor*, I found Japanese cartoons impoverished."[2]

Another aspiration of Imamura's cartoon theory, then, was to reform cartoon production in Japan. In this respect, Imamura's theory shows continuity with concerns of prior film criticism for reforming national production, particularly as articulated in the pure film movement that gathered steam from the late 1910s through the 1920s in Japan.[3] Yet Imamura's interest in reforming Japanese cartoons took a turn that seems, at least at first, to be at odds with his interest in realism. For his reflections turned toward how cinema might enable a practical repurposing of traditional Japanese art forms, which he himself does not deem realist. As a consequence, Imamura's work consistently flirts with forms of cultural nationalism or, more precisely, national culturalism in the form of traditionalism. In addition, insofar as Imamura turns to Japanese traditions in an attempt to take Japanese cartoons beyond received oppositions between Japanese tradition and Western modernity, his film theory verges on the modernist conceit commonly referred to as "overcoming modernity."[4]

In sum, Imamura's film theory operated between two modernist tendencies—traditionalism and realism. I propose to look at how Imamura resolved this tension through a conceptualization of photography that allowed him to produce an original variation on apparatus theory. Instead of the familiar emphasis on the monocular lens of the camera and regimes of one-point perspective, Imamura stressed the descriptive, explanatory, and even narrative force of the camera and photography, both in cartoons and documentaries. This emphasis allowed him to mobilize techniques of traditional Japanese arts as potential modes of realism that, because they were no longer standing in opposition to modern cinema, could actively reform or even move beyond it.

I also propose to explore the sociohistorical implications of Imamura's invention of a "transcriptive apparatus" to resolve the tension between traditional arts and realist cinema. As Irie Yoshirō notes, "Imamura's investigations into the essence of cinema began alongside his emerging consciousness of Marxism."[5] When Imamura leapt into film theory in earnest in 1934, contributing to the reader's column of *Kinema Junpō* and founding and contributing to the film magazine *Eiga Shūdan*, a series of mass arrests of communists and others deemed politically suspect (among them Marxists) was leading to the collapse of the Japanese Communist Party and to conversions (*tenkō*) of intellectuals and artists from Marxism to nationalism, among them Imamura. It is thus difficult to gauge the impact of Marxism on Imamura: for instance, where Irie calls attention to the Marxist currents of Imamura's film theory, Ōtsuka Eiji stresses Imamura's renunciation of Marxism.[6] It is consequently possible to see a tension between Marxism and nationalism within Imamura's theory, which is analogous to the tension between realism and traditionalism. Indeed, Imamura's goal of producing distinctively Japanese cartoons and documentaries might be seen as analogous to the formation of cultural nationalism out of cosmopolitanism and Marxism.

I will focus largely on his "For the Sake of Japanese Cartoon Films," for a number of reasons. First, although Imamura is best known for his 1940 book on documentary film, *A Theory of Documentary Film* (*Kiroku eiga ron*), and for the first book-length treatise on animation, *A Theory of Cartoon Film* (*Manga eiga ron*), which was first published in 1941, revised and published again in 1948 and 1965, and recently republished in 2005, "For the Sake of Japanese Cartoon Films" not only anticipates the arguments of the 1941 book but also presents them in a condensed form, making clear the connections between arguments that are sometimes held apart in the book.[7] Second, the 1938 essay addresses a specific moment in the history of animation: the introduction of new techniques for producing a sense of depth in animation, that is, the multiplanar camera system, which received a great deal of popular and critical attention in the context of Disney's *The Old Mill* (1937) and Fleischer's *Popeye the Sailor Meets Ali Baba's Forty Thieves* (1937). Imamura continued to evoke new Disney and American cartoons throughout his career, but there is a sense of historical urgency at this early stage in his career. Arguably, it was the critical buzz surrounding the technical achievements of American cartoons that spurred Imamura to focus attention on the apparatus and realism in animation. Third, this buzz about technical innovations in animation around 1937, in combination with the economic ascendency of American cartoons throughout the world, imparts a sense of urgency to Imamura's reflections on the relation between the technical and the economic, and to his concerns about how to produce cartoons in Japan.

Photography

Imamura opens "For the Sake of Japanese Cartoon Films" with praise for the vitality of movement in Disney cartoons, in contrast to which Japanese cartoons prove deficient, as the example of *Kaeru no kenpō* makes woefully clear to him.[8] As his discussion shifts to the practical matter of how to produce such vitality in cartoons, he takes a rather surprising tack. Imamura associates the vitality of animation with realism of movement, and at the same time he stresses the importance of photography over drawing or painting techniques.[9] He thus writes, adding emphasis to underscore his points: "The realism [*shajitsusei*] of Disney's cartoons—this wellspring of vital force—where does it come from? It comes from that fact that the drawings [*e*] are not just drawings; they are *drawings combined with photography* [*shashin to ketsugō shita e*]. In fact, in the cartoon, *photographic methods prevail over drawings* [*shishin teki na hōhō ga kaiga o shihai shite iru no de aru*]."[10] This may seem an obvious point: the distinctiveness of cartoons lies in movement, and movement takes precedence over techniques of drawing and painting, at once conjoining and governing the images. Yet discussions of the vitality of animation usually privilege the art of the hand over the "technical work" of photography. In Sergei Eisenstein's unfinished manuscript and notes, written in the late 1930s and early 1940s, on Disney cartoons, for instance, he calls attention to what he calls plasmaticness, that is, the plasticity and elasticity of line and figure in animation.[11]

Eisenstein deftly steers his discussion toward the stroke drawing, a drawing in which the line traces a continuous contour in a single stroke, in form rather like an amoeba.[12] Eisenstein highlights how this basic feature of cartoons—the stroke drawing—allows for a continual transformation and deformation of form, without an actual loss of form. At one point he refers to its "poly-formic capabilities." Eisenstein thus calls attention to the elasticity of shapes, the mobility of contours, and the fluidity and diversity of forms, which he frequently links to primordial protoplasm-like vitality, to primitive exuberance and ecstasy, and to animism: "The very idea, if you will, of the animated cartoon is like a direct embodiment of the method of animism."[13]

In contrast, while Imamura is similarly interested in the vitality and movement of animation, his account goes to great lengths to deemphasize the primacy of drawing: "Taken one by one the still drawings are not particularly attractive. A still image of something like Mickey Mouse tends rather to be ugly. How is it that an image crudely drawn in heavy lines without any particular charm, when set in motion, becomes full of life and spirit, and simply put, is no longer a drawing? The secret must lie in movement itself, that which moves the drawings."[14] But also in contrast to Eisenstein's emphasis on animism, animation for Imamura is above all a matter of the realism of movement, and that realism derives from photography and photographic methods—over and above techniques of drawing or painting. But what are these photographic methods?

Imamura calls attention to how photography allows for "parsing action" or "parsing movement." His turn of phrase is *dōsa no bunkai*, which might be translated in a number of different ways, among them

FIGURE 13.1 Still from *The Country Cousin* (1936).

"decomposing motion" or "breaking down movement," for Imamura's usage implies the decomposition and recomposition of the movement of distinct entities—in effect, his emphasis falls on character animation or object animation. Take, for instance, his example of the animation of the drunken mouse in Disney's *The Country Cousin* (1936), which, he claims, "is nothing other than photography of a person in an inebriated state," calling attention to how "each frame of film is rendered in drawings" (see figure 13.1).[15] In other words, although he does not directly refer us to rotoscoping, which was common practice in 1930s American cartoons, Imamura's emphasis on how the animation of the drunken mouse is rendered by drawing the photographed movement of a person frame by frame suggests that he has something like rotoscoping in mind. His subsequent example from Fleischer's *Popeye the Sailor Meets Sinbad the Sailor* (1936) similarly calls attention to the photographic parsing of movement, focusing on the scene in which the roc takes flight in the first reel. As Imamura notes, the roc's extended takeoff resembles that of a Douglas passenger plane (probably the Douglas DC-2, introduced in 1934, or the DC-3, introduced 1936). Indeed, the giant cartoon bird skips and bumps along its runaway, gaining elevation only to fall back to the ground, with the sound of engines buzzing over the music (see figures

13.2–13.4). But then Imamura adds, "The thoroughly realistic movement of its wings is clearly a pictorial rendering based on parsing the flight of a bird with photographic filming [*shashin satsuei*]."[16]

As such examples attest, Imamura's use of the term *shashin*, conventionally translated as "photography," is complex. His use of shashin implies two distinctive orientations. On the one hand, what he calls photography seems to be the same thing as filming, or at least seems practically indistinguishable from it. The term shashin appears in different combinations and contexts in which photography merges with filming, that is, producing film footage. Thus, we find Imamura restating his basic thesis about animation: "If the parsing of action did not proceed instant by instant through photography, the vitality of the mouse, duck, and dog [Mickey, Donald, and Goofy] could not be expressed. The parsing of a continuous chain of vital movement by means of moving photographs [*katsudō shashin*] begins with drawings to bring about movement-time."[17]

I will discuss Imamura's conceptualization of temporality, but I wish first to make two points about this first orientation of *shashin* in Imamura. First, his use of shashin moves easily between kinds of mediatic capture that are frequently held apart today. We often think of photography in terms of instantaneity, stills, and stopped time (snapping photos) in contrast to the continuity, movement, and temporal flow of filming sequences. Yet we do not resolve anything by concluding that shashin in Imamura really refers to filming and not to photography. Similarly, it won't fix matters to assume that he is really thinking of the movie camera rather than the still camera. We should not presume that we know what photography really is or what cinema really is. Rather, we should accept the challenge of the uncertainty of received distinctions afforded in Imamura's use of shashin. Let me begin by considering what is common to cinema and photography that might explain Imamura's conceptualization, if only by way of contrast.

In Japanese, both photographs and films are sometimes included under the rubric *eizō*, a term that is commonly translated as "image," but that refers more specifically to mechanically produced and reproduced images. Imamura occasionally uses this term near the end of "For the Sake of Japanese Cartoon Films." Although Imamura is interested in the scientific and technical aspects of cinema, he tends to separate its photographic methods from the domain of (capitalist) mass production and reproduction. His primary concern then is *not the reproducibility of images* that is often associated with the term eizō.

FIGURES 13.2, 13.3, AND 13.4 Stills from *Popeye the Sailor Meets Sinbad the Sailor* (1936).

In English usage, the term *shooting* refers both to taking photos and filming. This usage directs attention to the importance of capture, with emphasis on targeting and contacting, which is also very different in tone from Imamura's notion of "parsing action." Parsing movement with photographic methods for him is *not a matter of referentiality* in the sense of a one-point, one-moment contact between object and image, spatially or temporally. Nor is there a sense of the object captured, mummified, or frozen. On the contrary, Imamura associates the photographic parsing of movement with the expression of vitality. As such, his understanding of shashin stands in contrast to currents in film theory related to Bazinian realism as Phillip Rosen describes them: "Photographic and filmic images have normally been apprehended as indexical traces, for their spatial field and the objects depicted were in the camera's 'presence' at some point prior to the actual reading of the sign. The indexical trace is a matter of pastness."[18]

There is something similar to the indexical trace at work in Imamura's examples of the animation of the drunken mouse and the flight of the roc, and yet, rather than a matter of pastness, it is a matter of vitality. This makes sense if we consider the procedures of rotoscoping, already in use from the mid-1910s, in which animation was drawn frame by frame from film footage. Donald Crafton describes it as "a new process Max Fleischer called rotoscoping. Motion pictures of various mechanisms were made; then, by projecting the developed footage on frame at a time and tracing it on cels, a film of schematic clarity could be made."[19]

In rotoscoping, the "presence" of the camera is thus doubled. The camera is first present to film the live-action footage and then again to film the drawn images based on the live-action footage. In some currents of cinematic realism, the presence of the camera is often taken as a guarantee of one-point referentiality and thus of a linear relation capable of assuring that a photo, for instance, can be a document and therefore ground a historical relation. Consequently, the realism of animation, evident in rotoscoping, must grapple with multiple presences and cannot make claims for linearity. In this respect, it is telling that Imamura's example of the flight of the roc has two indexes: the Douglas airplane and the flight of a bird. And if, as Imamura suggests, both of them drew on photographic sources, then both entailed two camera "presences" during production. If we think of realism in terms of referentiality, there are already four points of camera presence.

As such, animation presents a profound challenge to theories of cinematic realism, which have tended to treat indexicality as a form of one-point referentiality based on a moment of indexical contact or capture, which is in turn grounded in the sense of photographic instantaneity. Animation automatically doubles and redoubles the index. This is surely one of the reasons why animation has so often been associated with the digital (the multiplication of sources within a single image or the multiplication of images from a single source) in contrast with the analog (one-point or one-moment presence). While the contrast between the digital and analog has often tended to exaggeration and thus to an unworkable opposition,[20] it does concisely point to the challenge of Imamura's theory of animation: its realism is based neither on reproducibility nor on one-point referentiality. What is more, animation does not stand in opposition to documentary, because realism for Imamura is not a matter of guaranteeing the one-point, one-instant presence of the camera.

Nonetheless, Imamura stresses the temporality of photographic methods. It is photography that transforms the spatiality of painting or drawing into the temporality of cartoons. He writes,

> What becomes evident here is that, conceptually, the cartoon [*manga*] is something fundamentally different from painting [*kaiga*]. Of course, individual images are paintings. Yet these paintings in cartoons, taken one by one, do not possess any particular artistic meaning. Painting is essentially a spatial art. However, while the paintings in the cartoon film may be spatial, they first take on artistic consistency on the strict condition of being *temporal paintings*. Accordingly, insofar as the arts of drawing and painting in cartoons are grounded in photographic methods and combined with photography [*shashin to ketsugōshi*], cartoons come into being as a temporal art, wherein lies their specificity.[21]

Once again, Imamura uses the verb *ketsugō suru* (to combine, join, or unite) in a manner that invites us to read the effect of photography in two ways. On the one hand, photography refers to the process of combining drawn images into a sequence that will move when projected. When Imamura insists that cartoons must be based in photographic methods and combined with photography, his account appears consonant with rotoscoping, and with using film photography to decompose motion and then to recompose that motion with drawings. On the other hand, there is some ambiguity in his description of drawings being combined or united with photography, for we have the impression that not only does photography connect one image with another but also the images themselves are becoming somewhat photographic, being combined or suffused with photography itself. Here we reach the limits of translating the term shashin as "photography" and arrive at the second orientation of photography in Imamura's film theory.

As has often been noted, photography in Japan did not give rise to a new term or neologism, as it did in Europe. Rather a term already in usage, shashin, was applied to photography. Photography was thus placed in a specific lineage of artistic practices and discursive frameworks. As Maki Fukuoka writes,

> In writing on the history of photography in Japan, scholars commonly note that the Japanese word *shashin* conveys different meanings than the English word *photography*. While the term *shashin* existed prior to the introduction of photography in Japan, only in the 1870s did it become a stable reference to the technology. Indeed, in the discourse on Japan's photographic history, *shashin* is a cumbersome term that does not yield valuable discussion. And yet *shashin* casts an unmistakable and enduring symbolic shadow on the field and is a distinct part of its history.[22]

Fukuoka goes on to explain that, if the cumbersome term *shashin* has not yielded valuable discussion, it is because commentators have remained content to indicate that, before the advent of photography, shashin signified something akin to "realism," and their investigations have stalled there, with a vague notion of realism. In contrast, to historicize the putative realism of shashin, Fukuoka explores the discourses and practices associated with shashin prior to the introduction of photography, showing how "the concept of *shin* and *shashin* that came to be associated with copper-etching prints, sketches, and ink rubbing underwent multilayered processes of intellectual challenge, confirmation, and authentication. As tensions in textual and pictorial representational systems were resolved, the concepts of *shin* and *shashin* congealed and symbolized ideas of fidelity between depicted subject and print."[23] It was within this epistemological and historical context that shashin came to serve as a stable reference to photographic technology in the 1870s, as in the writings of the translator Yanagawa Shunsan. Fukuoka thus concludes, "Yanagawa's characterization [of photography as shashin] stemmed from his concern for the process and his attention to the space between image and object, the level of fidelity maintained within this space, rather than the impression gathered from the photographs in and of themselves."[24]

While Imamura's concerns differ from Yanagawa's, Imamura's insistence on the realism of photography in the 1930s does inherit something of this sense of shashin that began to hold sway from the 1870s:

shashin as a process of maintaining fidelity between image and object rather than an impression imparted by the photographs themselves. In this respect, even though Imamura insists on a contrast between kaiga (drawing or painting) and manga (cartooning) on the basis of shashin, his use of *photography* or *photographic methods* is not antithetical to painting. Photography might even be characterized as another kind of drawing or painting, as indicated in Imamura's characterization of cartoons as "temporal painting" (*jikan teki na kaiga*). Moreover, Imamura subsequently situates photography in a lineage of materialist depiction that he associates with oil painting.

In sum, there are two orientations implicit in Imamura's use of shashin. Shashin feels closer to filming or cinematography than to photography insofar as it implies a cinematic decomposition and recomposition of movement or action. But shashin implies a practical sense of photography as a process of sustaining and guaranteeing fidelity between image and object. Such fidelity is a matter of indexicality, but this indexicality is not that of a one-point or one-moment contact with an object. Rather, in a manner reminiscent of the prephotographic association of shashin with etching, sketching, and ink rubbing, shashin in Imamura's work implies a sort of multipoint durational capture that is supposed to capture the temporal depth of movement rather than merely combining discrete instants.

Thinking with the Camera

In his 1940 essay, "A Theory of Documentary Cinema," included in his book on documentary film published the same year, *Kiroku eiga ron* (A theory of documentary film), Imamura builds to the provocative statement "the camera is human" to sum up his stance on cinematic documentation.[25] He opens his account by stressing: "To document something is not the same as having it mechanically recorded and unilaterally reflected in human consciousness."[26] This insight encourages Imamura to emphasize that documentation is a form of subjective expression, not objective recording. His theory initially appears intent on downplaying or even dismissing the role of the camera. As a consequence, at least initially, his account appears entirely at odds with apparatus theory. He writes, "The real significance of [the short documentary film] *Workers Leaving the Lumière Factory in Lyon* was not the birth of a new machine. Rather, it was the birth of something new that we do not fully understand—a more social form of human understanding or way of knowing. To document via film means to express only through film, to think things through only via film."[27] In other words, rather than positing the camera as a deterministic apparatus, Imamura finds something akin to a new machinic consciousness deriving from the entanglement of human consciousness with the new machine, the camera.

In his characterization of this new machinic consciousness as more social and collective, we perhaps see echoes of a Marxist sensibility. In his account of documentary, as in his discussion of cartoons, Imamura associates the studio with the factory as a new form of collective endeavor. Yet the Marxist concern that revolutionary transformations in modes of production have not lead to revolutionary transformation in social relations (due to the persistence of older forms of social relations that empower, for instance, the foreman at the expense of workers) does not register in Imamura's account. The idea that Japan in particular was not modernizing or "revolutionizing" due to the persistence of "feudal" social relations was a major concern in Marxist thought at the time. Imamura, however, does not address the persistence of uneven social relations or the exploitation of workers in factories. It is instead the social energies implied in the factory, as new collective social endeavor, that capture Imamura's imagination. In "For the Sake of Japanese Cartoon Films" he submits that the age of solitary artist is vanishing and suggests: "Wouldn't painting of greater social import [mottomo shakai teki na kaiga] be based on the industrial system and be built on the cooperative work of hundreds of artists, like the manufacturing studios for Disney cartoons?"[28] His account seems to assume that this new collective endeavor is inherently leveling or dehierarchizing in its social effects. As such, the potential of cinema and film theory for Imamura lies partly in their capacity to force an awareness of the new social energies implicit in this new machinic consciousness—thinking via the camera, socially.

Already we can detect a potential source of trouble in his approach: because contradiction and conflict are not situated within production or within Japan (they are subsequently situated between Japan and America), this new machinic consciousness will tend to be channeled into national consciousness, into the "people," and the reformation of Japanese modes of expression. Yet such a national populist outcome may not be inherent in or preordained by his approach.[29] It is imperative then to work through the different registers and tendencies of Imamura's film theory, to investigate how the social energies of this machinic consciousness become shunted into national reformation or "conservative revolution" via cinema.

Imamura places so much emphasis on the subjective side of documentation, writing for instance that "every document is an expression of some preexisting thought," that we are at a loss about how to take into consideration the objective side of cinema, not to mention its materiality. The very idea of objectivity is called into question, or at least, the priority of objectivity is. Consequently, there isn't much machine to Imamura's intimations of a machinic consciousness. Not surprisingly perhaps, he ultimately finds Dziga Vertov's efforts to "document the camera's movement" in *A Man with a Movie Camera* to be rather dull. A paradox arises: Imamura clearly thinks that cinema and the movie camera differ from other arts and modes of expression, yet he gives such priority to subjective expression, consciousness, and thought that his film theory is in danger of ruling out any form of materiality, verging on pure idealism. Indeed he is quick to conflate a de facto observation (filmmakers always have some thoughts about what they are filming) with a de jure situation (filmmakers *should* always organize their thoughts in writing before beginning to film).

It is here that Imamura turns to composition, construction, or structure (*kōsei*). This is also where Imamura situates the materiality of cinema in his essay on documentary film, almost by default—kōsei. But what sort of materiality is this kōsei, this composition or construction?

Imamura stresses the importance of writing a script before filming, and in fact, if he finds *Man with a Movie Camera* dull, it is because the film is not clearly structured or solidly composed. Generally speaking, in this context, Imamura sees composition as a process of clarifying and strengthening one's thoughts, and at the end of the essay on documentary film, he proposes the science film as a possible model. Although his examples, comparisons, and general discussion initially introduce a somewhat narrative or dramaturgical perspective, his characterization of composition ultimately steers away from fiction (and verbiage) toward scientific schematization, as if to compensate for the heavy emphasis on the subjective side of things in his critique of objectivity. In sum, a sense of objectivity is sustained, but largely at the level of a scientific mode of composition. Needless to say, such a move runs the risk of replacing or supplementing pure idealism with pure rationalism.

It is here that Imamura's discussion of cartoons proves interesting alongside his documentary film theory. Although his book on documentary and his book on cartoons were published nearly at the same time (1940 and 1941, respectively), the publications hold the two approaches apart. Yet reading between the two accounts provides a way to consider what sort of materiality is at stake in the suggestions for a machinic consciousness in Imamura's documentary theory. For where his account of documentary downplays the camera and lingers on the ordering capacity of (written) composition, his theory of cartoons focuses on the decomposition and recomposition of movement afforded by photographic methods. Reading between the two accounts offers a way to address the fundamental question posed by Imamura: what does it mean to think via the camera?

Accounts of the effect of the movie camera on thought or subjectivity, which are often grouped under the general rubric of "apparatus theory," thus afford some useful points of contrast with Imamura's approach. Jean Baudry, for instance, highlights how the monocular lens of the camera tended to make one-point perspective into the operative convention for the organization of visual space in cinema.[30] Jean-Louis Comolli provides a nice summary of this stance: "The camera is what produces the 'visible' in accordance with the system of 'monocular' perspective governing the representation of space: it is therefore in the area of the camera that we should seek, for the materials of cinema as a whole, the perpetuation of this code of representation and the ideology it sustains or reasserts."[31]

Because of its mechanistic and deterministic tendencies, apparatus theory quickly met with a host of objections. Noël Burch, for instance, took issue with those who "decreed that the optical properties of the photographic lens (and hence the cinematic lens), a monocular technology arising directly from bourgeois ideology, were a kind of 'original sin' of the seventh art, a historical fatality adhering to its very being and that only disruptive practices could free it from."[32] Noël Carroll objects to the mechanistic determinism that "appears to envision each art form on the model of a highly specialized tool with a range of determinate functions. A film, play, poem, or painting is thought of, it seems, analogous to something like a Phillips screwdriver."[33]

If something of apparatus theory has nonetheless persisted in film theory, it is not because of its mechanistic determinism but because of its promise to provide a way to move between material structures and subject formations. For instance, as Martin Jay reminds us in the context of art history, what we think of as Cartesianism is not simply a structurally determined outcome of the use of one-point perspective. It is the combination of one-point perspective with "Cartesian ideas of subjective rationality in philosophy" that served to make Cartesianism appear to be "the dominant, and even totally hegemonic, visual model of the modern era."[34] Similarly, when Laura Mulvey introduces Renaissance perspective into her account of the male gaze, it is part of an effort to ground Lacanian mechanisms of identity formation in the material structures of cinema.[35] Or, when Comolli takes up Baudry's notion of a basic apparatus, he highlights how economic demands and scientific developments conspired to transform the basic apparatus into an "ideological instrument."[36] In other words, one of the functions of apparatus theory has been to provide a sense of a material ground for analyses of subjectivity or ideology in risk of becoming overly rationalist or idealist. This is precisely the role that cartoons play in Imamura's film theory: they promise a material ground for the subjective emphasis of his documentary theory.

Imamura's film theory, which is deliberately, even stubbornly, contrary to expectations that documentary is objective while cartoons are fantastical, stresses subjective expression in the context of documentary, while his cartoon theory lingers on the realism stemming from photographic methods. In this respect, his cartoon theory appears not merely alongside his documentary theory. His cartoon theory affords a way to account for the material side of the machinic consciousness announced in, but eliminated from, the account of documentary film. In keeping with Imamura's reversal of received ideas about cartoons and documentaries, the cartoon serves as the ground not only for documentary but also for cinema. Animation takes the place of the basic apparatus, and it is in cartoons that we will find the objective side or the machine side of what it means to think via the camera.

Significantly, where *A Theory of Documentary Film* opens with a discussion of theatrical spaces and the relation between drama and cinema, *A Theory of Cartoon Film* begins thus:

> Histories of cinema usually begin in 1890 with Thomas Edison's invention of the kinetoscope or in 1895 with the Lumière brothers' development of the cinematograph. But the origins of cartoon films are much older. They go back as much as three hundred years prior to the kinetoscope and the cinematograph. The reason that today's very short cartoon films have been able to become so cinematic in comparison with live-action cinema [*shashin no eiga*] can be explained by the fact that, historically, making drawings move preceded making photographs move.[37]

Imamura's cartoon theory, then, begins not only with the history of cinematic apparatuses but also with the prehistory of cinema, with the history of optical toys and other devices for making moving images. In other words, there is something akin to apparatus theory in Imamura, but that something is not the monocular lens. For Imamura, because moving images (*ugoku e*) emerged in the era of Newton's classical mechanics and Descartes's mathematics, moving images entail a transformation of individualized entities into quantified mechanistic series, which is similar to the division of labor in industrial manufacturing.[38]

Despite this analogy between the Fordist assembly line and the series of images in cinema, in his discussion of Disney, Imamura resolutely separates the apparatus or techniques of animation from capitalism. For instance, when he poses the question that he feels absolutely crucial, of why cartoon films have developed on a large scale only in America, he muses that Lotte Reiniger's silhouette animations and Ladislaw Starevich's puppet films were very popular before the ascendency of Disney cartoons. What then explains the subsequent ascendency of Disney? Imamura acknowledges the importance of capital investment in Disney's success, only to conclude: "We cannot explain it only on the basis of capital investment. Clearly, at the basis of such success were techniques that were more cinematic. Capital merely brought them to light."[39]

Consequently, Imamura submits, film theory and film reform should focus first and foremost on cinematic techniques and not on capital investment. In support of this separation of techniques and capital, he cites the fact that, before the bank put up the necessary funds for his production studio, Walt Disney was a poor artist living in an attic. But Disney had grasped one principle, Imamura explains: "The principle was that of drawing images strictly in accordance with movement as parsed with film photography [*katsudō shashin*]. This is what 'animating' is all about. If I may speculate a bit, it seems likely that he parsed movement through close observation of the dynamics of the actions of various animals and humans. And film photography is the only way to show all the stages of such actions in still images."[40]

In brief, Imamura imagines Disney capturing in drawings the movements of animals as captured with cinematic photography. Imamura then drops the question of capital investment, leaving us to fill in the blanks. Apparently, in light of his prior comments, techniques that are more cinematic will prove more attractive to capital, precisely because they enable greater quantification and mechanization of the production process. As such, when Imamura gives advice for rendering Japanese cartoons more cinematic, he apparently takes the side of capitalist development or modernization. This makes sense in a context that he has characterized in terms of underdevelopment. Yet the impasse of Japan's underdevelopment in cartoons cannot be resolved with capital according to Imamura. The underlying problem is that of machinic consciousness—how to think with the camera.

Imamura uses terms as diverse as *aesthetics (bigaku), method (hōhō), technique (gijtusu* and *gikō),* and *principle (genzoku)* to describe the technical and artistic level of filmmaking that demands attention prior to financial investment and industrial development. I have been somewhat insistently reading Imamura's problematic with such terms as *apparatus* and *machinic consciousness* rather than, say, *aesthetics.* This is not because I think that aesthetics is beside the point. On the contrary, it is the fundamental point for Imamura. But there is nevertheless a technical inflection to his aesthetics, a profound concern for technical development, which I aim to highlight by recourse to such terms.

Imamura ends the first section of "For the Sake of Japanese Cartoon Films" with this advice: "All in all, the lack of creativity in Japanese cartoon films is a befuddled reflection of the contradictions of contemporary Japanese painting. It would be a mistake to set aside an examination of such aesthetic problems and to think that, if we invested as much capital as the Americans, we could produce Japanese cartoon films. Such an approach would only make for duplications of Mickey Mouse and Popeye."[41]

In sum, in Imamura's theory of cartoons, the question posed in his essay on documentary film—"how to think with the camera"—has transformed into a question about "how to overcome the contradictions of Japanese art," and about which contradictions arise from the effects of the apparatus. His confidence in clear or rational thinking to bring order to the human use of the camera in the context of documentary film has given way to a concern for potential dissonance or resonance between camera and image, between photography and art. In effect, the camera is no longer a tool for conscious manipulation or a cause-and-effect mechanism under rational control. It is closer to an apparatus in the Foucauldian sense of *dispositif,* a kind of ethico-aesthetic or techno-discursive paradigm whose positive effects include modes of spacing that also entail truth effects and resistance—prior to the division of labor and capital unevenness but potentially complicit with them. In Imamura's case, his discussion of cartoons will both acknowledge and resist a particular set of truth effects, those of Western painting as prolonged in photography, commonly associated with one-point perspective and Cartesianism.

Temporal Depth

For Imamura, photography defines the modern regime of visuality. He frequently reminds us of the challenge presented by the ubiquity of photography in contemporary Japan: "All around us mechanical techniques, not at all different from those in America, are developing; photography is flourishing, and everyone is learning to see things via photography [*shashin ni yoru mono no mikata*]."[42] Photography is for Imamura the inevitable standard for producing modern visuality or perception. As such, photography in his film theory confronts the two fundamental problematics of modernity: modernization (developmental progress) and the modern (the experience of a temporal lag or rupture, of time out of joint). Modernity is above all a temporal problematic, positing a break between past and present, between tradition and modernity. But it is a tricky temporal problematic because modernity at once names the goal and the break. Modernization is a matter of progressive movement toward modernity as the goal, while the modern or modernist experience dwells on modernity as temporal rupture, as a relation between past and present that does not go away. As such, because it conjoins two different temporal paradigms (progress and rupture), modernity is always impossible, and always already here.

Imamura struggles with the tricky temporality of modernity in the context of photography. His account strives to resolve the problem of modernity in a fairly familiar, and in retrospect, rather predictable manner. While Imamura sees technological progress and industrial development as necessary and inevitable, he discusses them in terms of different national techno-aesthetic regimes. In other words, he lays out or redistributes the temporal problem of modernity in spatial, geopolitical terms. He writes, for instance: "The success of American cartoons is rooted above all in the characteristics of this country, where there are no long established traditions of art, and mechanical techniques are the mostly highly advanced. Due to the lack of constraining traditions, drawings are most confidently combined with photography." In contrast, even though impressionist artists in France have moved painting closer to capturing the temporality of movement, Imamura concludes: "Nevertheless, insofar as not a single creator of cartoon films has appeared in France, we have to acknowledge the considerable and heavy constraints of its artistic traditions."[43]

This passing comment on the difference between America and France merits attention, because the essay otherwise gives the impression that photography follows naturally and inevitably from Western oil painting. For instance, immediately after he suggests that there are limitations to French traditions of oil painting, Imamura shifts his attention to the realism of oil painting, which he feels verges on photography. He writes, "In the history of development of oil painting techniques, as we enter into modern painting, it became so realistic [*genjitsushugi teki*] and materialist [*machiriaru teki*] that it seems to possess a tendency toward relief carving [*ukibori*]. In other words, oil painting is the formative matrix [*botai*] of photography. Rubens and Rembrandt come to mind in this context. Oil painting itself steadily advanced, verging on photography of things [*jibutsu no shashin*]."⁴⁴ To summarize, modern Western oil painting tends toward or verges on photography, and yet, if we take seriously Imamura's caveat about the lack of cartoonists in France being due to the constraints of its art traditions, oil painting does not automatically result in, or guarantee the advent of, photography. In other words, for Imamura, techno-aesthetic progress is a matter of tendency or potentiality rather than teleology or determinism.

It is interesting that Imamura describes this potentiality with the term *ukibori*, which refers to relief carving, embossing, or other techniques for raising the surface of the image to add a sense of dimensionality to it. This notion that shashin is able to capture something of the depth of things recalls Fukuoka's discussion of practices and discourses related to shashin prior to the introduction of photography into Japan, whereby techniques of copper etching, sketching, and ink rubbing came to assure the fidelity of the relation between object and image. But Imamura makes no reference to such prephotographic shashin practices. Either Imamura is not aware of them or he is so intent on the contradiction between Western and Japanese artistic techniques that he omits such practices. In any event, even as he posits a contradiction between Western photography and traditional Japanese arts, his usage of the term *shashin* potentially implies a zone of noncontradiction to be discovered, which will be realized in the multipoint indexical capture discussed earlier.

In conjunction with the term *ukibori*, Imamura's other examples give us a better sense of what kind of apparatus Imamura has in mind. In his evocation of impressionist art, for instance, Imamura calls attention to the capture of the transformations of an object over time: "It was surely Impressionism that first attempted a serious treatment of time within art. We may think of the Impressionist artist who tried to capture the essence of a haystack as it ceaselessly transformed with the changing light as one who investigated time with images. An artist like Degas who strove to grasp the pose of a ballerina in an instant was also an investigator of movement-time [undō—jikan] in painting."⁴⁵

In this instance as well, Imamura misses a potential connection between Western and Japanese art. After all, one important source for Degas's posed ballerinas was the poses of dancers in Hokusai's collection of block-printed sketches (manga); the first volume appeared in 1814.⁴⁶ Volumes of Hokusai's manga sketches and various *nishikie* (multicolored woodblock printing) circulated widely among European artists by the second half of the century, and the impressionists in particular made frequent reference to the photographic qualities of such art.⁴⁷ Of course, the particulars of these intersections and convergences, such as Degas's ballerinas being inspired by Hokusai's sparrow dancers, were probably not known to Imamura. Yet neither prehistory of photography in Japan—neither Edo shashin nor Edo nishikie—would serve Imamura's purposes, for his argument depends on establishing a contradiction between (Western) photography and Japanese arts—a contradiction that is to be overcome in cartoons. He is intent on the potential for the emergence of something entirely new from cartoons in Japan, which requires grappling with the effects of this cine-photographic apparatus.

Already in his brief account of impressionism, Imamura suggests that the photographic capturing of the temporal depth of something (or someone) entails a twofold procedure: it is not only a process of capturing something in the instant but also a process of capturing something instant by instant, as with Monet's series of haystacks. Imamura's sense of the photographic apparatus jives with Gilles Deleuze's conceptualization of cinema as a mode based on "any-instant-whatsoever."⁴⁸ And like Deleuze, Imamura is concerned with temporal depth. But because Deleuze is interested in an experience of duration through and beyond the organizing of any-instants-whatsoever into a consistent cinematic body (the movement-image), he introduces another wrinkle—making for a threefold process, as it were—wherein *stopping on the image* releases or explicates the temporal potentiality folded into the cinematically organized twofold process of capturing instants and arraying them in series. For Imamura, however, the pressing concern is the production of clear, solid films whose consistency derives from the photographic apparatus. In effect, despite its reference to time, Imamura's theory of "movement-time" is an effort to produce what Deleuze calls the movement-image, which happens in the form of national or "classical" cinema. It makes sense of course that Imamura, writing in the late

1930s in Japan, would be more concerned with the production of the movement-image and the politics of finding the people, while Deleuze, writing in the early 1980s in France, would be attentive to the emergence of the time-image and the politics arising when "the people are missing."

Consequently, Imamura lingers on the rupture between tradition and modernity, between Japanese art and American cartoons. America is now defined as a land where nothing has troubled the full and confident use of photographic methods, while Japan is emerging as a site where photography stands in contradiction to received pictorial practices. As implied in Imamura's constant use of the term *ketsugō* (combination or unification), his film theory is intent on a synthesis that promises to re-solve, overcome, or perhaps sublate the contradiction between painting and photography, between traditional Japanese artistic practices and modern American industrial cartoons. To ground such a synthesis, Ima-mura has to find within Japanese arts something analogous to, or con-sonant with, modern photographic methods, which will allow them to communicate. Insofar as he defines cartoons as "temporal painting," he naturally turns to Japan's traditions of temporal painting. As we have seen, he must rule out prephotographic shashin and nishikie or ukiyoe, for there is already too much intercourse with the West implicit in these arts. And so, to find materials appropriate for Japanese cartoons, Ima-mura turns to picture scrolls (*emaki*) dating as far back as the twelfth century, pictorial maps of Kyoto (*Kyōto zue*) on folding screens from the Edo period, and acting techniques found in the nō theater, as de-scribed by Zeami Motokiyo in the late fourteenth century. His range of examples is exceedingly eclectic—bringing them together entails a good deal of historical decontextualization and media deterritorialization, as does the resultant sense of Japaneseness implied in articulating their commonality.

To understand why and how Imamura chooses such examples, we must first note that his cartoon theory addresses two different aspects of animation under the aegis of "temporal painting." On the one hand, he begins and ends with character animation, and his cartoon theory initially focuses on how to produce realistic movement of figures, ob-jects, and characters. Indeed, as we have seen, his ideal for character animation is akin to rotoscoping. On the other hand, as the term *uki-bori* succinctly indicates, Imamura is concerned with the overall sense of depth to the image, with an emphasis on dimensionality. Although he does not refer to the multiplane-camera system per se, his examples make clear that he is addressing effects that came to be associated with it. The second part of his essay opens with examples of American cartoons in which the images verge on photography:

> In the recent cartoons of Disney and Fleischer, shading has been enhanced, imparting a sense of dimensionality, and coloring has become more nuanced, aiming for photographic reality. Take, for instance, the background for the ocean in the opening sequence of *Sinbad the Sailor* or the first scene of the desert in *Forty Thieves* (1937). The latter picture in particular might well be mistaken for photography. The silhouettes of the forty thieves appear running across the distant horizon. In the foreground are the scattered remains of a skeleton, and the depths of the undulating dunes, rendered with soft shading, are close to color cinema [see figure 13.5]. Such aspects are on par with *The Old Mill*.[49]

Imamura here refers to a series of recent cartoons, which were met with popular and critical acclaim: Disney's *The Old Mill* (1937), Fleischer's *Popeye the Sailor Meets Sinbad the Sailor* (1936), and Fleischer's *Popeye the Sailor Meets Ali Baba's Forty Thieves* (1937). He then refers us to Disney's *Lonesome Ghosts* (1937) and *Hawaiian Holiday* (1937).

Disney's *The Old Mill* is commonly credited as the first cartoon to use the multiplane-camera system, and Fleischer quickly followed suit with *Popeye the Sailor Meets Ali Baba's Forty Thieves*, released just weeks before Disney's *Snow White and the Seven Dwarfs* (1937). These films were touted for the realism and dimensionality of their images due to the multiplane-camera system. Yet, as Imamura's citations of other cartoons not directly associated with the multiplane system imply, efforts to produce such depth effects had long been under way, and the effects were palpable prior to the buzz about Disney's multiplane-camera system. As such, Disney's multiplane-camera system itself might be seen as an innovation upon the basic apparatus or invention of the animation stand used for cel animation, in which a camera fixed on a rostrum looks down through layers of painted celluloid.[50] The animation stand, like rotoscoping, had come into usage much earlier and had already undergone a great deal of experimentation.

Indeed, Imamura's account reminds us that these new effects of depth were not simply due to photographing through multiple celluloid layers or the use of the multiplane-camera system alone. The new effects were actually a result of sustained attempts to eliminate the sense of gaps between the celluloid layers, which is to say that the "artifacts" of the animation stand tended to disrupt the sense of a closed volumetric three-dimensional world. Eliminating such effects entailed a num-

FIGURE 13.5 Still from *Popeye the Sailor Meets Ali Baba's Forty Thieves* (1937).

ber of techniques for regulating the relation between layers, such as the differential shading and coloring of backgrounds, characters, and foregrounds; cinema-inspired effects of focal depth; and recalibration of relations between layers between shots. While Imamura draws attention primarily to artwork (shading and coloring), he also shows awareness of how American cartoons rely on one-point perspective and scalar proportions, for, when he contrasts these cartoons with Japanese *emaki* (picture scrolls), he comments that emaki "do not depict all parts equally as in Western painting."[51]

Imamura addresses the effects of photography at two levels in cartoons: character animation (decomposition and recomposition of movement) and dimensionality (the overall depth effect of the image in volumetric terms). The realism of cartoons has to be realized at both levels at once. Part of what makes Imamura's account challenging comes from the fact that he does not explicitly or operatively separate these two levels, but instead treats them as two faces of the same problematic of photography. It is as if rotoscoping and the multiplane-camera system, for instance, were but two faces of the same photographic realism. This assumption is what ultimately pushes him toward a theory of temporal depth: photography in cinema is a matter of both temporality and dimensionality, which are becoming more mechanized, scientific, and ubiquitous due to technical development and expansion.

Why then can't Japanese cartoonists just use photography as the Americans do? Imamura does not provide any theorization of sociohistorical conditions, but, to understand his concerns, we have to think in terms of underlying persistent material conditions. While his account of documentary gives the impression that the problem of Japan's temporal lag is largely a matter of subjectivity, Imamura doesn't think that ideological awareness alone will resolve the problem. Subjective expression has to pass through the camera, through photography. In effect, his account encourages us to think in terms of sociohistorical development and material conditions, but these conditions are posited in a techno-aesthetic, perceptual register rather than in socioeconomic terms. As we have seen, Imamura suggests that treating the problem of Japan in purely economic terms will not resolve anything: Japan would merely replicate American forms of expression. The problem for him is deeper than or prior to the purely economic, the limited economy. Such a stance is not entirely at odds with Marxism, or at least, certain currents of Marxism, since Marx formulated a critique of political economy that comprised the social beyond the purely economic.

At the same time, because Imamura makes no distinction between the social and the national, the overall tendency of his cartoon theory is toward the naturalization of the Japanese nation. Japan tends to appear homogeneous, self-identical, and immutable. In this respect, Imamura's film theory invites a variation on psychoanalytic, self-other dialectical reading in the manner of Slavoj Žižek: Imamura's account projects even development, that is, untroubled, unfettered techno-economic progress, onto America, which guarantees the temporal unevenness of Japan. Why is temporal unevenness desirable? It is desirable because modernity itself is organized around temporal progress and temporal rupture, that is, temporal unevenness. By imputing developmental evenness to America, Imamura assures that Japan is a site of temporal unevenness, and thus of modernity itself — and maybe *the* site of modernity, beyond received configurations of modernity. America then is the past of modernity, and Japan the future.

Interesting enough, in this case, the excess that is imputed to the other in order to disavow it is temporal evenness, or what Walter Benjamin called empty, homogeneous time. Therein lies the challenge of Imamura's cartoon theory: although it posits photography in American cartoons as the ideal apparatus for the production of temporal depth, the theory simultaneously resists that temporal depth (as if aware that it is ultimately nothing more than empty homogeneous time), seeking a deeper temporal depth, as it were — a twisted, distorted, weird temporal depth. And the temporal unevenness of modernity suddenly appears materialized in ancient picture scrolls and drama, transmuted, cinematized.

When Imamura turns to picture scrolls, for instance, he first comments: "I said that cartoons are temporal paintings. Japanese emaki are probably the oldest, most refined form of art striving for temporality in painting. Like contemporary cartoons, emaki develop a story with images. It is surprising how close they come to the temporal techniques of cinema."[52] In other words, Imamura begins by establishing the aesthetic parity of cartoons and emaki. The source for this argument about emaki is probably Hosokibara Seiki's general history of manga from 1924, *A History of Japanese Manga* (*Nihon manga-shi*), and as Ōtsuka Eiji points out, such a view of emaki only becomes possible once the conventions of modern cinema have been established and normalized.[53] In Ōtsuka's opinion, emaki are not the origin for modern manga. He argues instead that the cinematic sensibility established in the 1930s in Japan allowed critics and artists to project a sense of parity onto emaki and manga. The same may be said of Imamura's account of emaki: if he sees emaki as analogous to cartoon films, it is because he is already reading emaki in cinematic terms.

Imamura also finds some points of difference between modern photography and emaki: "Seen from the standpoint of Western painting, many of the pictures appear utterly chaotic in terms of perspective. One scroll of a warship loaded with warriors, for instance, shows not just the side facing us but the side facing away as well. As a result, the ship looks oddly twisted. To borrow from Hinago Motoo's discussion, it is exactly as if the artist had done a pan with a camera to show us both sides simultaneously."[54] Imamura concludes that showing two sides of an object on one surface, or upon a single plane, is exactly like the "mobile camera of cinema" (*idō satsuei*). Naturally, in keeping with Ōtsuka's point, this is precisely what we might question: do emaki really strive to make different views and different realities commensurable within a single plane of expression? Usually, as in Mikhail Bakhtin's account of the novel, bringing divergent realities into a single plane of expression is considered the hallmark of the modern.[55] Here again we clearly see that Imamura's film theory is resolutely modern and geared toward the present: he seeks divergence within the modern, not from it. As such, we need to think of his examples of traditional arts as temporal oddities existing in the present, producing spatio-temporal warps upon the single plane of the contemporary.

Imamura's account of pictorial maps of Kyoto agrees with that of emaki. In emaki he also finds temporal depth in discrepancies of the scalar or homogenous proportioning of space. The use of clouds to conceal insignificant parts of a building, for instance, is likened to temporal techniques in cinema such as fade-in, fade-out, and overlap.[56] Regarding pictorial maps of Kyoto painted on large folding screens during the Edo period, he speculates that their tendency to run counter to perspective is related to the temporal styles of emaki:

> Instead of overall spatial balance and proportion, the artists' goal was *to present distant sites in the same manner as nearby ones*. A small theater in Sanjō Kawara, for instance, had to be drawn as large as the Shimizudera temple complex. What was distant and what was close had to be shown in the same way. As a result, techniques of perspective run haywire. A path may become wider and wider as it goes from foreground into the distance. The image is clearly not drawn from the standpoint of equalizing spatial proportions; rather such techniques are designed to allow for temporal progress related to narrating—and explaining—things here and there in Kyoto. The picture scroll form seems to be one that rejects pictorial space in favor of narrative time.[57]

Imamura reads what diverges from one-point perspective in traditional Japanese arts as evidence of a form of temporal depth that is analogous to the photography of cinema. In the end, the temporal depth of art is transformed into a narrative force, and his cartoon film theory finally joins his documentary film theory. Cartoon theory has allowed Imamura to ground his documentary theory in the material apparatus of photography. The documentary theory approached cinema from the subjective side, proposing a solid script (scientific or schematized) in the place of an apparatus. Cartoon theory, approaching cinema from the materialist or objective side, finds the ground for schematized writing in the material effects of the photographic apparatus. Cartoon theory and documentary theory meet at the level of narrative, but narrative is now an effect of temporality and dimensionality of cinema, rather than a subjective structure imposed upon reality with the camera.

Imamura's attention to the temporality and dimensionality deriving from the use of photography in cartoon films has enlarged the apparatus of film beyond the deterministic mechanism of the camera and into a dispositif, that is, an apparatus-paradigm or diagram: the transcriptive apparatus. Photography does not commit cinema to objective documentation due to linear indexicality or referentiality. Photography instead suggests modes of transcription, in which multipoint indexicality allows for a form of realism. What is new or novel about Imamura's form of photography-centered realism is that, because it has passed through the crucible of cartoons, it entails plastic, elastic, and vitalist realism. Consequently, in Imamura the deformative potentiality of animation is not the antithesis of realism, nor is it a fantastical compensation for what Eisenstein called the "heartless geometrizing" and "formal logic of standardization" of capitalist modernity.[58] Cartoons become the past and future of realism for moving images.

Coda: Imamura Today

If many aspects of Imamura's film theory feel conservative, restrictive, or plainly fascist today, we should recall that his film theory was never intended to be revolutionizing, disruptive, or anarchic. It was reformative in impulse. Whatever revolutionary potential it discovered, it tended to harness to the national cause, in the service of national reformation geared to international rivalry. Imamura's film theory aimed to make Japanese cartoons that would compete with American cartoons in the international market. Not surprisingly then, after the start of the Pacific War, Imamura would frame that rivalry in fully militarist terms: "The former superiority of Disney cartoons as art lay in their superiority as weapons for propaganda warfare. In them we can see how fine art may play a powerful role in enlightening the public. If we are unable to produce cartoons like those of Disney, we will be overpowered."[59]

In his recent discussions on Imamura's film theory, Ōtsuka Eiji characterizes it in terms of fascism and reminds us that this impulse of film theory cannot be comfortably relegated to the past. Ōtsuka situates contemporary otaku culture as the direct heir to 1930s fascism, casting his net wide while singling out the films of Studio Ghibli as direct heirs. After all, Studio Ghibli was responsible for the republication of Imamura's *Theory of Cartoon Film* in 2005, and the Ghibli director and producer Takahata Isao builds directly on Imamura's discussion of cartoons and emaki in his book on twelfth-century Japanese picture scrolls as the origin on Japanese animation.[60] Ghibli's aesthetics is clearly a bid to establish a national aesthetic.

Yet Imamura's film theory is not nationalist or fascist in tendency simply because it explicitly aims to produce a national cinema. Nor can we effectively resist such fascist aesthetics by focusing attention on those thinkers or artists who adopt nationalist discourse, localizing the problem in specific individuals. Rather, as Imamura's theory attests, even if the theories or practices of specific individuals provide a point of departure for raising questions, the problem of resisting fascism entails more than identifying who adopts national allegiance or militarist discourse. The political challenge of Imamura's cartoon theory lies in how it opens the question of the production of cinema beyond the purely economic and into the social, and then strives to ground the production of the social in techno-aesthetic paradigms, that is, in the production of bodies rather than subjects. In effect, he is opening a physiology or "somatics" of power prior to ideology and subjectivity. "For the Sake of Japanese Cartoon Films," for instance, offers this odd and potentially disruptive analogy:

> Among the techniques of nō drama and puppet theater that had a profound impact on kabuki performance, there are also a couple of significant principles that Japanese cartoons films must adopt. As Watsuji Tetsurō has pointed out, in puppet theater, substantial reality lies in the material body of the puppet.[61] Because the puppeteer manipulates the puppet only with his fingers, the performance is exceedingly limited, largely directed into movements of the head and shoulders. The principle of the cartoon film is precisely the principle of puppet theater. Like the puppet, the image that is drawn sheet by sheet is but the material body. If manipulation of this material body is to impart the feeling that it is alive, one must select only the most distinctive actions. As in photography, in cartoons it is not possible to capture all movements equally, so it is necessary to draw the viewers' eyes only to the most significant movements of the actor. Close observation of Disney's animals confirms that the repetition of simple operations similarly has complicated effects on us. If you look at that Donald's action, for instance, the operation consists almost entirely of him wagging his rump back and forth.[62]

Ultimately, however, it is at this level that his theory shows its tendency toward corporatism. For Imamura shows absolutely no interest in nonlocalized movement in animation.[63] He consistently ignores any movement, temporal or dimensional, that cannot be localized in a body. Prior to his bid for enlightening the masses with animation, Imamura effectively pushed the transcriptive apparatus of cartoons into the production and mobilization of operative bodies. Indeed there can be no national propaganda or militarist propagation without such bodies.

Yet, in pushing the theory of cartoons toward the formation of bodies before subjects, Imamura highlights a central problematic for the study of animation today, perhaps inadvertently: insofar as the transcriptive apparatus of cartoon film entails multipoint capture, we begin to see how cinema indexes its own movement. This is what makes for the self-indexical worlds of cinema, whose generation and propagation become so salient in cartoons. If we do not constrain the use of the transcriptive apparatus to the localization of movement in operative, cooperative bodies, other cartoon worlds are still possible.

Notes

1. See Hansen, "Of Ducks and Mice," for a discussion of Benjamin's and Adorno's very different takes on Disney cartoons.
2. Imamura, "Nihon manga eiga no tame ni," 137. All translations mine unless otherwise indicated.
3. On the pure film movement, see Bernardi, *Writing in Light*; Gerow, *Visions of Japanese Modernity*; and LaMarre, *Shadows on the Screen*.
4. On "overcoming modernity," see Richard Calichman's introduction to, and translation of, the wartime conference entitled *Overcoming Modernity* at which Japanese scholars and writers addressed the impasses of modernity in Japan.
5. Irie, "Approaching Imamura Taihei."
6. Ōtsuka, "An Unholy Alliance of Eisenstein and Disney."
7. For instance, some of the points made in "For the Sake of Japanese Cartoon Films" appear in the final section of *A Theory of Cartoon Film* called "Cartoons and Japanese Art," while other parts of the argument appear in his sections on painting and on cartoons in general. A translation of the final section in the revised edition of *A Theory of Cartoon Film* was published as "Japanese Art and the Animated Cartoon." This is not only one of the rare translations of Imamura but also (as far as I know) the first into English. Michael Baskett recently published two translations, an essay on documentary film and a section on sound in cartoons, both of which I cite here. Nonetheless, I rely primarily on "For the Sake of Japanese Cartoon Films" because this essay, in its brevity, makes Imamura's basic arguments about cartoons and connections between them more lucidly and concisely than the book, which is after all a compilation of essays.
8. The Project on Toy Films website lists a cartoon film entitled *Kaeru kenpō* (Iwao Ashida, dir., 1933), which is probably the film that Imamura cites as *Kaeru no kenpō*.
9. Imamura uses a series of different terms that can be translated as "picture" or "image," "drawing" or "painting." I have chosen sometimes to translate *kaiga* as "drawing" and sometimes as "painting" (although in some contexts it might

equally well be glossed "art") in order to convey the nuance of his argument. I translate *e* sometimes as "drawing" and sometimes as "image." He later introduces the term *eizō*, which refers more specifically to images associated with mechanical reproduction, but which I translate simply as "image." Because of the potential difference in nuance in different contexts and my shifts in translation, I often include the Japanese term.

10. Imamura, "Nihon manga eiga no tame ni," 139–40.
11. Eisenstein, *Eisenstein on Disney* (1988).
12. Eisenstein, *Eisenstein on Disney* (1988), 43, 83–84.
13. Eisenstein, *Eisenstein on Disney* (1988), 41, 44.
14. Imamura, "Nihon manga eiga no tame ni," 138.
15. Imamura, "Nihon manga eiga no tame ni," 140.
16. Imamura, "Nihon manga eiga no tame ni," 140.
17. Imamura, "Nihon manga eiga no tame ni," 141.
18. Rosen, *Change Mummified*, 20.
19. Crafton, *Before Mickey* (1982), 158.
20. Rosen, *Change Mummified*, 302.
21. Imamura, "Nihon manga eiga no tame ni," 140–41.
22. Fukuoka, "Toward a Synthesized History of Photography," 571.
23. Fukuoka, "Toward a Synthesized History of Photography," 591–92.
24. Fukuoka, "Toward a Synthesized History of Photography," 592.
25. Imamura, "A Theory of Film Documentary," 56.
26. Imamura, "A Theory of Film Documentary," 52.
27. Imamura, "A Theory of Film Documentary," 56.
28. Imamura, "Nihon manga eiga no tame ni," 146.
29. See Driscoll, "From Kino-Eye to Anime-Eye / Ai"; and Furuhata, "Rethinking Plasticity," for additional accounts of the politics of production in Imamura's film theory.
30. Baudry, "Ideological Effects of the Basic Cinematographic Apparatus."
31. Comolli, "Technique and Ideology," 44.
32. Burch, *Life to Those Shadows*, 162.
33. Carroll, "The Specificity Thesis," 336.
34. Jay, "Scopic Regimes of Modernity," 4.
35. Mulvey, "Visual Pleasure and Narrative Cinema."
36. Comolli, "Technique and Ideology," 55.
37. Imamura, *Imamura Taihei eizō hyōron* 5, 3. The 1991 edition of Imamura's collected works includes the 1941 edition of *Manga eigaron*. The revised 1965 edition was republished in 2005 as Imamura Taihei, *Manga eigaron*.
38. Imamura Taihei, *Imamura Taihei eizō hyōron* 5, 5.
39. Imamura, "Nihon manga eiga no tame ni," 142.
40. Imamura, "Nihon manga eiga no tame ni," 143.
41. Imamura, "Nihon manga eiga no tame ni," 147.
42. Imamura, "Nihon manga eiga no tame ni," 146.
43. Imamura, "Nihon manga eiga no tame ni," 144.
44. Imamura, "Nihon manga eiga no tame ni," 145.

45. Imamura, "Nihon manga eiga no tame ni," 144.
46. See Wichmann, "Degas," in *Japonisme*, 26–33.
47. Evett, "The Critical Response: A Survey of General Reactions to Japanese Art," in *The Critical Reception of Japanese Art in Late Nineteenth Century Europe*, 27–59.
48. Deleuze, *Cinema 1: The Movement-Image*, 6.
49. Imamura, "Nihon manga eiga no tame ni," 148.
50. See LaMarre, "Animation Stand," in *The Anime Machine*, 12–25. The distinction between innovation and invention comes from James Utterbeck, as discussed by David Nye in *Technology Matters*, 33.
51. Imamura, "Nihon manga eiga no tame ni," 151.
52. Imamura, "Nihon manga eiga no tame ni," 150.
53. Ōtsuka, "An Unholy Alliance of Eisenstein and Disney."
54. Imamura, "Nihon manga eiga no tame ni," 150. In adapting his discussion of emaki in the book *A Theory of Cartoon Film*, Imamura omits this reference to Hinago Motoo and associates this technique with double exposure rather than panning.
55. Bakhtin, "Discourse in the Novel," in *The Dialogic Imagination*, 291–92. In addition, in "Superflat and the Layers of Image and History in 1990s Japan," Thomas Looser directly addresses the question of whether multiple perspectives within an image should be considered as evidence of different layers of realities or different realities. A similar question emerges in the context of magic lanterns and nishikie. See LaMarre, "Magic Lantern, Dark Precursor of Animation."
56. Imamura, "Nihon manga eiga no tame ni," 151.
57. Imamura, "Nihon manga eiga no tame ni," 151–52.
58. Eisenstein, *Eisenstein on Disney* (1988), 35, 42.
59. Imamura, *Imamura Taihei eizō hyōron 9*; cited in Ōtsuka, "An Unholy Alliance of Eisenstein and Disney." Originally published as *Sensō to eiga* (Tokyo: Geibunsha, 1942).
60. Takahata, *Jūni seki no animeeshon*.
61. Imamura appears to be drawing on Watsuji Tetsurō's essay "Bunrakuza no ningyō shibai," *Shisō* (August 1935), which is reprinted in *Watsuji Tetsurō zenshū* 17, 309–15. The term *keigai* is used to stress the materiality of the doll or puppet body, and *jittai* to indicate its substance or reality.
62. Imamura, "Nihon manga eiga no tame ni," 154–55.
63. Put another way, building on my ideas for how we might open the analysis of animation, Imamura is only interested in "closing" compositing, avoiding the issue of the nonlocalized movement related to compositing. See LaMarre, "Compositing," in *The Anime Machine*, 26–44.

14 :: African American Representation through the Combination of Live Action and Animation

CHRISTOPHER P. LEHMAN

African American animated caricature has a relationship with live-action African American images that is unique among depictions of ethnic groups in cartoon films. No other ethnic group appears in films that use both animation and live action to construct identity and culture as much as African Americans do. Animation studios used live-action footage to accurately illustrate popular and profitable images of African American performance, so that the studios could cash in on the established appeal of those images. In addition, between 1929 and 1974, commercial studios created several styles of African American filmed representation by combining animation and live action. Each style of representation is not unique to African Americans alone. On the other hand, the techniques of drawings "coming to life," live-action footage traced by animators for cartoon figures, live-action characters narrating animated stories, and interplay between live-action and animated characters collectively compose a significant portion of the history of African American animated images in the first forty-five years of sound in U.S. animated cartoons. Moreover, the uses of these techniques by studios did not remain static but instead evolved in tandem with advancements of African Americans in both the quality of actors' roles and the access to production of their own images. Because of the special relationship that African American imagery has to both kinds of film, any endeavor to study the ethnic group's appearances in the first sound films requires the inclusion of cartoons alongside live-action films as the primary sources.

When animation began in the United States in the first decade of the twentieth century, it was not only a film novelty but an exercise in vanity too. Animators themselves were stars of the earliest cartoons. They filmed themselves for live-action sequences, playing the role of the boss of the characters they drew. In many cartoons of the silent era, a live-action hand appears on screen to sketch a character and all of the character's props. Although the figure comes to life, it does not become independent of the animator. Instead, the figure conducts all of its actions on the paper on which it is drawn. In addition, it does whatever the animator tells it to do. The artists were like the ventriloquists of vaudeville; although their puppets were made of sketches instead of wood, the drawings still functioned as extroverted extensions of the animators.

No studios employed African Americans as animators at the time. As a result, the only animators on camera were European Americans. Moreover, the African American figures were extensions of the European Americans who drew them. Many animators were European immigrants or children of immigrants. The cartoon became a vehicle by which the artists became Americanized. They used visual and verbal ethnic stereotypes for jokes as a means of familiarizing themselves with all the different nationalities they had not seen in their countries of origin. Several of their gags poked fun at African Americans, which meant that African American representation in animated form had little to do with the ethnic group's experiences and more to do with how European Americans responded to them.

African American caricature, especially blackface, was a necessity to the early commercial cartoon studio. A studio contracted to animate a cartoon on a weekly basis had to simplify character designs as much as possible in order for artists to draw multiple pictures of figures and their "movements." As a result, many animators drew their characters with jet-black bodies, large eyeballs to more easily animate expression, and large mouths to more easily animate dialogue. To be sure, the medium of animation has a foundation of caricature. An animator has to stylize the appearance of any living being to an extent when sketching it in order to be able to make an animated figure. If an artist adds details to a figure, then the artist has to animate all the details associated with the character's movement. Animators of the 1910s and 1920s, therefore, stuck to basic character designs to produce as many cartoons for a given schedule as possible.

What differentiates cartoons from live-action movies at this time is that cartoons show the minstrel without makeup (the live-action animators) and the blackface figure (the cartoon character) at the same time. In live-action movies, a European American character demonstrates his authorship of an African American performance when he blackens his face, transforming into the blackface figure in front of the audience. The animator, however, has a different goal in presenting ownership of a drawing of an African American performance. Drawing the figure in front of the camera only partly accomplishes the task, because the figure is still stationary. To show control of the movements of the figure, he has to simultaneously appear with his figure and give it commands.

The California-based cartoonist Hugh Harman plays the role of the animating minstrel in *The Talk-Ink Kid*—the cartoon he and Rudolf Ising produced in 1929 to convince Warner Brothers to hire them. Harman sits at a desk and draws a picture of a blackface figure he names Bosko. The drawing then comes to life. As the artist proceeds to ask Bosko questions, the character answers them in a stereotyped "Negro dialect." The animator draws various props for Bosko to use, but the figure never leaves the paper on which it was drawn. At the end of the film, Harman reinforces his dominance over his character by sucking Bosko and the props back into his ink pen.

This test film proved successful for Harman and Ising, and Warner Brothers hired them to direct a new cartoon series starring Bosko—Looney Tunes. However, the partners disregarded the format of combining live-action and animation and made all-animated cartoons with the character over the next eight years. The lone exception was the installment *Ride Him, Bosko* from 1933, which features a scene that, although short, effectively shows that Bosko remained the product of the filmmakers' imagination four years later. The film largely consists of Bosko's adventures as a cowboy. In the final twenty seconds of the film, the shot of Bosko riding on a horse pans out to reveal a group of men watching the character on a small screen. One of the men establishes that the group is in control of the figures by slapping his thighs to make the horse's galloping sound. They discuss among themselves how to end the film before deciding to go home. Bosko watches in horror as the artists leave. He briefly continues to ride but then stops in his tracks, because the animators have not given him direction on what to do next.

The staff members of the cartoon producer Max Fleischer in New York also served as minstrels, but unlike Harman and Ising, they sought to appropriate African American performance as accurately as possible. The artists filmed entertainers and then traced over the footage to animate characters doing those movements—an animation process known as rotoscoping. Also, for the cartoons the studio featured live-action footage of the African Americans whom the artists tried to approximate in order to show how similar the animation of the performance was to the live-action version. Therefore, the animators themselves are not the stars, because they are not on camera; instead, the animated imitation of the performance is the main attraction. Fleischer's films of the 1930s with African American stars are cartoon short-subject versions of the "Negro talking pictures," as defined by the film historian Ryan Jay Friedman. In this genre African Americans performed the same acts in movies that they had done on records and on the stages of nightclubs. Studios produced these movies in the early years of sound, because they saw an audience for musical films starring African Americans. The genre petered out in 1931, when sound was no longer a novelty in live-action movies. On the other hand, cartoon studios continued to use famous voices as attractions, and African American acts were among the drawing cards selected. Plenty of studios used audio of African Americans to strengthen the cartoons in terms of humor and music. But only Fleischer let audiences *see* the African Americans whose talents the studio allowed.[1]

In a few of the studio's Betty Boop cartoons from 1932 to 1934, the caricatures cross social boundaries that are taboo for the live-action African Americans. African American culture is cartoon humor in this series, and the scenes featuring caricatures of African Americans not only dominate the length of each film but also compose most of the humor of each installment. The European American female character Betty Boop shares scenes with caricatures of the African American performers, who play various roles ranging from a ghost walrus to an African cannibal. As a result, the films dangerously flirt with the movie industry's banning of male-female relationships of different skin colors. More important, such closeness of European American women and African American men violated social customs of color-based segregation in the United States at the time. However, when the beginning of each installment shows a live-action scene of the African Americans to be caricatured later, the entertainers are on a stage by themselves. They appear to be separated from all other people and are entertaining either themselves or the people behind the camera filming. In addition, the entertainers' scenes are not part of the cartoons' narratives but rather consist of part of the opening's title sequence.

In the films starring the jazz singer Cab Calloway, live action and animation do not intermingle. The opening of each film shows a live-action Calloway performing his unique dance steps. When those same steps reappear later in the cartoon, a caricature of Calloway performs them for his fellow animated characters. In each of his Betty Boop installments, Calloway's caricatures do not resemble him. However, by having established Calloway's uniqueness as a dancer with the live-action opening, the cartoon presents a recognizable caricature not through the depiction of physical features but through the invocation of signature movements.

In *I'll Be Glad When You're Dead You Rascal You* (1932), the juxtaposing of live action and animation is the most obvious of all the Betty Boop films. It is the only installment of the series to feature live-action African Americans and cartoon characters in the same scenes. Consequently, the film flaunts the industry's cross-color boundary the most boldly. The jazz musician Louis Armstrong appears in animated form as a big-lipped, dark-skinned cannibal—thus associating the cannibal's African heritage with that of Armstrong—and chases Betty through the rain forest. The studio constantly reminds the viewers of the cartoon that they are seeing caricatures of Armstrong and his orchestra. As the cannibal pursues Betty, his head separates from the body, grows, and floats, so that the studio can switch the cartoon head with Armstrong's live-action head. After this scene, the cartoon establishes live action and animation as separate entities. The studio drops the pretense that the live-action musician and the cannibal are one and the same. Near the end of the film, a scene with a cannibal precedes a live-action shot of one of Armstrong's musicians performing the same gestures as his caricature. In this film the studio tries too hard to show its mastery of African American cultural appropriation. Live-action film is an overused crutch for animated characterization, perhaps because Armstrong lacked Calloway's unique movements *and* because the cannibal caricature looks nothing like Armstrong.

Installments from Fleischer's Screen Songs series that have the Mills Brothers as the stars do not feature animated imitations of African American culture; instead the installments sell live-action African Americans on their own terms—the "Negro talking pictures" in their truest form. These entries of the series, released in 1932 and 1933, are the only cartoons of the 1930s to have live-action African Americans address the audience and sing directly to the viewers. By doing this, the studio implied that there was a familiarity or comfort that the film's spectators would have had with engaging the African Americans who appeared on screen. It is as close to a flirtation with cross-color boundaries as the Betty Boop cartoons. But unlike the Betty Boop series, the live-action African American sequence is the centerpiece of each Screen Song installment, and African American performance without European American alterations through caricature or rotoscoping is completely segregated from the animation except for the superimposed bouncing ball and the text of the lyrics of the song that the group sings. Each film consists of assorted animated characters and their gags. Then halfway through the films, the Mills Brothers appear in live action to tell the audience to follow the bouncing ball that moves to each word of the on-screen lyrics as the group sings it. The song lasts for the second half of the installment. Unlike the caricatures of Calloway and Armstrong, the ball has no interaction with any characters sharing the screen with it. The ball is expressionless and completely divorced from the actions of the figures. It merely exists as a tool to guide willing viewers to sing.

The Screen Songs are not about European Americans showing mastery of the African American image, although some animation scenes do have characters voiced by the singing Mills Brothers. In addition, the Mills Brothers are not animated. Unlike Cab Calloway and Louis Armstrong, they incorporate no humorous gestures into their act for animators to caricature, with the exception of the member who replicates a trumpet sound by blowing into his cupped hands. They are notable for their voices, but the studio realized that it did not have to go through the expense of animating entertainers just for the sake of exhibiting their vocal talents. Just filming them and inserting the live-action shot in the cartoon sufficed.

When Fleischer stopped using African American entertainers after 1933, the first phase of the interaction between live action and animation ended. Paramount Pictures distributed Fleischer's films and wanted his studio to produce cartoons that resembled the Academy Award–winning films that Walt Disney was making for United Artists, and Disney did not use African American talent. Also, the industry had begun to enforce its production code more strictly, which meant that the cross-color flirtations had to go. Neither Fleischer nor other studios knew how to devise interactions between live action and animation featuring African American characters in the industry's new climate. For more than a decade such content simply disappeared.

Only Walter Lantz's *Voodoo in Harlem* in 1938 broke the hiatus for the rest of the 1930s, marking a return to the practice of highlighting the African American character as a product of European American creativity. Also, it is one of the few films to use both live action and animation to reinforce African Americans' secondary status to European Americans. In a live-action animation studio late at night, a toppled jar drips ink that transforms into animated cannibals. They proceed to sing "Voodoo in Harlem" while moving all over the live-action studio. This marks a technological advancement, because the figures, although still existing only in the world of the animator, are not restricted solely to the paper on which they are drawn. The film ends when the characters retreat to their papers as a live-action African American maid turns on the light. She sees the papers scattered on the floor and burns them as she cleans the studio, muttering in "Negro dialect" and shuffling while she does. By treating the art as garbage, she rejects the figures as valid representations of her ethnicity. Her discarding of the caricatures reveals that she sees them as worthless European American interpretations of her heritage.

When Disney used live-action and animated film to illustrate African American culture in 1946, he broke new ground. *Song of the South* is similar to the Bosko films, because live-action people are creating imaginary African American worlds. Just as Harman introduces Bosko, the fictional live-action ex-slave Uncle Remus introduces the animated "Br'er" animals when telling stories to the children of the plantation where he lives. The Br'er animals act out Remus's imagination in separate animated segments, just as Bosko is a product of the animator's imagination. However, the film marks the first occasion in which animation serves to illustrate the creativity of a live-action African American. The animated figures do what Remus says they do, because the ex-slave created the characters to act out his tales of morality. To be sure, the cartoon scenes are collectively a European American adaptation of a European American adaptation of African American culture, because Disney had based Remus's stories on the character's appearances in short stories by Joel Chandler Harris, who in turn had appropriated the folktales from African American ex-slaves. Still, the studio did not have the goal of boasting its mastery of animating African American folktales but instead of placing the folktales in a narrative about an African American character.

However, Disney uses live action to reinforce the African American's secondary social status during segregation. In contrast to the flirting with industry guidelines regarding male-female cross-color contact in Fleischer's cartoons, *Song of the South* depicts relations between the colors in manners that did not challenge the status quo. The movie shows Remus as a friendly, docile babysitter for European American and African American children. He only has authority in his ability to impart moral lessons to the children. Otherwise he remains resigned to his political and economic deprivation, and he comes nowhere nearly as close to a European American woman as various caricatures did to Betty Boop.

Song of the South was a commercial success upon its release, but it did not inspire imitations. Civil rights groups protested the continuation of the old Southern ethnic relations, and musicals that combined animation and live action were declining in popularity. The closest competitor to the movie was George Pal's short cartoon *Date with Duke* (1947). Like *Song of the South*, Pal's film uses animation to illustrate a live-action African American's creativity. The film stars the jazz musician Duke Ellington, who plays the song "Perfume Suite" on his piano on a stage as perfume bottles come to life as they hear the song. The bottles transform into animated figures and disrupt his performance.

Date with Duke is similar to the early, silent cartoons but with an ethnic twist. Ellington, just as the animators who served as stars of their own films, exhibits control of the animated figures. Unlike the early cartoons that showed animators controlling characters with their pens, the musician makes the bottles come to life by touching piano keys. In contrast to the early animators trying to prove that they knew how to illustrate African Americans and their culture, Ellington here does not attempt to show mastery of another ethnic group's culture by dominating bottles; he merely shows the fictional power of his musicianship over inanimate objects.

Over the next two decades, live-action sequences in cartoons were few and far between, due not only to the continued enforcement of industry standards but also to the decline of the theatrical cartoon itself. Then, starting in 1971, African Americans became involved in the production of African American animated caricature. European Americans still composed the ethnic majority of the employees of the animation studios. European Americans still animated, directed, and produced the cartoons. However, since 1970 the studios had refrained from using European American actors to voice African American characters. In addition, African American performers allowed studios to caricature them in exchange for control over how the animators depicted them. The performers made the greatest inroads in cartoons produced for television, especially the half-hour Saturday-morning programs. These series, including *The Jackson 5ive* and *Fat Albert and the Cosby Kids*, were the first cartoons coproduced by African Americans and among the few shows produced by African Americans at the time—live action or animated.

The input from African Americans in cartoons mattered greatly to studios in the 1970s. Protests from the civil rights movement during the previous two decades had turned cultural appropriation into a taboo, and television networks refused to broadcast cartoons with African American stereotypes, especially those derived from blackface minstrelsy. The banning of these films led studios to avoid drawing African Americans altogether, because they saw no other context for the ethnic group beyond that of broad caricature. However, as specific African American entertainers gained followings among children, studios wanted to capitalize on the performers' fame without insulting them with the caricatures. The involvement of the stars helped minimize the studios' risk of developing any demeaning images.

From the Rankin / Bass studio in 1971, *The Jackson 5ive* offered no original treatment of live-action African American footage. The series used live action very minimally in each episode and in ways having little to do with the plot, not unlike the Screen Songs. On the other hand, the aesthetic means by which the series integrates live action into the cartoon resembles the Betty Boop cartoons. The opening and closing of each episode merely identify band members by juxtaposing the live-action photograph of each one with particular caricatures—a trick from *I'll Be Glad When You're Dead You Rascal You.* In a few episodes, the live-action footage is of film negatives with animation superimposed whenever a recording of a song by the group plays. Such scenes are similar to the live-action shots of Calloway's dancing that appear before his animated caricature duplicates the moves in *Minnie the Moocher*, except that the live-action negatives are on screen at the same time that the cartoon Jacksons dance.

The main difference between the Betty Boop cartoons and *The Jackson 5ive* lies in the explanation of why each series contains both live action and animation. For the former, because the animators tried to approximate only the movements and gestures of the live-action performers, accuracy in terms of how the figures resembled the entertainers was not an issue. The Fleischer Studio never implied that Betty Boop was cavorting with Cab Calloway or Louis Armstrong but with cartoon characters looking and sounding like them. In contrast, for the latter, the animators precisely illustrated not only the Jacksons' movements but also the Jacksons themselves. Each live-action photograph in the opening introduces the performer to the audience, and the corresponding caricature informs the viewer that the image will represent the photographed person in the cartoon to follow. The program promised the Jacksons as the stars, which necessitated that the figures represent the group in animation. The series was part of a current wave of television cartoons starring animated versions of famous entertainers, ranging from the Beatles to the Harlem Globetrotters. In addition, with television networks monitoring the content they aired and Motown Records coproducing *The*

Jackson 5ive, the studio did not dare to make crude, broad caricatures of the singers. Rather, the Jacksons' caricatures lack the huge lips and bugged eyes that had plagued the caricatures of African American entertainers from before the 1950s.

In 1972 the television cartoon series *Fat Albert and the Cosby Kids* blurred boundaries between live action and animation in ways that previous cartoons starring African Americans had not. Bill Cosby coproduced the program with Filmation Associates, giving him control over the African American cartoon characters. The figures are characters from Cosby's stand-up comedy routines about his childhood friends from urban Philadelphia, and one of the protagonists is a caricature of him as a child. As a result, the show follows the lead of *Song of the South* in having animation represent an African American's thoughts or memories. However, in *Fat Albert and the Cosby Kids*, the live-action Cosby comments on the cartoon action while simultaneously acting as if he occupied the same junkyard as the cartoon characters. He is filmed on a "cartoony" junkyard set, with fences designed to resemble the scenery in the cartoon, and a variety of familiar continuity techniques are used to break down the distinctions between live-action and cartoon worlds. Cosby looks offscreen to the side in order to seem as if he is viewing what the cartoon characters are doing. He throws objects to that side, and the characters catch animated versions of those objects in the cartoon. Sometime they throw back the objects, and Cosby catches live-action versions of them. He is part of the cartoon world, unlike Bosko, who belongs to the human world. Cosby interacts with his "memories," which Uncle Remus did not do in *Song of the South*; indeed, Cosby's performance suggests that Remus may well be one of the memories with which Cosby interacts and to which he responds.

The show is also a throwback to the Screen Songs of four decades earlier, because the live-action Cosby addresses the audience. He tells the spectators what to do, which made him one of the most authoritative African Americans to appear in a live-action sequence of a film for children. He invites them to listen to his stories and hear Fat Albert's musical ensemble (the Junkyard Band) play songs that summarize the episodes. However, Cosby's instructions extend beyond the Mills Brothers' request for viewers to "follow the bouncing ball." He plays the role of a teacher, reminding the audience of the lesson he tries to instill in them through his childhood story.

Fat Albert and the Cosby Kids presents the most ambiguous integration of live action and animation of all the aforementioned works. The cartoon series leaves several questions unanswered. Cosby never intro-duces himself by name to viewers, nor does he specifically say that the characters in the cartoon are from his childhood. The opening sequence of the program mentions that it is "starring Bill Cosby," and Filmation calls the animated main figures the "Cosby Kids." But is the comedian starring as himself? If so, is he pretending not to be the adult, live-action version of one of the cartoon's cast members? Does the cartoon take place in the present with the live-action Cosby? Or does he exist in the past with his childhood friends' caricatures? Do the present and the past coexist, allowing the adult live-action Cosby to interact with his animated juvenile self? If Cosby is not playing himself, then is his live-action character an anonymous commentator on each episode?

Fat Albert and the Cosby Kids aired on Saturday mornings for twelve consecutive years and spawned many imitators, more for the blending of morality and humor than for the exclusive starring of African Ameri-can figures. One of its first derivative competitors aired only months after the debut of Cosby's show. However, Flip Wilson, a fellow African American comedian, coproduced and starred in a holiday-season special telecast instead of a weekly program. From the DePatie-Freleng cartoon studio, *Clerow Wilson and the Miracle of PS 14* features characters from Wilson's stand-up routines appearing as animated characters. As with Remus and Cosby, the live-action Wilson serves as a storyteller in scenes separate from the animated stories he tells.

There the similarities end between Cosby and Wilson. The latter does not pretend to appear in the same setting as his story, unlike Cosby in his cartoony junkyard. Rather, Wilson stands on the stage of his weekly live-action television series *The Flip Wilson Show* to introduce the story to viewers. He appears as himself and identifies the cartoon characters as part of his childhood. A sequel special aired in 1974, with the same format.

By this time studios had run out of novel approaches to African American imaging by integrating both live-action footage and anima-tion. Ralph Bakshi's 1975 movie *Coonskin* merely updated *Song of the South* by animating a live-action African American character's stories and featuring profanity and nudity while doing so. The experiment had simply run its course. For decades European Americans used live action to prove that they could conquer African American animated appropria-tion until the demand for such talent decreased. African Americans then took control of their own caricatures and starred in their own live-action clips to validate their creative stamps on the characters, whose animators were still largely European Americans. Live action in cartoons now is exclusively a gimmick, but it was once an extremely political means of illustrating and sometimes reinforcing ethnic relations.[2]

Notes

1. Friedman, *Hollywood's African American Films*, 7.
2. Several of the cartoons mentioned in this writing are also mentioned in Lehman, *The Colored Cartoon*, but the relationship in each film of live action to animation is not discussed.

15 :: Animating Uncommon Life: U.S. Military Malaria Films (1942–1945) and the Pacific Theater

BISHNUPRIYA GHOSH

But malarial fever is important not only because of the misery it inflicts on man-kind, but the serious opposition that it has given to the march of civilization in the tropics. Unlike many diseases, it is essentially an endemic, a local, malady; and one which unfortunately haunts more especially the fertile, well-watered and luxuriant, tracts—precisely those which are of the greatest value to mankind. There it strikes down, not only the indigenous barbaric population, but, with still greater certainty, the pioneers of civilization, the planter, the trader, the missionary, the soldier. It is therefore the principal and greatest ally of barbarism.

RONALD ROSS, *Researches on Malaria: Nobel Lecture, December 12, 1902*

Malaria (1898)

At the dawn of the twentieth century, a new actor arrives on the global stage. Its agency seems planetary, here before us, and perhaps . . . after us. Human history, civilization, is but a phase in the *longue durée* of the malarial parasite. Not so long ago, nineteenth-century miasma theories named the disease after "bad air," *mal aria*, before germ theory estab-lished the primacy of biological agents in states of infection. Bad air over in India, over in North Africa, yes; but then, the British and French colonial forces were *there*, exposed to a resilient nonhuman Other in the tropics. In 1878 Alphonse Laveran had identified plasmodium or spo-rozoites, little curved creatures swimming in the bloodstream of 148 out of 192 patients struck with cyclic fevers, and in 1897–98, Ronald Ross, studying bird malaria, had located the carrier, an agent percep-tible to the naked human eye, in the anopheles mosquito.[1] In his accep-tance speech for the subsequent Nobel Prize that he received for this re-search,[2] the specter of bad air reappeared: it was not just the nonhuman agents, plasmodium, and the anopheles that were responsible for the

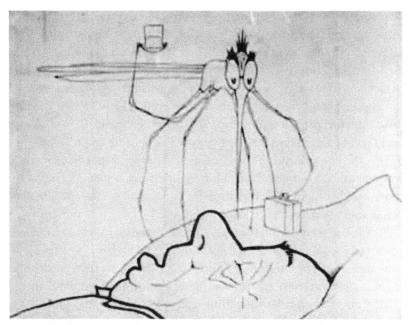

FIGURE 15.1 The first animated mosquito. Frame from *How a Mosquito Operates* (1912). Courtesy of Winsor McCay.

disease, but water, lush vegetation trapping water, humid air, the dim cool of the twilight—in fact, all of nature *over there* in malarial climes. Hence, the scale on which Ross articulates malarial infection astonishes: a planet where humans, the nineteenth-century premiere agents of history, find themselves in an agonistic struggle with nonhuman microbial life, "uncommon" in the sense of life forms antithetical to human survival.[3]

Animating Anopheles (1912)

A giant mosquito wearing a top hat flies through the open window. The outside infiltrates a domestic space suddenly vulnerable to tiny intruders. Casting knowing glances at the audience the anopheles feasts until he explodes. So goes the transformation of the mosquito, the nonhuman enemy par excellence in Winsor McCay's six-minute line-drawn animation *How a Mosquito Operates* (1912) (see figure 15.1).[4] A first in reverse animation (running the animated sketches backward in the latter part of the film), the film preceded McCay's better-known feature-length animation *Gertie the Dinosaur*, placing the mosquito within an iconography of marvelous creatures—dinosaurs, certainly, but also the winged lizards and sea serpents of McCay's running comic strip *The Land of Wonderful Dreams*. In fact, Gertie first appeared in the comic strip on September 13, 1913, before his appearance on film; and when the film was released, McCay combined live performance *with* the screening, talking to Gertie on stage before a wide-eyed audience when the film first screened at Chicago's Palace Theater on February 8, 1914. As we shall see, McCay's combinatory praxis of juxtaposing graphics, live performance, line-drawn, and, later, cel animation would persist in medical and scientific documentaries on life explicitly marked as *non*human. In turn, the thoroughfare between modes of animating nonhuman life impacts animation as a political technology.

These two scenes from the early twentieth century serve as a link between two seemingly unrelated domains that I hope to engage: (1) scientific animations of infection, a flourishing industry that sells pedagogic films to laboratories, educational institutions, and corporate media platforms at the present juncture; and (2) contemporary globalizing protocols, agreements, and treaties that seek to secure human populations against infection. Scientific animations, plunging us in cellular worlds, nurture the cellular agon of infection, the unending cellular hostilities, as a common human condition. Here the artifice of the self-contained universe, sketched, photographed, or digitized from the advent of single-cel animation (perfected by Earl Hurd in 1914), against which animated actors move, facilitates the act of enclosing us within a single scale of action. We wander in the cellular world, for instance, a marvelous autonomous universe with its own set of rules. We play according to rules of the game that simplify, classify, and differentiate our real enemy as the parasite—and only that. Gone are self-serving human interests that shape the biopolitical distributions of health that we know well from horrifying stories of clinical trials gone bad, *over there*, or indeed from reports on the Trade-Related Aspects of Intellectual Property Rights agreement of 1995 to limit the dissemination of cheap generic drugs for AIDS-related therapies.[5] Consequently, animation can come to constitute a cultural ethos that rationalizes globalizing biosecurity imperatives as benign collective projects. If we reinsert the global as a myth of totality back into the cellular-planetary axis, then the limitations of rules that serve the specific interests of corporations, institutions, and states become clear.

If the epistemology of infection, with its founding cellular agon, makes "worlds" in the name of science, animation media technologies, in particular, offer ample arsenal. From the moment of inception, the labor-intensive production process (McCay was reputed to draw four thousand sketches a month for his line-drawn work) modeled procedures for visualizing cellular life in the laboratory: for instance, while animation techniques layered image and background in a composite, scientists marked cells under scrutiny with dyes of cells to *foreground* them against the extracellular environment. More important, both scientist and animator obsessively focused on a microunit, a single cel image or an organic cell, *stilled* in action, attending to the minutiae of changes, modifications, and reconfigurations to the unit. McCay's "split system" of using "key frames" in his storyboards, before sketching in the transitional frames, exemplified the scientific effort to isolate snapshots in the life cycle of microbes. Certainly the microunit, copied and multiplied, proliferating and moving between discrete worlds, preoccupied both scientists and animators. In cel animation an image drawn on cellulose acetate could speed across painted or photographed backgrounds, from the tropics to the North Pole in a second. What better technology could one have to vivify uncontrolled *infection* sweeping across the hitherto discrete global environments? No wonder animation came to play a central role in the epistemology of infection by the second decade of the twentieth century. But that was a time of escalating human hostilities. Hence, animating infection would irrevocably become a militarized scientific enterprise at this historical juncture, and therefore instructive for present obsessions with biosecurity.

A fundamental part of the visualization of "life itself" (the prevailing critical shorthand for our biological existence) was cinematic malaria animations made for scientific research (mostly lab microcinematography in the early years) and for public health (military-training films during the Second World War). My underlying claim is that the *epistemology of infection* in mid-twentieth-century film animation was formative to the militarization of biosecurity regimes on a global scale, evolving as they did into "vital systems preparedness" for all catastrophes that are widely prevalent today.[6] If we live in constant terror of the next bioterrorist infraction, as the recent flap over lab-engineered flu viruses for research indicates, a return to the Pacific theater of war, where we see a consolidation of the first infrastructures of preparedness, is timely indeed. There the tropics, those infamous hot zones of rampant infections that haunt global public-health initiatives, appear as a dehumanized milieu that lays asunder human life. There both human hostilities and ecological disequilibria play a role in exacerbating our cellular agon.

My main argument concerns the animation of "life itself" at a moment of crisis, when life faces the possibility of catastrophic annihilation, and the corollary infection topologies constitutive of biosecurity as we understand it today. Animation turns infection, in its double articulation as ontological condition and scientific theory, into a concrete epistemological object, as Hans-Jörg Rheinberger has argued vis-à-vis the gene.[7] The object is concrete because the epistemology of infection is as dependent on laboratory techniques and procedures (e.g., changes in staining, dyeing, or freezing cells), advanced bioimaging technologies (e.g., new microscopes capable of amplifying protein fluorescence), and innovative software (e.g., three-dimensional reconstructions of the cell from sectional images) as it is on shifting scientific protocols and methods, adaptive public-health regulations, and a dynamic popular culture on human and nonhuman collectivities. Yet most scholarship on mediating life itself remains focused on exciting technologies and booming informatics, lightly skirting the *governance* of vital circulations through media technologies. There are complex analyses of molecular and cellular imaging that meticulously elaborate new possibilities offered by fluorescent microscopy, X-ray tomography, and confocal microscopy (mostly in laboratory pedagogy of the life sciences).[8] There is flourishing research on bioimaging as theory and practice (e.g., Christopher Kelty and Hannah Landecker's engagements with the material processes of capturing cellular life over the span of the twentieth century) and on the truth effects of the bioinformatic turn (e.g., Kirsten Ostherr's scrutiny of medical animation as documentary).[9] And there is rigorous interrogation of the globalizing force of prophylaxis, which includes collusions between big pharma, university laboratories, research institutes, local and supranational public-health agencies, policy wonks, and financial investors, in maintaining infection equilibriums (e.g., Melinda Cooper, Joe Dumit, and Kaushik Sunder Rajan's ongoing projects on biocapital).[10] Only on few occasions do theorists of global capital work alongside theorists of science and media technologies ask how imaging and informatics technologies produce value, in order to govern life within ecological networks. Such governance through biosecurity regimes is inextricable from the integrative processes of global capitalism.

The story of malaria, eclipsed when parasites receded before the march of illustrious and resilient viruses, elaborates this hitherto unexplored dimension: a cellular agon, with its specific modalities (its formal grammar, its techniques, and even its genres) manifesting as biosecurity. If war has been the touchstone for the expansion of industrial capital, what role does the mediation, and specifically the *animation*, of life itself play in this global history? I offer a theory of the cellular agon as a provisional starting point to make the theoretical connections between technological and political projects of securing life against unseen hostile forces within the ecological network. Imaging infection entails the vivification of what was once supplementary to the cell (the customary focal point): its milieu (conventionally construed as the extracellular environment). In cellular animations of microbial forms hostile to value-laden cells that are critical for human survival, such as red blood cells (microbial forms infiltrate, reconfigure, and finally kill these cells), the milieu bites back. A topology—a mathematical structure allowing for articulations of convergence, connectedness, and continuities—of infection emerges, galvanizing medical prophylactics aimed at restoring cellular and extracellular equilibrium. If, as in the case of malaria, that topology extends well beyond the human body and into the world, then we are faced with the politics of "to make live and let die," as Michel Foucault puts it—the backbone of biosecurity. It is thus critical to look at exactly how these cellular wars are vivified, because of what those processes illuminate about the contemporary shadows of biological warfare.

The roots of imaging infection as a state of war are firmly yoked to the history of film animation. It is in malaria film that a third layer of animation becomes readily apparent: not the bioengineered "making live" of dead matter, not bioimaging and consequent computational reconstruction, but the animation of dying human cells struggling to live (to repair and regenerate) against existing ecological hostilities. That dimension manifest as a cinematic cellular agon stabilized during the Second World War when U.S. forces found themselves *over there*, in the Pacific, where a nonhuman enemy proved to be their greatest threat. In 1943 for every wounded British and American soldier evacuated from the Pacific theater, there were 128 sick with malaria. Given this subliminal war that redrew battle lines between human and nonhuman armies, I focus on military training films made between 1942 and 1945 that contextualize the flourishing cellular agon we find in spectacular scientific edutainment today.

The Cellular Agon; or, When the Milieu Bit Back

Malaria animation has an unforgettable, iconic image: the delicate female anopheles mosquito poised on human skin, pointed proboscis penetrating the surface. Almost every malaria film from the 1940s to the present visualizes this moment of entry, the bite, as the opening sequence to human infection. Unlike the sporozoites that are only perceptible under the microscope, the anopheles is visible evidence of endemic hostilities. This cel-animated image from *The Winged Scourge* (1943) (see figure 15.2), the first among the educational shorts produced by Disney Studios under the aegis of the Office of Coordinator of Inter-American Affairs,[11] is followed by a series of diagrammatic sketches illustrating plasmodium passages (figure 15.3), static images of potential victims, and then the well-loved seven dwarfs heartily engaged in DDT spraying, assembling door screens, and eliminating pools of stagnant water. The combination of graphic forms and cel animation in this classic exemplifies the repertoire we find in most malaria animations. There are graphs, curves, and diagrams, the language of scientific instruction. There are well-loved cartoon figures, iconic humans as agents within the controlled, playful, cartoon universe. There are cel-animated moving images, as we see in the superimposed frame in figure 15.2, where the shot of the exposed human arm of a sleeping man fades into a close-up of anopheles on skin. There are static images of diagrams explained by the voice-of-god male narrator. There is cinematographic footage of swamps, of coming twilight, of plant-crowded water pools. And there is the inexorable sonic buzz of the coming mosquito before any close-up of the carrier. Such a combination of visual and sonic elements not just vivifies dynamic cellular processes but also codifies observation.[12] Consequently, these combinatory praxes effectively animate theories of the life, rendering them perceptible and intelligible.[13] Even as the sketches and diagrams slow down the processes of infection, reducing movement so we may better understand and calculate incidence, the second layer (the backdrop to the mosquito's antics) changes swiftly, generating the composite effect of speed. The animated mosquito zips across multiple global zones in a minute, conveying uncontrollable spreading infection. The viewer is caught in an experience of slowness and momentum that underscores the mammoth task of infection control that faces scientists, administrators, and the common man.

The combinations that Kelty and Landecker track in early twentieth-century films—time-lapse sequences of live cells writhing in preparations, hand-drawn images, line-drawn and cel-animated cartoons, and diagrams—recur in the military-training films, but with the one important difference.[14] These training films, "prophylactic media" as Kirsten Ostherr characterizes them, heavily rely on popular, culturally familiar cartoon figures to close the deal.[15] As a result, the films socialize us,

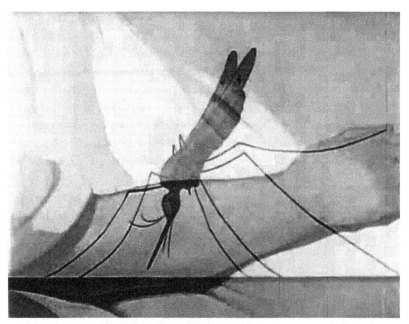

FIGURE 15.2 Cel animation of mosquito on human skin. Frame from *The Winged Scourge* (1943). Courtesy of Walt Disney Studios.

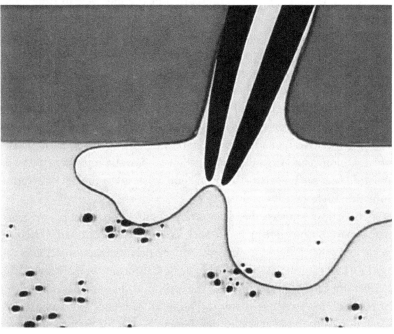

FIGURE 15.3 Diagram of mosquito bite. Frame from *The Winged Scourge* (1943). Courtesy of Walt Disney Studios.

teaching procedures and regulations for securing human life against infectious agents. Most of these films commence with codified scientific observation or realistic footage of the South Pacific, and then they introduce the cognitively estranging cartoon characters to animate what remains imperceptible to the eye: the larvae under water, the single hungry female anopheles too mobile to be visually captured, and the sporozoites within the bloodstream and liver. Ultimately, the cartoons codify the nonhuman world within and around us where the human is no longer the agent of change, of modifying life, even as the cartoon universe simplifies the complex topologies of infection.

But how do these films animate a cellular agon? Here it is constructive to return to Kelty and Landecker's argument regarding the status of bioimages in relation to knowledge. Less concerned with the ontological status of bioimages, the scholars sketch the scientific debates over the accuracy of capturing life in its dynamism that erupted after Julius Ries's famous film on the sea urchin in 1909: arguments over histological dyes that "killed" living cells; over the problem of fixing preparations that could sustain a cell through all its cycles; over the stitching of several different cells, shot at different moments of cell cycles, to represent one cell cycle; and over the compression of the life cycle in time-lapse photography. It is more important that such conversations testify to the denaturing of life itself under the microscopic gaze. Hence, argue Kelty and Landecker, there is greater continuity than we think between early twentieth-century microcinematographic manipulations of cellular imaging and the seemingly more artificial algorithmic reconstructions of cellular life at the close of the century. My interest is in articulating these perspectives on cellular life in terms of the imaging of infection or the colonization of a host organism by a parasite. If cellularity is the epistemology of *an* organism as the sum of discrete, repetitive parts, as Aristid Lindenmayer theorized it in 1968, what is the impact of imaging infection on animating cellularity?[16]

After all, the microcinematography of infection emerges over the same span of time, dating as far back as 1912, when commercial houses such as Pathé, Edison, Gaumont, and British Instructional Films, as well as laboratories at the University of California, Berkeley, and the University of Rochester in New York, produced scientific animations of malaria. The 1928 *Life History of Mosquito Aëdes Aegypti*, an Eastman classroom film made at the Kodak Research Lab, for instance, deploys time-lapse photography to track the life of the mosquito and shuttles between static and mobile images to make a case for the necessary restoration of ecological equilibrium. In this regard, unlike cel animations, an urgency pervades these projects of securing human life against the vicious carrier of malaria. There is already a strong perception of an elemental agonistic war, necessitated by malaria and yellow fever outbreaks among U.S. and British military units during the first two decades of the twentieth century. And we already see the beginnings of a cellular agon, the war within the cell, planetary in proportion, demanding public-health interventions. By 1927 W. Allen Daley, a British medical officer, coauthored a book on the efficacy of film as a public-health tool.[17] By 1933 President Roosevelt had funded the Tennessee Valley Authority and charged it with controlling malaria, which was impeding regional economic development; and between 1934 and 1940, corporations such as the German Bayer AG pharmaceuticals company (which developed the antimalarial chloroquine in 1934) and the British Shell Corporation had begun to produce malaria animations. The forces marshaled against the parasite were on the upswing when the war in the Pacific broke out.

I will turn to the public-health documentaries during the Second World War shortly. But what does this history of malaria animation reveal? Certainly it makes the unfolding of a cellular agon constitutive of cellular epistemology. Originally understood as a struggle for victory in the Olympic Games, the Greek term *agonia* underwrites the notion of the cellular agon that I theorize here, a war that unfolds in states of infection. If one confines oneself to biophysical or biochemical analyses of cellular processes, the term might seem a stretch. After all, cells are irrevocably porous and changeful; they routinely divide, separate, multiply, reconfigure, and die. But I am after an epistemological moment when the scientific gaze differentiates unicellular and multicellular biological organisms that live off human cells from value-laden human cells, and externalizes them as enemies engaged in hostile takeovers of a human host. Such a gaze is called forth by the frenetic activity of living organisms that catalyze mass human-cellular death. Animation not only theoretically reanimates the state of affairs before death but also remains integral for the mediation of this external object. The production of a composite layered image central to animation, multiplying and superimposing a single microunit (say, a mosquito) upon different background layers, enhances the possibilities of creating the sharp foreground-background distinctions attractive to scientists interested in differentiating, freezing, and then calculating cellular processes. The composite image further enables visualizing infection as a topographical assemblage, as cellular exchanges transpire between insect, human, and parasite. The nonhuman agent (parasite and mosquito) is differentiated and jettisoned as belonging outside the human cell but still threateningly close, in the *milieu intérieur* (as Claude Bernard named it) or in the extracellular environment that ensures stability for multicellular living organisms. Of course, we have been long disabused of the notion of the human body as a separable "organic edifice," because contemporary science routinely positions the human within a network of organic and inorganic matter.[18] The idea of a dynamic network is resonant in Georges Canguilhem's elaboration of the milieu as the dynamic *medium* within which living organisms exist—an ensemble of actions rather than a passive environment.[19] Hence, the moment of the cellular agon is also when the milieu comes alive. It reveals itself in combinations of interacting agents: parasites and carriers but also water, plants, temperature, humidity, and bad airs.

In the recursive and highly symbolic icon of the hungry pregnant anopheles of the mid-twentieth-century malaria films, the milieu bites back. The instructional animations vivify the struggle between human and nonhuman cells that have irreconcilable differences, even as scientists, doctors, public-health specialists, and medical officers theorize the potentiality of cells to repair and regenerate against uncommon microbial life. In this regard, these animations are speculative technologies, warnings and predictions of rising infection. Calculations arise: What are the levels of the external agent within the milieu intérieur? How does the agent penetrate and reconfigure the cell? What is its lifespan? How can we secure its multiplication in order to stave off human-cell catastrophe? Interventions follow: What panacea is at hand? And, in the absence of a panacea, what medical prophylactics can be advanced? These questions jettison us back to the mid-twentieth century when infection topologies and security measures became inextricable, the one unthinkable without the specter of the other.

Securing Life; or, Once upon a Time in the Pacific, 1942–1945

The images still transfix. The sultry, blowsy Annie, the most dangerous criminal at large and on the lookout for lonesome U.S. soldiers on their patriotic sojourn over in the Pacific. In 1943 the U.S. armed forces commissioned Ted Geisel (Dr. Seuss) to do an educational pamphlet for American troops serving in the Pacific theater. The result was the "This Is Ann!" pamphlet, which introduced the cartoon femme fatale just dying to drink "your" blood in her sojourn *over there*: "She's at home in Africa, the Caribbean, India, the South and Southwest Pacific, and other hot spots!" ran the accompanying caption, at once binding "Enemy Number Two" to the tropics. The cultural codification of an experienced, even rapacious, sex worker salaciously eyeing young American men would stick, making its way into animated medical instructional films for military training. In 1942 Colonel Frank Capra was already at the helm of the Armed Forces Motion Picture Unit, with Geisel in charge of the animation branch. The upshot was the memorable Private Snafu animated instructional films, featuring a boyish, hapless soldier bumbling along (through multiple snafus) in forgivable ways. Shortly after Capra created Private Snafu, mainly for a biweekly newsreel just for the armed forces, the Armed Forces Motion Picture Unit decided to let Disney Studios have the first crack. The results are unforgettable, especially with regard to developing a formal grammar, the *langue* of the cellular agon. With a "trail of broken men" in her wake, Ann / Annie surfaced in *Private Snafu: "Its Murder She Says"* (1945), educating younger sex workers by recounting her glorious sexual past (see figure 15.4). The campy voice-over turned nonhuman biological drives into human motives, even as the humor of the cartoon form defanged the hostility; moreover, the customary fun of violent clashes, chases, crashes, explosions of the toon universe absorbed the *ur-trauma* of the mosquito penetrating human skin. Even in scientific animations of anopheles, the voice-over often underscores a voracious *female* appetite, as the pregnant mosquito goes for a "blood meal" before laying eggs. Life itself, unleashed biological drives, becomes the motivation for the hostile act; hence, both reproduction and the sexual drive provide culturally recognizable rationales for nonhuman action. The human figure, embodied in the raw, young soldier, also has a healthy sex drive, an ungovernable youthful vitality that "opens" him, as the mosquitoes often murmur while licking their chops, to nonhuman penetration. The female anopheles seduces Snafu, while Malaria Mike (see figure 15.5), an older man who eyes Snafu's baby butt (calling it his "filet mignon") in *Private Snafu and Malaria Mike* (1944), penetrates the *unsuspecting* soldier as he takes a dip. Both the seduction and rape are featured as acts of sexual hostility, personalizing infection trauma and localizing threat to the prostitute and the war profiteer; and yet, in this characteristically homophobic codification, it is suggested that while Annie might snare a willing Snafu, Mike's imagined rape is unalterably sex without consent.

Dreaming of scuttling American victories in the Pacific, Malaria Mike fantasizes the appropriate answer to his son's plaintive question "what

FIGURE 15.4 Annie recounting her sexual adventures to younger colleagues. Frame from *Private Snafu: "It's Murder She Says"* (1945). Courtesy of Warner Bros.

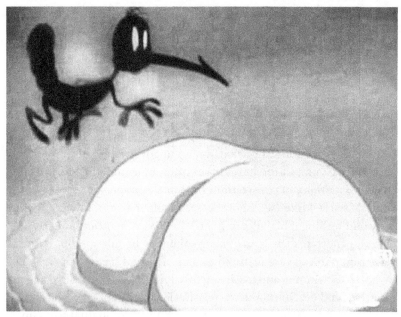

FIGURE 15.5 Malaria Mike targeting Snafu's butt. Frame from *Private Snafu and Malaria Mike* (1944). Courtesy of Warner Bros.

did you do in the great war, Daddy?" to be "I did my share!" Here the iconic sexually threatening figure becomes a saboteur who lays American bravery to waste, preying on the young, the future of the nation. This mobilization against America associatively grows across the ensemble of the animated cartoon films, with *The Six-Legged Saboteurs* (1940), an early short made by the U.S. Department of Agriculture, first introducing the idea. The spectator is privy to a secret meeting of the "Insect Axis," made up of mosquitoes, boll weevils, and fruit flies that hope to inflict $150,000 in economic damage to America; at the head, of course, is the anopheles as Hitler, complete with his *Mein Malaria*. With these warnings, mosquitoes are perceived as heralding not just military defeat but massive economic catastrophe (from crop failures to the shutting down of factories), solidifying links between disease, capital, and war. By the close of the war, in films such as *Criminal at Large* (1945), the blowsy Annie has morphed into a global female terrorist hunted by a young foreign correspondent on the lookout for new battle zones.

The cultural iconography around the mosquito as the visible, if minute, malarial agent is critical to the orientation of infection as agonistic struggle. I begin with these symbolic codifications, intentionally, in order to critique the assumption that the study of media materiality—media technologies, instruments, institutions, and infrastructures—need not involve a rigorous scrutiny of representation. Cellular materiality is to be found in preparations, tissue cultures, technological instruments, and software programs, *as well as* in signifiers (images, sounds, and words). All these media practices contribute to animating the cellular agon as the epistemology of infection.

The cartoons codify in order to socialize, strategically securing American bodies against the abnormal as nonhuman. The cartoons form a part of a vast audiovisual repertoire of the cellular agon that includes instructional films for clinical training and for preparedness drills, such as *Malaria: Cause and Control* (1942) and three documentaries from 1944: *Malaria, Personal Health in the Jungle*, and *Clinical Malaria*.[20] Of these, *Clinical Malaria* offers the widest range of animation techniques and strategies and serves as the paradigmatic instance. Made for medical instruction on identifying malaria symptoms, the film commences with a live-action shot of a scientist peering through a microscope as the voice-over introduces malaria as the "greatest invader in history." Then there is a cut from the observing scientist (an image that makes us anticipate a cut to what he sees, the slide under the microscope) to a rotating globe, while the narration catalogs all the regions (Asia, Latin America, Africa) that fall under the shadow of the anopheles. Cut to the iconic mosquito on skin, a line-drawn image, before moving to static sketches of a patient infected with malaria; then a zoom under the skin, cutting to a line-drawn animated diagram of the artery's interior where sporozoites swim. For the next fifteen minutes of this documentary, with a total running time of twenty-five minutes and thirty seconds, a "slide" of mobile sporozoites coursing through infected blood shot in time-lapse photography runs along the bottom of the screen. In the meantime, a part on the top of the screen features several other animated forms: a rising and falling temperature graph (the primary image), a line-drawn static cartoon of a patient, the diagram of the human body with arrows marking the liver (where the merozoites develop), and sometimes cel-animated enlarged versions of the parasite in its many avatars (sporozoites, merozoites, and gametocytes). The combination effectively explains malaria to the common viewer, with the laboratory microcinematography acting as an authenticating trace despite everything we know about sectioning, preparations, imaging, and motion capture. The running slide at the bottom of the screen further signals the motility of the nonhuman agent, its silent movement through vectors of transmission (open drains, mosquito saliva, human bloodstream). All this is mixed in with cinematographic footage of tents, landscapes, doctors, and medical assistance, mixtures of live action and animation that we see in almost all the instructional documentaries. The image production of malaria, then, arises at the intersection of live action and animation, and therefore prompts the question: do these modes act in concert to enact the calculative rationality behind militarized biosecurity? Or are the relations between them more complex? It would be difficult to generalize, given the diversity of the combinations we encounter in these instructional documentaries. But, by and large, graphic, line-drawn, and cel-animated forms, together with indexical microcinematographic footage in these documentaries, tend to reduce movement, slowing and stilling action, even freezing moments for further analysis. Against such efforts, cinematic live-action footage and a soundscape tailored for each milieu produce a sense of flux: of perceptions of speed, of changing scales (switching between body, social space, and environment), and of meteorological and geological differences. The world is not the same everywhere, and what happens elsewhere will inexorably come home to roost, goes the story of uncontrollable flux. Hence, quixotically, in these scientific animations of life itself, live action implicitly emerges as a beneficent media.[21]

But there is another significant effect of this combinatory praxis worth noting in these efforts to create an image of life itself: the curious emergence of an insect vision, to see as the mosquito does in order to know it better. This is profoundly present in the complex observational mode of the documentaries. If we take *Clinical Malaria* as our example, observation is one of the four procedures (techniques and protocols) for animating life; codification, vivification, and translation are the others. Observation includes microcinematographic footage of the mosquito and parasite life cycles. Sequences of the cellular change are foreshortened in time-lapse photography in order to artificially produce these life cycles for running durations of three to six minutes; the temporality of life, in this instance, requires artificial splicing for scientific intelligibility. In virtually all the films, the visual temporality is recast as prediction: while the voice-over prolepses constantly look ahead to what is to come ("these tiny sporozoites will one day . . ."), the indexical images anchor predictions to an authoritative scientific calculus. On the other hand, there is live-action footage in wide pans of marshes, swamps, puddles, ponds, and pools; of troops marching; of planes swooping down; and of verdant trees, bushes, and water plants. The back-and-forth cuts, within this observational mode, assemble this tropical geography into the field of the microscopic gaze, and the scale switching turns cellular infection into an ever-widening gyre. A critical part of this observation is what cannot be seen—"the jungle you can't see," as one film remarks—but what registers as the sonic trace of the enemy, an unrelenting buzz. The mosquito approaches, unseen but heard. A roaming speculative eye, poised against abstracted indexical images of life itself, can only inductively calibrate an image of the mosquito. The ensuing image is a composite culled from multiple images and sounds, a calibration that makes the viewer see like an insect. Insects register multiple images of a single source in the compound eye, and these are subsequently neurologically processed into one image for the brain; the multiplicity of images characteristically enhance the sense of motion important to perceiving danger. The combinatory praxis of these instructional films effectively induces such insect vision, even as other graphic elements attempt to arrest speculative processing through codification. This observational mode is complemented by the signaling of a social *and* scientific theory of infection. Arrows, graphs, curves, and other scientific markings indicate what our focal point should be (often the tiny parasite differentiated as the catalyst for catastrophic cellular decay), while the cultural iconography of the cartoons spurs us to hold common human interests dear against uncommon life.

While observation and codification work toward intelligibility, uncommon life (mosquito and parasite) becomes perceptible (sensory and affective) in a series of vivifications that "bring to life" the imperceptible. Vivifications enlarge, magnify, zoom in, distend, and amplify: there are close-ups of hand-drawn images that superimpose the specter of the mosquito over realist footage; shots of massive physical models of the mosquito towering among trees; amplified images of parasites under the microscope; and the magnified buzz of the mosquito indistinguishable from the drone of attacking airplanes. More than any other technique, vivified sounds and images are most successful in the affecting agon in these audiovisual transcriptions of an identifiable enemy. Finally, the instructional films recursively translate a set of key messages — enemy, danger, preventive action — through flexible translations of content in multiple formats: the cinematic image is vivified in static hand-drawn images, then sketched on a blackboard, and, sometimes, transcribed into a cartoon character. The iterative structure turns mosquito and parasite into a multiheaded hydra: the enemy is a cellular terrorist, an economic drain, a military saboteur, and a social deviant. The attack comes at many levels, on multiple scales. In this way, these processes animate the cellular agon, mobilizing sight, sound, slide, footage, artwork, models, camera speeds and apertures, dyes and stains, and biological preparations. By the close of the films, Enemy Number Two has become intelligible, legitimizing the move toward biosecurity.

That move is accomplished by a topological articulation of malaria, which establishes an enduring link between the preservation of human life and the military control of territory made urgent during the Pacific War. Malaria outbreaks were already a recognizable security threat during the U.S. actions in Panama, Puerto Rico, and the Philippines, and with the acquisition of new military bases in the Caribbean. By the time the Tropical Disease Control Section was established in 1942, malaria had become *the* premiere threat to the U.S. military. Consequently, the Malaria Control in War Areas was formed to prevent malaria infection in wartime areas, and later to prevent civilian infection as the troops demobilized. After the war, the U.S. Public Health Service saw the need to create an organization whose primary charge would be biosecurity, leading to the formation of the Communicable Diseases Center in 1946 (renamed the Centers for Disease Control in 1980). By 1950 the center had developed the Epidemic Intelligence Service, and the wartime scientific films became valuable archival material for further strategic interventions. Between 1947 and 1951, malaria was eradicated in the United States after the successful mass manufacture of DDT and less toxic antimalarial drugs.[22] The eradication was so successful, in fact, that U.S. models for malaria prevention, including audiovisual pedagogy, became transposable interventions across the world, and the World Health Organization launched a global campaign against malaria in 1955. The history tells us that the struggle over malaria, cellular or otherwise, is inextricable from the rhetoric of war. A war that, in the 1960s, had been won — at least, so it was thought in the historical West. That myth would persist, as Melinda Cooper has shown, until the eruption of ungovernable viruses (e.g., Ebola, HIV, West Nile) in the late 1970s to the early 1980s.[23]

The Pacific War theater was one of the historical junctures when the scientific and the popular intelligibility of life itself became bound to its ontological preservation through what Foucault characterizes as the "apparatuses of security." Much has been said regarding the famous Foucauldian formulation in his Collège de France lectures, so my allusion to that genealogy will be rather cursory.[24] In those lectures, Foucault offers a third articulation of power, the apparatus of security, which does not punish or kill (as sovereign juridical power does) or correct, survey, or observe (as the law dies) but calculates and intervenes in the vital circulations of human life. Security apparatuses adjust balances and check overflows, quantifying the risk distributions in a population. The target is not this body or that population but a form of life itself, our very biological existence without which there would no longer be any human societies; the target is a modification of the biological destiny of the species. Looking at smallpox-inoculation campaigns of the eighteenth century, Foucault argues that security is manifest in the logic of inoculation where the pathogen is not eradicated but its levels in the body are maintained at a minimum. Security is a calculative rationality that speculates on probable infections in the near future. A part of the calculation is estimating internal borders within populations and separating certain social aggregates (high-risk cases, such as the elderly) from others (low-risk, healthy individuals). The latter, as productive subjects, are central to our biological destiny, to social reproduction. In the cartoon animations discussed here, we see the recursive figures of the young soldier, the teenage girl (her neck exposed to the mosquito), and the hard-working father as the potential victims; no middle-aged woman past her child-bearing years or elderly citizens make an appearance. In this way, the cartoons effortlessly link economic productivity, social reproduction, and biological equilibrium.

More important perhaps is that security always territorializes, Foucault insists, and we see such a move across the mid-twentieth-century military-training films. The topology of infection becomes culturally codified as a particular topography of (malarial) infection. The cellular agon is unmistakably territorialized: the organic edifice of the body initially violated by the mosquito on skin is immediately secured through a series of boundaries visualized in close-ups of protective clothing (socks, uniforms), mosquito nets, tents, and screen doors. These prophylactic surfaces act as deterrents, lines of militarized control, against a perversely porous natural landscape booming with sonic disturbances of unseen presences. Sometimes diagrammatic idioms such as arrows and circles highlight imperceptible flows and flights, directing our gaze to hidden vectors of disease transmission. The difference between live-action footage and graphic forms creates a disjunctively layered visual space, making a quotidian milieu palimpsestically live, in active ferment. The live-action sequences are where we find a nonhuman world as changeful, mutable, and impossible to contain; the graphic elements and cel-animated forms freeze particular moments, such as entry into the body or the movement into the liver. We can only access the nonhuman enemy (mosquito and parasite) if we inductively calibrate a composite image, carefully directed by diagrammatic forms. In several films, live-action footage also features men or machines at war against the nonhuman enemy, painstakingly dousing the hostile milieu with chemicals (aerosol cans and equipment for spraying DDT) as if to keep nature at bay. Voice-overs underscore these agonistic acts as necessary calculative measures intervening in the balance of life itself, which is now a vast ecological network of nonhuman agents. We are told *how much* DDT should be sprayed, what *grade* of mosquito net is best, how *many* tablets to take, how *much* insect repellent to rub, how *high* the fevers can get, how *often* the sweat breaks—a calculative rationality at the heart of security measures. Security does not kill, to echo Foucault, but strives to restore equilibrium; security divides, contains, and territorializes to distribute quantified risks—this time, across global regions. Globes, maps, and shots of newspaper headlines (reporting malaria in India and China) territorialize the natural world into global zones ready for biosecurity interventions, even as the films reinforce incommensu-

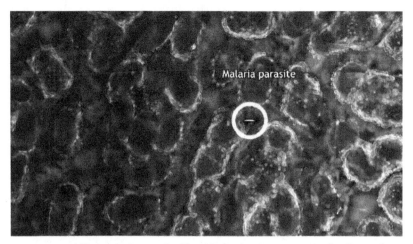

FIGURE 15.6 The malaria parasite identified as luminescent microbe. Frame from *Life Cycle of Malaria: The Human Host* (2011). Courtesy of Howard Hughes Medical Institute.

rable differences between the "godforsaken hole" of the outpost (as Private Snafu puts it) and the home front. The hot spots where "Anopheles Annie" rules the roost, slugging back her martinis, recede into the jungles, into the verdant tropics. Within the narrative of security, calculations and intervention pay off as those wild regions, the sketched or photographed backdrops to the antics of the animated mosquito, are steadily brought to order by the onward march of the U.S. armed forces. And so the cellular agon becomes expressive as topography marked by division, segregation, and containment. The cellular agon unfolds as unending antagonism, immortalized in the recursive image of the anopheles treading human skin.

And yet our *knowledge* of the mosquito remains partly speculative, always a composite projection cobbled together from multiple sources that signal an unseen enemy. Animation freezes, stills; but its artifice — its multiple forms and its radical estrangement from realistic footage — also brings home the impossibility of capturing life itself.

Coda: The Coming of the Cellular Fantastic

If in mid-twentieth-century films, a strong sense of incommensurable differences between the vital interests of parasites, mosquitoes, and humans endures (and with it the unhomely topos of hostile nature) past the late twentieth-century ecological movements, then that cellular agon is now recast as inevitable, even pleasurable, incommensura-bility. We live with viruses; we depend on synthetic technologies to play the game within our cellular systems. The cellular agon now manifests not as spectral terror but as a domain of the marvelous: the cellular fantastic (to echo Akira Lippit's "optical fantastic" in the first half of the twentieth century) emergent in present-day scientific edutainment.[25] Advanced imaging technologies and software enable immersive 3-D animations of cellular and extracellular environments in film shorts that take us on voyages reminiscent of intergalactic passages. Malaria animations still commence with eschatological narrations of parasites that once brought the world's most valorous (Genghis Khan, Alexander the Great, and George Washington) to their knees; the imaging techniques and software for image transcriptions are, however, radically different.[26] Cells glow while lit with luminescent proteins, sectional images become three-dimensional, and a mobile camera surfs the cellular galaxies. Still, the focal point in the immersive field remains the nonhuman (see figure 15.6; the tiny sporozoite is diagrammatically circled), the dark passenger of our extracellular environment. The cellular agon arrives zoning the fluid 3-D universe. Incommensurable differentials appear in our field of vision, and epic journeys turn into war games. The film's abiding pull "worlds" once more, securing the human as the premiere subject of history.[27]

Notes

1. Malaria infection has double articulation in the human host (which experiences cellular catastrophe) and an infected mosquito, the carrier. The bite of an infected mosquito passes the plasmodium in the mosquito's saliva into the human bloodstream; there the plasmodium travels to the liver, where it multiplies and differentiates into merozoites in human liver cells. These leave the liver to reenter the bloodstream and enter and explode red blood cells, replicating and multiplying in the process. They eventually develop into male or female gametocytes. When a mosquito bites an infected human, a blood meal necessary for the pregnant female anopheles, the mosquito absorbs the gametocytes from the infected human; these further develop into gametes (new plasmodium) within the mosquito. When the infected mosquito bites again, the cycle begins anew.

2. There is a great deal of controversy over the patrimony of malaria research: Alphonse Lavern certainly, but also Patrick Manson and Italian malariologists, led by Giovanni Battista Grassi, described in the 1890s how human malaria was transmitted by the anopheles mosquito. Because Ross was a colonial administrator, malaria was an endemic problem in his view, a genocidal force in the

tropics (as early as 1852, a malaria epidemic had wiped out the entire village of Ula in Bengal, where Ross conducted much of his research).

3. In his provocative essay "Uncommon Life," Eugene Thacker pursues the new ecological collectives where microbial and human organisms are placed in equivalence.

4. The short is also known as *The Story of the Mosquito* and comprised of six thousand cel drawings. An early innovator, Winsor McCay's contributions have been eclipsed by cultural figures such as Max Fleischer and Walt Disney. Before his animated films, McCay published comic strips in the Sunday section of newspapers: *Little Nemo in Slumberland* in 1905 and, later, "Dreams of a Rarebit Fiend" (both were published under a pseudonym, Silas); he later gained renown for traveling with his animated shorts and accompanying screenings with vaudeville acts in which he held out his hand to his animated creations.

5. For details on the agreement, see "WTO and the Trips Agreement," World Health Organization, accessed February 12, 2012, http://www.who.int/medicines/areas /policy/wto_trips/en/index.html.

6. See Lakoff, "Preparing for the Next Emergency."

7. Rheinberger, *An Epistemology of the Concrete*.

8. Rogerio Amino et al., "Imaging Parasites in Vivo," in Shorte and Frischknecht, *Imaging Cellular and Molecular Biological Functions*, 345–64.

9. See Kelty and Landecker, "A Theory of Animation." For more on epistemologies of life itself, see Landecker, *Culturing Life*; and Rheinberger, *An Epistemology of the Concrete*. Regarding Ostherr, I am referring to an unpublished essay that she is crafting for *The Blackwell Companion to Contemporary Documentary Studies* (forthcoming in 2014), titled "Animating Informatics: Scientific Discovery through Documentary Film," as well as her monograph *Cinematic Prophylaxis*.

10. The cluster of works include Cooper, *Life as Surplus*; Dumit, *Picturing Personhood*; and Sunder Rajan, *Biocapital*.

11. The Office of the Coordinator of Inter-American Affairs, a U.S. agency appointed by Roosevelt with Nelson Rockefeller at its head, was formed to promote inter-American cooperation during the 1940s, especially in commercial and economic areas.

12. Kelty and Landecker, "A Theory of Animation," 38.

13. Kelty and Landecker, "A Theory of Animation," 33.

14. Kelty and Landecker, "A Theory of Animation," 40.

15. Ostherr, *Cinematic Prophylaxis*.

16. The biologist Aristid Lindenmayer developed the formal grammar of plants that came to be known as L-systems: see "Mathematical Models for Cellular Interaction in Development," *Journal of Theoretical Biology* 18 (1968): 280–315.

17. Daley and Viney, *Popular Education in Public Health*.

18. Landecker, *Culturing Life*, 62–63.

19. Canguilhelm, *Knowledge of Life*.

20. Right after the war, a few prophylactic films continued to be made to prevent malaria infection in the U.S. South, particularly in humid Tennessee (e.g., *Mosquito Proofing for Malaria* from 1949, a documentary that ran for ten minutes

and eighteen seconds and was made by the Tennessee Valley, Malaria Control in War Areas, and the U.S. Public Health Services). When malaria was eradicated in the United States, similar documentaries were made for dissemination all over the world (for example, *India's War against Malaria* and *Malaria Prevention* in the late 1960s).

21. I am indebted to Karen Beckman for encouraging me to attend closely to the cultural work of live action in these documentaries.

22. DDT (dichlorodiphenyltrichloroethane) is a pesticide once widely used to control insects in agriculture, especially insects that carry diseases such as malaria. Its use in the United States was banned in 1972 because of damage to wildlife, but it is still used in some countries.

23. Cooper, *Life as Surplus*.

24. See Foucault, *Security, Territory, Population*.

25. Akira Lippit's account in *Atomic Light (Shadow Optics)* of the "optical fantastic" triangulates the development of X-ray technologies, the splitting of the atom, and psychoanalysis.

26. For more on new imaging technologies, and therein a newly transparent body, see Dijck, *The Transparent Body*.

27. A recent diptych of malaria documentaries—the *Life Cycle of Malaria: The Human Host* (four minutes and seventeen seconds) and *Mosquito Host* (three minutes and fifty-nine seconds)—was funded by the Howard Hughes Medical Institute, a nonprofit organization advancing biomedical research. The institute spent as much as $825 million on research in 2011, which included $60 million for a film-production unit.

16 :: **Realism in the Animation Media Environment: Animation Theory from Japan**

MARC STEINBERG

Realism and animation? Realism *in* animation? The association of the two terms may seem incongruous to those more familiar with notions of filmic realism. *Realism* is undoubtedly a term much more closely associated with film than with animation.[1] In part we can understand this to be a product of film's relationship with profilmic reality; film offers an image and style of movement that is an iconically and indexically faithful portrait of the profilmic events that occurred in front of the camera. This also comes in part from the greater prominence of debates around realism at various stages within film discourse, criticism, and theory. Film's phenomenological reproduction of reality, or its artificial or semiotic construction of realism (depending on whom you ask), was one of the key dividing lines between the supposed naive phenomenological approach of André Bazin and the more critical approach of writers associated with 1970s screen theory. Finally, the link between film and realism is made all the stronger by the multiple film movements that have evoked concepts of realism — from Italian neorealism to the kitchen-sink realism of the British new wave to the long-take, long-shot aesthetic of what is sometimes called slow cinema or contemporary contemplative cinema that informs contemporary transnational art cinemas.

Animation has traditionally had a far more tenuous relationship to realism. It is not in any obvious way a realist form. While there is no inherent contradiction between drawing and realism — indeed realism as a concept emerges from both literary studies and painting in the nineteenth century — animators have tended to embrace nonrealistic styles of drawing and movement in their creations.[2] Similarly, realism has historically not been a key component to animation criticism or theory. What theoretical works on animation there were tended to emphasize the nonrealistic quality of animation—one need only think of Sergei Eisenstein's fragments on Disney, wherein the theorist-filmmaker finds the plasmaticness of animation of the greatest interest.[3]

One site where theoretical, critical, and practical interest in realism in animation first comes together is around the work of Disney. Walt Disney famously pushed his animators toward a greater verisimilitude of movement and weight displacement in the drawing of their characters. Disney's drive toward realism was also taken to new levels in his attempt to reproduce the filmic production of depth in the form of the multiplane camera, a camera with multiple levels of glass separated spatially, allowing animators to produce a cinematic illusion of depth (from differentiation between foreground, middle ground, and background to the simulation of racking focus and the creation of out-of-focus parts of the shot). Disney aimed for the production of what Paul Wells, borrowing a term from Umberto Eco, calls "hyper-realism."[4] *Hyperrealism* is an appropriate term because it implicitly traces a lineage of animation from Disney to the three-dimensional computer-generated imagery (3-D CGI), a more recent development in animation wherein we encounter the problematic of realism. This heightened form of realism is often known as hyperrealism, or, in Andrew Darley's coinage, "second order realism."[5]

What makes Darley's term *second-order realism* so useful is that it clearly states what is sometimes ambiguous: that the referent for CGI's realism is not "the real world" or the profilmic but rather cinematic conventions of realist representation: the perspective of objects recorded by a monocular camera lens, lens flare, perspectival depth, motion blur, and so on. This distinguishes Darley's work from that, say, of Stephen Prince, whose seemingly similar term, "perceptual realism," ultimately refers to what the referent of the image, *if it had existed*, would have looked like to the perceiver. Prince's interest lies in how "even unreal [i.e., animated] images can be perceptually realistic"—how nonindexical, nonphotographic images could still seem to us to be perceptually real.[6] When Darley defines second-order realism as "an attempt to produce old ways of seeing or representing by other means," he ultimately takes one step further and forward by suggesting that animated realism—in Disney as in contemporary CGI—is in fact a representation of an older form of representation: the animated reproduction of standard photographic techniques.[7]

Realism and Animation: Japanese Debates

This brief sketch of the state of debates on realism in animation studies provides us with a ground from which to approach the place of realism and animation within Japanese critical discourse of the 2000s. Two of Japan's main animation critics and public intellectuals, Ōtsuka Eiji and Azuma Hiroki, have organized part of their critical work around the question of realism in animation.[8] However, the principal manner in which these writers engage with realism resembles (and exceeds) Darley's conception of second-order realism. Animation, for these writers, is not a medium capable of reproducing realism as much as it is a medium that itself provides the basis for "animation-like" work within a different media form. Realism is first and foremost a set of conventions proper to a historically produced configuration of a given medium, rather than a visual resemblance to a given reality. Moreover, Ōtsuka and Azuma push the debate one step further by suggesting that realism applies not to animation's imitation of another medium (cinema) but rather another medium's imitation of animation styles and problems.

In addition to providing this different take on the relation between animation and realism, my discussion of Ōtsuka and Azuma's writings also provides a gateway into the ways that animation has been engaged with and theorized within recent Japanese critical discourse. Beginning in the late 1990s and really taking off in the early 2000s, public intellectuals such as Ōtsuka and Azuma, as well as Saitō Tamaki, Kasai Kiyoshi, Uno Tsunehiro, Itō Gō, and others, organized their critical activities in part around commentary on Japanese animation, its associated forms of media (comics, novels, and games), its cultures of consumption, and the critical terminology that often develops out of its fan cultures.[9] In this sense the trend in critical thought known as *zeronendai no shisō* (thought of the oughts) has seen the unprecedented prominence of animation as a critical node around which much criticism, commentary, and theorization were organized. Granted, one may argue that something similar occurred in the Anglophone world as well around the beginning of the millennium. This trend is embodied in Lev Manovich's famous claim that animation, previously cinema's maligned twin, would become *the* moving-image category par excellence, with live-action cinema becoming a mere subset of animation.[10] The appearance of journals such as *animation: an interdisciplinary journal* and the increasing number of scholars working on some aspect of animation are certainly proof of a rise in the extent and purview of animation scholarship in the Anglophone world.

Yet the parallels also offer some instructive contrasts. While Manovich and many of the contributors to debates around animation in the Anglophone world come from the field of film and media studies, the Japanese critics I have mentioned come from the fields of literary studies, critical theory, and criticism. While many now have academic positions, they come as much from the world of criticism as from academia, a positionality that is reflected in their writing.[11] They write for a broad public readership and frame their discussions of animation very much within wider debates around contemporary "expressive cultures," as they are often called. To be sure there are also a growing number of more academic animation scholars in Japan, often with close ties to film studies, such as the film and animation scholar Katō Mikiro and the animation historian Tsugata Nobuyuki (both, interestingly, based in Kyoto, while Azuma, Ōtsuka, and others are based in Tokyo—leading to the suggestion that the latter group's work should be called Tokyo criticism rather than Japanese criticism). Here I would like to focus on the Ōtsuka-Azuma debate around realism in order to provide a clearer sense of the approach to animation adopted by these writers and to highlight the prominent place of animation within Japanese cultural criticism since the late 1990s. Indeed, the significance of these debates lies both in their theory of realism and in their manner of situating animation within wider cultural and media spheres—in their manner, that is, of situating animation as the environment for a wider media culture. This work on animation debates in Japan will not undertake the rereading of the existing film theory canon for traces of animation criticism, but it will create a portrait of other spaces, milieus, and media ecologies in which animation criticism is being developed, and from which film theory may itself learn. Let us turn then to an examination of the animation criticism in Japan since the late 1990s, with an eye to what it may teach us about the specificity of animation's media ecologies and the critical discourses developed around them.

Ōtsuka Eiji's Three Realisms

Ōtsuka's importance lies in his intervention in two fields: manga criticism and the development of a theory and practice of what he dubbed "narrative consumption." I have introduced and discussed the latter aspect of his work elsewhere, but to sum up briefly: Ōtsuka worked as an editor since the late 1980s for one of the main producers of books, comics, magazines, and animation programs for the hard-core fans known as *otaku*, Kadokawa Books. During this time he also formulated a theory of narrative consumption that has been a constant reference for Azuma and others within the zeronendai group.[12] The second principal field of his critical work lies in his manga criticism, and in his reinterpretation of the development of postwar Japanese manga (comics), anime (animation), and otaku culture. From his award-winning early book *Sengo manga no hyōgen kūkan: Kigōteki shintai no jubaku* (The expressive space of postwar manga: The spell of the semiotic body) through his seminal *Atomu no meidai: Tezuka Osamu to sengo manga no shudai* (The Atomu thesis: Tezuka Osamu and the main theme of postwar manga) to his most recent project on the importance of the prewar and wartime periods on the aesthetics, cinematic style of montage, and themes of postwar manga, found in his *Eiga shiki mangaka nyūmon* (An introduction to cinematic manga artists), Ōtsuka aims to bring to light the historical conditions for the development of manga style and themes that, along with anime as its offshoot, constitute the principal media of otaku culture.

Within this work on the aesthetic and conceptual parameters of postwar manga and anime—the two are often treated as interchangeable and possessing a common expressive base—Ōtsuka develops three conceptions of realism. The first is most fully developed in *Atomu no meidai* and is what we may, for lack of a better term, call *biological realism*. Ōtsuka had long been dealing with a particular tension in postwar manga between the generic, nonrealistic, *semiotic* drawing style and the importance of interiority within much postwar manga, and *shōjo* (girls' manga) in particular. The "semiotic theory of manga" was first elaborated by Tezuka Osamu, in an interview in the magazine *Pafu* where he describes his drawings as mere signs or patterns.[13] According to Tezuka, his drawings are completely detached from any referent or external reality, and insofar as they refer to anything, merely refer to drawing styles developed within Disney animation or Tagawa Suihō's wartime manga (both major influences on a young Tezuka).

The twist that Tezuka gives to these signs is to be found in what is for Ōtsuka a representative scene from an unpublished manga that a young Tezuka wrote in 1945, wherein the so-called semiotic body of a character is shot—and actually bleeds. For Ōtsuka this single comic frame, wherein a sign bleeds, becomes the defining moment of postwar manga and anime. What is born here is the tension between semiotic abstraction "completely cut off from a referent" and "a fleshly body that bleeds if shot."[14] This tension between a character that is a semiotic drawing that has no relation to a real-world referent and yet somehow also possesses a fleshly, physical body that can bleed, die, and have sexual relations with other characters forms the expressive basis for postwar manga and anime.[15] This is the "main topic of postwar manga," which is also the birth of "a new kind of realistic [riarizumu teki] expression that is not dependent on realistic [shajitsu] illustrations."[16]

The second conception of realism that Ōtsuka develops is a much more conventional one: the realism of mechanical objects, particularly vehicles and weapons, that Ōtsuka refers to as "scientific realism," "the realism of the depiction of weapons," and "graphical realism."[17] If the first form of realism is a nonpictorial realism—a realism of bodies or biological realism whose referent is the real-world body that can die—the second form of realism is a pictorial realism, or photo-realism; this is a drawing style that deploys linear perspective to generate a sense of visual resemblance to real-world objects, or their photographic representations. This latter form of realism is deployed most often in the drawing of technical objects such as fighter planes, guns, and military gear. In keeping with his thesis that the roots of the otaku arts of animation and manga are to be found in fascist, wartime Japan, Ōtsuka traces this realistic depiction of machines to the photography and technical drawings of the wartime period, a style quickly imitated by animation and comics of the time and adopted by postwar manga and animation artists like Tezuka. Indeed, there continues to be a tendency toward the realistic depiction of guns, weapons, and military gear in contemporary animation, which often uses 3-D CGI selectively to represent warships, planes, and the like, while cel-style animation is used for characters.[18] The distinction Ōtsuka notes between the semiotic realism of characters and the graphical realism of machines is alive and well to this day.

The third form of realism that Ōtsuka identifies fundamentally differs from the first two: it is neither a realism whose referent is the biological body nor a realism whose referent is the machinic or its photorealistic depiction. It is, rather, a realism whose premise is the environmental ubiquity of animation and manga; a realism whose referent is anime and manga: "manga-anime realism." Ōtsuka first introduces the term at the end of his Monogatari no taisō (Narrative exercises), published in 2000, and further develops the concept in his 2003 book, Kyarakutā shōsetsu no tsukurikata (How to make character novels).[19]

Ōtsuka first develops this concept as a way of grappling with the specificity of what he calls "character novels" but which have since become known as "light novels" (*raito noberu*, or *ranobe* for short). Light novels are a new genre or supergenre of pulp fiction that takes the worlds and characters of manga, anime, and video games as their objects. These novels are generally breezily written, have covers with drawings in the style of manga or anime characters, and include periodic illustrations of these characters throughout the books. They are an extension of young-adult literature, but have, since the 2000s, become widely read and an integral part of the expressive universe of manga-anime and their otaku consumers. These novels' form is also related to the main form of high literature in Japan, known as the "I-novel" (*shishōsetsu*), called such for its first-person narration and characterized by its naturalism or realism.

Whereas the I-novel was based on the naturalistic mode of copying or sketching the world of the author-as-I (with a presumed transparent relationship between the two worlds within critical commentary), the character novel is based on the "copying" of the fictional world of (actual or potential) anime, manga, or video games. As Ōtsuka writes: "Character novels are novels that adopt 'characters' instead of the I-novel's 'I' and use anime-manga realism instead of naturalistic realism."[20] I-novels and the naturalistic form of literature associated with them are "ways of writing prose that transcribe the reality that we live in as a sketch [*shasei*]."[21] Light novels deploy the techniques of capturing reality — sketching, transcribing, copying — proper to the I-novel yet turn them on the worlds of anime and manga; they are novels that sketch the fictional world of anime rather than that of reality, "applying the techniques of naturalism not to 'reality' but rather to 'anime.'"[22] Unlike I-novels, which assume a relation between the real world and the world of fiction as mediated by the interiority of the first-person protagonist, light novels based on the principles of anime-manga realism assume that the world of fiction has a relation to the world of anime or manga and that the "I" is in fact an anime or manga character.[23]

The realism of anime-manga realism is then not a matter of fidelity to a real-world referent — the perceptual realism that Prince sees operating within 3-D CGI, for instance. Rather, it is a style of writing that imports the nonnaturalistic, nonrealist media of Japanese animation and comics into a literary form that operates according to principles of naturalism. It is an operational realism that, in writing anime-manga characters into the naturalistic style of the I-novel, produces a sense that the character itself — a mere conglomeration of codes or patterns, as Tezuka first suggested — has an "I" and hence possesses interiority. This manner of writing characters as if they had interiority is then an interesting evolution of the first form of realism that Ōtsuka identifies as the legacy of Tezuka: the intersection of the semiotic body with the fleshly body. However, it is also the product of a particular form of medial transposition whose effects become most apparent through the theoretical work of Azuma.

Azuma Hiroki's Transmedial Realism

Anime-manga realism is a realism produced by the intersection of a particular expressive milieu (anime and manga and their production of a specific media environment) and the naturalistic formal devices associated with the I-novel. With the ascendency of the light novel in the first decades of the 2000s, a set of highly stylized media forms seemingly quite distant from realistic depiction—animation and comics— becomes the ground for a realism that depends less on these forms' visual proximity to a real-world referent and more on their constitution of a consistent and self-contained media milieu. The environmental pervasiveness of anime and manga styles throughout at least one segment of the Japanese media ecology gives rise to the sensation of realism. That codes can become naturalized and are subsequently experienced as real is a lesson we have known at least since Roland Barthes's *Mythologies*; the twist here is that the naturalization takes place through a particular subgroup of closely interlinked media forms: animation and comics. Hence, what we have is a distinctly transmedial realism: a realism that depends on, first, the aesthetic consistency of anime and manga styles, and, second, the migration to a form of literature whose presumption is a naturalistic relation to the real world.

What about video games, that other medium so closely linked to the media ecologies of manga and anime? Are games also open to the realism associated with anime and manga? For Ōtsuka the answer is clear: no. Video games have a reset button, which goes against the importance of flesh and blood and the possibility of death that is at the heart of the anime-manga expressive world and is the basis for its realism.[24] This is the point at which Azuma Hiroki enters the debate.

Azuma, a relatively younger scholar in a critical milieu where interventions are often defined around generational divides, rose to prominence after publishing *Dōbutsuka suru posutomodan* (The animalizing postmodern; translated into English as *Otaku: Japan's Database Animals*). Azuma's importance comes in part from his mentoring of younger scholars, and from his creation of journals and book series that publish critical debates relating to anime, manga, games, light novels, and the consumer group—otaku—that has become the privileged focus of their analyses.[25] But his importance also comes from his own critical interventions into and creation of debates around areas ranging from anime consumer cultures to Internet architecture and the security state post-9 / 11. His critical work has, as Endō Toshiaki has written in an overview of Japanese critical debates of the 2000s, become "the very 'environment' within a particular sphere of the world of criticism."[26] One of Azuma's most important contributions in this regard was his *Gēmu-teki riarizumu no tanjō: Dōbutsukasuru posutomodan 2* (The birth of game-ic realism: The animalizing postmodern 2).

As the title suggests, the core of this work revolves around an engagement with Ōtsuka's concept of anime-manga realism. Against Ōtsuka, Azuma argues that there *is* such a thing as "game-ic realism."[27] Video games, and the logic of the "replay" that informs them, have completely permeated light novels and so-called novel games (text-heavy computer games with a minimum of branching and a limited degree of user input). The most noticeable manifestation of this is the prevalence of the trope of the loop in light novels throughout the 2000s, though the transformation of the position of the reader, brought in line with the point of view of the player, is also another place that the game-ic is observed within the light novel. If anime-manga realism deals with the "paradoxical theme of expressing the fleshly body through the use of signs," then game-ic realism deals with the paradoxical feat of using a content or meaning-oriented medium such as the novel to express the experience of games—an experience whose primary feature is, according to Azuma, two-way communication, or communication for communication's sake.[28]

Exploring Azuma's theory of game-ic realism would lead us too far astray from the topic of animation and realism. What I would like to hone in on here is the theoretical framework that Azuma develops for understanding how trends such as anime-manga realism and game-ic realism can come into being. For while Ōtsuka develops a theory of what anime-manga realism is, he does not offer a sense of the media processes at work in this transformation. And it is precisely here that Azuma's significant contribution is to be found. The very condition for the development of anime-manga realism or game-ic realism is the permeation of the imagination by the logic of these media forms. The imagination these media inspire has been environmentalized to such a degree that the media's defining traits become the basis for the operation of other media forms. Azuma writes:

> We all live in a specific environment of the imagination. In premodern societies people lived among the accumulation of myths and folktales told by storytellers, the modern author or reader or citizen lived within naturalism, and the postmodern otaku live within the database of characters. These various environments determine the author's forms of expression, as well as the form of consumption of the works.
>
> Moreover, what is important here is that this environment functions across works and across genres.[29]

This environment also functions across media forms. In a move evocative of debates around realism in animation, and particularly of the term *second-order realism*, Azuma suggests that what we encounter in postmodern works grounded in the animation cultures of Japan is *"the realism of an artificial environment."*[30]

This move is not only of interest in the context of the Japanese debates. It also promises to take us one step beyond debates around realism in much Anglophone scholarship on animation and realism insofar as the basis for this realism is not to be found in an adherence either to the perceptually real (with its insistence on the fidelity of the representation to "our" phenomenological perception of real things) or to the filmic real (a second-order realism or photo-realism that insists on filmic representation as the ground, or as the first-order realism). In part because they are far removed from any imperative to portray people or things with fidelity to phenomenological reality or photographic representations, the vibrant worlds of Japanese anime, manga, and games form the basis for an alternative sphere of expression. Anime, manga, and game-ic realisms develop as forms of fidelity to nonrealist modes of representation. This is not the hyperreal, in the sense of a realm of representation that replaces the real. Nor is it of necessity an unreal world, going with the popular and critical assumption that animation must be about the fantastical or the nonexistent. It is a different realm of expression that, as Azuma properly emphasizes, *is* real, that is, has a reality of its own, as well as a form of causality proper to it (here we may recall Azuma's comment to the effect that imaginative environments determine the forms of expression and consumption of works).[31] Realism, then, designates the operation of transcription or transposition from one medium to another, and references the existence of the consistent yet nonrealist realm of expression of anime and manga.

Conclusion

The work around animation and realism in recent Japanese criticism is of interest for two reasons. The first is for the ways the work differs from common discussions of animation and realism that start with the premise that animation can realistically depict the world (whether in terms of the visual level through movement style and 3-D CGI or, as is also claimed for animation, on the emotional level). These discussions instead presume that the environmental pervasiveness of animation's style or theme within a given expressive media ecology can, when its principles or problematics are translated through a different regime of expression (the naturalist novel), lead to a form of expression (the light novel) whose style can be called anime-manga realism, or, under different conditions, game-ic realism.

Second, this work is of interest for the way it takes up an issue—realism—that has played a central role in film theory, and in animation studies in the Anglophone world, and shifts the register at which the issue is considered. Film studies started from and, in some respects, has recently returned to questions of realism from the premise that cinema's force comes from the automaticity of film's recording of reality.[32] The primary engagements of animation studies with realism have been equally organized around issues of second-order realism and photo-realism in the consideration of CGI. Azuma's and Ōtsuka's writings shift the ground from a question of fidelity of representation to realism as a technique of transmedia transcription that assumes anime-manga as an expressive regime or referent that is autonomous (not referentially bound to the real) yet visually and thematically consistent. If one of the problems with this Japanese criticism is its emphasis on literature and other media instead of dealing with the specificity of animation, then this is also the criticism's greatest contribution: to put animation (and its cultures of consumption) in dialogue with a wider media ecology, one that includes literature, comics, and games more than film. Perhaps the end result is that these theories animate media theory more than they do film theory. But these critics should not be faulted for ending up in a different place (a transmedia theory of animation environments) after starting from a different problem (an examination of the impact of anime and manga on literature): both animation studies and film studies can benefit from this transmedia approach to realism. Indeed, this group of writers and the problematics they develop in their debates shows the value of expanding the canons of film and animation theory to include writers from as yet underexplored critical milieus. For it is in these milieus that we may find the potential to overturn some of the most naturalized assumptions in the canons of film and animation theory—such as the continued presumption that realism has to relate to the perceptually "real."

Notes

All translations from Japanese sources are my own, unless otherwise indicated.

1. At this point I am content to assume the common understandings of animation and cinema. Animation will hence be understood to be frame-by-frame work, most commonly encountered as cel, puppet, or CGI animation; cinema will be the automatic recording of some profilmic real. It is the existence of this real, in some form, that marks the common understanding of cinema as bound (by ethics if not by nature) to some form of realism. For a classic display of this association of animation with the unreal and cinema with the real (or a particular form of "rapport with the real"), see Andrew, *What Cinema Is!* I do not share this view; indeed this chapter is about thinking through the particular forms of realism that animation develops, and asks us to theorize.
2. Hayward, *Cinema Studies*, 311.
3. Eisenstein, *The Eisenstein Collection*.
4. Wells, *Understanding Animation*, 25. Wells's discussion of realism and animation in *Understanding Animation* is both thorough and wide-ranging, and this chapter is indebted to it.
5. Darley explicitly sees the realistic CGI animation of Pixar as "continuing a tradition of cartoon realism stretching back to the early efforts of Disney and his animators." Darley, *Visual Digital Culture*, 83. Debates about the stakes and implications of the extension of filmic realism (or *photorealism*) into animation gained fruitful food for thought in *Final Fantasy: The Spirits Within* (Hironobu Sakaguchi, 2001), an early attempt at a full-length, full-CGI animated film that attempts to replicate filmic realism. It was an instructive failure (critical, box-office, and aesthetic) that also formed the basis for several important critical interventions into questions of CGI realism. See LaMarre, "New Media Worlds"; Monnet, "A-Life and the Uncanny in *Final Fantasy: The Spirits Within*"; and Sobchack, "Final Fantasies."
6. Prince, "True Lies," 32.
7. Darley, *Visual Digital Culture*, 83.
8. While I call Ōtsuka and Azuma "animation critics," they are perhaps better described as "subculture media critics"—animation being one of the principal media forms around which the subculture of anime-manga-game fandom is organized.
9. For instance, the term *sekai-kei* (world style), which describes a particular genre of animation and became a flashpoint for critical debate in the mid-2000s, first

developed out of web-based fan discussions in 2002. See Maejima, *Sekai-kei to wa nanika*, 27–28.

10. Manovich, "What Is Digital Cinema?"; a revised and extended version of this essay was included in Manovich, *The Language of New Media*.

11. By "criticism" (*hihyō*) I refer to the general category of critical writing aimed toward a general public by authors who are as likely to be unaffiliated freelance writers as they are to be academics. In the case of this subculture criticism in particular, it must be kept in mind that the forums of discussion are monthly magazines, collections of debates and essays, and paperback books aimed at an interested general audience, rather than an academic audience. Moreover, one of the features of criticism in Japan at least since the 1980s is what we might call its market orientation. Azuma, for instance, has explicitly made "winning" at the marketplace the measure of good criticism. By this measure a bestseller becomes the sign of good criticism. While certainly more critics would decry this position than accept it, Azuma is not alone in taking this stance. On criticism and the market, see Endō, *Zeronendai no ronten*, 53. See also Marilyn Ivy's "Critical Texts, Mass Artifacts"—an analysis of the consumption of theory in the 1980s, which continues to be of critical importance to this day.

12. For a brief introduction to this aspect of Ōtsuka's work, see my "Translator's Introduction" to his "World and Variation," 99–104; I give a fuller account of his work at Kadokawa in chapter 5 of *Anime's Media Mix*.

13. Tezuka uses the words *kigō* (sign) and *patān* (pattern). Cited in Ōtsuka, *Sengo manga no hyōgen kūkan*, 6.

14. Ōtsuka, *Atomu no meidai*, 63, 158.

15. The question of sex is an important one for Ōtsuka for two reasons, which become most clear in a later work, coauthored with Ōsawa Nobuaki, *"Japanimēshon" wa naze yabureru ka*. First, Ōtsuka sees the problem of the relation between the semiotic and the corporeal or biological body playing itself out in the development of shōjo girls' manga in the 1970s with the "1949er" (*24 nen gumi*) generation of women manga artists, whom Ōtsuka understands to be artists who both "inherit and develop" Tezuka's problematic. Second, the doubled semiotic-corporeal body is at the heart of the *moe* phenomenon of so-called two-dimensional love—the sexualization of and attraction to manga, anime, game, and other drawn characters within contemporary male otaku culture. See Ōtsuka and Ōsawa, *"Japanimēshon" wa naze yabureru ka*, 157, 169. For a theoretical treatment of moe that situates it as a postmodern phenomenon (and against which Ōtsuka is writing) see Azuma, *Otaku*.

16. Ōtsuka, *Atomu no meidai*, 171.

17. Ōtsuka, *Atomu no meidai*, 144–48; Ōtsuka and Ōsawa, *"Japanimēshon" wa naze yabureru ka*, 54. The last term, *graphical realism*, is a translation of *shajitsuteki riarizumu*, which could also be rendered "realistic realism"—here mobilizing the two senses of the term *realism*: the convention of realism (the transliteration *riarizumu*) as produced by the tradition of realistic (*shajitsuteki*) depiction, most notably through the technique of linear perspective.

18. On the politics and geopolitics of the use of 3-D CGI in otherwise cel-style animation, see Bolton, "The Quick and the Undead."

19. Ōtsuka, *Monogatari no taisō*, 210; Ōtsuka, *Kyarakutā shōsetsu no tsukurikata*. Ōtsuka is a peculiar writer in the sense that much of his theory is presented in the form of how-to books, reflecting his belief in the need for a close relationship between theory and practice.

20. Ōtsuka, *Monogatari no taisō*, 210.

21. Ōtsuka, *Kyarakutā shōsetsu no tsukurikata*, 22.

22. Ōtsuka, *Monogatari no taisō*, 209–10.

23. Ōtsuka, *Kyarakutā shōsetsu no tsukurikata*, 27.

24. Ōtsuka, *Kyarakutā shōsetsu no tsukurikata*, 142–43.

25. This focus on the male otaku and the exclusively male group of academics and commentators organized around Azuma have fostered a sense that gender critique is unnecessary, or irrelevant. Not surprisingly, this stance has provoked some outrage, as well as also a countertrend that focuses on the female otaku (*fujoshi*) instead. See, for instance, Sugiura, *Fujoshika suru sekai*.

26. Endō, *Zeronendai no ronten*, 22.

27. While the term *ludic realism* may be a smoother translation of the term *geemu-teki*, I opt for *game-ic* to keep the resonances with the term (video or computer) *game* that Azuma is unambiguously referring to.

28. Azuma, *Gēmu-teki riarizumu no tanjō*, 175.

29. Azuma, *Gēmu-teki riarizumu no tanjō*, 64.

30. Azuma, *Gēmu-teki riarizumu no tanjō*, 72.

31. Azuma suggests that while the character database is a "virtual existence that may only exist within the minds of otaku," its economic effects in terms of the sales of hit light novels mean that "it is unmistakably a real existence." Azuma, *Gēmu-teki riarizumu no tanjō*, 44–45.

32. Andrew's *What Cinema Is!* and Rodowick's *The Virtual Life of Film* rather remarkably agree on the fact of film's digital transformation, all the while reaffirming cinema's relation to the real—through the mediation of Bazin, in the former, and Stanley Cavell, in the latter.

17 : : **Some Observations Pertaining to Cartoon Physics; or, The Cartoon Cat in the Machine**

SCOTT BUKATMAN

From Stephen Millhauser's short story "Cat 'n' Mouse," published in the *New Yorker* in 2004:

> The cat is chasing the mouse through the kitchen: between the blue chair legs, over the tabletop with its red-and-white checkered table-cloth that is already sliding in great waves, past the sugar bowl falling to the left and the cream jug falling to the right, over the blue chair back, down the chair legs, across the waxed and butter-yellow floor. The cat and the mouse lean backward and try to stop on the slippery wax, which shows their flawless reflections. Sparks shoot from their heels, but it's much too late: the big door looms. The mouse crashes through, leaving a mouse-shaped hole. The cat crashes through, replacing the mouse-shaped hole with a larger, cat-shaped hole.[1]

Alain Robbe-Grillet meets Tom and Jerry. Millhauser meticulously maps the illogics of a typical funny animal cartoon, producing a calm, dispassionate appraisal of what is usually experienced as seven minutes of frenetic anarchy. The brilliance of the piece lies in its lack of distortion, its accuracy in detailing the causal chains that constitute the gags in a typical chase cartoon. Millhauser's cool, detached prose also has the salutary effect in pointing out just how strange those cartoons actually were. Does the surprise lie in Millhauser's act of making them strange, or is it stranger that these cartoons didn't seem all that strange in the first place?

Anything can happen in a cartoon, as cartoon characters frequently remind us as they blithely ignore the fourth wall and a rather significant ontological gap to address us directly (as, for example, Sylvester the Cat does in 1945's *Peck Up Your Troubles*). But Hollywood cartoons do not give us an entirely disordered universe of chaos and entropy. They give us a world that is ordered, but ordered differently: hence, *cartoon physics*. The term, though not the concept, was introduced in an *Esquire* magazine article in 1980, which formalized a series of laws that would be recognized and accepted by anyone who'd ever spent their formative years watching cartoons. Further amendments have been added along the way, aided by the crowdsourcing made possible by the Internet (not to mention fan cultures: there are laws of cartoon physics that are specific to manga, for example). Some examples, many of which are exemplified by the scenes described by Millhauser:

- Any body suspended in space will remain in space until made aware of its situation.
- Any body in motion will tend to remain in motion until solid matter intervenes suddenly.
- Any body passing through solid matter will leave a perforation conforming to its perimeter.
- Certain bodies can pass through solid walls painted to resemble tunnel entrances; others cannot.
- Any violent rearrangement of feline matter is impermanent.
- A cat will assume the shape of its container.

There is also something that has come to be called "hammerspace," which is the realm behind a character's back from which any object (often an oversized hammer) can be pulled.

Cartoon physics may have its genesis in the animation principle of "squash and stretch"—a phenomenon at least as old as phenakistoscopes. A bouncing ball will squash along the vertical axis and stretch along the horizontal. Overall mass is preserved, and movement can be rendered more realistically and with more fluidity. But this realist principle, exaggerated, produced a comedic effect, and voilà, the Hollywood cartoon was born. Winsor McCay put two of his characters from *Little Nemo in Slumberland* through their squashing and stretching paces in his first animated film, produced in 1911.

So cartoon physics has been with us for nearly as long as cartoons have existed, but it becomes important to write about now because its alternative universe of unnatural laws is threatened by the encroachments of the physics of the real world into the realm of animation in the digital age, a shift I'll address toward the end of this chapter.

Cartoon Physics and Cartoon Bodies

There is something uncanny going on in Millhauser's story: a part of our childhood experience is being returned to us in a way that makes the cartoon's homey familiarity most unhomey. It's a bit disturbing. It's also hilarious, and reminiscent, in a way, of that other act of cartoon-ish estrangement—the opening of Robert Zemeckis's *Who Framed Roger Rabbit* (1988). Recall (for I can't imagine that anyone reading this volume hasn't seen it) that the film begins with a Baby Herman and Roger Rabbit cartoon, replete with flying knives, preternaturally slippery soap, eyeballs popping from heads, and all the rest, until a director's yell of "cut!" reveals to us that these actions were actually happening in real space and time, performed by a cast of "Toons" who coexist, uncomfortably, with humans and in human space. Both Millhauser's story and Zemeckis's film return us to the cartoons of our childhood, their strangeness newly highlighted for our contemplation.

Who Framed Roger Rabbit thematizes what usually goes unremarked on within the works themselves, which is that the diegesis of the Hollywood cartoon is governed by its own set of physical laws, a new set of restrictions that operate in the service of humor. When the private detective Eddie Valiant tries to saw off the handcuffs that bind him to Roger Rabbit, Roger easily slips out of his cuff to help steady things. A predictable (and I mean that in a good way) double take ensues: "Do you mean to tell me you could've taken your hand out of that cuff at any time?" To which Roger replies, "Not at any time! *Only* when it was funny!"

There are a few laws that I want to add—fondly remembered tropes from my childhood, adolescent, and adult viewing experience(s):

- Pepper will *always* make one sneeze.
- Billy goats eat anything and have a special fondness for tin cans.
- Eyeballs are detachable.
- Heads are empty, and smaller creatures can run around inside of them.
- Any explosion will turn a face into an African American caricature.

All of these perhaps belong more properly to the realm of what could be called cartoon *biology*, but, when you get right down to it, all of cartoon physics is ultimately about the body. The laws propose an alternative set of means by which bodies navigate space: momentum trumps inertia, gravity is a sometime thing, solid matter often isn't. And cartoon bodies are possessed of a nearly infinite pliability, which allows them to weather the vicissitudes of cartoon physics (this idea of cartoon characters as differently, miraculously, abled is wonderfully articulated by *Who Framed Roger Rabbit*).

If there is a privileged body within the universe governed by cartoon physics, it undoubtedly belongs to Goofy. Indeterminate biology (what kind of an animal *is* Goofy?) has yielded an infinitely pliable body that seems constantly subject to operations of physical law, both actual and cartoony. He becomes the exemplar of the industrial body that David Kunzle has called "machined almost beyond recognition."[2] Squashed and stretched by gymnastic equipment, or by the act of pitching a baseball (an act that stretches his body nearly to home plate),[3] Goofy demonstrates that what is really at work in the world of cartoon physics is a reimagining of the body and its relation to the world. If my work has centered on such reimaginings (cyberspace, Jerry Lewis movies— *The Nutty Professor* even features another battle with gymnastics equipment—Winsor McCay comics, morphing), then it should be said that cartoon physics is the ur-phenomenon that undergirds them all.

But the Disney sensibility of the 1940s—Goofy's heyday—was a far cry from the animistic wonderland that Sergei Eisenstein celebrated in the earliest Mickey Mouse cartoons. Cartoon physics cannot be allowed free reign in Disney's cartooniverse, and so the laws of physical reality are gently teased rather than mercilessly mocked or overturned. Tom and Jerry cartoons, produced for MGM by William Hanna and Joseph Barbera, blend some of the realism of Disney's technique with a healthy indulgence in the principles of cartoon physics. The world depicted is appealingly solid, making the transgressions of physical law that much more . . . I can't decide whether to write *profound* or *funny*. The suburban decor of the house in which Tom and Jerry dwell and do battle provides an important quotidian backdrop. That bourgeois domesticity (Millhauser is right about the gleaming linoleum floors and polished surfaces) emphasizes the uncanniness of the goings-on—an effect already partly achieved through defamiliarizing perspectives (mouse-eye views from floorboard level or magisterial gazes from atop grandfather clocks) (see figure 17.1).[4]

Cartoon physics is fundamental to the world of Tom and Jerry and informs what happens to both cat and mouse in equal measures. An undulating tablecloth will carry a luscious-looking sundae directly to Jerry's mouth without spilling a drop. Tom's eyebrows, pupils, and the whites of his eyes will pop from his head and float in midair.[5] But the Roadrunner series presents something quite different, and we should pause

FIGURE 17.1 Bourgeois estrangement.

to acknowledge the tragic figure of Wile E. Coyote, who always gets the lit end of the dynamite stick in his struggle to catch that nameless road-runner. Wile E. has a particularly tortured relation to physics, which begins with his unshakeable faith in its predictability. His is an eminently rational mind, and he knows it. In his one guest-starring role in a Bugs Bunny cartoon, *Operation Rabbit* (1952), he announces himself with his card, which reads, "Wile E. Coyote. Genius." Declaring his intention to eat Bugs, he cautions, "Now don't try to get away! I am more muscular, more cunning, faster and larger than you are—aaaaand, I'm a genius!" A bit later in the proceedings he considers a promotion. "Wile E. Coyote—SUPER genius! I like the way that rolls out. Wile E. Coyote, *Super-Genius.*" (He then proceeds to be blown to smithereens.) His plans are meticulous, often carefully mapped and blueprinted, and their reliance on basic principles of physics makes their success seem inevitable. Attach a boxing glove to a massive rock with a giant spring. Lock in place. Release spring. Aaaaaand, in contravention of all the laws governing the properties of mass, the glove remains in place as the rock springs backward, right where a certain coyote has been confidently lurking (figure 17.2). (The coyote's faith in causal relations and step-by-step planning lends itself to the kind of precise descriptive mapping that marked Millhauser's narrative voice in "Cat 'n' Mouse.")

Physics is not his only betrayer, however. In advance of *Duck Amuck*, by the same writer and director team, the very makers of the cartoon itself seem allied against him. Screen space is made complicit with the slipperiness of cartoon physics. In the first Roadrunner cartoon, *Fast and Furry-ous* (1949), Wile E. pulls the old "fake tunnel" trick. Painting a deceptive white line up to a cliff face, he then paints a perfect perspectival painting of a long tunnel, the white line continuing to its ultimate vanishing point, a hint of blue sky marking the tunnel's end in the seeming distance. The camera is placed behind him, giving us a lovely view of what the Roadrunner will see as he approaches, and it's obvious that he'll be fooled. The coyote clears out of sight, taking his painting paraphernalia with him, and an offscreen "beep beep" denotes the bird's approach. The shot continues as the Roadrunner sails onscreen from behind the camera and blithely continues on into the tunnel's simulacral space. The coyote has done his job too well. Cut to a lateral view of the coyote, his face stretched in dismay and disbelief. But he is nothing if not adaptable. Emerging with a look of fierce determination, he rears back and launches himself in pursuit, only to smash up against that all-too-physical rock wall (as it sometimes says on Wile E. Coyote's own

FIGURE 17.2 Spring-loaded.

blueprints, "Ha ha!"). But the coyote's failure has been anticipated, indeed, preordained, by the cut from an axial to a lateral view that demolishes the trompe l'oeil effect, the image's two-dimensionality now evident to us all (figure 17.3). Similarly, in *Beep Beep* (1952), Wile E. lays a short stretch of track laterally across the highway to fake a railroad crossing, but then makes the mistake of camouflaging both ends with some shrubbery to create the illusion of the tracks extending, not just beyond the road, but beyond the boundaries of the *screen*. Cue the train.

Topsy-Turvydom Redux

If I were the kind of person who did research, I'd be interested in learning how frequently kids tried to mimic the behavior that they witnessed in cartoons. Apparently television's Superman, George Reeve, became distraught over stories of children trying to replicate Superman's ability to fly out of windows. But I've yet to hear about kids trying to blow up roadrunners with dynamite (much less with any of the more esoteric products sold by the Acme Company). I suspect that children understand that they are watching something from a world apart, something not mimetic of reality, and therefore not something that they would

FIGURE 17.3 Betrayed by screen space.

seek to mimic in turn. Cowboys and Indians was a popular game. Playing superheroes—of course! But Roadrunner and Coyote, Tom and Jerry, Bugs and Elmer—not so much.

But I wonder what, more specifically, children "get" from cartoon physics. It's tempting to think that it speaks to an anxiety over bodily development and control (what *doesn't?*), but let's remember that kids think next to nothing of falling—skinned knees and elbows are the body art of childhood. Perhaps cartoon physics speaks to a utopian condition of bodily invulnerability then, and all the coyotes, cats, and ducks represent more of an attempt to hold on to (for kids) or return to (for adults) the body that could take a lickin' and keep on tickin'. While I think there's something to this, I'm more tempted to find the utopianism of cartoon physics in the state of licensed topsy-turvydom that it instantiates. The cartoon represents an other space—the screen already separates it from our reality, and its animated status positions it as "other" to the more dominant live-action cinema—in which other rules apply, in which the seemingly immutable laws of the here and now are no longer so determinate. This shares many of the conditions recognized as endemic to the world of play, an activity that often takes place in a magic circle with its own rules and codes of behavior.[6]

In *The Poetics of Slumberland*, I argue that cartoon physics speaks to the key ontological difference between live-action film and animation: a shot in the former is filmed in real time, with the camera recording the movement that occurs before it, while in the latter, the camera only records a series of still images, with the suppression of the real-time movement of switching images as the caesura on which the illusion depends.[7] Projecting live-action cinema reconstitutes the movement that occurred in profilmic space, while projecting filmed animation generates an illusion of movement where there was none. This inversion of the filmic process has, I think, its sly analogue in cartoon physics. If the production of animation is a topsy-turvy version of the production of live-action cinema, then the topsy-turvydom of cartoon physics is its onscreen equivalent, a visible sign of its otherness. And if the animated beings onscreen are marked by their disobedience and unruliness—early cartoon characters seem to exist in a continuous state of rebellion against their animator creators—then cartoon physics maps that disobedience onto the natural world itself.

Millhauser takes up this condition in another story that I've cited elsewhere in my writing, this one a fictionalized version of Winsor McCay's forays into animation: in the story, the artist, forced to abandon his innovative comic strips in favor of meticulously rendered editorial cartoons, finds increasing solace in his nocturnal production of drawings for elaborate animated films. I can't not cite this passage again:

> The animated cartoon was nothing but the poetry of the impossible — therein lay its exhilaration and its secret melancholy. For this willful violation of the actual, while it was an intoxicating release from the constriction of things, was at the same time nothing but a delusion, an attempt to outwit mortality. As such it was doomed to failure. And yet it was desperately important to smash through the constriction of the actual, to unhinge the universe and let the impossible stream in, because otherwise — well, otherwise the world was nothing but an editorial cartoon.[8]

There is a melancholic dimension, but presumably more pronounced for adults. Children, I'd like to think, are simply taking it for granted that there is a realm where all kinds of punishments can be inflicted without consequence. A few bandages, some circling stars, then on to the next adventure, fully restored. Or is Millhauser more correct, and do children see in cartoons a condition to which they know they cannot aspire, and so do not?

I have written about the licensed topsy-turvydom represented by special effects and their destabilizing of perceptual norms, a notion borrowed from Terry Castle's writing on the function of masquerade in the eighteenth-century British novel. These presented "a world of endless, enchanting metamorphosis" and introduced a touch of carnival to a culture sorely in need of one.[9] Castle argues, "In a rigidly taxonomic, conceptually polarized society, it [masquerade] opened up a temporary space of transformation, mutability, and fluidity. It embodied, one might say, a gratifying fantasy of change in a world that sanctioned few changes."[10] This seems almost ridiculously appropriate to the world of animation, and more specifically to the world of the Hollywood cartoon with its re-formations, or overturnings, of physical law.

I had originally pressed this into the service of theorizing how the spectacular elements of cinema might constitute a resistance to narrative's authority — narrative, with its causal logics, containments, and more or less tidy closures. In Hollywood cartoons, however, the narrative is hardly the thing: they revolve instead around a set of situations that will be repeated throughout the series.[11] Settings might change (Yosemite Sam might be a pirate instead of an outlaw), variations might be rung (Bugs and Elmer might be singing opera), but the themes retain their familiarity. Even the comparatively reflexive *Duck Amuck* (1953) can be understood as belonging to the genre of the Daffy Duck cartoon, in which Daffy will try and fail to play his assigned role (western gunfighter, space explorer, detective, Robin Hood). When Michael Maltese and Chuck Jones tried to repeat the formula of *Duck Amuck* with Bugs Bunny now the victim rather than the tormenting animator in *Rabbit Rampage* (1955), the results fell flat; the formula did not work for the genre of the Bugs Bunny cartoon. And whatever stability is represented by the cartoon's finale, the audience knows that the next cartoon will simply reanimate the same conflict, with nothing changed, nothing learned, nothing gained, and nothing lost.

So the topsy-turvydom of cartoon physics represents no threat to narrative power, since the narrative really serves to frame a set of gags that may or may not be specific to this particular variant. No, what is being challenged by cartoon physics, as Millhauser demonstrates in both of the writings cited here, is the logic of the cosmos itself. Eisenstein's celebration of early Disney concentrated on the "rejection of once-and-forever allotted form, freedom from ossification, the ability to dynamically assume any form,"[12] and this was a freedom, he hypothesized, particularly attractive to those laboring in the factories of America. He further explored the animistic attractions of the cartoon, which aligned it with other phenomena, such as children's literature. Everything in the cartoon potentially possesses a life force: inanimate objects possess life, while flowers and trees and cats and mice take on anthropomorphic qualities. Both the cartoon's plasmatic possibilities and its animistic tendencies are reflected in cartoon physics, despite their more rule-bound nature: in a world where a cat will assume the shape of its container, there is clearly a rejection of allotted form, while the capriciousness of the very laws of nature gives those laws something of a life force of their own, which some characters and not others can harness to their own ends. The freedom claimed for the cartoon by Eisenstein here becomes a freedom from traditional causality, freedom from natural law, and freedom from consequence (punishment, death, skinned knees).

The Cartoon Cat in the Machine

If animation is newly popular, either through entirely animated films (*Ratatouille*) or through the incorporation of animated beings into real-world settings (*The Golden Compass*), or the incorporation of captured movement into animated forms (*King Kong*), it is specifically digital animation that dominates. While the occasional hand-animated films may appear from overseas or, even more rarely, from Hollywood (*Fantastic Mr. Fox* [2009], *Coraline* [2009]), digital technology has been largely responsible for animation's renaissance. And digital animation has, historically, had a different set of concerns—its task defined, more often than not, by replicating (and perhaps tweaking) real-world physics.

What Paul Wells has called "realist animation," animation that replicates the formal and stylistic structures of live-action film, has become so much the norm that it frequently goes unremarked.[13] And digital animation extends beyond the cinema—much of the software for rendering physics comes from the world of computer games. Playability, rather than comedy, is the goal, and the immersive experience of console gaming is all too easily interrupted when bodies in space fail to move properly.

The intersection of modeled physics and computer gaming stretches all the way back to the medium's beginnings, with Spacewar (1962). Using crude vector graphics, two players fire at one another's spaceships, but a central body exerts a gravitational pull that affects the ballistics and threatens the ships themselves. The first successful "home" video game was Pong (1975), which was nothing more than angles and trajectories of movement.[14] The subsequent history of console gaming is largely the history of simulation, and as Microsoft and Sony competed for a lucrative market, their machines became increasingly powerful, and this power was dedicated to the modeling of physics in real time.

Books on game design stress physics as a crucial component of a game's realism, and entire books are dedicated to game physics, instructing designers in the modeling of not only gravity and momentum but also light refraction, air and water resistance, friction, collisions, and wave behaviors. To generate more realistically moving bodies for procedural (real-time) animations in games, bodies were composed of rigid body parts connected with virtual joints whose articulations were similarly constrained to those in human bodies. They could thus fall believably, and improvements in programming produced increasingly realistic simulations of human collapse. Real-time animation is thus overwhelmingly placed in the service of the real—never mind whether the world created is historical, alien, or fantastic.

But these "ragdoll physics" simulations had their problems: if issues such as weight, flexibility, and mass weren't properly factored in, bodies could bounce, flounce, and jounce in exaggerated and painfully humorous ways. Machinima examples abound on YouTube of computer-animated characters sailing through the air, bouncing off walls, or sliding head first for the length of city blocks, always to end up unscathed and unbruised, in a heap of articulated limbs, like the ragdolls that gave the phenomenon its name. Ragdoll physics, Gamespot's Vocabularium tells us, became associated with "wild flailing and exaggerated reactions to physical forces," and its accompanying video features actual people mimicking those loose-limbed, bobble-headed pratfalls.[15] What was thus originally a programming glitch, a pothole on the road to realism, became, on the part of gamers, a kind of *détourned* embrace of the resulting cartooniness.

Gamers further exploit programming glitches when performing speedruns—zipping through the levels of a game in the minimum possible time. This mode of play often depends on working against the normal sequence of events in the game ("sequence breaking") or exploiting glitches in the game engine that may involve using a weapon to propel yourself through space in unexpected ways, or that may yield, for example, a suddenly permeable wall under certain, accidentally encountered, conditions ("glitch usage"). It would be nice if any body passing through the glitchy wall would leave a perforation conforming to its perimeter, but you can't have everything.

Speedruns are meticulously planned exhibitions of hacker skill, and they are based on a combination of accidentally discovered phenomena and meticulous analyses of the physics of the game engine. And the possibilities for cartoony fun don't stop there. Gamers able to manipulate the game's programming code can modify variables such as gravity or attraction, exaggerating effects still further: manipulating the "PushActorAway" script, for example, can send adversaries flying into walls with the lightest tap. Hilarity ensues. Thus, cartoon physics still lurks within the more realistic physics of game engines, as its uncanny, playful double: the cartoon cat in the machine. It could even be argued that real physics is actually a mere subset of cartoon physics in the world of gaming—a specific set of computational restrictions imposed on the vast variability of which the technology is capable. I find this somehow reassuring.

It does make one wonder what a game explicitly based on cartoon physics would be like. Would you choose your weapon with an eye toward what shape your adversary will be after the blow is struck? Would a change in your knowledge-state affect what happens to your body, as you discover that your avatar is actually poised high above an abyss that leads to an abrupt descent? After all, there actually is an equivalent to "hammerspace"—in some games you're allowed to carry an unlimited number of weapons, with no consideration of their weight or bulk.

The software that generates the physics in console games has its analogs in the world of cinema. Here too the ability to convincingly animate a body moving through space depends on a consistent physics—objects and beings should behave in a way that makes sense. Even in the genre that most celebrates alternative kinds of bodies—the superhero film— physical laws must be respected, even as a few of them are being revised. As I argue in *The Poetics of Slumberland*, animation in the superhero film represents a kind of constrained plasmatic, one that speaks to the "freedom from allotted form" while unable to fully embrace it.[16]

Perhaps the difficulty arises when cartoon characters or animated figures have to share screen space with live elements. With the signal exception of *Who Framed Roger Rabbit*, animated characters in these films can be seen to have left the world of pure animation, their special realm, to exist in a hybridized reality, and in that reality their playful, internally consistent physics are trumped by those of the real world. Even Jerry the Mouse, in his celebrated partnering with Gene Kelly in *Anchors Aweigh* (1945), loses much of his elasticity, his movements now tethered to those of the undeniably compelling but strictly physical body of Kelly.[17] Similarly, Spider-Man is tethered to Peter Parker, with his frail aunt and unrewarding day job. The emergence of a physics more like the cartoonish becomes a more temporary thing that occurs at more or less predictable intervals when danger threatens.[18] A significant exception to this is Brad Bird's *The Incredibles* (2004), which pairs off interestingly with *Who Framed Roger Rabbit*. Here again there is the existence of differently abled bodies, superheroes now rather than Toons, and a profound suspicion and dis-ease surrounding them. But *The Incredibles* is entirely animated, and so it is free to celebrate those bodies in ways that elude most superhero films.

Strange as it sounds, speedruns and game modifications introduce something similar to a level of *play* to the act of gaming. The rules of the game are jettisoned in favor of something more improvisational and original—the whole point is to elude or elide the rules.[19] And the reemergence of play in the form of a return to cartoon physics makes me wonder whether there isn't a deeper connection between them. Might the supersession of cartoon physics by the comparatively constrained plasmatics of CGI and game engines have its echo in another shift with significance to the world of children: the supersession of unregulated, "free" play by the hyperregulated world of contemporary childhood. Gabrielle Principe cites current neurological research and declares: "If parents and teachers wanted to design a way of life counter to the needs of developing human brains, they'd invent something like modern child-hood."[20] Scheduled play dates, "Mozart effects," prekindergartens, after-school activities, team practices, music lessons, chess clubs, "teaching to the test," abundant achievement awards—all of this mitigates against the improvisational, the playful, the exploratory, the imaginative.[21]

Adults might decry the level of violence in your classic Tom and Jerry or Roadrunner cartoons—it's difficult to make the case that explosion, electrocution, decapitation, defenestration, immolation, and all the rest are the kinds of things that kids *should* be seeing. But this is to con-sider the content of these cartoons on only the most blatant narrative plane, which ignores the cartoonishness of it all, and which ignores the bodily imagination that exists around and through these "violent" dis-plays. Here is the body deformed and reformed—elastic in every sense of the word, an alternative body that is itself the product of imaginative play. Wile E. Coyote and his brethren live, breathe, and blow up in that "magic circle" of play.[22]

The advent of digital animation in Hollywood has yielded films of sometimes great beauty and humor, rich (paradoxically enough) in the textures of the world. But their great achievements can come at the ex-pense of what truly characterized the Hollywood cartoon in its seven-minute heyday—its playful remaking of the world. Of course this ten-dency greatly predates Pixar—from the moment Disney turned its attention to the production of feature films, the realist aesthetic came to the fore. But *Snow White and the Seven Dwarfs* had its Dopey, *Pinocchio* its Gideon, *Dumbo* its pink elephants on parade (not to mention its flying elephant)—physical laws and bodies were transcended *somewhere*. Most of the press around Disney-Pixar's *Brave* (2012) focused on new computer algorithms that could effectively simulate the lead character's unruly *hair*. Somehow that doesn't seem enough (although, truth to tell, it's pretty awesome hair). Meanwhile, in the real world, creative, unstructured, ex-ploratory play has been supplanted by the deeply goal-oriented telos of computer gaming, which is more limiting even in its most "open world" iteration. I miss the impossible. With apologies to William Burroughs, it's time to storm the reality studio—and unleash the cartoon cat.

Notes

1. Millhauser, "Cat 'n' Mouse," 175.
2. Kunzle, *The History of the Comic Strip*, 357.
3. Oddly, the day I wrote this, the guest on National Public Radio's *Fresh Air* pro-

gram was the major-league pitcher Bob Ojeda, who discussed the extraordinary amount of pain his noncartoon body experienced with each and every pitch.

4. Sometimes an African American woman intervenes in the chaos, her role provocatively ambiguous (hausfrau or maid?).

5. Both examples are from *The Million Dollar Cat* (1944).

6. See Huizinga, *Homo Ludens*.

7. Bukatman, *The Poetics of Slumberland*, 47, 155.

8. Millhauser, "The Little Kingdom of J. Franklin Payne," 107.

9. Castle, *The Female Thermometer*, 107.

10. Castle, *The Female Thermometer*, 104.

11. There is some debate about this in film studies circles. Brian Henderson downplays the place of narrative in the Hollywood cartoon short, while Richard Neupert finds the shorts to have all the hallmarks of classical Hollywood narrative, albeit in condensed form. I have to side with Henderson—narrative elements are present, but they hardly represent the same kind of determinant structure as in feature films. I also can't imagine the viewer of a Pepé Le Pew cartoon focusing on, say, issues of closure. For the Hollywood cartoon built around repeating characters, narrative provides an ersatz unity, one that, more than anything else, allows the cartoon to end in its allotted seven minutes. See Henderson, "Cartoon and Narrative in the Films of Frank Tashlin and Preston Sturges"; and Neupert, "We're Happy When We're Sad."

12. Eisenstein, *Eisenstein on Disney* (1986), 21. I believe that all scholarly essays on animation are required to cite this work.

13. See Wells, *Understanding Animation*, 24–28.

14. For a thoughtful history of this period, see Lowood, "Videogames in Computer Space." Thanks to Henry for his assistance on this essay.

15. "Vocabularium—Ragdoll Physics," posted by gamespot, uploaded May 1, 2012, accessed June 9, 2013, http://www.youtube.com/watch?v=9LIhGBB3RdM.

16. Bukatman, *The Poetics of Slumberland*, 205.

17. Jerry's movements are clearly rotoscoped from the footage of Kelly, and so the sequence is actually a disguised version of Kelly partnering with himself.

18. As I've argued in *The Poetics of Slumberland* (203–4), the exception here is the origin sequence, when the body's new abilities are still indeterminate and surprising.

19. To clarify: I'm not implying that something such as a speedrun is a real-time improvisation, but rather that it represents a kind of riff played against the "score" of the game world as its designers envisioned it.

20. Principe, *Your Brain on Childhood*, 17.

21. Henry Jenkins has addressed the relation between computer play and outdoor play in "'Complete Freedom of Movement.'"

22. Huizinga, *Homo Ludens*, 10.

Bibliography

Adorno, Theodor W. "Criteria of New Music." In Theodor W. Adorno, *Sound Figures*, translated by Rodney Livingstone, 145–96. Stanford, CA: Stanford University Press, 1999.

———. "Ernst Kurths 'Musikpsychologie.'" In *Gesammelte Schriften*, vol. 19, *Musikalische Schriften VI*, edited by Rolf Tiedemann, 350–58. Frankfurt am Main: Suhrkamp, 2003.

———. "Musikalische Aphorismen." In *Gesammelte Schriften*, vol. 18, *Musikalische Schriften V*, edited by Rolf Tiedemann, 11–53. Frankfurt am Main: Suhrkamp, 2003.

Adorno, Theodor W., and Walter Benjamin. *The Complete Correspondence, 1928–1940*. Edited by Henri Lonitz and translated by Nicholas Walker. Cambridge, MA: Polity Press, 1999.

Adorno, Theodor W., and Max Horkheimer. "The Culture Industry: Enlightenment as Mass Deception." In *Critical Visions in Film Theory: Classic and Contemporary Readings*, edited by Timothy Corrigan, Patricia White, and Meta Mazaj, 1016–31. Boston: Bedford / St. Martin's, 2011.

Alberti, Walter. *Il cinema di animazione, 1832–1956*. Turin: Edizione Radio Italiana, 1957.

Anderson, Joseph, and Barbara Anderson. "The Myth of Persistence of Vision Revisited." *Journal of Film and Video* 45, no. 1 (Spring 1993): 3–12.

Andrew, Dudley. "The Neglected Tradition of Phenomenology in Film Theory." *Wide Angle* 2, no. 2 (1978): 44–49.

———. *What Cinema Is! Bazin's Quest and Its Charge*. Chichester, West Sussex, UK: Wiley-Blackwell, 2010.

Aristotle. *The Basic Works of Aristotle*, edited by Richard McKeon and translated by R. P. Hardir and R. K. Gaye. New York: Random House, 1966.

Aronowitz, Stanley. "Film: The Art Form of Late Capitalism." *Social Text* 1 (Winter 1979): 110–29.

Asenin, Sergei. *Volshebniki ekrana: Esteticheskie problemy sovremennoi multiplikatsii*. Moscow: Iskusstvo, 1974.

Augustine. *Confessions*. Translated by Rex Warner. New York: New American Library, 1963.

Auriol, Jean-George. "Les premiers dessins animés cinématographiés: Emile Cohl." *La Revue du Cinéma*, no. 6 (January 1930): 12–19.

Awazu Kiyoshi. *Dezain ni nani ga de kiruka*. Tokyo: Tabata shoten, 1969.

———. *Dezain Yakō*. Tokyo: Chikuma shobō, 1974.

———. "Dezain o nen: Kotowari aratame gurafizumu." *Dezain Hihyō* 11 (April 1970): 16–24.

———. "Hōhō to hyōgen ni tsuite: Tōtaru dezain kō." *Dezain Hihyō* 3 (June 1967): 78–87.

Azuma Hiroki. *Dōbutsuka suru posutomodan*. Tokyo: Kodansha, 2001.

———. *Gēmu-teki riarizumu no tanjō: Dōbutsukasuru posutomodan 2*. Tokyo: Kōdansha, 2007.

———. *Otaku: Japan's Database Animals*. Translated by Jonathan E. Abel and Shion Kono. Minneapolis: University of Minnesota Press, 2009.

Bakhtin, Mikhail. *The Dialogic Imagination: Four Essays by M. M. Bakhtin*. Edited by Michael Holquist and translated by Caryl Emerson and Michael Holquist. Austin: University of Texas Press, 1981.

Balázs, Béla. *The Spirit of Film*. In *Béla Balázs: Early Film Theory*, edited by Erica Carter and translated by Rodney Livingstone, 91–234. New York: Berghahn Books, 2010.

Barrier, Michael. *Hollywood Cartoons: American Animation in Its Golden Age*. New York: Oxford University Press, 1999.

Barthes, Roland. "Non Multa Sed Multum." In *Writings on Cy Twombly*, edited by Nicola del Roscio, 88–101. Munich: Schirmer / Mosel, 2002.

Baudrillard, Jean. *The Perfect Crime*. Translated by Chris Turner. London: Verso, 1996.

———. *The Vital Illusion*. Edited by Julia Witwer. New York: Columbia University Press, 2000.

Baudry, Jean-Louis. "Ideological Effects of the Basic Cinematographic Apparatus." In *Film Theory and Criticism: Introductory Readings*, 6th ed., edited by Leo Braudy and Marshall Cohen, 355–65. Oxford: Oxford University Press, 2004.

Bendazzi, Giannalberto. *Cartoons: One Hundred Years of Cinema Animation*. London: John Libbey; Bloomington: Indiana University Press, 1994.

Benjamin, Walter. *Fukusei gijutsu jidai no geijutsu*. Translated by Kawamura Jirō, Takagi Hisao, Takahara Kōhei, and Nomura Osamu. Tokyo: Kinokuniya shoten, 1965.

———. *Gesammelte Schriften*. Vol. 4.2. Edited by Tillman Rexroth. Frankfurt am Main: Suhrkamp, 1991.

———. *Illuminations*. Edited by Hannah Arendt and translated by Harry Zohn. New York: Schocken Books, 1969.

———. *Selected Writings, Volume 2: 1927–1934*. Edited by Michael W. Jennings, Howard Eiland, and Gary Smith and translated by Rodney Livingstone and others. Cambridge, MA: Belknap Press of Harvard University Press, 1999.

———. *Selected Writings, Volume 3: 1935–1938*. Edited by Howard Eiland and

Michael W. Jennings and translated by Edmund Jephcott, Howard Eiland, and others. Cambridge, MA: Belknap Press of Harvard University Press, 2002.

———. *Selected Writings, Volume 4: 1938–1940*. Edited by Howard Eiland and Michael W. Jennings. Translated by Edmund Jephcott and others. Cambridge, MA: Belknap Press of Harvard University Press, 2003.

———. *The Work of Art in the Age of Its Technological Reproducibility, and Other Writings on Media*. Edited by Michael W. Jennings, Brigid Doherty, and Thomas Y. Levin and translated by Edmund Jephcott, Rodney Livingstone, Howard Eiland, and others. Cambridge, MA: Belknap Press of Harvard University Press, 2008.

Bernardi, Joanne R. *Writing in Light: The Silent Scenario and the Japanese Pure Film Movement*. Detroit, MI: Wayne State University Press, 2001.

Bloch, Ernst. *The Utopian Function of Art and Literature: Selected Essays*. Translated by Jack Zipes and Frank Mecklenberg. Cambridge, MA: MIT Press, 1988.

Bolton, Christopher. "The Quick and the Undead: Visual and Political Dynamics in *Blood: The Last Vampire*." *Mechademia* 2: *Networks of Desire* (2007): 125–42.

Boorstin, Daniel. *Gen'ei no jidai: Masukomi ga seizō suru jujitsu*. Translated by Hoshino Ikumi and Gotō Kazuhiko. Tokyo: Sōgen shinsha, 1964.

Bordwell, David, and Noël Carroll, eds. *Post-theory: Reconstructing Film Studies*. Madison: University of Wisconsin Press, 1996.

Bordwell, David, and Kristin Thompson. *Film Art: An Introduction*. 6th ed. New York: McGraw-Hill, 2001.

Boytler, Mikhail. *Reklama i kino-reklama*. Moscow: Teakinopechat, 1926.

Braudy, Leo, and Marshall Cohen, eds. *Film Theory and Criticism: Introductory Readings*. 6th ed. Oxford: Oxford University Press, 2004.

Braun, Ludwig. *Über Herzbewegung und Herzstoss*. Jena, Germany: Gustav Fischer, 1898.

Braun, Marta. *Picturing Time: The Work of Etienne-Jules Marey (1830–1904)*. Chicago: University of Chicago Press, 1992.

Brinckmann, Christine N. *Die anthropomorphe Kamera und andere Schriften zur filmischen Narration*. Edited by Mariann Lewinsky and Alexandra Schneider. Zurich: Chronos Verlag, 1997.

Buchan, Suzanne, ed. *Animated "Worlds."* Eastleigh, UK: John Libbey Publishing, 2006.

———. *The Quay Brothers: Into a Metaphysical Playroom*. Minneapolis: University of Minnesota Press, 2011.

Bukatman, Scott. *The Poetics of Slumberland: Animated Spirits and the Animating Spirit*. Berkeley: University of California Press, 2012.

Burch, Noël. *Life to Those Shadows*. Edited and translated by Ben Brewster. Berkeley: University of California Press, 1990.

Bushkin, A. I. *Triuki i multiplikatsiia*. Edited with an introduction by Lev Kuleshov. Moscow: Kinoteapechat, 1926.

Calichman, Richard F., ed. and trans. *Overcoming Modernity: Cultural Identity in Wartime Japan*. New York: Columbia University Press, 2008.

Canales, Jimena. *A Tenth of a Second: A History*. Chicago: University of Chicago Press, 2010.

Canguilhelm, George. *Knowledge of Life*. Translated by Stefanos Geroulanos and Daniela Ginsburg. New York: Fordham University Press, 2008.

Carroll, Noël. *On Criticism*. New York: Routledge, 2009.

———. "Prospects for Film Theory: A Personal Assessment." In *Post-theory: Reconstructing Film Studies*, edited by David Bordwell and Noël Carroll, 37–68. Madison: University of Wisconsin Press, 1996.

———. "The Specificity Thesis." In *Film Theory and Criticism: Introductory Readings*, 6th ed., edited by Leo Braudy and Marshall Cohen, 332–38. Oxford: Oxford University Press, 2004.

———. *Theorizing the Moving Image*. Cambridge: Cambridge University Press, 2001.

Cartwright, Lisa. *Screening the Body: Tracing Medicine's Visual Culture*. Minneapolis: University of Minnesota Press, 1995.

Cartwright, Lisa, and Brian Goldfarb. "Radiography, Cinematography and the Decline of the Lens." In *Incorporations*, Zone 6, edited by Jonathan Crary and Sanford Kwinter, 190–201. New York: Zone, 1992.

Castle, Terry. *The Female Thermometer: 18th-Century Culture and the Invention of the Uncanny*. New York: Oxford University Press, 1995.

Cavell, Stanley. *The World Viewed: Reflections on the Ontology of Film*. Enlarged ed. Cambridge, MA: Harvard University Press, 1979.

Chadarevian, Soraya de, and Nick Hopwood. "Dimensions of Modelling." In *Models: The Third Dimension of Science*, edited by Soraya de Chadarevian and Nick Hopwood, 1–15. Stanford, CA: Stanford University Press, 2004.

Cholodenko, Alan. "The 'ABCs' of B, or: To Be and Not to Be B." *Film-Philosophy* 14, no. 2 (2010): 84–112.

———. "Animation—Film and Media Studies' 'Blind Spot.'" *Society for Animation Studies Newsletter* 20, no. 1 (Spring 2007).

———. "The Animation of Cinema." *The Semiotic Review of Books* 18, no. 2 (2008): 1–10.

———. "Animation (Theory) as the Poematic: A Reply to the Cognitivists." *Animation Studies* 4 (2009).

———. "Apocalyptic Animation: In the Wake of Hiroshima, Nagasaki, *Godzilla* and Baudrillard." In *Baudrillard West of the Dateline*, edited by Victoria Grace, Heather Worth, and Laurence Simmons, 228–44. Palmerston North, New Zealand: Dunmore Press, 2003.

———. "'The Borders of Our Lives': Frederick Wiseman, Jean Baudrillard and the Question of the Documentary." *International Journal of Baudrillard Studies* 1, no. 2 (July 2004).

———. "'The Crypt, the Haunted House, of Cinema." *Cultural Studies Review* 10, no. 2 (September 2004): 99–113.

———. "(The) Death (of) the Animator, or: The Felicity of Felix," part II: "A Difficulty in the Path of Animation Studies." *Animation Studies* 2 (2007).

———. "(The) Death (of) the Animator, or: The Felicity of Felix," part III: "Death and the Death of Death." In *Selected Writings from the UTS: Sydney International Animation Festival 2010 Symposium*, edited by C. Bowman, 9–32. Sydney: Faculty of Design, Architecture and Building, University of Technology, Sydney, 2010.

———, ed. *The Illusion of Life: Essays on Animation*. Sydney: Power Publications in association with the Australian Film Commission, 1991.

———, ed. *The Illusion of Life 2: More Essays on Animation*. Sydney: Power Publications, 2007.

———. "The Illusion of the Beginning: A Theory of Drawing and Animation." *Afterimage* 28, no. 1 (July / August 2000): 9–12.

———. "Jean Rouch's *Les maîtres fous*: Documentary of Seduction, Seduction of Documentary." In *Three Documentary Filmmakers: Errol Morris, Ross McElwee, Jean Rouch*, edited by William Rothman, 157–77. Albany, NY: SUNY Press, 2009.

———. "The Nutty Universe of Animation, the 'Discipline' of All 'Disciplines,' and That's Not All, Folks!" *International Journal of Baudrillard Studies* 3, no. 1 (January 2006).

———. "'OBJECTS IN MIRROR ARE CLOSER THAN THEY APPEAR': The Virtual Reality of *Jurassic Park* and Jean Baudrillard." In *Jean Baudrillard: Art and Artefact*, edited by Nicholas Zurbrugg, 64–90. London: Sage Publications, 1997.

———. "Speculations on the Animatic Automation." In *The Illusion of Life 2: More Essays on Animation*, edited by Alan Cholodenko. 486–528. Sydney: Power Publications, 2007.

———. "Still Photography?" *Afterimage* 32, no. 5 (March / April 2005): 5–7.

———. "*Who Framed Roger Rabbit*, or the Framing of Animation." In *The Illusion of Life: Essays on Animation*, edited by Alan Cholodenko, 209–42. Sydney: Power Publications in association with the Australian Film Commission, 1991.

———. "Why Animation, Alan?" *Society for Animation Studies Newsletter* 21, no. 1 (2008).

Chong, Doryun, ed. *Tokyo 1955–1970: A New Avant-Garde*. New York: Museum of Modern Art, 2012.

Clarens, Bernard [and André Martin]. *André Martin: Ecrits sur l'animation; Tome 1, Pour lire entre les images*. Edited by Bernard Clarens. Paris: Dreamland, 2000.

Clark, T. J. *Farewell to an Idea: Episodes from a History of Modernism*. New Haven, CT: Yale University Press, 1999.

Coates, Paul. *The Story of the Lost Reflection: The Alienation of the Image in Western and Polish Cinema*. London: Verso, 1985.

Coe, Brian. *The Birth of Photography: The Story of the Formative Years 1800–1900*. New York: Taplinger Publishing Company, 1977.

Comolli, Jean-Louis. "Technique and Ideology: Camera, Perspective, Depth of Field." In *Movies and Methods: An Anthology*, vol. 2, edited by Bill Nichols, 40–57. Berkeley: University of California Press, 1985.

———. "Technique et idéologie (3)." *Cahiers du Cinéma*, no. 231 (August–September 1971): 42–49.

Cooper, Melinda. *Life as Surplus: Biotechnology and Capitalism in the Neoliberal Era*. Seattle: University of Washington Press, 2008.

Courtet-Cohl, Pierre, and Bernard Génin. *Émile Cohl: L'inventeur du dessin animé*. Paris: Omniscience, 2008.

Crafton, Donald. *Before Mickey: The Animated Film, 1898–1928*. Cambridge, MA: MIT Press, 1982.

———. *Before Mickey: The Animated Film, 1898–1928*. Chicago: University of Chicago Press, 1993.

———. *Emile Cohl, Caricature, and Film*. Princeton, NJ: Princeton University Press, 1990.

———. "The Veiled Genealogies of Animation and Cinema." *animation: an interdisciplinary journal* 6, no. 2 (July 2011): 93–110.

Cubitt, Sean. "The Cinema of Attractions: Review Essay." *animation: an interdisciplinary journal* 2, no. 3 (November 2007): 275–86.

Curnow, Wystan. "Lye and Abstract Expressionism." In *Len Lye*, edited by Jean-Michel Bouhours and Roger Horrocks, 205–12. Paris: Centre Pompidou, 2000.

Curtis, Scott. *The Shape of Spectatorship: Art, Science, and Early Cinema in Germany*. New York: Columbia University Press, forthcoming.

———. "Still / Moving: Digital Imaging and Medical Hermeneutics." In *Memory Bytes: History, Technology, and Digital Cultures*, edited by Lauren Rabinowitz and Abraham Geil, 218–54. Durham, NC: Duke University Press, 2004.

Daley, W. Allen, and Hester Viney. *Popular Education in Public Health*. London: H. K. Lewis, 1927.

Darley, Andrew. "Bones of Contention: Thoughts on the Study of Animation." *Animation: An Interdisciplinary Journal* 2, no. 1 (March 2007): 63–76.

———. *Visual Digital Culture: Surface Play and Spectacle in New Media Genres*. London: Routledge, 2004.

Deleuze, Gilles. "The Brain Is the Screen: An Interview with Gilles Deleuze." Translated by Marie Therese Guirgis. In *The Brain Is the Screen: Deleuze and the Philosophy of Cinema*, edited by Gregory Flaxman, 365–73. Minneapolis: University of Minnesota Press, 2000.

———. *Cinema 1: The Movement-Image*. Translated by Hugh Tomlinson and Barbara Habberjam. Minneapolis: University of Minnesota Press, 1986.

———. *Cinema 2: The Time Image*. Translated by Hugh Tomlinson and Robert Galeta. Minneapolis: University of Minnesota Press, 1989.

———. *Frances Bacon: The Logic of Sensation*. Translated by Daniel W. Smith. Minneapolis: University of Minnesota Press, 2003.

Denslow, Philip Kelly. "What Is Animation and Who Needs to Know? An Essay on Definitions." In *A Reader in Animation Studies*, edited by Jayne Pilling, 1–4. London: John Libbey and Co., 1997.

Deriabin, Aleksandr. "Vertov i animatsiia: Roman, kotorogo ne bylo." *Kinovedcheskie zapiski* 52 (2001): 132–44.

Derrida, Jacques. "*Fors*: The Anglish Words of Nicolas Abraham and Maria Torok." Translated by Barbara Johnson. In Nicholas Abraham and Maria Torok, *The Wolf Man's Magic Word: A Cryptonymy*, translated by Nicholas Rand, xi–xlviii. Minneapolis: University of Minnesota Press, 1986.

Dickerman, Leah. "The Propagandizing of Things." In *Aleksandr Rodchenko*, edited by Magdalena Dabrowski, Leah Dickerman, and Peter Galassi, 62–99. New York: Museum of Modern Art, 1998.

Dijck, José van. *The Transparent Body: A Cultural Analysis of Medical Imaging.* Seattle: University of Washington Press, 2005.

Dorfman, Ariel, and Armand Mattelart. *How to Read Donald Duck: Imperialist Ideology in the Disney Comic.* New York: International General, 1975.

Driscoll, Mark. "From Kino-Eye to Anime-Eye / Ai: The Filmed and the Animated in Imamura Taihei's Media Theory." *Japan Forum* 14, no. 2 (September 2002): 269–96.

Drost, Wolfgang. "La photosculpture entre art industriel et artisanat: La réussite de François Willème (1830–1905)." *Gazette des Beaux-Arts* 106, no. 1,401 (October 1985): 113–29.

Dufoix, Stéphane. *La dispersion: Une histoire des usages du mot diaspora.* Paris: Amsterdam Editions, 2012.

Dulac, Germaine. "Aesthetics, Obstacles, Integral *Cinégraphie.*" Translated by Stuart Liebman. In *French Film Theory and Criticism: A History / Anthology, 1907–1939*, vol. 1: 1907–1929, edited by Richard Abel, 389–97. Princeton, NJ: Princeton University Press, 1988.

———. "From 'Visual and Anti-visual Films.'" In *The Avant-Garde Film: A Reader of Theory and Criticism*, vol. 3 of the Anthology Film Archives Series, edited by P. Adams Sitney, 31–35. New York: New York University Press, 1978.

Dumit, Joseph. *Picturing Personhood: Brain Scans and Biomedical Identity.* Princeton, NJ: Princeton University Press, 2003.

Durie, Robin, ed. *Time and the Instant: Essays in the Physics and Philosophy of Time.* Manchester: Clinamen Press, 2000.

Eder, Josef Maria. *Die photographische Camera und die Momentapparate.* Halle a. S.: Knapp, 1892.

Eisenstein, Sergei. *The Eisenstein Collection.* Edited by Richard Taylor. London: Seagull Books, 2006.

———. *Eisenstein on Disney.* Edited by Jay Leyda and translated by Alan Upchurch. Calcutta: Seagull Books, 1986.

———. *Eisenstein on Disney.* Edited by Jay Leyda and translated by Alan Upchurch. London: Methuen, 1988.

———. *Non-indifferent Nature: Film and the Structure of Things.* Translated by Herbert Marshall. Cambridge: Cambridge University Press, 1987.

Eisner, Lotte H. *The Haunted Screen: Expressionism in the German Cinema and the Influence of Max Reinhardt.* Berkeley: University of California Press, 1969.

Ellenbogen, Josh. "Educated Eyes and Impressed Images." *Art History* 33, no. 3 (June 2010): 490–511.

———. *Reasoned and Unreasoned Images: The Photography of Bertillon, Galton and Marey.* University Park: Pennsylvania State University Press, 2012.

Elsaesser, Thomas. "Digital Cinema: Delivery, Event, Time." In *Cinema Futures: Cain, Abel or Cable? The Screen Arts in the Digital Age*, edited by Thomas Elsaesser and Kay Hoffmann, 201–22. Amsterdam: Amsterdam University Press, 1998.

Endō Toshiaki. *Zeronendai no ronten: Webu kōgai karuchā.* Tokyo: Soft Bank, 2011.

Enzensberger, Hans Magnus. "Media ron no tame no tsumikibako." Translated by Nakano Kōji. *Bungei* 10, no. 9 (1971): 236–57.

Epstein, Jean. "The Cinema Seen from Etna" (1926). Translated by Stuart Liebman. In *Jean Epstein: Critical Essays and New Translations*, edited by Sarah Keller and Jason N. Paul, 287–92. Amsterdam: Amsterdam University Press, 2012.

———. "On Certain Characteristics of *Photogénie*" (1924). In *French Film Theory and Criticism: A History/Anthology, 1907–1929*, vol. 1, edited by Richard Able, 314–18. Princeton, NJ: Princeton University Press, 1988.

Ermanski, J. [Osip]. *Wissenschaftliche Betriebsorganisation und Taylor-System.* Translated by Judith Grünfeld. Berlin: J. H. W. Dietz Nachf., 1925.

Evett, Elisa. *The Critical Reception of Japanese Art in Late Nineteenth Century Europe.* Ann Arbor, MI: UMI Research Press, 1982.

Foster, R. B. *Hopwood's Living Pictures.* 2nd ed. London: Hatton Press, Ltd., 1915.

Foucault, Michel. *The Archaeology of Knowledge.* Translated by A. M. Sheridan Smith. New York: Pantheon, 1972.

———. *Security, Territory, Population: Lectures at the Collège de France, 1977–1978.* Edited by Michel Senellart and translated by Graham Burchell. New York: Picador, 2009.

Freud, Sigmund. "Drei Abhandlungen zur Sexualtheorie." In *Gesammelte Werke*, Band V (1904–1905), 27–145. Frankfurt am Main: S. Fischer, 1968–1978.

Friedberg, Anne. *The Virtual Window from Alberti to Microsoft.* Cambridge, MA: MIT Press, 2006.

Friedman, Ryan Jay. *Hollywood's African American Films: The Transition to Sound.* New Brunswick, NJ: Rutgers University Press, 2011.

Frizot, Michel. *Etienne-Jules Marey chronophotographe.* Paris: Nathan, 2001.

———. "Le temps de l'espace: Les préoccupations stérégnosiques de Marey." In *Le relief au cinéma*, edited by Thierry Lefebvre and Philippe-Alain Michaud, special issue, *1895, revue de l'Association française de recherche sur l'histoire du cinéma*, 58–81. Paris: Association française de recherche sur l'histoire du cinéma, 1997.

———. *Le temps d'un mouvement: Aventures et mesaventures de l'instant photographique.* Paris: Centre National de la Photographie, 1986.

Fukuoka, Maki. "Toward a Synthesized History of Photography: A Conceptual Genealogy of Shashin." *positions: east asia cultures critique* 18, no. 3 (Winter 2010): 571–97.

Furniss, Maureen. *The Animation Bible: A Practical Guide to the Art of Animating, from Flipbooks to Flash.* New York: Abrams, 2008.

———. *Art in Motion: Animation Aesthetics.* London: John Libbey and Co., 1998.

———. *Art in Motion: Animation Aesthetics.* Rev. ed. London: John Libbey and Co., 2007.

Furuhata, Yuriko. "Rethinking Plasticity: The Politics and Production of the Animated Image." *Animation* 6, no. 1 (March 2011): 25–38.

Fusco, Coco. "Fantasies of Oppositionality—Reflections on Recent Conferences in Boston and New York." *Screen* 29, no. 4 (1988): 80–93.

Gadamer, Hans-Georg. *Wahrheit und Methode. Grundzüge einer philosophischen Hermeneutik.* Tübingen: Mohr Siebeck, 1972.

Gadassik, Alla. "Ghosts in the Machine: The Body in Digital Animation." In *Popular Ghosts: The Haunted Spaces of Everyday Culture*, edited by María del Pilar Blanco and Esther Peeren, 225–38. New York: Continuum, 2010.

Gall, Jean-Luc. "Photo / Sculpture: L'Invention de François Willème." *Etudes Photographiques* 3 (November 1997): 64–81.

Gassner, Hubertus. "The Constructivists: Modernism on the Way to Modernization." In *The Great Utopia: The Russian and Soviet Avant-Garde, 1915–1932*, 298–319. Exhibition catalogue. New York: Guggenheim Museum, 1992.

Gauthier, Christophe. "Une composition française. Histoire de la mémoire du cinéma en France des origines à la Seconde Guerre Mondiale." PhD diss., Université de Paris 1, 2007.

———. "L'invention des 'primitifs' à l'orée du parlant: Le cas Méliès." In *Cahiers Parisiens / Parisian Notebooks*, vol. 2, edited by Robert Morrissey, 148–75. Paris: University of Chicago Center in Paris, 2006.

Gautier, Théophile. *Photosculpture*. Paris: Paul Dupont, 1864.

Gaycken, Oliver. "The Cinema of the Future: Visions of the Medium as Modern Educator." In *Learning with the Lights Off: Educational Film in the United States*, edited by Dan Streible, Marsha Orgeron, and Devin Orgeron, 67–89. New York: Oxford University Press, 2011.

———. "'The Swarming of Life': Moving Pictures, Education, and Views through the Microscope." *Science in Context* 24, no. 3 (September 2011): 361–80.

Gerow, Aaron. *Visions of Japanese Modernity: Articulations of Cinema, Nation, and Spectatorship, 1895–1925*. Berkeley: University of California Press, 2010.

Ginzburg, S. *Kinematografiia Dorevoliutsionnoi Rossii*. Moscow: Iskusstvo, 1963.

Gough, Maria. *The Artist as Producer: Russian Constructivism in Revolution*. Berkeley: University of California Press, 2005.

———. "Constructivism Disoriented: El Lissitzky's Dresden and Hannover *Demonstrationsräume*." In *Situating El Lissitzky: Vitebsk, Berlin, Moscow*, edited by Nancy Perloff and Brian Reed, 77–125. Los Angeles: Getty Research Institute, 2003.

Gräper, Ludwig. "Die Methodik der Stereokinematographischen Untersuchung des lebenden vitalgefärbten Hühnerembryos." *Wilhelm Roux' Archiv für Entwicklungsmechanik der Organismen* 115 (1929): 523–41.

Grierson, John. "First Principles of Documentary." In *Grierson on Documentary*, edited and with an introduction by Forsyth Hardy, 78–89. New York: Harcourt, Brace, 1947. Republished in *Film: A Montage of Theories*, edited by Richard Dyer MacCann, 207–15. New York: E. P. Dutton and Co, Inc., 1966.

Grieveson, Lee. "The Work of Film in the Age of Fordist Mechanization." *Cinema Journal* 51, no. 3 (Spring 2012): 25–51.

Grossman, Jeffrey. "The Reception of Walter Benjamin in the Anglo-American Literary Institution." *German Quarterly* 65, nos. 3/4 (Summer 1992): 414–28.

Gunning, Tom. "An Aesthetic of Astonishment: Early Film and the (In)credulous Spectator." *Art and Text* 34 (Spring 1989): 31–45.

———. "The Cinema of Attraction: Early Film, Its Spectator and the Avant-Garde." *Wide Angle* 8, nos. 3–4 (1986): 63–70.

―――. "Moving Away from the Index: Cinema and the Impression of Reality." *Differences: A Journal of Feminist Cultural Studies* 18, no. 1 (2007): 29–52.

―――. "Never Seen This Picture Before: Muybridge in Multiplicity." In *Time Stands Still: Muybridge and the Instantaneous Photography Movement*, edited by Phillip Prodger, 222–72. Oxford: Oxford University Press, 2003.

―――. "New Thresholds of Vision: Instantaneous Photography and the Early Cinema of the Lumière Company." In *Impossible Presence: Surface and Screen in the Photogenic Era*, edited by Terry Smith, 71–100. Sydney: Powers Publications, 2001.

―――. "The Play between Still and Moving Images: Nineteenth-Century 'Philosophical Toys' and Their Discourse." In *Between Stillness and Motion: Film, Photography, Algorithms*, edited by Eivind Røssaak, 27–43. Amsterdam: Amsterdam University Press, 2011.

Halberstam, Judith. *The Queer Art of Failure*. Durham, NC: Duke University Press, 2011.

Hall, Stuart. "Cultural Studies and Its Theoretical Legacies." In *Stuart Hall: Critical Dialogues in Cultural Studies*, edited by David Morley and Kuan-Hsing Chen, 262–75. London: Routledge, 1996.

Hansen, Miriam Bratu. *Cinema and Experience: Siegfried Kracauer, Walter Benjamin, and Theodor W. Adorno*. Berkeley: University of California Press, 2012.

―――. "Of Ducks and Mice: Benjamin and Adorno on Disney." *South Atlantic Quarterly* 92, no. 1 (Winter 1993): 27–61.

Harding, Colin, and Simon Popple, eds. *In the Kingdom of Shadows: A Companion to Early Cinema*. London: Cygnus Arts, 1996.

Hartungen [C. Herting], Ch. [Christoph] von. *Psychologie der Reklame*. Stuttgart: C. E. Poeschel, 1921.

Hayward, Susan. *Cinema Studies: The Key Concepts*. 2nd ed. London: Routledge, 2003.

Hegel, Georg Wilhelm Friedrich. *Lectures on the History of Philosophy, Volume 1: Greek Philosophy to Plato*. Translated by E. S. Haldane. Lincoln: University of Nebraska Press, 1995.

Henderson, Brian. "Cartoon and Narrative in the Films of Frank Tashlin and Preston Sturges." In *Comedy / Cinema / Theory*, edited by Andrew S. Horton, 153–73. Berkeley: University of California Press, 1991.

Hinata Akiko. "Gurafikku aato: Erekutoronikusu jidai." *Bijutsu Techō* 293 (January 1968), 106–7.

Hogarth, William. *The Analysis of Beauty*. Pittsfield, MA: Silver Lotus, 1909.

Hopwood, Nick. "'Giving Body' to Embryos: Modeling, Mechanism, and the Microtome in Late Nineteenth-Century Anatomy." *Isis* 90, no. 3 (September 1999): 462–96.

Horrocks, Roger. *Len Lye: A Biography*. Auckland, New Zealand: Auckland University Press, 2001.

Huizinga, Johan. *Homo Ludens*. London: Routledge, 2002.

Hutcheon, Linda. "Postmodern Afterthoughts." *Wascana Review of Contemporary Poetry and Short Fiction* 37, no. 1 (2002): 5–12.

Hutchings, Peter. "The Work-Shop of Filthy Animation." In *The Illusion of Life: Essays on Animation*, edited by Alan Cholodenko, 161–81. Sydney: Power Publications in association with the Australian Film Commission, 1991.

Imamura, Tahei. *Imamura Taihei eizō hyōron 4: Kiroku eiga ron*. Tokyo: Yumani shobō, 1991.

———. *Imamura Taihei eizō hyōron 5: Manga eiga ron*. Tokyo: Yumani shobō, 1991.

———. *Imamura Taihei eizō hyōron 9: Sensō to eiga*. Tokyo: Yumani shobō, 1991.

———. "Japanese Art and the Animated Cartoon." *The Quarterly of Film, Radio, and Television* 7, no. 3 (Spring 1953): 217–22.

———. *Manga eigaron*. Kyoto: Daiichi geibunsha, 1941.

———. *Manga eiga ron*. Tokyo: Tokuma shoten, 2005.

———. "Nihon manga eiga no tame ni." In Imamura Taihei, *Imamura Taihei eizō hyōron 2: Eiga geijutsu no seikaku*, 137–59. Tokyo: Yumani shobō, 1991.

———. "A Theory of Film Documentary." Translated by Michael Bassett. In "Decentering Theory: Reconsidering the History of Japanese Film Theory," edited by Aaron Gerow, special issue of *Review of Japanese Culture and Society* 22 (December 2010): 52–59.

Irie Yashirō. "Approaching Imamura Taihei: Film Theory and Originality." Translated by Philip Kaffen. In "Decentering Theory: Reconsidering the History of Japanese Film Theory," edited by Aaron Gerow, special issue, *Review of Japanese Culture and Society* 22 (December 2010): 60–79.

Iser, Wolfgang. *The Fictive and the Imaginary: Charting Literary Anthropology*. Baltimore, MD: Johns Hopkins University Press, 1993.

Ivanov-Vano, Ivan. *Kadr za kadrom*. Moscow: Iskusstvo, 1980.

Ivy, Marilyn. "Critical Texts, Mass Artifacts: The Consumption of Knowledge in Postmodern Japan." In *Postmodernism and Japan*, edited by Masao Miyoshi and Harry D. Harootunian, 21–46. Durham, NC: Duke University Press, 1989.

Jameson, Fredric. *Postmodernism, or The Cultural Logic of Late Capitalism*. Durham, NC: Duke University Press, 1991.

———. "Reading without Interpretation: Postmodernism and the Video-Text." In *The Linguistics of Writing: Arguments between Language and Literature*, edited by Nigel Fabb, Derek Attridge, Alan Durant, and Colin MacCabe, 199–223. Manchester, UK: Manchester University Press; New York: Methuen, 1987.

Jay, Martin. "Scopic Regimes of Modernity." In *Vision and Visuality*, edited by Hal Foster, 3–23. Seattle, WA: Bay Press, 1988.

Jenkins, Henry. "'Complete Freedom of Movement': Video Games as Gendered Play Spaces." In *From Barbie to Mortal Kombat*, edited by Justine Cassell and Henry Jenkins, 262–97. Cambridge, MA: MIT Press, 1999.

Jones, Caroline A. *Eyesight Alone: Clement Greenberg's Modernism and the Bureaucratization of the Senses*. Chicago: University of Chicago Press, 2005.

Joubert-Laurencin, Hervé. "Le cinéma d'animation n'existe plus." *Acme*, no. 1 (Autumn 2008): 106–11.

———. *La lettre volante: Quatre essais sur le cinéma d'animation*. L'œil vivant. Paris: Presses de la Sorbonne Nouvelle, 1997.

Kai Yoshiaki. "'Akushidento' no shōgeki nao." In *Moriyama Daidō ron*, edited by Tokyo-to Shashin Bijutsukan. Tokyo: Tankōsha, 2008.

Kamiyama Ryōko. "1970 nendai shotō no Nihon no zerogurafii aato: Takamatsu Jirō o chūshin ni." In *Zerogurafii to 70 nendai*, edited by Tokyo Publishing House, 21–24. Tokyo: Fuji Xerox, 2005.

Kaplan, E. Ann. "Theories and Strategies of the Feminist Documentary." *Millennium Film Journal*, no. 12 (Fall / Winter 1982–83): 44–67.

Kelty, Christopher, and Hannah Landecker. "A Theory of Animation: Cells, L-Systems, and Film." *Grey Room* 17 (Fall 2004): 30–63.

Klee, Paul. *Notebooks, Volume 1: The Thinking Eye*. Edited by Jürg Spiller and translated by Ralph Manheim. Woodstock, NY: Overlook Press, 1992.

———. *Notebooks, Volume 2: The Nature of Nature*. Edited by Jürg Spiller and translated by Heinz Norden. Woodstock, NY: Overlook Press, 1992.

Koch, Gertrud. "Cosmos in Film: On the Concept of Space in Walter Benjamin's 'Work of Art' Essay." In *Walter Benjamin's Philosophy: Destruction and Experience*, edited by Andrew Benjamin and Peter Osborne, 205–15. London: Routledge, 1994.

Kracauer, Siegfried. "'Marseiller Entwurf' zu einer Theorie des Films: IV; Mit Haut und Haaren." In *Werke: Theorie des Films*, vol. 3, edited by Inka Mülder-Bach, 559–89. Frankfurt am Main: Suhrkamp, 2005.

———. *Theory of Film: The Redemption of Physical Reality*. Introduction by Miriam Bratu Hansen. Princeton, NJ: Princeton University Press, 1997.

Krauss, Rosalind. "Video: The Aesthetics of Narcissism." *October* 1 (Spring 1976): 50–64.

———. *A Voyage on the North Sea: Art in the Age of the Post-medium Condition*. London: Thames and Hudson, 1999.

Kubelka, Peter. "The Theory of Metrical Film." In *The Avant-Garde Film: A Reader of Theory and Criticism*, vol. 3 of the Anthology Film Archives Series, edited by P. Adams Sitney, 139–59. New York: New York University Press, 1978.

Kunzle, David. *The History of the Comic Strip: Volume 2; The Nineteenth Century*. Berkeley: University of California Press, 1990.

Lakoff, Andrew. "Preparing for the Next Emergency." *Public Culture* 19, no. 2 (Spring 2007): 247–71.

LaMarre, Thomas. *The Anime Machine: A Media Theory of Animation*. Minneapolis: University of Minnesota Press, 2009.

———. "Magic Lantern, Dark Precursor of Animation." *Animation: An Interdisciplinary Journal* 6, no. 2 (July 2011): 127–48.

———. "New Media Worlds." In *Animated "Worlds,"* edited by Suzanne Buchan, 131–50. Eastleigh, UK: John Libbey Publishing, 2006.

———. *Shadows on the Screen: Tanizaki Jun'ichirō on Cinema and "Oriental" Aesthetics*. Ann Arbor: University of Michigan Press, 2005.

———. "Speciesism, Part I: Translating Races into Animals in Wartime Animation." *Mechademia* 3: *Limits of the Human* (2008): 75–95.

Landecker, Hannah. *Culturing Life: How Cells Became Technologies*. Cambridge, MA: Harvard University Press, 2010.

Latour, Bruno. "Drawing Things Together." In *Representation in Scientific Practice*, edited by Michael Lynch and Steve Woolger, 19–68. Cambridge, MA: MIT Press, 1990.

———. *Science in Action*. Cambridge, MA: Harvard University Press, 1987.

Lehman, Christopher P. *The Colored Cartoon: Black Representation in Animated Short Films, 1907–1954*. Amherst: University of Massachusetts Press, 2007.

Leslie, Esther. *Hollywood Flatlands: Animation, Critical Theory and the Avant-Garde*. London: Verso, 2002.

Leyda, Jay. *Kino: A History of the Russian and Soviet Film*. London: Allen and Unwin, 1960.

Lindenmayer, Aristid. "Mathematical Models for Cellular Interaction in Development." *Journal of Theoretical Biology* 18 (1968): 280–315.

Lindsay, Vachel. *The Art of the Moving Picture*. Rev. ed. New York: Macmillan, 1922.

Linhart, Robert. *Lénine, les paysans, Taylor: Essai d'analyse matérialiste historique de la naissance du système productif soviétique*. Paris: Éditions du Seuil, 1976.

Lippit, Akira M. *Atomic Light (Shadow Optics)*. Minneapolis: University of Minnesota Press, 2005.

Lodder, Christina. *Russian Constructivism*. New Haven, CT: Yale University Press, 1983.

Lo Duca, Joseph-Marie. *Le dessin animé: Histoire, esthétique, technique*. Paris: Prisma, 1948.

———. *Technique du cinéma*. 1st ed. Paris: Presses Universitaires de France, 1943.

———. *Technique du cinéma*. 4th ed. Paris: Presses Universitaires de France, 1956.

———. *Technique du cinéma*. 7th ed. Paris: Presses Universitaires de France, 1971.

Looser, Thomas. "Superflat and the Layers of Image and History in 1990s Japan." In "Emerging Worlds of Anime and Manga," edited by Frenchy Lunning, special issue, *Mechademia* 1 (2006): 92–101.

Lowood, Henry. "Videogames in Computer Space: The Complex History of Pong." *IEEE Annals of the History of Computing* 31, no. 3 (July–September 2009): 5–19.

Lutz, E. G. *Animated Cartoons: How They Are Made, Their Origin and Development*. New York: Charles Scribner's Sons, 1926.

Lye, Len. *Figures of Motion: Len Lye, Selected Writings*. Edited by Wystan Curnow and Roger Horrocks. Auckland, New Zealand: Auckland University, 1984.

———. "Len Lye Speaks at the Film-Makers' Cinematheque." *Film Culture* 44 (Spring 1967): 48–51.

Lyotard, Jean-François. "L'acinéma." In "Cinéma: Théorie," special issue, *Revue d'Esthétique* 26, nos. 2–4 (1973): 357–69.

MacDonald, Scott. "Desegregating Film History: Avant-Garde Film and Race at the Robert Flaherty Seminar, and Beyond." In Scott MacDonald, *Adventures of Perception: Cinema as Exploration, Essays / Interviews*, 10–80. Berkeley: University of California Press, 2009.

Mach, Ernst. "Bemerkungen über wissenschaftliche Anwendungen der Photographie." In *Jahrbuch für Photographie und Reproductionstechnik* 2, edited by Josef Maria Eder, 284–86. Halle, Germany: W. Knapp, 1888.

MacKay, John. "Vertov and the Line: Art, Socialization, Collaboration." In *Film,*

Art, New Media: Museum without Walls?, edited by Angela Dalle Vacche, 81–96. London: Palgrave Macmillan, 2012.

Maejima Satoshi. *Sekai-kei to wa nanika*. Tokyo: Soft Bank, 2010.

Mair, Victor H. "Danger + Opportunity ≠ Crisis. How a Misunderstanding about Chinese Characters Has Led Many Astray." http://www.pinyin.info/chinese/crisis.html, accessed June 26, 2013.

Manovich, Lev. "After Effects, or the Velvet Revolution." *Millennium Film Journal*, nos. 45 / 46 (Fall 2006): 5–19.

——. *The Language of New Media*. Cambridge, MA: MIT Press, 2001.

——. "What Is Digital Cinema?" In *The Digital Dialectic: New Essays on New Media*, edited by Peter Lunenfeld, 172–92. Cambridge, MA: MIT Press, 1999.

Marcuse, Herbert. *One-Dimensional Man: Studies in the Ideology of Advanced Industrial Society*. Boston: Beacon Press, 1964.

——. *One-Dimensional Man: Studies in the Ideology of Advanced Industrial Society*. London: Routledge, 2002.

Marey, Etienne-Jules. *Le mouvement*. Paris: G. Masson, 1894.

Marotti, William. "Simulacra and Subversion in the Everyday: Akasegawa Genpei's 1000-Yen Copy, Critical Art, and the State." *Postcolonial Studies* 4, no. 2 (2001): 211–39.

Martin, André. "Films d'animation au festival de Cannes." *Cahiers du cinéma*, no. 25 (July 1953): 38–39.

Marx, Karl. *Das Kapital: Kritik der politischen Oekonomie*. Vol. 1. Hamburg: Verlag von Otto Meissner, 1867.

Mast, Gerald, and Marshall Cohen, eds. *Film Theory and Criticism: Introductory Readings*. New York: Oxford University Press, 1974.

McLuhan, Marshall. *Understanding Media: The Extensions of Man*. London: Routledge, 2001.

Mehrtens, Herbert. "Mathematical Models." In *Models: The Third Dimension of Science*, edited by Soraya de Chadarevian and Nick Hopwood, 276–306. Stanford, CA: Stanford University Press, 2004.

Merleau-Ponty, Maurice. "Eye and Mind." Translated by Carleton Dallery. In *The Primacy of Perception: And Other Essays on Phenomenological Psychology, the Philosophy of Art, History and Politics*, edited by James M. Edie, 159–90. Evanston, IL: Northwestern University Press, 1964.

Metz, Christian. "*Trucage* and the Film." Translated by Françoise Meltzer. In *The Language of Images*, edited by W. J. T. Mitchell, 151–69. Chicago: University of Chicago Press, 1980.

Millhauser, Steven. "Cat 'n' Mouse." *New Yorker*, April 19, 2004, 174–83.

——. "The Little Kingdom of J. Franklin Payne." In *Little Kingdoms*, 11–115. New York: Vintage Books, 1993.

Mishima Mari. *Kōhōshi ga kataru kigyōzō*. Tokyo: Nihon hyōronsha, 2008.

Mitry, Jean. *The Aesthetics and Psychology of the Cinema*. Translated by Christopher King. Bloomington: Indiana University Press, 1997.

Mjolsness, Lora Wheeler. "Dziga Vertov's *Soviet Toys*: Commerce, Commercialization and Cartoons." *Studies in Russian and Soviet Cinema* 2, no. 3 (2008): 247–67.

Monnet, Livia. "A-Life and the Uncanny in *Final Fantasy: The Spirits Within*." *Science Fiction Studies* 31, no. 1 (March 2004): 97–121.

Mori Takuya. *Animēshon nyūmon*. Tokyo: Bijutsu shuppansha, 1966.

———. "Sōgetsu anime fesutibaru o mite." *Eiga Hyōron* (January 1965): 45–47.

Morin, Edgar. *The Cinema, or The Imaginary Man*. Translated by Lorraine Mortimer. Minneapolis: University of Minnesota Press, 2005.

Mulvey, Laura. "Visual Pleasure and Narrative Cinema." In *Movies and Methods: An Anthology*, vol. 2, edited by Bill Nichols, 303–14. Berkeley: University of California Press, 1985.

Nakahira Takuma and Moriyama Daidō. "Shashin to iu kotoba o nakuse." In *Nakahira Takuma: Kitaru beki shashinka*, 102–7. Tokyo: Kawade shobō shinsha, 2009.

Nead, Lynda. *The Haunted Gallery: Painting, Photography, Film, c. 1900*. New Haven, CT: Yale University Press, 2007.

Neer, Richard. *The Emergence of the Classical Style in Greek Sculpture*. Chicago: University of Chicago Press, 2010.

Nelle, Florian. "Im Rausch der Dinge: Poetik des Experiments im 17. Jahrhundert." In *Bühnen des Wissens: Interferenzen zwischen Wissenschaft und Kunst*, edited by Helmar Schramm, 140–68. Berlin: Dahlem University Press, 2003.

Neupert, Richard. "We're Happy When We're Sad: Comedy, Gags, and 1930s Cartoon Narration." In *Funny Pictures: Animation and Comedy in Studio-Era Hollywood*, edited by Daniel Goldmark and Charlie Keil, 93–108. Berkeley: University of California Press, 2011.

Ngai, Sianne. *Ugly Feelings*. Cambridge, MA: Harvard University Press, 2007.

Nichols, Bill. *Blurred Boundaries: Questions of Meaning in Contemporary Culture*. Bloomington: Indiana University Press, 1994.

———, ed. *Movies and Methods: An Anthology*. Vol. 2. Berkeley: University of California Press, 1985.

———. *Representing Reality: Issues and Concepts in Documentary*. Bloomington: Indiana University Press, 1991.

Nicholson, Linda, and Steven Seidman, eds. *Social Postmodernism: Beyond Identity Politics*. Cambridge: Cambridge University Press, 1995.

Nicolet, J. L. *Intuition mathematique et dessins animés: Causerie pédagogique*. Paris: Payot, 1942.

Norling, John A., and Jacob F. Leventhal. "Some Developments in the Production of Animated Drawings." *Transactions of the Society of Motion Picture Engineers* 3 (September 1926): 58–66.

Nye, David. *Technology Matters: Questions to Live With*. Cambridge, MA: MIT Press, 2006.

Ostherr, Kirsten. "Animating Informatics: Scientific Discovery through Documentary Film." In *The Blackwell Companion to Contemporary Documentary Studies*, edited by Alisa Lebow and Alex Juhasz. West Sussex, UK: Wiley-Blackwell, 2014.

———. *Cinematic Prophylaxis: Globalization and Contagion in the Discourse of World Health*. Durham, NC: Duke University Press, 2005.

Ōtsuka Eiji. *Atomu no meidai: Tezuka Osamu to sengo manga no shudai*. Tokyo: Tokuma shoten, 2003.

————. *Kyarakutā shōsetsu no tsukurikata*. Tokyo: Kōdansha, 2003.

————. *Monogatari no taisō: Mirumiru shōsetsu ga kakeru muitsu no resson*. Tokyo: Asahi shinbun-sha, 2003.

————. *Sengo manga no hyōgen kūkan: Kigōteki shintai no jubaku*. Kyoto: Hōsōkan, 1994.

————. "An Unholy Alliance of Eisenstein and Disney: The Fascist Origins of Otaku Culture." Translated by Thomas LaMarre. *Mechademia* 8, "Tezuka Osamu: Manga Life" (2013): 251–77.

————. "World and Variation: The Reproduction and Consumption of Narrative." Translated and with an introduction by Marc Steinberg. *Mechademia 5: Fanthropologies* (2010): 99–116.

Ōtsuka Eiji, and Ōsawa Nobuaki. *Japanimēshon wa naze yabureru ka*. Tokyo: Kadokawa, 2005.

Panofsky, Erwin. "Style and Medium in Motion Pictures." In *Film Theory and Criticism Introductory Readings*, edited by Gerald Mast and Marshall Cohen, 151–69. London: Oxford University Press, 1974.

Passek, Jean Loup, ed. *Dictionnaire du cinéma*. Paris: Libraire Larousse, 1986.

Plato. *Theaetetes*. Translated by F. M. Cornford. In *Plato: The Collected Dialogues*, edited by Edith Hamilton and Huntington Cairns. Princeton, NJ: Princeton University Press, 1961.

Plessner, Helmuth. *Conditio humana. Gesammelte Schriften* VIII.1. Auflage, Suhrkamp Taschenbuch Wissenschaft. Frankfurt am Main: Suhrkamp Verlag, 2003.

————. *Die Stufen des Organischen und der Mensch*. Berlin: de Gruyter, 1975.

Polan, Dana B. "Brecht and the Politics of Self-Reflexive Cinema." *Jump Cut: A Review of Contemporary Media*, no. 1 (1974): n.p. http://www.ejumpcut.org/archive/onlinessays/JC17folder/BrechtPolan.html. Accessed June 1, 2013.

Polanyi, Michael. *The Tacit Dimension*. Chicago: University of Chicago Press, 2009.

Pozzo, Thierry. "La chronophotographie scientifique: Aux origines du spectacle du monde vivant." In *Images, Science, Mouvement: Autour de Marey*, 11–28. Paris: L'Harmattan, 2003.

Prince, Stephen. "True Lies: Perceptual Realism, Digital Images, and Film Theory." *Film Quarterly* 49, no. 3 (Spring 1996): 27–37.

Principe, Gabrielle. *Your Brain on Childhood: The Unexpected Side Effects of Classrooms, Ballparks, Family Rooms, and the Minivan*. Amherst, NY: Prometheus Books, 2011.

Prodger, Phillip, ed. *Time Stands Still: Muybridge and the Instantaneous Photography Movement*. Oxford: Oxford University Press, 2003.

Quart, Alissa. "The Insider: David Bordwell Blows the Whistle on Film Studies." *Lingua Franca* 10, no. 2 (March 2000): 34–43.

Reicher, Karl. "Kinematographie in der Neurologie." *Verhandlungen der Gesellschaft Deutscher Naturforscher und Ärtzte* 79, no. 2 (1907): 235–36.

Renov, Michael. *The Subject of Documentary*. Minneapolis: University of Minnesota Press, 2004.

Rheinberger, Hans-Jörg. *An Epistemology of the Concrete: Twentieth-Century Histories of Life*. Durham, NC: Duke University Press, 2010.

———. "Wissensräume und experimentelle Praxis." In *Bühnen des Wissens: Interferenzen zwischen Wissenschaft und Kunst*, edited by Helmar Schramm, 366–82. Berlin: Dahlem University Press, 2003.

Ries, Julius. "Kinematographie der Befruchtung und Zellteilung." *Archiv für Mikroskopische Anatomie* 74 (1909): 1–29.

Rodowick, D. N. "A Care for the Claims of Theory." *Cinema: Journal of Philosophy and the Moving Image*, no. 1 (2010): 14–68.

———. *The Virtual Life of Film*. Cambridge, MA: Harvard University Press, 2007.

Roffat, Sébastien. "L'émergence d'une école française de dessin animé sous l'Occupation (1940–1944)." PhD diss., University of Paris 3, Sorbonne Nouvelle, 2012.

Roque, Georges. *Qu'est-ce que l'art abstrait?* Folio essais inédit. Paris: Gallimard, 2003.

Rosen, Philip. *Change Mummified: Cinema, Historicity, Theory*. Minneapolis: University of Minnesota Press, 2001.

Roshal', Lev. *Nachalo vsekh nachal: Fakt na ekrane i kinomysl "serebrianogo veka."* Moscow: Materik, 2002.

Russett, Robert and Cecile Starr. *Experimental Animation: Origins of a New Art*. New York: Da Capo Press, 1976.

Saar, Martin. *Genealogie als Kritik: Geschichte und Theorie des Subjekts nach Nietzsche und Foucault*. Frankfurt am Main: Campus Verlag, 2007.

Schoonover, Karl. "*The Cinema, or The Imaginary Man* and *The Stars* by Edgar Morin." *Senses of Cinema*, no. 39 (May 5, 2006): n.p. http://sensesofcinema .com/2006/book-reviews/edgar_morin/. Accessed June 1, 2013.

Shiozawa Minobu. *Sengo shuppanshi: shōwa no zasshi, sakka, henshūsha*. Tokyo: Ronsōsha, 2010.

Shorte, Spencer L., and Friedrich Frischknecht, eds. *Imaging Cellular and Molecular Biological Functions*. Berlin: Springer, 2007.

Sifianos, Georges. "The Definition of Animation: A Letter from Norman McLaren." *Animation Journal* (Spring 1995): 62–66.

Simmel, Georg. "The Metropolis and Mental Life." In *The City Cultures Reader*, edited by Malcolm Miles, Tim Hall, and Iain Borden, 12–19. London: Routledge, 2003.

Sitney, P. Adams, ed. *The Avant-Garde Film: A Reader of Theory and Criticism*. Vol. 3 of the Anthology Film Archives Series. New York: New York University Press, 1978.

———. "Harry Smith Interview." In *The Avant-Garde Film: A Reader of Theory and Criticism*, vol. 3 of the Anthology Film Archives Series, edited by P. Adams Sitney, 94–95. New York: New York University Press, 1978.

Smoodin, Eric Loren. *Animating Culture: Hollywood Cartoons from the Sound Era*. New Brunswick, NJ: Rutgers University Press, 1993.

Snyder, Joel. "Visualization and Visibility." In *Picturing Science, Producing Art*, edited by Caroline A. Jones and Peter Galison, 379–97. New York: Routledge, 1998.

Sobchack, Vivian. *The Address of the Eye: A Phenomenology of Film Experience*. Princeton, NJ: Princeton University Press, 1992.

————. "Final Fantasies: Computer Graphic Animation and the (Dis)illusion of Life." In *Animated "Worlds,"* edited by Suzanne Buchan, 171–82. Eastleigh, UK: John Libbey Publishing, 2006.

————. "The Line and the Animorph or 'Travel Is More Than Just A to B.'" *Animation: An Interdisciplinary Journal* 3, no. 3 (November 2008): 251–65.

Sobieszek, Robert. "Sculpture as the Sum of Its Profiles: François Willème and Photosculpture in France, 1859–1868." *The Art Bulletin* 62, no. 4 (December 1980): 617–30.

Sōgetsu Aato sentaa no kiroku kankō iinkai, ed. *Kagayake 60 nendai: Sōgetsu aato sentaa no zenkiroku.* Tokyo: Firumu aatosha, 2002.

Solhdju, Katrin. "L'expérience 'pure' et l'âme des plantes: James lecteur de Fechner." In *Vie et Expérimentation: Peirce, James, Dewey,* edited by Didier Debaise, 77–99. Paris: J. Vrin, 2007.

Sorel, Philippe. "Photosculpture: The Fortunes of a Sculptural Process Based on Photography." In *Paris in 3D: From Stereoscopy to Virtual Reality 1850–2000,* in association with the Musée Carnavalet, edited by Françoise Reynaud, Catherine Tambrun, and Kim Timby, 81–89. London: Booth-Clibborn Editions, 2000.

Souriau, Etienne. "Die Struktur des filmischen Universums und das Vokabular der Filmologie." Translated by Frank Kessler. *Montage / av* 6, no. 2 (1997): 140–57. Originally published as "La structure de l'univers filmique et le vocabulaire de la filmologie." *Revue Internationale de Filmologie* 2, nos. 7–8 (1951): 231–40.

Steinberg, Marc. *Anime's Media Mix: Franchising Toys and Characters in Japan.* Minneapolis: University of Minnesota Press, 2012.

Stiegler, Bernd. "Ernst Machs 'Philosophie des Impressionismus' und die Momentphotographie." *Hofmannsthal Jahrbuch zur Europäischen Moderne* 6 (1998): 257–80.

Sugiura Yumiko. *Fujoshika suru sekai: Higashi Ikebukuro no otaku shojo tachi.* Tokyo: Chūō shinsho, 2006.

Sukharebsky, Lazar. *Uchebnoe kino.* Moscow: Teakinopechat, 1928.

Sunder Rajan, Kaushik. *Biocapital: The Constitution of Postgenomic Life.* Durham, NC: Duke University Press, 2009.

Tada Michitarō. *Fukusei geijutsuron.* Tokyo: Keisō shobō, 1962.

————. "Fukusei geijutsu to wa nani ka." In *Gurafikēshon Bessatsu: Fukusei jidai no shisō,* 113–43. Tokyo: Fuji Xerox, 1971.

Takahata Isao. *Jūni seiki no animeeshon: Kokuhō emakimono ni miru eigateki—animeteki naru mono.* Tokyo: Tokuma shoten, 1999.

Thacker, Eugene. "Uncommon Life." In *Tactical Biopolitics: Art, Activism, and Technoscience,* edited by Beatriz da Costa and Kavita Philip, 309–21. Cambridge, MA: MIT Press, 2008.

Thompson, Richard. "Duck Amuck." *Film Comment* 11, no. 1 (January–February 1975): 39–43.

Tode, Thomas. "Absolute Kinetika: From Absolute Film to Kinetic Art of the 1950s." In Thomas Tode et al., *Le Mouvement: Vom Kino zur Kinetik,* 81–97. Basel: Museum Tinguely, 2010.

Tomii, Reiko. "State v. (Anti-) Art: *Model 1,000-Yen Note Incident* by Akasegawa Genpei and Company." *positions* 10, no. 1 (Spring 2002): 141–72.

Tortajada, Maria. "The 'Cinematographic Snapshot': Rereading Etienne-Jules Marey." In *Cinema beyond Film: Media Epistemology in the Modern Era*, edited by François Albéra and Maria Tortajada, 79–96. Amsterdam: University of Amsterdam Press, 2010.

Tosi, Virgilio. *Cinema before Cinema: The Origins of Scientific Cinematography*. Translated by Sergio Angelini. London: British Universities Film and Video Council, 2005.

Trahair, Lisa. "For the Noise of a Fly." In *The Illusion of Life: Essays on Animation*, edited by Alan Cholodenko, 183–208. Sydney: Power Publications in association with the Australian Film Commission, 1991.

Tsivian, Yuri. "Turning Objects, Toppled Pictures: Give and Take between Vertov's Films and Constructivist Art." *October* 121 (Summer 2007): 92–110.

———. "Vertov's Silent Films: An Annotated Filmography." In *Lines of Resistance: Dziga Vertov and the Twenties*, edited by Yuri Tsivian, 403–9. Sacile: Le Giornate del Cinema Muto, 2004.

Turvey, Malcolm. "Theory, Philosophy, and Film Studies: A Response to D. N. Rodowick's 'An Elegy for Theory.'" *October* 122 (Fall 2007): 110–20.

Tyagai, A. *Kino v pomoshche tekhnicheskomu podkhodu*. Moscow: Teakinopechat, 1930.

Vertov, Dziga. *Iz naslediia: Dramaturgicheskie opyty*. Edited with a foreword by Aleksandr S. Deriabin and an introduction by V. S. Listov. Moscow: Ejzenshtejn-Tsentr, 2004.

———. *Kino-Eye: The Writings of Dziga Vertov*. Edited by Annette Michelson and translated by Kevin O'Brien. Berkeley: University of California Press, 1984.

Vignaux, Valérie, and Pierre Courtet-Cohl, eds. *Emile Cohl*, special issue, *1895, revue de l'Association française de recherche sur l'histoire du cinéma*, no. 53. Paris: Association française de recherche sur l'histoire du cinéma, 2007.

Vimenet, Pascal, ed. *Emile Cohl*. Montreuil: Musées d'Annecy / Editions de l'œil, 2008.

Völker, Jan. *Ästhetik der Lebendigkeit: Kants dritte Kritik*. Munich: Wilhelm Fink, 2011.

Wallon, Henri. "De quelques problèmes psycho-physiologiques que pose le cinéma." *Revue Internationale de Filmologie* 1, no. 1 (July–August 1947): 15–18.

———. "Le réel et le mental (A propos d'un livre recent)." *Journal de Psychologie Normale et Pathologique* 32, nos. 5–6 (1935): 455–89.

Watsuji, Tetsurō. "Bunrakuza no ningyō shibai." In *Watsuji Tetsurō zenshū*, 17: 309–15. Tokyo: Iwanami shoten, 1963.

Weber, Max. "Zur Psychophysik der industriellen Arbeit." In *Gesamtausgabe I: Schriften und Reden*, vol. 11: Zur Psychophysik der industriellen Arbeit, edited by Wolfgang Schluchter, 162–380. Tübingen, Germany: J. C. B. Mohr, 1995.

Wells, Paul. *Understanding Animation*. London: Routledge, 1998.

Whitehead, Alfred North. *Process and Reality: An Essay in Cosmology*. Edited by

David Ray Griffin and Donald W. Sherburne. Corrected ed. New York: Free Press, 1978.

Wichmann, Siegfried. *Japonisme: The Japanese Influence on Western Art since 1858*. London: Thames and Hudson, 1981.

Widakowich, V. "Über kinematographische Vorfürung von Serienschnitten durch Embryonen." *Zentralblatt für Physiologie* 23 (1907): 784–85.

Williams, Linda. "Mirrors without Memories: Truth, History, and the New Documentary." *Film Quarterly* 46, no. 3 (Spring 1993): 9–21.

Williams, Raymond. *Television: Technology and Cultural Form*. Edited by Ederyn Williams. London: Routledge, 2003.

Williamson, Colin. "Watching Closely with Turn-of-the-Century Eyes: Obscured Histories of Magic, Science, and Animation in the Cinema." Ph.D. diss., University of Chicago, 2013.

Williamson, Judith. "Two Kinds of Otherness—Black Film and the Avant-Garde." *Screen* 29, no. 4 (1988): 106–12.

Wittgenstein, Ludwig. *Philosophical Investigations*. Translated by G. E. M. Anscombe, P. M. S. Hacker, and Joachim Schulte. Rev. 4th ed. West Sussex, UK: Wiley-Blackwell, 2009.

Worringer, Wilhelm. *Abstraction and Empathy: A Contribution to the Psychology of Style*. Translated by Michael Bullock and with an introduction by Hilton Kramer. Chicago: Ivan R. Dee, 1997.

———. *Form in Gothic*. Rev. ed. Edited and translated by Herbert Read. New York: Schocken, 1964.

Zielinski, Siegfried. *Deep Time of the Media: Toward an Archeology of Hearing and Seeing by Technical Means*. Translated by Gloria Custance. Cambridge, MA: MIT Press, 2006.

Zola, Émile. *Mes haines*. Texte de l'édition du Cercle du Livre précieux. Paris: A. Faure, 1866.

Zone, Ray. *Stereoscopic Cinema and the Origins of 3-D Film, 1838–1952*. Lexington: University Press of Kentucky, 2007.

Contributors

KAREN BECKMAN is the Elliot and Roslyn Jaffe Professor of Cinema and Modern Media in the Department of the History of Art and the Program in Cinema Studies at the University of Pennsylvania. She is the author of *Vanishing Women: Magic, Film, and Feminism* (Duke University Press, 2003) and *Crash: Cinema and the Politics of Speed and Stasis* (Duke University Press, 2010), and she is now working on a new book, "Animation and the Contemporary Art of War." She has coedited two volumes: *Still Moving: Between Cinema and Photography* with Jean Ma (Duke University Press, 2008) and *On Writing with Photography* (2013) with Liliane Weissberg. For several years she served as a senior editor of the journal *Grey Room*.

SUZANNE BUCHAN is a professor of animation aesthetics at Middlesex University London. Until 2012 she was a professor and director of the Animation Research Centre at the University for the Creative Arts in the United Kingdom. Her research investigates interdisciplinary approaches to animation as a pervasive moving-image form across a range of platforms and media, and she is also active as a film and exhibition curator. Buchan was a founding member and codirector (1994–2003) of the Fantoche International Animation Film Festival in Switzerland. Her publications include *Pervasive Animation: An AFI Reader* (2013), *The Quay Brothers: Into a Metaphysical Playroom* (2011), and *Animated "Worlds"* (2006). She is the founder and editor of *animation: an interdisciplinary journal*. She continues to work on her wider "pervasive animation" project, which includes a forthcoming curated exhibition for the Museum of Design, Zurich.

SCOTT BUKATMAN is a professor in the Film and Media Studies Program in the Department of Art and Art History at Stanford University and the author of *Terminal Identity: The Virtual Subject in Postmodern Science Fiction* (Duke University Press, 1993 — still in print two decades later); a monograph on *Blade Runner* commissioned by the British Film Institute and recently reprinted as one of a small number of commemorative anniversary editions; and a collection of essays, *Matters of Gravity: Special Effects and Supermen in the 20th Century* (Duke University Press, 2003). His latest book is *The Poetics of Slumberland: Animated Spirits and the Animating Spirit*

(2012), which celebrates play, plasmatic possibility, and the life of images in cartoons, comics, and cinema. The book begins with Winsor McCay's *Little Nemo in Slumberland* to explore how and why the emerging media of comics and cartoons brilliantly captured a playful, rebellious energy characterized by hyperbolic emotion, physicality, and imagination. Slumberland becomes more than a marvelous world for Nemo: it's an aesthetic space defined through the artist's innovations; an animated space that opens to embrace the imaginative sensibility of a reader; and a temporary space of play.

ALAN CHOLODENKO is an Honorary Associate of the University of Sydney, and prior to that he was a senior lecturer in film and animation studies in what is now known as the Department of Art History and Film Studies at that university. He has pioneered in the articulation of film theory, animation theory, and poststructuralist and postmodernist French thought through his publications as well as his organizing of landmark events—notably for *The Illusion of Life*, the world's first international conference on animation, held in Sydney in 1988. He is the editor of *The Illusion of Life: Essays on Animation*, the world's first book of scholarly essays theorizing animation (1991); Samuel Weber's *Mass Mediauras: Form, Technics, Media* (1996); and *The Illusion of Life 2: More Essays on Animation* (2007).

YURIKO FURUHATA is an assistant professor in the Department of East Asian Studies and the World Cinemas Program at McGill University. She is the author of *Cinema of Actuality: Japanese Political Avant-Garde Filmmaking in the Season of Image Politics* (Duke University Press, 2013). She has also published in journals such as *Animation*, *Screen*, *Semiotica*, and *New Cinemas*.

ALEXANDER R. GALLOWAY is a writer and computer programmer working on issues in philosophy, technology, and theories of mediation. He is a founding member of the Radical Software Group and the creator of the Carnivore and Kriegspiel projects. An associate professor of media, culture, and communication at New York University, he is author or coauthor of five books on digital media and critical theory, most recently *The Interface Effect* (2012) and *Les nouveaux réalistes: Philosophie et postfordisme* (2012). In his future work he intends to focus more closely on French philosophy and the Continental tradition.

OLIVER GAYCKEN is an assistant professor of English and comparative literature at the University of Maryland, College Park. He has published on aspects of the intersections of cinema and science in the *Journal of Visual Culture*, *Science in Context*, *Historical Journal of Film, Radio, and Television*, and several edited collections. His monograph, *Devices of Curiosity: Early Cinema and Popular Science*, is forthcoming.

BISHNUPRIYA GHOSH teaches postcolonial theory and global media studies at the University of California, Santa Barbara. Much of her scholarly works, including the two books *When Borne Across: Literary Cosmopolitics in the Contemporary Indian*

Novel (2004) and *Global Icons: Apertures to the Popular* (Duke University Press, 2011), investigate contemporary cultures of globalization. She is currently working on two monographs on speculative knowledge: a book on spectral materialism in global cinemas ("The Unhomely Sense: Spectral Cinemas of Globalization") and a comparative study of pandemic media in the United States, South Africa, and India ("The Virus Touch: Living with Epidemics").

TOM GUNNING is the Edwin A. and Betty L. Bergman Distinguished Service Professor in the Department on Cinema and Media at the University of Chicago. He is the author of *D.W. Griffith and the Origins of American Narrative Film* (1991) and *The Films of Fritz Lang: Allegories of Vision and Modernity* (2000), as well as more than a hundred articles on early cinema, film history and theory, avant-garde film, film genre, and cinema and modernism. With André Gaudreault he originated the influential theory of the "cinema of attractions." In 2009 he was awarded an Andrew A. Mellon Distinguished Achievement Award, the first film scholar to receive one, and in 2010 he was elected to the American Academy of Arts and Sciences. He is currently working on a book on the invention of the moving image.

ANDREW R. JOHNSTON is a visiting assistant professor in the English Department and the Program in Film and Media Studies at Amherst College. His forthcoming book, *Pulses of Abstraction: Episodes from a History of Animation*, explores the history of abstract animation in cinema and new media from the 1920s through the 1970s. He has also published articles and chapters on animation, avant-garde film, color aesthetics, and the history of digital technology and computer graphics in books and journals such as *Color and the Moving Image* (2012), *Animation: Behind the Silver Screen* (forthcoming), and *Discourse*.

HERVÉ JOUBERT-LAURENCIN is a professor of aesthetics and film history at the University of Paris, Nanterre-La Défense, where he directs the International Master of Cinema Studies program. He specializes in the cinematic, political, poetic, and theatrical works of Pier Paolo Pasolini, which he also translates into French. He specializes in the writings of André Bazin and animation cinema as well. He is currently directing the triennial international research program Traverser Bazin: Ecrits suscités par le cinéma. His works on Pier Paolo Pasolini include *Salò ou les 120 journées de Sodome* (2012), *Le dernier poète expressionniste: Ecrits sur Pasolini* (2005), *Pasolini Portrait du poète en cinéaste* (1995), and *Théâtre (1938–1965)*. His works on poetry include *Le dada du sonnet* (2005), and his political writings include *Contre la télévision* (2003), *Écrits sur la peinture* (1997), and *Écrits sur le cinéma* (1987). Works on André Bazin include *Opening Bazin* (2011) and *Le sommeil paradoxal: Écrits sur André Bazin* (forthcoming). Works on animation cinema include *La lettre volante: Quatre essais sur le cinéma d'animation* (1997) and *Quatre films de Hayao* (2012).

GERTRUD KOCH teaches cinema studies at the Free University in Berlin, where she is also the director of a research center on aesthetic experience: Sonderforschungsbereich 626. She has taught at many international universities and was a research fellow at the Getty Center, as well as at the University of Pennsylvania in 2010 and at Brown University's Cogut Center for Humanities in 2011. Koch has written books on Herbert Marcuse and Siegfried Kracauer, feminist film theory, and the representation of Jewish history. She has edited numerous volumes on aesthetics, perception, and film theory. She is also a coeditor and board member of the journals *Babylon*, *Frauen und Film*, *October*, *Constellations*, and *Philosophy and Social Criticism*.

THOMAS LAMARRE teaches East Asian studies and communications studies at McGill University. His books include *Shadows on the Screen: Tanizaki Jun'ichirô on Cinema and Oriental Aesthetics* (2005), *Uncovering Heian Japan: An Archaeology of Sensation and Inscription* (2000), and *The Anime Machine: A Media Theory of Animation* (2009).

CHRISTOPHER P. LEHMAN is a professor of ethnic studies at St. Cloud State University in Minnesota and has held the position of visiting fellow at the Summer Institute of the W. E. B. Du Bois Institute for African and African American Research at Harvard University. His book *The Colored Cartoon: Black Representation in American Animated Short Films* won a *Choice* Outstanding Academic Title award.

ESTHER LESLIE is a professor of political aesthetics at Birkbeck, University of London. Her first book is *Walter Benjamin: Overpowering Conformism* (2000). She is also the author of the biography *Walter Benjamin* (2007). Her book *Hollywood Flatlands: Animation, Critical Theory, and the Avant Garde* (2002) excavates the historical relationships between critical theory, European intellectuals, and animation, in its avant-garde and commercial varieties. Since then she has written and lectured extensively on all types of animation. A subsequent book, *Synthetic Worlds: Art, Nature and the Chemical Industry* (2005), investigates the industrial manufacture of color and its impact on conceptions of nature and aesthetics. She runs a website together with Ben Watson, Militant Esthetix, www.militantesthetix.co.uk.

JOHN MACKAY is a professor of Slavic languages and literatures and film studies and is the chair of the Film Studies Program at Yale University. He is the author of *Inscription and Modernity: From Wordsworth to Mandelstam* (2006), *Four Russian Serf Narratives* (2009), and *True Songs of Freedom*: Uncle Tom's Cabin *in Russian Culture and Society* (2013), as well as articles on Soviet film, film theory, and biography. In 2013 he completed *Dziga Vertov: Life and Work* (forthcoming).

MIHAELA MIHAILOVA is a PhD student in the joint Film Studies and Slavic Languages and Literatures program at Yale University. Her academic interests include animation, film theory, media studies, comic books, early Soviet cinema, Russian cinema, and translation. Her article on Anna Melikyan's 2007 film *Mermaid*—"I Am Empty Space: A *Mermaid* in Hyperreal Moscow"—is published in *Kino Kultura*, no. 34 (October 2011). Her translation of Sergei Tretyakov's "The Industry Production Screenplay" is included in *Cinema Journal* 51, no. 4 (2012). An article titled "The

Mastery Machine: Digital Animation and Fantasies of Control" appeared in *animation: an interdisciplinary journal* 8, no. 2 (July 2013).

MARC STEINBERG is assistant professor of film studies at Concordia University, Montreal. His book *Anime's Media Mix: Franchising Toys and Characters in Japan* (2012) chronicles the development of transmedia convergence in Japan. He has published articles in *Japan Forum, animation: an interdisciplinary journal, Journal of Visual Culture, Theory, Culture and Society, Mechademia,* and *Canadian Journal of Film Studies.*

TESS TAKAHASHI is an assistant professor in the Department of Film at York University in Toronto, where she teaches classes on technologies of the image, experimental film, animation, and documentary cinema. She is a member of the editorial collective of the *Camera Obscura: Feminism, Culture, and Media Studies.* Her writing has appeared there, as well as in *animation: an interdisciplinary journal, Millennium Film Journal,* and *Cinema Journal.* She is currently working on a book titled "Impure Film: Medium Specificity in the North American Avant-Garde (1968–2008)."

Index

NOTE: Page numbers followed by *f* indicate a figure.

200n48; on homogeneous time, 244; influence of, 198n3; Japanese reception of, 181–82, 190–92, 197nn2–3, 200n50; on plasmaticness, 18, 138; on play and innervation, 10, 182, 195–96; on technological reproduction, 181–83, 187–97, 197nn1–2, 199n34, 199n37

Benning, Sadie, 201

Berger, John, 17

Bergman, Alan, 26

Bergson, Henri, 50

Bernard, Claude, 274

"Better Castles in the Sky" (Bloch), 28–29

Betty Boop, 255–56, 258, 260

Bijutsu Techō journal, 190

biological realism, 291–92, 299n15

biosecurity regimes, 266–69; animation and, 266, 268–69; epistemology of infection in, 267–68

Bird, Brad, 314

blackface, 253–54, 259–60

Blade (Lye), 178

Blake, Jeremy, 125

Blinkety Blank (McLaren), 3, 86, 88–89, 93

Bloch, Ernst, 28–29

"Bones of Contention" (Darley), 124

Boorstin, Daniel, 188, 189

Bordwell, David, 12–13, 16, 22n47, 116, 126n19

Born, Gustav, 74, 75*f*

Boschet, Pierre, 91–92

Bosko series, 254, 258, 261

Bourdieu, Pierre, 95n4

Boytler, Mikhail, 149–50

Braderman, Joan, 201, 211

Brakhage, Stan, 38

Braun, Ludwig, 71–72, 80nn12–14

Braune, Christian Wilhelm, 61–66

Brave (Disney-Pixar), 315

Bray Studios, 69

"Brecht and the Politics of Self-Reflexive Cinema" (Polan), 16–17

Breer, Robert, 176

Brinckmann, Christine N., 120

Bromberg, Betsy, 204

Brumberg, Valentina, 149

Brumberg, Zinaida, 149

Buchan, Suzanne, 1–2, 20n1

Bugs Bunny, 306, 309, 311

Bukatman, Scott, 6–7, 8, 14

Burch, Noël, 234

Burroughs, William, 315

Bushkin, Aleksandr, 13, 22n47, 149, 163n2, 164n11

Byrne, David, 215

Calder, Alexander, 170

Calloway, Cab, 255–56, 257, 260

cameraless animation, 18–19; of Jodie Mack, 38–39; of Len Lye, 38, 167–79

camera obscura, 42–43

Canales, Jimena, 44, 45

Canguilhem, Georges, 274

Cannes festival: first public displays of animation at, 86, 88, 89; Palme d'Or winners at, 89

"Cat 'n' Mouse" (Millhauser), 301–3

Capra, Frank, 275

caricature. *See* African American portrayals

Carroll, Lewis, 139

Carroll, Noël, 111, 117; on the activities of criticism, 114, 126n19; on apparatus theory, 234; on homospaciality, 121; on physical noncompossibility, 120–21, 127n34; on piecemeal theorizing, 116

cartoon physics, 6–7, 14, 301–15; of cinema superheroes, 314; in Disney Studio cartoons, 304; gaming realism's suppression of, 311–15, 316nn18–19; primacy of the body in, 303–7, 316n4; squash and stretch principle of, 302, 304; topsy-turvy utopian freedom in, 307–11, 315, 316n11, 316n21

cartoons: Balázs on line in, 7; Imamura's theory of realism and, 221–49; Japanese production of, 221–22, 236–47; multiplane-camera system in, 223, 251n50, 251nn54–55; stroke

emaki, 241, 243, 245–47, 251n54
embryological modeling, 73–74, 75f,
    76, 79n6
empathy, 48
Endō Toshiaki, 295
Energy journal (Esso), 191, 199n34
Eno, Brian, 215
Enthusiasm: Symphony of the Donbass
    (Vertov), 156
Enzensberger, Hans Hangnus, 199n37
epistemology of infection, 267–68
Epstein, Jean, 5, 8, 14, 78–79
Ermanskii, Osip, 155, 166n28
Esso, 191, 199n34
evolution and change, 8
"Experience and Poverty" (Benjamin),
    30–31
experimentation, 131–42; definition
    of, 131; Eisenstein on plasmatic-
    ness and, 135–38; film aesthetics
    of, 135–38; human theorizing in,
    131–34, 143n11; of identity-politics
    documentary videos, 201–16; of
    Japanese xerox artists, 15, 181–97;
    of Lye's scratch animation tech-
    niques, 167–79; of Rodchenko's
    mobile intertitles, 145–48, 163; of
    Vertov's frame shooting, 145–63,
    164n9, 166n28
"Eye and Mind" (Merleau-Ponty),
    174–75

Fade to Black (Cokes and Trammel),
    208, 213–15
Fanon, Frantz, 17
Fantasmagorie (Cohl), 86, 90–91, 176
Faraday, Michael, 47
Fast and Furry-ous, 306
Fat Albert and the Cosby Kids, 259,
    261–62
Fechner, Gustav Theodor, 135, 136
Feldman, Seth, 217n8
La fete blanche (Uno), 183
FIAF *Index to Film Periodicals*, 112
Film Art: An Introduction (Bordwell and
    Thompson), 12–13, 22n48
Filmation Associates, 261–62

film theory, 16–18; apparatus (screen)
    theory of, 231–32, 234–36, 287; cog-
    nitive approaches to, 108n1; on
    digital transformations of cinema,
    117, 297, 300n32; documentary
    theory of, 205–8; Eurocentrism of,
    208; on experimentation, 131–34;
    on first principles of animation in,
    98–108, 108n5, 108n7; on the his-
    torical a priori, 54–55; ideological
    concerns in, 17–18; on the instant,
    49–51; interdisciplinary approaches
    in, 111–26, 127n34; marginalization
    of animation in, 1–2, 16–17, 19, 28,
    98–101, 108n5, 114, 121; materialist
    theory in, 135–42; postmodernism
    in, 201–2, 205–8; on time-lapse
    photography, 77–78. *See also* ani-
    mation theory; Japanese animation
    theory
Finkelstein, Lois, 168
Fischinger, Oskar, 33, 61–63, 93, 125
Flack, Roberta, 210
Fleisch, Thorsten, 124
Fleischer, Max, 33, 228, 285n4; African
    American portrayals by, 254–57;
    Screen Songs series of, 256–57
Fleischer brothers/Fleischer Studios,
    69; *Popeye* cartoons of, 221, 223,
    225–28, 242; self-reflexivity in work
    of, 40, 151
Flip and Two Twisters (Lye), 178
The Flip Wilson Show, 262
Fonoroff, Nina, 204
Form in Gothic (Worringer), 175–76
"For the Sake of Japanese Cartoon
    Films" (Imamura), 221, 223–49,
    249n7; on American cartoon-
    ing, 223–26, 238–45; on collective
    social endeavor, 232; on Japan's
    underdeveloped cartoon industry,
    236–37, 244; localized bodily focus
    of, 248–49, 251n63; on movement-
    time, 240–41; on the multiplane-
    camera system, 241–44, 251n50,
    251nn54–55; on photographic pars-
    ing of movement, 221, 223–31, 234,

Tanaami Keiichi, 183, 186
Taylor, Frederick Winslow, 155
temporal contexts, 133; of cameraless animation, 38–39; of human visual perception, 45–47; Imamura's account of, 238–47; of the instant, 49–51; modernity's transformation of, 41–42, 238–47; in scientific modeling, 76–79; of 3-D animation, 56–66; time-lapse photography and, 76–79, 81n30
Tennessee Valley Authority, 273
Tezuka Osamu, 291–94, 299n13, 299n15
Theaetetes (Plato), 52n11
Théâtre Optique, 99
theory. *See* animation theory; experimentation; film theory; Japanese animation theory
A Theory of Cartoon Film (Imamura), 223, 233–36, 247, 249n7
"A Theory of Documentary Cinema" (Imamura), 231–37
A Theory of Documentary Film (Imamura), 223, 233–34, 235
Theory of Film (Kracauer), 136–37
thing theory, 10
Third Cinema, 17
"This is Ann!," 274–75, 276f
Thompson, Kristin, 12–13, 16, 22n47
Thompson, Richard, 16
Thornton, Leslie, 209
"Thoughts on Total Design" (Awazu), 187–88, 199n17
3-D animation, 14, 25, 26; in Braune and Fischer's modeling, 61–66; in Marey's chronophotography experiments, 61–63, 65–66; origins of, 54–66, 67n18; for scientific visualization, 14–15, 17–18, 68–79, 284; in Willème's photosculpture, 14–15, 56–61, 67n10. *See also* computer-generated imagery (3-D CGI)
time-lapse photography, 81n30; Mach's observations of, 76–77; in scientific modeling, 76–79; in slapstick, 6
Tom and Jerry, 304, 305f, 309, 315, 316n4

tomographic photography, 79n6
Tongues Untied (Riggs), 208, 209–11
the trace, 187
Tracy, Spencer, 212
Trammel, Donald, 208, 213–15
translation, 279–80
transmedial realism, 15, 294–98, 300n27, 300n31
Trinh T. Minh-ha, 201, 211, 216, 217n8
Triumph of the Will (Riefenstahl), 28–29
Tsivian, Yuri, 145
Tsugata Nobuyuki, 290
Two Bagatelles (McLaren), 88–89

Uchebnoe kino (Sukharebsky), 154
Uncle Remus (character), 258, 261–62
Uno Akira, 183, 185, 186
Uno Tsunehiro, 289
the "ur" experience, 105–6, 110n28
utopian theories of animation, 8, 18

Valéry, Paul, 93
Vanderbeek, Stan, 40, 125
variable-speed cinematgraphy, 8, 9–10
Vertigo (Hitchcock), 213–14
Vertov, Dziga, 7, 21n28, 22n47, 145–63; animation experiments of, 148–63; educational animation of, 153–55, 165n27; frame shooting practices of, 156–63, 164n9, 166n28; *Kino-Pravda* newsreels of, 145–49, 164n5; self-reflexivity in work of, 151–53, 161, 233; on Taylorist labor practices, 155–56
video games, 294–98
visual change, 3
vivification, 279–80
Völker, Jan, 142
Voodoo in Harlem (Lantz), 257–58

Wada Makoto, 183–84, 186
walk cycles, 80n16
Wall-E, 111
Wallon, Henri, 136–37
The Walt Disney Studios. *See* Disney Studios
Ward, Paul, 20n4